RIFLES

Mark Urban is the Diplomatic Editor of the BBC's *Newsnight* and was formerly defence correspondent for the *Independent*. He has covered many wars as a journalist and is the author of *Big Boys' Rules: The SAS and the Secret Struggle against the IRA*, *UK Eyes Alpha: Inside British Intelligence* and, most recently, the bestselling *The Man Who Broke Napoleon's Codes*. He lives in London with his wife and three children.

Further praise for *Rifles*:

'A superb study of the unit that effectively created the modern British Army's infantry tactics.' Nicholas Fearn, *Independent on Sunday*

'Fans of Bernard Cornwell's Sharpe series have a real treat here. In a deeply researched, beautifully crafted and captivating volume, Mark Urban recounts the story of the 95th Rifles – the elite regiment who provided the Duke of Wellington with his crack troops and helped to win the Peninsular War against Napoleon's marshals . . . After his previous work on codebreaking in the Peninsular War, Urban must now be accounted one of the leading scholars of the period but the ordinary reader will find this a riveting slab of derring-do and high adventure.' Frank McLynn, *Daily Express*

'A delight, wise in its judgements and clear-headed in its approach to the painful field of battle.' Trevor Royle, *Sunday Herald*

'As though Mark Urban, the diplomatic editor of BBC2's *Newsnight*, did not have enough to do in his day job, he is fast carving out a second career for himself as a first-class military historian of the Napoleonic wars. His recent biography [*The Man Who Broke Napoleon's Codes*] was critically acclaimed, and now he has followed it up with a history of the 95th Rifle Regiment that is as dashing and unconventional as the legendary unit itself.' Andrew Roberts, *Literary Review*

'A colourful history of that daredevil corps, the Royal Greenjackets . . . A must for Sharpe fans.' John Crossland, *Sunday Times*

'Urban's book is war unplugged – vicious, immediate, chaotic and raw. Well known as a *Newsnight* reporter, he brings to his subject the journalist's sense of drama. But the book is not just a lurid story; he has spent the requisite time in the archives, among neglected diaries and correspondence. The evidence he has collected enables him to tell the story of the 95th through six soldiers: two officers and four lowly privates. This gives the battles a humanity usually lacking in studies of war.' Gerard DeGroot, *Scotland on Sunday*

'Should be read by everyone who has an interest in soldiering and warfare.' Gary Sheffield, *Living History*

'[*The Man Who Broke Napoleon's Codes*] was very good. This is even better. How he finds the time, with his broadcasting commitments, to research and write quality history in under two years is a mystery. Somehow he does – and it won't only be Sharpe fans who are grateful for this brilliant warts-and-all depiction of Wellington's famous riflemen.' Saul David, *Daily Telegraph*

RIFLES

RIFLE CORPS!

COUNTRYMEN!

LOOK, BEFORE YOU LEAP:

Half the Regiments in the Service are trying to persuade you to Enlist:
But there is ONE MORE to COME YET!!!

The 95th; or,

Rifle REGIMENT,

COMMANDED BY THE HONOURABLE

Major-General Coote Manningham,

The only Regiment of RIFLEMEN in the Service:

THINK, then, and CHOOSE, Whether you will enter into a Battalion Regiment,
or prefer being a RIFLEMAN,

The first of all Services in the British Army.

In this distinguished Service, you will carry a Rifle no heavier than a Fowling-Piece. You will knock down your Enemy at Five Hundred Yards, instead of missing him at Fifty. Your Clothing is GREEN, and needs no cleaning but a Brush. Those men who have been in a RIFLE COMPANY, can best tell you the comfort of a GREEN JACKET.

NO WHITE BELTS; NO PIPE CLAY!

On Service, your Post is always the Post of Honour, and your Quarters the best in the Army; for you have the first of every thing; and at Home you are sure of Respect - because a BRITISH RIFLEMAN always makes himself Respectable.

The RIFLE SERGEANTS are to be found any where, and have orders to Treat their Friends gallantly every where.

If you Enlist, and afterwards wish you had been a RIFLEMAN, do not say you were not asked, for you can BLAME NOBODY BUT YOURSELF.

GOD SAVE the KING! *and his Rifle Regiment!*

Rifles

Six Years with Wellington's Legendary Sharpshooters

MARK URBAN

faber and faber

by the same author

THE MAN WHO BROKE NAPOLEON'S CODES
BIG BOYS' RULES
UK EYES ALPHA
SOVIET LAND POWER
WAR IN AFGHANISTAN

First published in 2003
by Faber and Faber Limited
3 Queen Square London WC1N 3AU
This paperback edition published in 2004

Typeset by Faber and Faber Limited
Printed in England by Mackays of Chatham plc,
Chatham, Kent

A CIP record for this book
is available from the British Library

ISBN 0-571-21681-1

2 4 6 8 10 9 7 5 3 1

for my beloved Sol

Contents

List of Illustrations

Preface

The 95th Rifles became the British Army's best-known regiment at a time of some very potent national myths. Wellington's riflemen have found a niche in the military historical pantheon alongside Cromwell's Ironsides or the Desert Rats.

In modern times they have been lionised by popular culture in novels as well as television drama. C. S. Forester featured riflemen in his books, and Bernard Cornwell's Sharpe series has brought tales of the Green Jackets' derring-do to millions.

It is apparent then that their exploits have been recounted in more or less embroidered forms quite a few times before. Surprisingly, though, nobody has ever written a proper history of the regiment, and in particular of its 1st Battalion through the period of maximum drama – 1809–15. A colonel in the Rifle Brigade, Willoughby Verner, attempted to tell the full story of all three battalions of his regiment, but never completed his narrative, which ends abruptly two years before the campaigns do.

What's more, although Verner's efforts were deeply impressive for their time, he began publishing his history in 1912. It was a very different age and he wrote for the glory of his regiment. Although he was prepared to confront a few difficult issues, Verner self-censored in a way that would be unacceptable to most readers today.

I knew that if I was to push this narrative well beyond Verner or any other previous account, I would have to exploit many new sources of information, as well as looking again at the old ones. My starting point was the existing published memoirs of several soldiers of the 95th, as well as Verner's account.

Then I was able to get to most of Verner's working papers, which allowed me to revisit his research, including some vital primary sources that had for many years been unavailable to other writers. After that I dug out some other primary material such as letters or journals that he did not have access to and which has never been used in published form before. Then the various claims of authors or diarists had to be checked against official records, such as the Muster Lists or Casualty Returns at the Public Record Office in Kew. Having performed all of these tasks, I had to search for the French Army version of various key engagements, in order to try to gauge the real effectiveness of the Rifles.

After going through all of these different sources, I needed to find a coherent way of telling the 95th's story. I chose to write it as the saga of the men who embarked at Dover on 25 May 1809. This really gets to the core of Rifles mythology and to all of the legendary regimental characters. There were various compromises inherent in this decision – not least that some epic moments in the year prior to this, as well as the stories of the 2nd and 3rd Battalions, could not be told in great detail. Be that as it may, the 1st Battalion in May 1809 was a substantially different unit to the one that had fought a few months earlier and it is the interaction between veterans and newcomers that forms a vital subtext to the early part of the book. Also, I have mentioned the 2nd and 3rd Battalions' most celebrated exploits in the campaign.

Many soldiers' stories are told in this book, but six individuals are flagged up at the start. This book is not the story of these six men *per se*, but their fate provides a useful reference point as the narrative unfolds.

In recounting the six-year journey to Waterloo with them it is also my aim to give the lay reader a great deal of information about the realities of life in Wellington's Army and to establish the 95th's pivotal role in creating what we might now recognise as a modern British soldier. It is not a general history of the Iron Duke's campaigns nor of soldiering in the Napoleonic era, so the wider themes are always tackled through the experience of soldiers of the 95th Rifles. I make no apology for dispatching the Battle of Salamanca, perhaps Wellington's greatest battle, in a few short sentences, since the 1st/95th played almost no part in it.

The result is, I hope, an account of these campaigns that shears away the distortions or recycling of other authors, providing a vivid, truthful account of how these extraordinarily tough men lived, fought and died. It is inevitable, I think, when going back to so many primary sources, that much of the new material that comes to light concerns issues that later authors wanted to screen out such as cowardice, theft or bungling. Because of this, some who rush to judgement may see my book as a debunking or knocking job on the 95th. It is certainly not intended as such, and I hope that my admiration for the courage, stoicism and thoughtfulness of many of its officers and men is clear throughout.

I owe many people a debt of gratitude. My editor at *Newsnight*, George Entwistle, has to be thanked for allowing me to embark on the journey in the first place, and my agent Jonathan Lloyd for making sure it was worth my while to do so! Phyllis Mendoza started me off with a very kind gift of several Rifles memoirs that her late husband had collected.

Lieutenant General Sir Christopher Wallace was the key that opened the door of the Royal Green Jackets Archive in Winchester for me. Once there, I relied time and again on the extraordinary recall and patience of Major Ron Cassidy who, in retirement, administers this vital resource as a labour of love for his regiment. It was here that Verner's notes and many other vital accounts were found.

For some new material, I have a debt to Caroline Craufurd, a descendant of Major General Robert Craufurd, who helped me to much information about that tormented figure. In working on the official records, I sometimes deployed the skills of professional researchers in the shape of Eileen Hathaway and Roger Nixon. George Caldwell and Robert Cooper gave freely of their particular expertise on the 95th. On the French accounts, Cyril Canet assisted in the Vincennes archives. John Montgomery, librarian of the Royal United Services Institute in London, rallied to the cause this time just as energetically as he did with my last book.

Throughout the research, I benefited enormously from the kindness of John Sandler, the leading collector of Napoleonic literature in Britain, whose library, amassed over more than sixty years, contains fifteen thousand volumes. I was able to consult this vast resource at will and draw on his great expertise. The Sandler Collection was particularly useful for digging up early French published accounts.

The task of licking my tract into shape fell to Julian Loose and Angus Cargill at Faber and I am delighted to complete this fourth collaboration with that house. Dr Rory Muir once again did me the enormous favour of vetting my text for more egregious errors – but of course I alone take responsibility for any that remain. Many others – too numerous to mention – have shared their knowledge or books, often through virtual communities such as the Napoleon Series internet forum.

Finally I must also thank those who have had to put up with me while I got this obsession out of my system: my wife Hilary, as well as daughters who showed an understanding far in advance of their years, Isabelle and Madeleine.

Mark Urban
London, October 2003

ONE

Departures

May 1809

Just before 6 a.m. the head of the battalion entered Dover. There were many people watching from upstairs windows as the green phalanx wound its way down to the port. Of course they drew onlookers; the battalion's buglers had seen to that by shattering the twilight stillness as they arrived. A good blast on the horns was usually used to announce them and to tell ignorant civilians that, having heard a strange cacophony, their eyes were about to register something quite unusual too: the first regiment of British riflemen.

At the head of the column rode several officers resplendent in their dark-green uniforms, with a pelisse, that fashionable braided jacket beloved of hussars and other cavalry dandies, thrown over one shoulder. On their crowns, tall caps with a bugle badge and a tuft of green. Behind them about 1,100 troops tramped along, the thumping cadence of their marching echoing through narrow streets.

They had already been going for four hours when they filed into Dover, having quit their barracks a little further down the coast after the briefest of nights. Many of them were bursting with anticipation, for they were embarking on foreign service. In a letter that he posted that morning, 25 May 1809, Second Lieutenant George Simmons wrote home to Yorkshire, 'This, my dear parents, is the happiest moment of my life; and I hope, if I come where there is an opportunity of showing courage, your son will not disgrace the name of a British soldier.'

Simmons, with all the patriotic fervour of the military virgin, marched behind his captain, Peter O'Hare, a grizzled veteran who had fought in a dozen battles around the world. Putting the newest officer under one of the oldest; that, of course, was the commanding officer's intent.

The whole battalion had been formed on the same principle. It had returned from campaigning against the French in Spain just three months earlier, but it had been remade. Such were the exigencies of the service. Of the ten captains at the head of their companies that 25 May, only O'Hare and one other had filled the same positions in January.

Dead men's shoes had been filled and many experienced officers and soldiers marched out of the 1st Battalion in order to give a backbone of experience to the newly formed 3rd, who were staying behind while they were trained to some sort of acceptable standard. In the pell-mell of regimental reorganisation, the 1st Battalion had not been able to refuse its quota of new men.

Private Robert Fairfoot marched in the ranks of O'Hare's company down to Dover docks. He was tall, a well-made man of twenty-six years, but he was Johnny Raw in the eyes of the old riflemen. Granted, Fairfoot had done his time in the militia – there was no way they'd have let him into the 1st Battalion at all without some knowledge of the soldier's way of life – but he'd never heard a shot fired in anger. Fairfoot had been in the 95th for less than four weeks. One of the old hands commented contemptuously that when the orders to embark that morning had been received, 'the men who had joined us from the militia had scarcely learned the rifle drill'.

Each of the ten companies in that battalion contained its sprinkling of Johnny Raws and its quota of veterans. They had not been blended yet. Months would be required to get those men messing happily together. The extra recruits had been drafted from the militia because Britain's generals had been roused from their usual indifference in professional matters by the regiment's performance in several foreign expeditions. Just a few weeks before its 1st or senior battalion embarked at Dover, the 95th had been rewarded by being allowed to form a 3rd Battalion. There was a buzz of excitement about this new form of warfare – of green-jacketed men using the rifle – but its apostles knew that there was much still to be proved. The Rifles had generally been employed in brief little campaigns against second-rate troops. They had only faced Napoleon's legions fleetingly the previous summer and in the early part of 1809. So just as the likes of Simmons and Fairfoot were setting out to prove themselves, the entire battalion and its tactics would now be on trial. By the end of the campaign, the 1st Battalion of the 95th would be held up by some as one of the finest war bands in all history.

There was fighting in store for Simmons and the others all right: there would be five years of it before the survivors would see the white cliffs of Old England again. Of course, they had no way of knowing that as they caught sight of the ships at anchor. In fact, they did not even know where they were going. One rifleman would say with great conviction that the battalion was headed back to Spain or Portugal, but another, with equal fervour and a 'damn yer eyes', would assert they were going to help the Austrians, whose legions were locked in a new battle with Napoleon. The British government had been locked in a sporadic global competition with the French since their revolution, and as the Emperor Napoleon's armies triumphed on the Continent, ministers in London wanted to use the small expeditionary army they could scrape together to make mischief for their Gallic enemies. They had selected the 95th's destination as the most profitable place to do that.

As the tail of the column arrived on the dockside, a gaggle of dozens of women and small children brought up the rear. There was no set drill about the embarkation of wives for a foreign expedition. Sometimes there would be a quota of five or six per company. Sometimes, with a quartermaster's nod and wink, it would be more than that. But the commanding officer had issued strict orders this time: no women.

There had been wives on the last expedition, and not a few of them had ended up being left in Spain. Some had dropped dead from exhaustion trying to keep up on long marches through winter snows. Others had fallen behind to be violated by half a dozen French dragoons before having their throats cut. And there were a few who fell behind and might be alive or dead, nobody knew. So the colonel had been most adamant on this point: there would be no women with the regiment, and, as for those services like sewing repairs or fetching provisions, the men would fend for themselves.

As embarkation started, so did the wailing and oaths of women who saw that the dread moment of leave-taking had arrived. 'It was such a parting scene that I never wish to witness it again,' one of the soldiers later wrote. 'The women clung round the necks of their husbands, so that the officers had much ado to part them. There was such a ringing of hands, tearing of hair and crying that I was glad to jump on the boat, thankful that I had no wife to bewail my loss.'

The men, loaded down with anything up to eighty pounds of fighting kit, clambered gingerly into the rowing boats that awaited them at the base of the quay. The tars then heaved away on the oars, pulling their human cargo one mile out into the middle of the harbour where a squadron of transports lay at anchor.

Among the married soldiers, there were some last lingering looks at the waving figures on the quay. Then, putting a brave face on their misery, the wives sent up three cheers for the 95th, and many bystanders joined in. The women's cries were all the more poignant, one officer wrote, for 'knowing well that numbers must never return to their native land'. Not to be outdone, the soldiers returned their own huzzas before the stiff breeze carried away their shouts.

O'Hare's 3rd Company, including Simmons and Fairfoot, went aboard the *Fortune*, one of three transports needed to carry the battalion. The masters of *Fortune*, *Malabar* and *Laurel* wasted little time. The tide and wind were with them. They slipped their cables and stood out to sea.

The confidence with which the squadron had set off soon ebbed away. The wind had rounded on them, frustrating any progress down the Channel, and the entire group of ships found itself, by 5 June, close in to Cowes with heavy squalls pushing the transports about their anchorage. There they were to remain for six days.

For some of the men, like Private Joseph Almond, these unforeseen checks hardly excited surprise. Three years before, he'd been one of a small number in the present party who'd set sail from Portsmouth. Their journey had taken six months: six months of confinement on a ship, eating hard tack and suffering the company of poxy tars. They had disembarked in South America emaciated and short of puff, having to fight a hard and ultimately futile battle against the Spaniards.

While they remained confined afloat, four hundred riflemen and any number of matelots on board each little transport, the chances of rows and altercations multiplied. Almond, a big Cheshire man in his midthirties, was one of those unfortunates who had twice had corporal's stripes but lost them again through misdemeanours. Perhaps he might get them back in this new campaign.

Those who officered the 95th knew that even the brighter soldiers like Almond – and you needed some reading and writing to make corporal – had to be kept away from drink as far as possible. For the chances of fighting, mutinous language or even general insolence multiplied with each slug of liquor. So while some of the young officers took the opportunity to go ashore and strut like peacocks in front of the fair Isle of Wight girls, the same indulgence could not be granted to the rank and file.

Allowing the men off would also have carried some risk of desertion. Generally, fighting corps like the 95th did not suffer from it much. But you never knew when some militia hero might repent his decision to sign on to the regulars and steal away with his ten guineas' bounty. Private Fairfoot knew a fair bit about desertion: he had decamped three times from the Royal Surreys. He'd always been caught: twice they had busted him back from drummer to private and locked him up. Desertion was rarely a capital offence in England – it was too common for one thing, they'd have ended up executing dozens of Fairfoot's mates for it. Now, on board the *Fortune*, Fairfoot had changed his colours from the red coat of the Royal Surrey Militia to the green jacket of the 95th. Volunteering into this new regiment had also given him one more chance to make a proper soldier of himself, for if he was caught deserting on service it would be a capital offence.

It was not until almost three weeks had passed since leaving Dover that the convoy got properly under way. Happily for the commanding officer and his company commanders like O'Hare, nobody had been left behind through desertion or serious infractions of discipline.

As it sailed towards the open Atlantic, the convoy had swelled. Transports carrying two other battalions had joined them, as had *Nymph*, a frigate carrying the brigadier general who was commanding the whole enterprise. The veterans knew him well: Black Bob, a fierce flogger who taught them to fear their master. Old sweats could have pointed out their brigadier as he strolled on the frigate's deck or dined near the big windows of its captain's cabin. The brigadier was one of the few officers who knew the squadron's destination. Fierce reputation or not, he had been given a real plum of a job in command of this crack brigade, made up of some of the most highly trained troops in the Army.

Even among these three battalions, the Rifles were unique. Their green uniforms marked them out, as did their blackened leather cross-belts (for the other two battalions hung equipment whitened with pipe clay over their red coats). Their weapons were different too, the barrels grooved or rifled to spin the ball, giving greater accuracy and allowing them to attempt aimed fire at long range.

Just as many of the men in the 95th were yearning to prove them selves, so their commanding officer knew the present expedition would allow a chance to demonstrate a new sort of soldiering; a different approach to training, discipline, tactics and fighting. The higher reaches of the Army were notoriously conservative, and many generals, while they could appreciate the value of a sprinkling of sharpshooters here and there, could see no value in deploying an entire regiment of riflemen *en masse* for they must soon be driven from the field by formed infantry or cavalry. 'A very amusing plaything': that was how one of the Army's most experienced generals had ridiculed the Rifles.

As the ships passed the Needles, the foam frothing against their bows, gulls and all variety of seabirds dived and wheeled about them. And this is when some of the 95th's veterans showed their true colours. Officers and men alike drew their rifles and started shooting the creatures. What on earth did the sea officers make of the crackle of gunfire that built into a cacophony? Every now and then a cheer would go up as one of the Green Jackets found his mark and some unfortunate gull plopped into the brine.

'The order of the day was to bombard the sea-fowl which swarm at this season on the rocks. Rifles and fowling pieces were brought into full play on this occasion,' one of the company commanders wrote. It was no mean feat to drill a bird at any sort of distance; add to that the rapid movements of both ship and prey. For a seaman this was a barbaric thing to do, unless you'd been driven mad by hunger. But for the riflemen killing was sport, the best there was, and as soon as they got to wherever they were going, they intended to show how good they were at hunting men too.

Tom Plunket, in 3rd Company, along with Fairfoot, had bagged a rare prize during the last campaign: he had potted a French general. The commanding officer had singled Tom out in front of the paraded regiment after that, and told them all, 'Here, men, stands a pattern for the battalion!' And Tom's deadly shot wasn't repaid just in lip service: he'd been given a purse of money and a corporal's stripes too.

Private Edward Costello, twenty years old, another new man in the company, studied his corporal with something akin to worship. During the long period of waiting, Tom had kept them all laughing by joking, telling stories and dancing hornpipes on top of a barrel. He had the kind of celebrity that Costello, a squat little Irishman from Queen's County, valued: the corporal was a good soldier, but a hilarious character too, as ready with a deadly quip as he was with his rifle.

Among the rank and file, few things were prized more than courage and the facility for capers or laughter. Private William Brotherwood was another wag. He was the veteran of a couple of campaigns, a wry Leicester boy with a wicked way with words. At the Battle of Vimiero he'd run out of balls for his rifle. So with a torrent of abuse, he'd loaded his razor and fired that at the French. It was the kind of jape that the men told the Johnny Newcomers about and which ensured he was notorious in the best sense of the word.

What were they looking for, those men like Fairfoot, Almond, Costello and Underwood? Their bounty had seemed like a lot when they joined: ten guineas was more than a year's pay for the ordinary soldier. But many boozed that away quickly enough and then they had to live by their sixpence a day. When you'd been in more than seven years, like Almond and Brotherwood, you got the princely sum of another penny a day.

On campaign, as those two veterans knew well, there were also chances for plunder. A prisoner would soon be stripped of his valuables, and in all probability, his clothes too: most would yield a few coins but an officer might be unburdened of a watch or silver snuffbox. Such were the fortunes of war: the French hadn't hesitated to do it to the 95th's men who fell behind in January so why should the riflemen hold back if they clapped hands on some Frenchie, alive or dead?

They did not see themselves as mercenaries, though. Many had joined through a craving for adventure. Costello had been seduced by the yarns his uncle spun, as they sat back in Ireland making shoes together. The old soldier's tales of campaigning in Egypt made him 'red hot for a soldier's life'. Fairfoot too had been suckled on tales of derring-do, for his father had been a soldier for more than twenty-eight years and he had grown up to the echoes of the drill square. His initiation into military life, in the 2nd Royal Surreys, had gone badly wrong, for it was a deeply unhappy battalion run on the lash and fear. Now Fairfoot was given a new opportunity to advance his soldier's career. As for Brotherwood, he had originally been driven into the Leicestershire Militia through need. He had been a stocking-weaver but the fickle dictates of fashion led to hundreds like him being cast out of work. Having tasted a soldier's life and liked it, he had been determined to transfer into the Rifle Corps, with its hard-fighting reputation.

For officers things were a little different. They had dreams of glory too, of course, but for the most part those were inextricably linked with their craving for advancement. They were a rough lot, the 95th's officers, mostly, in the words of one of them, 'soldiers of fortune'. Out of nearly fifty sailing with the 1st Battalion, the great majority had never purchased a commission and for many, their patent of rank, signed by the sovereign, was their only real mark of gentility.

Captain O'Hare was one of the original riflemen, going back to the regiment's formation in 1800, and he had got his two promotions by seniority alone. Nobody had done him any favours or bestowed any patronage, which may have been one of the reasons why brother officers and men alike knew him as a foul-tempered old Turk. It had taken fifteen years of hard soldiering to creep his way up the lists of regimental officers until he arrived at the front of the promotion queue. Now he was the regiment's senior captain, and thirsting for the step to major, but that was not an easy thing, especially when some better-connected or richer officer might jump over his head and secure the prize.

As for Simmons, he had not purchased either, being granted his second lieutenancy for encouraging dozens of men from his militia regiment, the South Lincolns, to volunteer with him for the 95th. His commission was a prize for helping fill the ranks. This was just as well, for there was no question of purchase. It was a shortage of money that had caused Simmons to join the Army in the first place, giving up his medical studies and ending the dream of being a surgeon.

Having joined the 95th, George, the eldest of nine brothers and three sisters, saw his duty as helping to pay for the education of his siblings. In the letter he had posted from Dover, Simmons explained his motivation thus: 'As a soldier, with perseverance, I must in time have promotion, which will soon enable me to be of use to my family; and at all times it will be my greatest pleasure and pride to take care that the boys go regularly to a good school, and I have no doubt of seeing them one day men of some experience through my interposition.'

For some sprig of the gentry, a second lieutenant's pay, of just under £160 per annum, was not considered enough to live on. An allowance of £70 or £80 was considered quite normal, and some truly rich young men drew on their families for vastly more than that. Simmons, by contrast, not only intended to live within his means, but to remit £20 or £30 home to his parents each year, and his was not the most extreme case by any means. One young lieutenant of the 95th sailing with him was the main provider for his widowed mother and eight siblings back in County Cork.

Many of the 95th's officers, then, could be described as desperate men. Their hunger for promotion arose from the harshness of their personal and family circumstances. The little flotilla of transports and warships was therefore bursting with anticipation for the new campaign. There was a ceaseless hubbub about what the coming months might bring, and nobody, right up to the brigadier in command, could really have described himself as immune to this febrile atmosphere. But the officers' search for advancement, and that of many ordinary riflemen for fame among their peers, would soon expose them to horrible dangers.

Each man may have wanted to prove himself in battle, but there was also a collective will at work, a desire to show that a regiment of British riflemen could perform wonders on the battlefield, when all manner of *savants* believed no such thing was possible. Just a few months before the 95th's departure, a veteran light infantry officer had declared in print that people such as the Germans and Swiss made the best sharpshooters, whereas the British rifleman, through upbringing and temperament, 'can never be taught to be a perfect judge of distance'. Disproving this thinking would cost the regiment dear.

Only a minority of those who had sailed on 25 May 1809 would still be in the battalion's ranks when it returned five years later. Many would be dead, others sent home as invalids to beg on the street, and some would have disappeared without trace, presumed deserted.

What of Captain O'Hare, Second Lieutenant Simmons, and Privates Almond, Brotherwood, Costello and Fairfoot? Of those six, half would never come home: one dying a hero's death, another paying the price for a commander's mistake and the third suffering the ultimate disgrace of execution at the hands of his own comrades. And the survivors? They would gorge themselves on fighting, experience some of the most intense hardships imaginable and, between the three of them, be wounded ten times. In the process of those campaigns, the 95th would become a legend and its soldiers a pattern for what a modern warrior should be.

TWO

Talavera

July–August 1809

It was hard to say which disturbed their first night ashore more: the din of bullfrogs, the churning of empty stomachs or the aching of limbs confined too long on the passage. The battalion landed at dusk on 3 July. After weeks on the transports they had been disgorged in Lisbon – for Portugal was indeed their destination – the previous day. Their relief at escaping the smelly old tubs on which they had been shut up throughout June was short-lived, because it was followed immediately by a passage up the River Tagus in shallow-draught river boats. They were packed together on narrow benches, rifles between their legs, as the boats scraped and wobbled across sand bars, the soldiers expecting at any moment to be capsized into the river and consigned to a watery grave.

Once they had got off for the night at Vallada, the new men began to realise what life on service involved. Their short passage on the river boats had deposited them a little up the Tagus, saving them a couple of marches on their way to the Spanish frontier. The baggage was not yet organised, so no camp kettles appeared for cooking. There were no tents, for the 95th had not been issued with them.

As the sun slipped down, a hot day gave way to cool, damp night, the dew impregnating their woollen clothing. Second Lieutenant Simmons jotted in his journal, 'Hungry, wet, and cold and without any covering, we lay down by the side of the river. I put one hand in my pocket and the other in my bosom, and lay shivering and thinking of the glorious life of a soldier until I fell fast asleep.'

To the man not used to channelling his body between tree roots or stones, the night offered little refreshment. A mere three hours after they had sought refuge in sleep, the bugles sounded reveille. The men fell in by companies, began their march, and as they went, the sun, climbing into the Portuguese sky, heated the dew out of their clothing. They reached the town of Santarem, where matters began to look up a little.

The new campaigners soon discovered that it only takes a day without food to re-educate a soldier's stomach. So upon reaching the town, the officers piled into little restaurants and coffee houses and paid with their own money for the meal with which the military commissariat had not provided them. The realisation, barely a day into their campaign, that the individual rifleman would often have to dip into his own pocket to provide for the essentials of life, would be reinforced many times in the coming years.

The quartermaster and a party of helpers soon appeared with dozens of mules they had bought in Lisbon and the rudiments of a regimental baggage train began to form. There was an official allowance of pack animals for each regiment, and some in addition for the more senior officers. Captains commanding companies were entitled to a horse to ride and a mule or donkey to carry their valises and canteens. The subaltern officers – thirty-three of them in the battalion – were allocated just a single beast of burden between two from the public purse.

There was nothing to stop those lieutenants with an extensive equipage and ample funds buying their own mules or indeed their own riding horses. For Simmons, this was out of the question. A pack animal might cost ten or twelve pounds, a good horse considerably more. He would be walking.

From Santarem they headed off towards the Spanish frontier, in pursuit of the main British army. Their brigade commander may have had highly trained men under his command, but he appreciated they had been weeks at sea. Things began in measured stages: from Santarem to Golegao, four Spanish leagues (getting on for sixteen or seventeen miles); then more gently from Golegao to Punhete, three leagues; Punhete to Abrantes, two leagues.

As they marched along the dusty Portuguese roads, all became aware of their brigadier, Robert Craufurd. He rode back and forth along the column, watching them, measuring them. Every straggler claiming he couldn't keep up aroused Craufurd's notice. Every officer who fussed about leading his column across bridges or fords excited stronger emotions.

Craufurd was a small man, the product of a well-connected Scottish family. Sitting behind a large cloak rolled on the front of his saddle, his 'black muzzle' peered over. However freshly shaven, his chin always carried a blue-black tinge of stubble. His actions were quick, his eye missed little. There was something terrier-like about him. When he was angered by what he saw, which was often on this march, he would let fly with imprecations and abuse. The greater his rage, the reedier or squeakier his voice became.

Craufurd's character was sufficiently well known even in 1806 for him to have been described by one newspaper as 'an opinionated, an ungracious and even ill tempered man'. And that was before the disgrace.

During the 1806–7 expedition to the River Plate in South America, one in which both Captain O'Hare and Private Almond had served, Craufurd had been obliged to surrender his brigade. Surrounded by enemy troops in the streets of Buenos Aires, Craufurd's force had made its stand in a convent before, under a heavy fire of sharpshooters, its commander was forced to capitulate.

A court martial had exonerated Craufurd for the failure, blaming the expedition's overall commander instead. But the distinction of having surrendered a British brigade in action was an odious one, and he knew it would always cling to him. Even as this new campaign continued, he would find himself again and again coming back to the memory of Buenos Aires, writing home to his wife, 'In that very town, the capture of which would have raised me to the height of military glory if I had been left to myself, I, two days afterwards, found myself in the humiliating situation of a prisoner.'

Whatever his temperament, those who ran the Army, at Horse Guards in London, knew Craufurd as an officer of unusual education and vision. He had attended reviews of the Prussian Army and served as a British representative in the field with Archduke Charles of Austria. His German and French were fluent and he had the self-confidence necessary to discuss military theory with any of the great captains of the day. After Buenos Aires, Craufurd was saved from obscurity by the court-martial verdict, political connections, and a reputation for being a scientific soldier.

Lieutenant General Sir Arthur Wellesley, who would shortly become known as Lord Wellington, commanding the British forces in the Iberian Peninsula, knew that these qualifications made Craufurd a very rare creature indeed among a pedestrian corps of generals. What better man to entrust with the outposts at the front of his army?

For those marching in Craufurd's brigade, this grasp of military theory counted for little, of course. Old soldiers chatting around the campfire could piece together certain chapters in the brigadier's turbulent career. Captain O'Hare and a few of the others had been in Buenos Aires, where they too had been subjected to the ignominy of surrender and a few months' captivity before returning home. William Brotherwood had been with the 2nd Battalion of Rifles in Craufurd's brigade during the campaign of that previous winter. The wholesale reorganisation of the 95th had brought Brotherwood, his captain Jonathan Leach and many others into the 1st Battalion for this new campaign. Brotherwood could tell the others some stories: he was among the riflemen who'd seen Craufurd beat his men and order floggings for the most frivolous of disciplinary offences. During that long retreat to Corunna seven months before, the lads called him Black Bob.

Craufurd's strictness arose from a conviction that he must rule the brigade entrusted to him with the greatest zeal. He did so because it was the vehicle for the resurrection of his reputation. Its every movement and evolution must be calculated to excite the admiration of Sir Arthur Wellesley and the envy of his peers. Its marches must be regulated with the precision and predictability of a fine timepiece.

To this end, Craufurd issued a series of Standing Orders on the morning of 10 July, as the brigade had a day of rest in Abrantes. Less than a week into the campaign proper, this set of instructions confirmed his reputation for strictness in the eyes of the 95th's officers and established the commander as their enemy. Captain Jonathan Leach, commander of 2nd Company, wrote in his diary: 'Brigadier General Robert Craufurd (damn him) issued this day to the Light Division an immensity of the most *tyrannical* and *oppressive standing orders* that were ever compiled by a British officer [emphasis in original].'

Craufurd's system was designed to govern the troops' behaviour from their first waking moment to their last. Reveille, the blowing of a bugle horn, would sound an hour and a half before any intended march got under way. The Standing Orders set out what had to happen before a second horn blast an hour after the first, noting, for example, 'the baggage must be loaded at least ten minutes before the second horn sounds'. A quarter of an hour later, at the third horn, companies were to form, ready to set up. On the fourth blast, the head of the column would begin its march.

At the other end of the day, everything was prescribed, from the posting of a guard to catch stragglers who'd fallen behind without leave, to the choice of correct sites for cooking and measures to stop 'the men easing themselves in improper places'. In order to prevent the excrement piling up, ditches would have to be dug, 'covered over daily and fresh ones made as often as expedient'. Craufurd, it could truly be said, intended to regulate his brigade's every motion.

Standing Orders reached their most pedantic extreme when describing arrangements for what was usually the day's main business: marching. Article 3 No. 4 stipulated that 'any man who, for the sake of avoiding water or other bad places, or for any other reason, presumes to step on one side, or quit his proper place in the Ranks, must be confined.'

The reasoning for this last injunction was contained in Article 3 No. 7: 'the defiling of one Regiment on the march . . . will cause a delay of ten minutes; one such obstacle, if not passed without defiling, would, therefore, delay a Brigade consisting of three Regiments, half an hour, and in the winter, when obstacles of this kind are frequent, and the days short, a column, which is constantly defiling without cause will arrive at its quarters in the dark.'

Craufurd's orders ran to many pages, which officers were expected to learn by rote. While they were the product of much careful reflection on military science by their author, they were tainted by obsessions such as his conviction that small deviations on the line of march ruined all calculations. Furthermore, his ideas would be enforced with such harshness that they excited the unbridled hatred of almost every officer in the 95th, who had been infused in the newest and most liberal notions of disciplining and motivating soldiers.

If the Rifle officers found Craufurd especially insufferable, then he seems to have regarded them and their ideas with similar disdain. There was something so different about the 95th – its appearance, its weaponry, its conduct – that offended Craufurd's sense of order. He tried to use fear to change their ways. During the Corunna campaign, the whole brigade had often been paraded to witness floggings. He'd struck his soldiers with his own hand, too, for what he saw as insolence. The veterans of that campaign knew well that at one point, after beating a man of the 95th to the ground, Craufurd had shouted at the soldiers around him: 'You think, because you are riflemen, you may do whatever you think proper, but I'll teach you the difference before I have done with you!'

In July, many riflemen regarded the prospect of serving under Craufurd for the foreseeable future with dread. One captain in the 95th, who knew him from the previous campaign, wrote home, 'You have heard how universally General Craufurd was detested in the retreat to Corunna. If possible he is still more abhorred now and has been so ever since we landed in Portugal.'

For the next fortnight they fell into a daily routine of marching. Reveille was usually sounded in the early hours of the morning and the troops would trudge along until about 11 a.m. As the July heat reached its peak, they would be resting and cooking up their main meal of the day.

Craufurd had to reconcile his desire gradually to build up the marching powers of his Light Brigade (so that he did not leave too many stragglers behind or kill off soldiers with heatstroke) with his determination to catch up with the main army he'd been sent to reinforce. General Wellesley had moved his small force of sixteen thousand through the mountainous country of the Hispano-Portuguese frontier, in the direction of Madrid, linking up on the way with a Spanish force of thirty-five thousand under General Cuesta, together with which they now threatened their common enemy, the French. The aim of all this was to stop the French from pushing into the south of the country by threatening Madrid, the centre of their operations.

On most days the Light Brigade marched between twelve and sixteen miles. This was tough enough, and it killed a couple of the weaker men through heatstroke. Craufurd took to inspecting the soldiers' water bottles to make sure they were full. He did not want the rogues to fall out fetching water, or a whole column to halt at some stream while they filled up. The soldiers saw things differently: a full bottle added several pounds to your marching kit and they already felt crushed by the burden of full regulation equipment:

We each had to carry a great weight during this long and harassing march. There was a knapsack and straps, two shirts, two pair of stockings, one pair of shoes, ditto soles and heels, three brushes, a box of blacking, razor, soap box and strap, and also at the time an extra pair of trousers. There was a mess tin, centre tin and lid, haversack and canteen, greatcoat and blanket, a powder flask filled, a ball bag containing thirty loose balls, a small wooden mallet used to hammer the ball into the muzzle of our rifles, belt and pouch – the latter containing fifty rounds of ammunition – sword belt and rifle . . . thus we were equipped with from seventy to eighty pounds of weight in the melting month of July.

This already difficult situation changed decisively on the morning of 28 July, when a dusty rider, carrying an express from Sir Arthur Wellesley, found Craufurd. In it, the commander of forces told Craufurd that he was in the presence of a large French army and that a general action was to be expected at any moment. Any limits that the chief of the Light Brigade had placed on his men had to be thrown to the wind.

Craufurd did not intend to lose what might be his only chance to redeem his reputation in battle. What's more, everyone from private soldier to the commanding officer of the 95th shared the desire to measure himself against the French. So with little delay, Craufurd's brigade was launched into a series of crushing forced marches into the mountains of Iberia.

They began at 2 a.m. on the 28th and stopped at 11 a.m., as usual. Now, instead of resting for the remainder of the day, they started marching again, at about 5 p.m., as the early-evening cool began. 'Every man seemed anxious to push on, and all were in high spirits, hoping soon to be on the field of battle,' one of the marchers wrote. They kept going until 10 p.m., when they stopped for a few hours.

As the Light Brigade struggled up the mountain roads of the border-lands, Wellesley's army was attacked by the French at Talavera de la Reyna. The British general had chosen his ground with the care that was to become one of his most celebrated trademarks. On his right was the River Tagus and the city of Talavera: these obstacles would prevent the French simply going around, or turning, this wing of the Allied Army. Spanish troops occupied that right section of the line, and at the seam where their forces met the British – the junction of two armies being often a weak point – a defensive fieldwork had been built, a small fort bristling with cannon.

The left of Wellesley's position was anchored on another natural obstacle, the hills of the Sierra de Segurilla. Although these were no lofty peaks, the ground itself, being strewn with huge boulders and rocky outcrops, denied any movement to formed troops.

The French would have no choice but to attack in the centre, so this is where Wellesley placed his most powerful formation, the four brigades of General Sherbrooke's 1st Division. In front of them was a stream, the Portina, which ran down from the Sierra, above their left, to the Tagus down on the right. Although it wasn't deep, its banks were difficult in places, which hopefully would break the formation of the French regiments, leaving them vulnerable to a British countercharge.

As the Light Brigade was still marching up behind Wellesley's main army, the battle they fought on 28 July demonstrated very well the military orthodoxies of the day – precisely those ideas that the 95th and the other Light Brigade battalions would revolutionise.

For much of the morning of the 28th, Sherbrooke's men were forced to stand under the fire of French cannon. Their armies, under King Joseph (Napoleon's brother), had lined up their guns on some ground across the Portina and proceeded to batter away at the British line. In many places, particularly higher up the gradual slope to the Sierra, the nature of the ground allowed Wellesley to pull back his troops a little and get them to lie down, so that the ground protected them against the cannon balls.

Much of Sherbrooke's division, though, being deployed on the plain of the Tagus, had no such shelter. They had to put up with the cannonade at about six hundred yards' distance. Fortunately for them, this was not close enough for the really murderous effects of canister or grapeshot and the French gunners were obliged to hurl standard iron cannon balls at them, knocking down the redcoats like some devilish game of skittles. For the targets, this was an unpleasant experience, but it was not necessarily catastrophic, since the British battalions had deployed their companies in line abreast, so that their formation was only two soldiers deep. Only the most exceptional cannon ball could therefore carry off more than two men at a time. Every now and then, with the growling of sergeants making itself heard above the bombardment, the men shuffled a little from both wings towards the middle so that the gaps made by the French cannon were closed. It was vital to preserve a compact formation, both so that the battalion could fire effectively and so that it could defend itself against infantry and cavalry.

At about 3 p.m., it became clear that a general advance had been ordered by the French generals Lapisse and Sebastiani, who began moving twenty-four battalions towards Sherbrooke's eight. These two gentlemen had served long apprenticeships under their imperial master: having humbled Austrians, Prussians and Russians, they were skilled exponents in the French art of war. They had drawn up their forces in two waves. The first, of twelve battalions, marched forward with companies in line, matching the British formations. Behind this first echelon were the other battalions, deployed in columns, each of about forty to fifty men across the front and nine deep. Each of these French battalions had its own company of light soldiers and they were sent ahead of both waves. They ran forward taking potshots, ducking down in cover while they reloaded and then moving off again.

The French intent, with both the skirmisher fire and the artillery that had preceded it, was as much to unsettle the British troops as it was to kill them. Napoleon's victories had demonstrated that this long-range firing often unbalanced an enemy: many soldiers would begin shooting back perhaps at two hundred yards or even further, others might leave the ranks and try to save themselves. In this way, those facing a French charge would be goaded into a spontaneous, ineffective, long-range musket fire which would do nothing to check the onslaught, which in turn would so damage the defender's nerve that they often ran away before the Emperor's advancing regiments reached them. If not, a close-range French volley and the bayonet would usually decide the matter.

Sherbrooke's men watched the French formations moving down to the Portina in front of them, and loaded. Each man took a cartridge, and bit the top off the paper packet of gunpowder. He trickled some of the powder into a small pan on the right of his musket's barrel and then snapped shut the metal lid that covered this priming. Then the remaining powder, the bulk of it, was poured down the barrel, the paper packet scewed up and placed into the same hole, followed by the musket ball itself. The soldier then drew the ramrod from under the barrel, using it to force the ball down to the bottom so that powder, paper and ball were packed snug together.

While he was performing these actions, the soldier kept the hammer or cock sprung back in a half-open position: half-cock. On loading the cartridge, he would make the weapon ready by bringing it up to his chest and pulling the hammer back to full distance (you did not want to go off at half-cock). On hearing the command 'Present!' he would bring the musket up to the firing position.

When the order to fire was eventually given, he would pull the trigger, causing the hammer of his weapon to fly forward with the flint it held striking the cover. This in turn produced a spark that ignited the initial priming charge; which, burning through a small hole on the side of the barrel in a fraction of a second, then caused the main explosion which sent the ball out of the weapon and towards the enemy.

General Sherbrooke had given very strict orders that his men should not fire until the enemy was just fifty yards away. It should be a single volley, and it should be followed by a cheer and a charge with fixed bayonets. Sherbrooke's orders showed that he well understood the limitations of the musket and of his soldiers' training.

Muskets were so inaccurate that those carried by the British, the famed Brown Bess, had no sights. The men were not taught to aim them either. In fact, some regulations of a few decades before had even encouraged them to close their eyes at the moment of firing: packed together shoulder to shoulder in firing formation, the flash from their neighbour's priming, coming momentarily before the shot itself, might cause them to flinch and fire wildly. They were ordered not to aim but to 'Present!', which meant pointing in the enemy's direction. In theory, they were taught to 'level' their weapon for different ranges, firing at their enemy's waist at very close range, the chest when a little further away and so on. In practice, very few private soldiers knew anything about this. Once firing began, most soldiers tried to load as quickly as possible, discipline broke down and a ragged contest of ineffective musketry took place, with both sides rooted to the spot. The chances of hitting anything would be further reduced by the thick smoke that billowed about the field with each discharge of powder.

As the French marched up towards Sherbrooke's battalions, his orders were followed exactly. The French came forward with their customary shouting and calling, while the British line waited impassively. They waited indeed until the enemy formations were so close that their skirmishers could no longer provide any effective screening for them. In the process, a British screen of light troops, including a few dozen mercenary riflemen of the 60th, had been easily beaten back by the French and done little to trouble the advancing French heavy infantry.

When they were barely fifty yards away, so close that the lines of French troops would almost fill his battalions' field of view, the redcoats presented their pieces and fired. The slaughter was tremendous – hundreds of French troops dropped, perhaps one-third of the attacking echelon. The Brown Bess might be inaccurate but a man hit by its great slug of a ball suffered terrible trauma, often being hurled backwards several feet or having a limb ripped off by its shock.

Then came the cheer, in order to remind Sherbrooke's men not to get carried away in their musket shooting, the common soldier's delusion being that making a lot of noise and smoke was a substitute for more decisive action. Of course, the cheer was also intended to frighten the reeling Frenchmen.

As the Guards and King's German Legion of the 1st Division rushed forward, Lapisse and Sebastiani's men did not wait to be impaled on their bayonets: they broke, turned around and started running back towards their own lines. Six of Sherbrooke's battalions hurtled forward, many of the men going beyond the Portina in pursuit. Their blood was up and their commanders lacked the experience or ability to check their headlong rush.

It was at this point that the second echelons of Lapisse and Sebastiani's divisions came into play: fresh troops with an unbroken formation. What was worse for the British was that two regiments of enemy dragoons were also close at hand. As the horsemen careered into the clumps of redcoats streaming across the ochre plain they began sabreing them mercilessly. Two battalions of the German Legion, mercenaries serving the British crown under mostly Hanoverian officers, got the full impact. In rushing forward, the Legion had lost all formation or order. Once cavalry appeared there was no way they could be rallied into the virtually impregnable defensive square. Half of this Legion brigade of 1,300 men were lost, even the brigade commander paying with his life for his moment of impetuous pursuit.

The survivors among Sherbrooke's battalions came running back to their own lines, exhausted, many bearing sabre wounds, and prepared to meet a fresh French assault. This, somehow, they succeeded in seeing off. Sherbrooke's division ended the day with almost 1,700 killed, wounded and captured; the opposing French suffered similar losses despite their much greater initial numbers. The Battle of Talavera concluded with a British victory, but with heavy losses that Wellesley felt he could ill afford.

The lessons of Sherbrooke's fight would seem to have justified most of the British Army's orthodoxies: effective musketry could only be delivered at very short range; at these distances fire achieved its devastating effect with a blast like a ship's broadside, not with each man aiming; skirmishers capering about, trying to choose their own targets with inherently inaccurate weapons, would never decide the outcome of a battle between two forces of infantry formed in battle lines; steadiness was everything and to keep men in line required the maintenance of fierce discipline; once infantry lost their formation, they could be easily annihilated by charging infantry or cavalry. All of these principles, strongly held by Wellesley and his fellow generals, seemed to offer only an incidental role in battle for the Rifles.

The 95th set out on the morning of 29 July from Oropesa, where they'd rested for two or three hours, for a five-hour march to Talavera. One young officer recorded that over 'the last ten miles the road was covered with Spanish wounded and fugitive soldiers'.

The final stage of the march saw the men struggling forward against the incline. Their leather straps cut into shoulders, the stock or collar on their necks partially throttled them. Within an hour or two of starting, tongues were lolling about parched mouths, and haversacks bobbing on top of sweat-soaked backs. As the battalion halted for a moment by a fetid pool, garnished with cow dung, many fell flat on their bellies and lapped at the greenish water like animals.

When Craufurd's column appeared near Talavera around 7 a.m., it was cheered by the exhausted British battalions that remained on the field after a battle that had left something like twelve thousand men of the two sides dead or wounded. In some places the dry grass had caught fire, touched off by the smouldering cartridge papers, and many wounded men, unable to crawl away, had been badly burned.

Few of the French soldiers witnessed the scene on the 29th, for they had pulled back several miles from the battlefield. Wellesley wasted little time in pushing forward Craufurd's brigade to secure this new front, as surgeons and stretcher parties struggled to answers the plaintive cries of the wounded.

While the 95th had not tasted battle on the 28th, they most certainly saw its bloody consequences, one of the new soldiers remarking, 'The horrid sights were beyond anything I could have imagined. Thousands dead and dying in every direction . . . and, I am sorry to say, Spaniards butchering the wounded Frenchmen at every opportunity, and stripping them naked, which gave admission to myriads of pernicious flies and the heat of a burning sun.'

During the next two days, riflemen were posted on picket duty to observe the French scouts. Sometimes they exchanged fire, but to little effect. It took no more than a meal or two for everyone to realise that Wellesley would not be able to supply his army in this position. It was a horribly poor part of Spain, and its slender resources had already been stripped by the French. The British commissaries, inexperienced in operations of this scale, soon showed themselves incapable of acquiring either transport or the required number of rations.

While General Wellesley was deciding on his best course of action, attempts were made to burn hundreds of the putrefying bodies that still littered the field. Recalling this miserable stay, one officer of the 95th remembered that 'the feelings which constant hunger produces were, however, in some degree counteracted two days after the battle by the insufferable stench arising from hundreds of dead bodies of men and horses still unburied.'

If the battalion's recent arrivals had now seen a battlefield for the charnel house it was, not a few also took advantage of its fruits, plundering the dead. Second Lieutenant Simmons relieved one fallen Frenchman of his backpack: as an officer he'd not been issued with one, but he'd keenly felt the need for such a contraption during his march.

That dash was already the subject of comment in the brigade and the Army at large. During the last twenty-four hours they had covered something between twenty-nine and thirty miles on atrocious stone-strewn roads that were little better than goat tracks. Their whole journey over the previous twenty-five days was something like 360 miles. Men had dropped dead trying to keep pace with that. The rest of the Army was deeply impressed by this march, so much so that the final day's mileage was exaggerated as reports circulated on how Craufurd had driven his men onwards.

For Craufurd, though, it had all been futile. He had not made it in time to share in the laurels of a hard-fought general action. Like many officers in Wellesley's army, he suspected that this campaign would last no longer than the previous one in Iberia – a matter of several months – and then they would be embarked and taken home again, and it was to home that the despondent brigadier's thoughts turned. Craufurd was a faithful and loving correspondent with his wife Fanny. His letters to her were full of a tenderness and sympathy of which his many detractors would never have imagined him capable. They ended with passages like, 'God of Heaven bless you, my dearest love, Ever your most affectionate husband, R. C.' On 31 July he sat down to write her

a swift note from his bivouac near Talavera. Noting his brigade's failure to reach the town in time for the battle, it ended, 'This will perhaps
be a subject of joy to you, though you will at the same time find it natural that it should have mortified us.' Craufurd's desire to prove himself and his brigade burned with an undiminished intensity.

THREE

Guadiana

August–December 1809

Early in August the Army redeployed back to the Portuguese frontier. The 95th found itself marching in stages just as harsh as those before the Battle of Talavera. But whereas the chance of meeting the enemy had motivated that earlier struggle, they were now tramping away from him as quickly as their blistered feet and aching legs could carry them. Instead of a shot at glory, they had Craufurd hovering about them, taking the names of men who fell foul of Standing Orders and promising to punish them.

The diary of one company commander read:

3rd August. The whole British Army marched at two this morning to Oropesa where we arrived at 2 p.m. This day's march excessively severe; being twelve hours on the road; a suffocating heat, clouds of dust and not a drop of water to be got . . .

5th August. We finished our march this day about 2 p.m. The weather was immoderately hot and a great scarcity of water on the road. We were thirteen hours marching on the worst roads I ever travelled.

6th August. Marched at half past three this morning and did not reach our position until six in the evening. This day's march was remarkably harassing. Numbers of men of different regts. dropped on the road from excessive fatigue and the heat of the sun.

The mountainous borderland was bare at the best of times, and it could not sustain tens of thousands of hungry soldiers. One evening during that march, with the troops bivoaucking dejectedly in clumps of trees by the roadside, Brigadier Craufurd allowed his Light Brigade soldiers to shoot some pigs rooting around the groves. Mad with hunger, they had instantly set upon the animals, shooting and clubbing them, their death squeals filling the dark forest. The men had little doubt that this herd of swine must belong to somebody and had appreciated Craufurd's relaxation of the usual strictures against plundering civilians. But if the brigadier was normally a pedant about rules, he was also a man of volatile temper and he had been driven to distraction by the failure of the Army's commissaries to supply his men.

On 7 August, the Rifles reached Almaraz, a dusty crossroads in the sierra where they were to spend the next two weeks. The importance of the place derived from a bridge across the Tagus, which is sufficiently broad, even this high in its course, to form a serious obstacle to movement. The river's shape and that of the surrounding peaks made it a key point in both east–west and north–south communications. Although Almaraz had great strategic value, few people lived around the river, so the Rifles' arrival there did little to ease the supply shortage.

In order to guard the crossing, two companies of the 95th were deployed in turn as pickets, with the remainder of the battalion camped nearby and able to support them, should the French try to rush the place. From the moment they arrived at Almaraz, it became clear to the officers that the swampy ground about the Tagus and the heavy dews made this an unhealthy place, charged with ill vapours and miasmas.

'Here we remained a miserable fortnight,' one young lieutenant wrote in his journal, 'moving at sunset to a damp valley near the river (where the seeds of ague were sown in hundreds) and returning at daybreak to repose under the shelter of some cork trees which indifferently sheltered us from a scorching sun – no regular issue of rations – which never amounted to more than a handful of coarse flour, a little goat's flesh and neither wine nor spirits.'

The main bivouac, with its precious shade, was on a low hill a few hundred yards back from the river. Officers had chosen this spot because they believed it healthier than the low-lying land. Some of the flour that the men were supplied was actually made from grain, but much of it consisted of ground dried peas. They mixed it with water, and sometimes a little straw for binding, and formed it into little dumplings they called dough boys. They boiled or grilled them on flat stones. As often as not, the dough boys gave them cramps and the flux – but they still failed to sate their hunger. The riflemen named their camp Dough Boy Hill.

Every soldier, from private to captain, had noticed a dramatic change in himself since their disembarkation a little more than a month before. The hot sun had tanned their faces and cracked their lips. Constant marching and poor diet meant their clothes had begun to hang loose on them. One officer, deploying trademark Rifles irony, wrote, 'If any corpulent person despairs of reducing his weight by the means usually adopted, I strongly recommend a few weeks' change of air and scene at Almaraz.'

As the 3rd Company men sat one evening looking over the river and trying to stay their hunger pangs, two countrymen who'd volunteered into the 95th from the Leicestershire Militia considered their plight.

'Bill, I think we shall be kept on this Dough-boy Hill till we shall all die of want,' said the first.

'I think so too,' Private Green replied, before reflecting wistfully, 'it is Lutterworth feast today. Our friends will be eating plum pudding and roast beef!'

'Ah! They little think what we pass through and suffer.'

The Leicestershire Militia boys like Green and William Brotherwood in the 2nd Company were perhaps more alive to the misery of their situation than many others. The weavers who made up their bulk had joined up through need, having lost a good living. They were also bright men, having worked looms and been proud of their craftsmanship.

It took until 15 August for the French, following up Sir Arthur Wellesley's withdrawal, to appear on the other side of the Tagus. They placed their own pickets, in case the British should try to surprise *them*, and the two sides observed one another across the waters. The Rifle company commanders were sure enough of one thing: that while neither side intended to attack the other and while life remained as miserable as it was there, night alarms and other symptoms of the presence of an enemy could safely be dispensed with. By calling out to their French opposite numbers and using sign language, they evolved a system of signals to ensure a quiet stay. As one officer wrote, 'So far from a single shot being exchanged, our men and the French had the best possible understanding; and it frequently happened that the officers of both parties took off their hats and saluted each other across the river.'

This system was suspended several days later, when the 95th received orders to march almost a hundred miles south-east to the town of Campo Maior. With this movement, the campaigning season would effectively end, Wellesley deciding to abandon any further diversion on behalf of the Spanish and concentrate instead on solving the supply and other problems that debilitated his army while readying them for the defence of Portugal. Napoleon's attempts to take over Spain and Portugal had triggered such widespread resistance that a quarter of a million French troops were being tied down. Britain was doing its best to exacerbate these difficulties by landing expeditionary forces in Portugal and southern Spain, at the extremes of the Iberian Peninsula furthest from the French border. In this way they hoped to stiffen local resistance while forcing Napoleon's commanders to extend deeper and deeper into guerrilla-infested country.

The march down to Campo Maior required the riflemen to traverse some high mountains – known as the Sierra de Guadalupe – all the time under the eye of Black Bob Craufurd. Captain Jonathan Leach wrote in his diary on 27 August,

The Division paraded at six this evening when we got volleys of abuse and blasphemous language from that infernal scoundrel Brigadier Robert Craufurd, who, after flogging half a dozen men for some very frivolous offences committed on our late harassing marches, we were dismissed. Lay down to sleep at nine o'clock but not without offering hearty prayers for the discomfiture of our cursed commander.

Eight days later, the 2nd Company commander noted the flogging of a soldier from one of the other Light Brigade battalions and another 'long harangue from General Craufurd'.

As the battalion snaked its way down one of the steep mountain tracks leading from the sierra to the river plain that was their destination, Second Lieutenant George Simmons marched towards his brigadier, just off the road and in full flow, heaping scorn and abuse upon the head of the provost marshal. Before Simmons knew it, he'd been collared by Craufurd, taken out of the line of march, and, in one of the brigadier's squeaking furies, told to arrest the provost marshal, the man who himself was meant to be the brigade's enforcer of military discipline. Taking some riflemen to assist, Simmons found himself escorting the provost marshal, several soldiers already under arrest in his charge as well as some baggage. As for Craufurd, he galloped off to the head of the column.

A little further down the road, as it sloped steeply downhill, two of the mules, pulling one of the carts, decided to stop. After pushing, pulling and cajoling but all to no avail, one of the riflemen detached the sling from his weapon, got astride one of the beasts, and smacked it about the rump with the leather strap. The animals stampeded down the precipitous road, throwing the rifleman clear. Simmons and the others watched dumbstruck as the cart bounced about the narrow track, gathering speed until eventually the inevitable happened and it was hurled over a precipice, dashed to pieces on rocks below. It had been carrying Brigadier Craufurd's personal supply of wine and other delicacies.

Simmons found Craufurd that evening in a commandeered house at the end of their march:

He had a party at dinner, and was expecting his light cart every moment with its contents in the best possible order. When I related the sad catastrophe he became nearly furious, and directed me to march up the prisoners to their various regiments, to obtain drummers, and in front of each regiment to flog the culprits – in fact, to become a provost marshal for the occasion.

The young subaltern, the most junior officer in the 95th, found himself the instrument of his brigadier's fury. 'I was highly indignant at such usage,' Simmons wrote in his journal, 'having exerted myself zealously to serve him.' Noting that Black Bob 'never forgave me', Simmons resolved not to obey his brigadier's order. Instead he went off to locate his own commanding officer, Lieutenant Colonel Sidney Beckwith.

In Beckwith, Craufurd found his match and the 95th its idol. As someone opposed to flogging on principle, Beckwith simply went outside and verbally admonished the men under arrest, soldiers who had been caught by Craufurd straggling behind the line of march. The colonel then told Simmons to go to his company and that he would be answerable to Craufurd.

Once the brigade had arrived in Campo Maior, a battle of wills between Craufurd and Beckwith made itself apparent almost every day. Both men were determined to train their soldiers to a peak of professional efficiency and both were apostles of a new creed, one in which light infantry should become the pattern for the whole Army. Everything else about them, however, contrasted: Beckwith was a model of self-control, whereas Craufurd often became apoplectic with rage; Beckwith only raised his voice when it was necessary to make himself heard above gunfire, then it was described as being 'like thunder', whereas Craufurd did so frequently and squeakily; being more than six foot tall, Beckwith towered over his diminutive brigadier; Beckwith believed soldiers were best motivated either by positive encouragement or by shaming them in the eyes of their messmates, Craufurd believed in coercion.

Beckwith took a dim view of Craufurd, but he was sufficiently sensitive to the needs of military subordination to express his true feelings only to his equals. One evening the commanding officer of the 95th was standing in the Campo Maior camp talking to Lieutenant Colonel Barclay of the 52nd Light Infantry, another of Craufurd's battalions, when a gift arrived from the brigadier. He had sent Barclay a bottle of cherry brandy, and the colonel wasted no time easing its cork and pouring himself a glass.

Not a little disgusted, Beckwith asked him, 'What, Barclay, do you drink anything from such a fellow as that?' Barclay emptied the glass and replied, 'Don't I, indeed? Here's damnation to him!' There was a roar of complicit laughter.

At the age of thirty-seven, Beckwith was reaching the peak of his powers. He was a veteran of half a dozen campaigns and had been on intimate terms both with the founders of his regiment and with Sir John Moore, the general who had commanded the Light Brigade several years before in Shorncliffe, making it the crack corps it was. Moore, who had been killed at Corunna early in 1809, was a keen advocate both of new tactics and of a more humane attitude towards the rank and file.

Not only was Beckwith a natural leader, he also understood soldiers' mentality perfectly. All commanders were concerned, for example, by men falling out of the line of march. They would say they were going to answer nature's call, shake a stone out of their shoe or whatever else, but sometimes they were going to rob civilians. This problem drove Wellesley to distraction during the 1809 campaign, because hundreds of soldiers were doing it and he feared violent reactions from the populace.

While Craufurd frequently applied the lash to stragglers, the 95th had developed its own approach. As they fell out, riflemen were told to hand their weapon and haversack to their marching comrades. One 95th officer described why it worked so admirably: 'first, the soldier was enabled, not being encumbered with either knapsack or musket, more speedily to overtake the column on its march; and secondly, if he loitered unnecessarily on the way to rejoin his comrades, who were doubly burdened with his arms and pack, he would be certain to incur their displeasure.' The rifleman who left his weapon with his mates might receive verbal or physical abuse from them if he held back too long, and he would also have lost his instrument for threatening the locals.

The difference between Beckwith's and Craufurd's approaches manifested themselves almost as soon as the brigade made its bivouac in Campo Maior and the brigadier announced his programme of daily training.

Craufurd instituted a march, four miles to the nearby River Caya, where the men would bathe, before marching the four-mile return leg. The brigadier ordered that each man dress in full kit for this drill, carrying his weapon, a shako on his head, woollen regimental coat, leather stock around his neck, crossbelts, etc. 'Every corps did harness and march forth to the river in that form except our own,' wrote an officer of the 95th. 'Colonel Beckwith on the contrary always ordered our men on these occasions, to take . . . foraging caps and a stick.'

Beckwith shared his commander's belief that it was necessary to maintain his battalion's marching powers while in cantonments, and indeed to keep them clean, but he did not intend to vex them with petty regulations. On the contrary, he wanted officers and men to enjoy themselves. The riflemen were carrying sticks so that they could go beating in the grasslands around the Caya, while their officers murdered the duck, snipe, plovers and bustards that teemed there for sport and, of course, for the pot.

Another of Craufurd's preoccupations during that September of 1809 was shooting practice. Very few commanders in the British Army (and none in the French) paid any real attention to marksmanship. What need was there for it, if you only intended to open fire at fifty yards, as Sherbrooke had done at Talavera, and if the men had no clue about aiming? Craufurd understood though that his light troops would often be posted ahead of the army, observing the enemy in small groups, where they might have to defend themselves against superior numbers.

During the 1775–83 war against the American rebels, British generals had learned many valuable lessons: that sharpshooters could stop a battalion functioning properly by picking off its officers; that using cover was sometimes the key to defending yourself; that by allowing the soldier to choose his moment of firing, rather than doing it by rote commands, he might stand a better chance of picking his own target; and that by placing your men with a bigger distance between them, perhaps two feet apart instead of shoulder to shoulder, you made it easier to choose a target without being distracted by your neighbour's firing.

Craufurd felt the Army was guilty of forgetting many valuable lessons of the American war. Its veterans were too old to be involved in fighting Napoleon, and it lacked the professional journals or institutions needed to propagate this kind of knowledge. There had been attempts to foster professional study and debate during the early 1800s, with imprints like Egerton's Military Library publishing many books on the latest theories and practice, but too many officers, alas, were more interested in drinking and playing cards than in earnest professional debate. Even if some understood the need for training in marksmanship there was another problem: the Army failed to furnish its garrisons with sufficient ammunition to make target practice possible. As soon as his brigade reached Campo Maior, Craufurd set about trying to secure a vast stock of cartridges that had reportedly been written off as spoiled during the recent campaign. Some weeks after arriving at Campo Maior, a letter from Headquarters announced success: 'His Lordship [Sir Arthur Wellesley had lately received a peerage and taken the title Wellington] approves of your expending, for practice, as much ammunition as you may think proper, reporting from time to time to this office the quantity expended.'

Shooting was one of those areas where the officers of the 95th had very particular views. Many of the battalion's subalterns and even captains carried a rifle, whereas other officers, including in the red-coated battalions of the Light Brigade, considered that somewhat uncouth, for they regarded the sword as the only weapon truly becoming of a gentleman. Rifle officers justified their shooting prowess, and reconciled it with the gentility of rank, by portraying themselves as fellows who were simply bringing their love of sport to the battlefield.

In the hands of a private soldier, the rifle presented an interesting social conundrum and one less easily explained away as sport. The regulations for riflemen which were central to the 95th's training made it clear: 'As soon as the rifleman has fixed upon his object, he fires without waiting for any command.' Not only was the common rifleman made an arbiter of life and death, but the 95th was explicitly founded to emulate those sharpshooters of the previous century's American war who, 'posted behind thickets, and scattered wide in the country, frequently picked off the officer, and galled and annoyed the King's troops in their march'.

By contrast, General Sir David Dundas, the author of the Rules and Regulations for the Army as a whole, an officer who had reached the summit of his profession in 1809 as the Commander in Chief, had spelt out that one of the purposes of his tract was 'to enable the Commanding Officer . . . to be capable of restraining the bad effects of such ideas of independent and individual exertions as are visonary and hurtful', and instead to foster 'regulated obedience'. Dundas used his rules to impose a uniform system of drill on the British Army in the 1790s, one which was based on the Prussian school of Frederick the Great. Although most British officers recognised his achievement in imposing some kind of standardisation, by the early 1800s quite a few regarded Dundas and his regulations as a dead hand, holding the Army in a vice of formal, inflexible movements, slowing the evolution of light-infantry or rifle tactics.

Dundas thought any large-scale skirmishing a 'great danger', something that might have 'fatal consequences'. But many younger officers derided him as 'Old Pivot', a reference to his insistence on a slow system of manoeuvre practised by the Prussians in which companies of men turned on fixed points known as pivots. General Sir John Moore, for example, fumed about Dundas's 'damned eighteen manoeuvres' and their stultifying effect. Moore had already set about subverting Dundas's rules and regulations with new tactics introduced at Shorncliffe. The Guadiana plain contained representatives of both sides of the schism, between those who wanted all infantry to 'ape grenadiers' and others who wanted to free light troops from strict regulation. Craufurd, another admirer of Frederick the Great, was doing Dundas's bidding. Beckwith believed that freeing the soldier's spirit was essential. The great irony of it all was that Dundas, by a quirk of the Army's patronage system, had ended up a few months earlier as the titular head or Colonel of the 95th Regiment. He thus skimmed a lucrative side income from the administration of the very regiment whose tactics in Spain would undermine some of his most cherished ideas.

This tension between giving the rifleman power to kill on his own initiative and instilling complete obedience in the ordinary infantryman was resolved by generals and military theorists in two main ways.

One was to stress the limited roles of the light-infantry soldier, and particularly riflemen, in combat. The other was to insist that this type of fighter was born rather than made. It was infinitely less threatening to social order to believe that the rifle soldier was found among the natural hunters of mountain, forest and frontier.

At first, during the American wars, British generals had subscribed to the notion that only the born huntsman could make an effective rifle soldier, so they had hired German auxiliaries and enlisted loyalist frontiersmen. Even in 1798, when Britain had formed its first battalion armed with rifles, the 5th or Rifle Battalion of the 60th Regiment, it employed mercenaries – mainly Swiss and German – under a lieutenant colonel formerly of the Austrian service. The Austrians themselves chose to arm their Tyrolean *montagnards* with rifles. Even the French, whose swarms of *voltiguers* or *tirailleurs* operating free from the usual formations had become a hallmark of their revolutionary armies, had come to see the light infantry as a service which naturally suited inhabitants of their country's mountainous extremities.

British apostles of the rifle claimed that this new weapon would allow the nation to indulge once more in the passion for sport and marksmanship that had distinguished the English yeoman with his longbow centuries earlier. One officer of the 95th wrote in 1808, 'The rifle, in its present excellence, assumes the place of the bow, and the time is arrived when arms are again committed to the hands of Englishmen; the plains of Egypt and Calabria have witnessed deeds worthy of Cressy and Agincourt!'

Notions of national character had become a powerful influence on military debates at this time, so it should not be surprising that officers of the 95th Rifles used history to assert that the Englishman should face no obstruction in becoming as fine a marksman as the Swiss or German. To many military men, only those whom modern life had made too soft should be disqualified from service in light troops. One experienced practitioner wrote, 'No printers, bookbinders, taylors, shoemakers or weavers should be enlisted, as from their business they contract habits of effeminacy, and are unable to support the fatigues of war.'

The former shoemaker Costello and weaver Brotherwood would doubtless have objected loudly to such notions – for in their shooting or marching they intended to show they could be just as good a William Tell as any Swiss of the 60th. Costello, Fairfoot and the other new militia drafts sharpened their rifle skills, firing at marks on the grasslands around Campo Maior, thus unwittingly demonstrating the conviction of those who had founded the 95th that riflemen were not born but made. They were taught not just how to fire at man-sized target boards – 'if it were smaller the unpractised recruit would be apt to miss so often as to despair of hitting it' – but also more advanced techniques.

The rifle placed in their hands was a superbly designed weapon, both robust and practical. Ezekiel Baker, its inventor, had demonstrated his invention's superiority in competitive trials organised by the Board of Ordnance. Not only had the Baker rifle shown its accuracy, but it had also managed to overcome the prejudice against such weapons by being robust enough for field service, simple to reload, and less likely to foul after a few dozen shots than the designs it had vanquished. Baker's gun had sights along its barrel that allowed easy adjustment of long-range shots (so that you lifted the muzzle a little higher at ranges of, say, three hundred yards, to compensate for the droop in the shot at those distances). The more experienced riflemen had trained in techniques for shooting at running enemy soldiers with specially constructed moving targets on their ranges in England. In the field, they also learnt – for their officers did nothing to discourage the rank and file from shooting at birds, rabbits and other prey – how to lead a fast-moving target, so as to compensate for the gap between the shot being fired and it finding its target.

Many of the riflemen who had served in other regiments marvelled at the superiority of the 95th's techniques and instruction, one such commenting: 'Eight out of ten soldiers in our regular regiments will aim in the same manner at an object at the distance of three hundred yards, as at one only fifty. It must hence be evident that the greater part of those shots are lost or expended in vain; indeed the calculation has been made, that only one shot out of two hundred fired from muskets in the field takes effect, while one out of twenty from rifles is the average.' In this way, the Green Jackets hoped to more than compensate for the rifle's rate of fire, which with perhaps one shot per minute was two or three times slower than a smooth-bore musket.

Men like Beckwith believed that new qualities of initiative were required from the soldiers who wielded the rifle, and these were not best fostered by corporal punishment or drilling him until he became an automaton. One of the 95th's founders had written in 1806,

'Ambition and the love of distinction are the ruling passions of soldiers, prompting them to encounter every hardship.' In fostering that
ambition, the regiment believed in teaching its soldiers to read and
write – an essential qualification for promotion, but a step considered
highly suspect by many of the Army's more reactionary generals,
including Wellington himself.

The 95th's raw material, though, was not much different from that
of any other regiment, despite the wish of some officers to develop a
more selective recruitment system. Its founders had tried, in the early
days, to recruit among the tougher men on the country's Celtic fringes.
As a result the regiment had, for a while, been almost equally divided
between English, Scots and Irish. The admission of hundreds of militia
volunteers (mainly from Leicestershire, Lincolnshire and Surrey) early
in 1809 had changed the 95th's character, bringing in more English,
many of them former tradesmen. When setting out from Dover earlier
that year, its composition had been roughly six Englishmen to two
Scots and two Irish.

In the ranks of the 95th, there were soldiers with all the vices Lord
Wellington associated with British or Irish recruits. Many officers felt
the Irish were particularly prone to thieving. They almost all plundered, of course, especially when the failures of supply drove them mad
with hunger. They also loved to drink, and it was liquor that gave
Beckwith a particularly difficult problem of command while his battalion was in Campo Maior.

Tom Plunket, the Irish crack shot so admired on the passage out by
Ned Costello, had by this stage been promoted from corporal to sergeant, and got blind drunk one day after training had finished. When
his messmates tried to restrain his increasingly outrageous behaviour,
Plunket became violent, grabbed his rifle and barricaded himself into a
small hut. There was no choice but to send for an officer. Plunket, however, swore blind he would shoot the first person sent to arrest him.
The stand-off continued until his passions cooled and some officers
were able to persuade him to come out.

Under a draconian disciplinary regime, it is quite clear that Plunket
could have ended up charged with mutiny, being marched in front of a
general court martial. Such bodies tried the most serious offences,
including capital ones, and had Plunket been convicted he might well
have ended up on a rope. Beckwith's dilemma was all the more disturbing, given that just a few months before he had singled out Plunket

for shooting the French general and called him a 'pattern for the whole battalion'.

Many of the older soldiers knew that back in 1805 Beckwith had proved his aversion to flogging in the most remarkable way. When a party of drunken Irish recruits to the battalion had chanced upon two women near the camp, abusing them verbally and physically, Beckwith had soon discovered the culprits and paraded the battalion. The regiment had learned with shock that the ladies, who had been treated in the most indecent manner, were none other than the colonel's wife and one of her maids. Beckwith told his men that he would have flogged them had it been anyone else, but since the injury had been done to his own wife he did not wish the punishment to have the appearance of personal vengeance.

Although Beckwith and the other founders of the 95th considered flogging both degrading and pointless, they did not rule it out under all circumstances. His predecessor as commanding officer of the 1st Battalion, for example, had campaigned publicly for the abolition of corporal punishment, 'except in cases of infamy'. Such was Plunket's case, for the battalion could not be allowed to see such an example of riot go unpunished.

Plunket's company commander and Beckwith evidently resolved to settle the matter within the battalion. Officers of the 95th were sensitive to cases which might damage the regiment's good name going before a general court martial, because such proceedings would inevitably come to the notice of Lord Wellington and, since they were published, of newspapers back in England. Plunket's punishment – the loss of his sergeant's stripes and three hundred lashes – was instead decided *instanter* by a rapid regimental court martial.

'When the sentence became known, sorrow was felt for him throughout the regiment, by the officers almost as much as the men,' according to Private Costello, who had worshipped Plunket since joining O'Hare's company. The battalion was paraded to witness the punishment. Plunket was stripped to the waist, tied to a tree and two buglers stepped forward with their cats. After Beckwith refused a last appeal, the first bugler swung his whip onto the prisoner's back.

After a few strokes, the colonel suspected that Plunket's popularity was making the bugler lay it on a little light. 'Do your duty fairly, sir!' he shouted at the bugler, who completed the first ration of twenty-five lashes. But Beckwith could not stand the whole procedure, and after thirty-five had been administered, he ordered that Plunket be taken down. Beckwith spoke to the bloodied prisoner in a clear, loud voice, for the benefit of the whole battalion: 'You see now, sir, how very easy it is to commit a blackguard's crime, but how difficult to take his punishment.'

The training at Campo Maior reached a peak on 23 September. A little after dawn, the 95th was joined by the other two battalions under Craufurd's command (the 43rd and 52nd Light Infantry) for a brigade field day. This was an opportunity for the brigadier to watch how quickly his men responded to his commands to change formation while moving across country. The more swiftly and precisely these evolutions were carried out, the greater the brigade's chance of prevailing on the battlefield.

The tactics taught to the 43rd and 52nd by Moore back in England, and drilled by Craufurd under that blazing Iberian sun, were a hybrid of orthodox and Rifle ones. They helped the battalions to change formation more quickly, to extend many companies in skirmish order (not just one, as was more usual in normal infantry battalions), and they encouraged a new type of shooting which gave the redcoats the added destructive power that the 95th had achieved through aimed fire, while retaining the devastating short-range potential of the volley. The Light Brigade system pioneered by the 52nd instructed men: 'On the word "Present!" . . . each man slowly and independently levelling at the particular object his eye has fixed upon, and as soon as he has covered it, fires of his own accord.'

For new soldiers like Simmons, Fairfoot and Costello, running about the dusty scrub was hard, thirsty work, particularly as the day became ferociously hot. At least, though, they were learning the tactics of their chosen corps, something that was new to them. For the old hands such as O'Hare, Almond and Brotherwood, these field days could be tiresome in the extreme: they had done it a hundred times before and were only likely to catch Craufurd's notice if they fouled up. They knew the difference, too, between the textbook evolutions of the training ground and the real business of staying alive once the balls were flying.

As week after week of intense training went on, the Light Brigade found its preparations for war being sapped by a sinister disease. The plain where they had bivouacked belonged to the Guadiana River, and the Caya, where they bathed, was one of its tributaries. The Guadiana marked Portugal's frontier and Wellington had chosen to keep his army there because it would allow him to re-enter Spain on another raid in support of the Spanish armies. However, the flatlands around this great river were known to be 'proverbially unhealthy'.

Privates Robert Fairfoot and Ned Costello and Second Lieutenant George Simmons all came down with Guadiana fever. Simmons, who had once been destined for a medical career himself, believed he had been stricken with 'the typhus', but the army's surgeons had their own diagnosis of intermittent fever. Once a man was stricken with this malady, he could be laid out for weeks, each apparent improvement of his condition giving way to some recurrent bout of sweats and delirium.

The number of cases built up quickly and the regimental hospital, manned by the 95th's surgeon and his two mates, soon proved inadequate for the care of more than a few dozen patients, so the feverish riflemen were transported to a general hospital established in a convent in the nearby garrison of Elvas. One patient noted, 'My case was really pitiable, my appetite and hearing gone; feet and legs like ice; three blisters on my back and feet untreated and undressed; my shirt sticking in the wounds caused by the blisters . . . a little sympathy would have soothed, but sympathy there was none.' Private Costello, finding himself in the convent, recorded, 'I fortunately recovered after an illness of nearly six weeks, thanks to my good constitution, but none to the brute of an orderly, who, during a delirium of the fever beat me once most furiously with a broom stick.'

The surgeons were at a loss for a specific cause of the outbreak. Since the fever had evidently arisen because of the sickly miasmas that pervaded the Guadiana plain, they kept fires burning in the wards, so the smoke might keep out these noxious vapours. One of O'Hare's riflemen, dragooned into acting as an orderly, recorded another treatment for the raging fever: 'We were ordered to sit up with the sick in our turns, and about midnight to take each one out of bed (they all lay without shirts), lead them to a flight of steps, and pour two buckets of cold water on each. They were so deranged they knew nothing about it.'

Private Brotherwood, a fellow of iron constitution in his mid-twenties, was one of the minority not to succumb to Guadiana fever at all. Simmons, of similar age, managed to beat off the fever after three bouts of it. By mid-October he was on the mend. But by the time orders came through for an imminent march to northern Portugal, Guadiana fever had carried off thousands of Wellington's soldiers. Dozens died in the 95th, with O'Hare's company, for example, losing twelve soldiers.

Three of the eight Royal Surrey Militia men who had joined O'Hare's company with Fairfoot were among that dozen carried off by the fever. Fairfoot himself remained dangerously ill when the battalion joined the rest of the Light Brigade heading towards northern Portugal on 16 December. Costello was also too sick to march, languishing in the convent that the army had turned into a general hospital.

Before it had even crossed swords in earnest with the French, the 95th had lost a company's worth of men. Many of those who had sought the glories of a military career found themselves interred in unmarked graves in the dusty soil of Alemtejo. In Guildford or Dublin, mothers received an official notification of death, often with a promissory note for a few shillings of back pay, a last reminder of a rifleman son they would never see again.

The 95th would have many days on the road before it reached its destination on the northern Portuguese frontier of the Baixa Beira. The weather was turning, with increasingly heavy rains. Snows dusted the peaks of the sierras. At least the cooler temperatures made the marching easier, as did the knowledge that they were quitting that damnable Guadiana plain – and heading, perhaps, for the trial with the French for which so many of them yearned.

FOUR

Barba del Puerco

January–July 1810

On 6 January, the Rifles crossed the River Coa, on Portugal's northern border. It was their first glimpse of the deeply incised gorge, its fast-flowing torrent, and the ancient arched bridge that crossed it, leading to the fortress of Almeida guarding the gateway to the north of the country. The barrier of the Coa, with its few crossing points, and the poor peasant villages of the mountain country around it were destined to be the setting for many of the 95th's exploits in the coming years.

The journey north from Campo Maior had taken the Rifles three hundred miles through the dramatic peaks of the Sierra d'Estrella and up onto the barren plateau of the frontier. There, great lumps of rock littered the ground like giants' playthings and the few, poverty-stricken inhabitants lived in hovels with earthen floors and smoking chimneys. The driving rain and the covering of heather and ferns, as well as the frosts, reminded many riflemen of western Ireland or the Yorkshire moors.

As the battalion tramped away from the infernal Guadiana, many of the soldiers had come to appreciate the pleasures of life in the field. Each day as they marched up through the mountains, some ravishing new prospect greeted them – they experienced a host of sensations that the boyhood playmates they had left behind in Yorkshire or Chester would never know. One novice marching with the battalion wrote of the scenery, 'It was beyond anything I could have conceived, and it has highly compensated me for my labour.'

Craufurd pushed his troops beyond the Coa, closer to Ciudad Rodrigo, a fortified town on the Spanish side of the uplands. There they would take up a line of observation posts along another river, the Agueda, which ran parallel to the Coa and like it flowed down into the

Douro, the great river of northern Portugal. For the most part, this upland landscape consisted of open plains or rolling groves of black oaks and other trees. In places, though, the underlying rock burst through this covering, providing vantage points, and where the Agueda cut its way down to meet the Douro, a deep gorge many miles long presented itself.

The Light Brigade had been posted to this remote corner of Portugal to guard Wellington's army against the possibility of surprise. It was well known that tens of thousands of French troops lurked not far away in Spain, and everybody predicted it would not be long before these *corps d'armée* marched into Portugal to throw out the British. Brigadier Craufurd convinced his leader that posting a chain of lookouts on the peaks of this highland would provide warning of any hostile movement, allowing the rest of the army to train and rest in comfort many miles to the rear. One of Craufurd's staff noted, 'This extraordinary undertaking was in a great measure one of his own bringing about. He almost led the Commander in Chief into it by the enthusiastic zeal with which he carried it through.'

There were great dangers to occupying scattered posts so far ahead of friendly lines. The principal one was that enemy cavalry might pass the Agueda by some ford and cut off Craufurd's parties: then they would not only fail to give warning, but fall into the French bag to boot. For this reason, the forward line of outposts was to be occupied by Allied cavalry, two squadrons of the 1st Hussars of the King's German Legion, who might make good their escape just as quickly as any enemy tried to move on them. In one place, though, Craufurd posted infantry: he sent four companies of the 95th to the Agueda gorge and a small Spanish village called Barba del Puerco. Here the terrain was so rocky that enemy cavalry could not approach the little bridge across the river and Craufurd considered that if the Rifles were sufficiently hard-pressed, they could defend the pass for long enough for him to bring reserves up to cover their withdrawal.

In late January 1810, Craufurd started posting his observation parties. Most of them consisted of a few hussars. In key places, a British officer was attached. These groups could alert the reserves some miles behind them by lighting beacons or firing off their guns. Craufurd instructed these mustachioed veterans of the German Legion in great detail and in their own language. He told them how to conduct themselves and how to take daily measurements of the Agueda, so that he could reassure himself that the river remained high enough to protect his posts against surprise. 'General Craufurd in fact worked out the most difficult part of the oupost duty with them,' wrote James Shaw Kennedy, a staff officer who was one of the brigadier's few real admirers in the Army at the time. 'They knew his plan for each space they covered, but not his general plan; and each worked out his part most admirably. The General communicated with them direct. He had the advantage of possessing, with great abilities and activity and energy, uncommon bodily strength, so that he could be on horseback almost any length of time.'

Craufurd was skilled at working out complex problems of time and distance. When he applied this to his brigade's marching, and how small deviations might hold up the whole, he drove many of his officers to distraction. But in his appraisal of the time it would take the French to move on his people, and then how long his reserves of the 43rd and 52nd would need to extricate the forward parties, his ideas were perfectly sound. They would allow the Light Brigade to fulfil its warning role for the army as a whole without endangering itself unduly. Shaw Kennedy summed up the scheme and the 95th's role within it: 'He kept his infantry back entirely with the exception of the infantry post of four companies of the Rifles at Barba del Puerco, upon the *calculation* of the time that would be required to retire the infantry to the Coa . . . the *calculation*, as above stated, must never be lost sight of; for it was upon that *calculation* that he acted all along [emphasis in original].'

Lord Wellington wanted his outposts to frustrate French reconnaissance of his deployments, as well as warning of any large-scale attack. The scheme worked out by him and Craufurd thus threw a chain of light or Rifle companies across the front of his army – in much the same way as he screened the battalions of his army in battle, by using lines of individual skirmishers and undulations of the ground. Wellington was evidently very impressed with the way Craufurd supervised his observing parties, although in time he would become anxious for the safety of his forward scouts.

This use of Craufurd's troops in this way was novel in its scale, and Wellington was quite open to new ideas on how a Rifle regiment might act on the battlefield. There had been Rifles under his direct command in Denmark three years earlier, and his first battle against the French in Portugal during the brief 1808 campaign had been touched off 'by the

over-eagerness of the riflemen'. Wellington did not resent them for this
wild spirit – on the contrary, he had already come to value the 95th as
soldiers. They in turn thought highly of him. Although Wellington's
manners were of the eighteenth-century school, and his politics dis-
tinctly conservative, he was all for developing the use of light troops.
He rejected, for example, the old system of forming ad hoc battalions
from the light companies of several line regiments, favouring instead
the deployment of specially trained corps of these men like those under
Craufurd's command. Wellington soon realised that these regiments –
the 43rd, 52nd and 95th – were among the very best troops he had. He
also rejected the doctrine of many conservative generals that riflemen,
owing to their slower rate of fire and skirmishers' vulnerability to cavalry, could only ever be deployed in penny packets, supporting regular
infantry. Craufurd, although a conservative in many matters, accepted
that the 95th could be used as a regiment rather than being broadcast
about like the riflemen of the 60th were. Wellington and the commander of the Light Division between them came to the conclusion
that the way to nullify clouds of French light infantry on the battlefield
was to use their own Green Jackets or red-coated light infantry in large
numbers too.

In the early part of 1810, though, they were not contemplating a
general action; rather, they needed to frustrate the various French
probing movements on the upland frontier. The Rifles were posted in
villages about the uplands with savage-sounding names like Mata de
Lobos (Death of Wolves), eventually taking up their position in Barba
del Puerco (Pig's Beard) towards the end of February. This followed
two months in which they had been marching hither and thither almost
constantly, time which had afforded Second Lieutenant Simmons a
chance to see the less likeable side of Captain Peter O'Hare, his company commander.

O'Hare was a rough diamond typical of the Irish adventurers who
made up much of the 95th's officer cadre. If he was harsh with the
young officers, that was because this was the Rifles system and because
he had never gained anything easily in his military career. O'Hare had
joined the Rifles when they formed and served under Beckwith's predecessor, a man who believed in tough superintendence of his officers,
one of them commenting, 'With him the field officers must first be
steady, and then he goes downwards: hence the privates say, we had
better look sharp if he is so strict with the officers.'

For someone who had experienced O'Hare's slow rise through the ranks, beasting some young puppy of a subaltern came all too easily. Simmons noticed that each time they were quartered in a Portuguese household during their march up from Campo Maior, O'Hare would take the best sleeping quarters and give the next best to his company's two lieutenants. 'Being the junior officer,' Simmons noted, 'I consequently got the last choice of quarters, which too frequently was a dirty floor with my blanket only. Captain O'Hare did not show me much kindness.'

The captain's rough speech and slow advancement marked him out to officers and men alike as someone bereft of even the smallest quantum of patronage. O'Hare's soldiers believed him to be such a rough one that he must have started his career in the ranks. This was not quite true, for he had begun his military career as a surgeon's mate in the 69th Foot. This post was a sort of halfway house between the rank and file and an officer's commission. However, O'Hare's men were right in one essential: a surgeon's mate could be flogged for his misdemeanours, something quite out of the question for an officer.

He was not long in that lowly station: having been commissioned in the 69th, O'Hare had taken the opportunity offered by the creation of the Rifle Corps to transfer out of his original regiment and reinvent himself. His officers in this new corps appreciated his diligence and bravery, providing him at last with patrons to fight for his advancement. O'Hare had served as adjutant, a sign of his commanding officer's favour but a post also requiring him to police the regiment's young subalterns, acting as his colonel's truncheon. He had been promoted to captain in 1803 after that same commanding officer wrote of his 'anxious wish that the eldest lieutenant of the Rifle Regt, Adjt O'Hare, should be recommended to the succession to the 3rd . . . company . . . Lieut. O'Hare is a subaltern of very long standing and a very good officer.'

By early 1810, O'Hare was in a similar situation to that of seven years earlier. He had served longer in his rank than any other regimental officer and he was next on the list for promotion, unless he was overtaken by another captain who had the money to purchase a majority or had shown heroism on the field of battle. O'Hare had grown quite used to these vicissitudes, and was of course aware that now he was on campaign, he might secure the coveted major's post through heroics of his own.

In order to make the best of his chances, O'Hare had to ensure that his company's every duty was carried out punctiliously. He also intended to keep certain things about his own origins and his private life to himself. His brother officers were ignorant of the wife, Mary, and daughter, Marianne, that O'Hare left behind in England. To little Marianne, he was something of a stranger, his campaigns having kept him overseas for around half of her six years. As for Mary, he chose not to introduce her into regimental society.

When 3rd Company soldiers supping their grog gossiped about their captain, they talked about his love of wine and women. Before their departure, O'Hare had spent some time pursuing a young lady in Hythe, not far from Shorncliffe camp. As the couple walked arm in arm along the sea promenade, they would be greeted by soldiers from the company, many of whom would ask favours of their captain, knowing that he dare not decline, lest he forfeit her good opinion. O'Hare was not the brightest spark, but even he eventually tumbled to their tactics and swore to 'flog the first man who made another attempt'. In his pursuit of the maid of Hythe, O'Hare had eventually antagonised a rival in the form of a militia officer who challenged him to a duel. The captain sent word back to his challenger that he was a fool, and in any case the 95th was imminently departing on service.

The Irish captain was no oil painting – he was characterised by one of his riflemen as having an 'extremely ugly countenance'. Having sprung from obscure origins to the status and pay of a captain of the Rifles, he intended to make the most of his position, particularly when it came to the opposite sex. On campaign, he took many a chance to enjoy good wine and company.

During their march north, on Christmas night, O'Hare had been drinking with fellow officers and retired to his quarters, in the words of one of the party, 'having enjoyed the wine very much'. A rifleman, taking advantage of O'Hare's deep sleep, stole his boots. The intention, presumably, was to sell them for drink, since he could never have worn them publicly. The soldier was caught and ordered to be flogged. O'Hare supervised the punishment, 'gave the man every lash, and recommended the buglers to lay it on lustily and save the fellow from the gallows'.

Someone like O'Hare, having entered the Army as a surgeon's mate with Irish Catholic origins, could not claim to have started life at a station any higher than had most of the rankers. Many of the soldiers found it harder to defer to such a man. One private of the 95th summed it up pithily: 'In our army the men prefer to be officered by gentlemen, by men whose education has rendered them more kind in manners than a coarse officer who has sprung from obscure origins, and whose style is brutal and overbearing.'

From the officers' side of the divide – for O'Hare's predicament in this regard was far from unique in the Rifles – it was difficult to overcome the familiarity which many soldiers showed to someone of low birth. The riflemen could detect a natural gentleman easily enough by his manners. Whereas, for example, Lieutenant Harry Smith, a dashing young English subaltern who had bought his commission in the 95th, was addressed as 'Mr Smith', 'Your Honour' or 'Lieutenant Smith, Sir', O'Hare's men often called him by his first name.

'We had but a slender sprinkling of the aristocracy among us,' one officer of the 95th wrote later, perceptively summing up the difficult question of social status. 'They were not braver officers, nor were they better or braver men than the soldiers of fortune, with which they were mingled; but there was a degree of refinement in all their actions, even in mischief, which commanded the respect of the soldiers, while those who had been framed in rougher moulds, and left unpolished, were sometimes obliged to have recourse to harsh measures.' Such was the medicine that O'Hare had been obliged to give to the man who stole his boots.

Once serving on the frontier between the Coa and the Agueda, the captain and several other officers had come to enjoy what modest social opportunities the little Spanish villages could give them. They soon took over the small *cantinas*, inviting local girls to join them in nightly drinking, dancing and song.

The rankers also benefited from a relaxation of discipline in Barba and the other villages they had occupied since 1810 began. This was in part the result of the distance of their billets from the main Army and its officious staff men. One captain of the 95th noted in his journal, 'Various amusements were exhibited this morning in our village. Jack ass racing, pig hunting, fighting all the cocks in the village was also introduced. I afterwards shot one of the cocks with a single ball at one hundred and seven yards. Several matches at football were also played.'

Lieutenant Colonel Beckwith, who took personal command of the four companies in Barba, was quite content for these amusements to take place. His calculation, one officer surmised, was 'that to divert and to amuse his men and to allow them every possible indulgence compatible with the discipline of the battalion . . . was the surest way to make the soldiers follow him cheerfully through fire and water, when the day of trial came.'

As a Christmas treat, Beckwith bought a hog and had it greased and set loose through the narrow alleys of one village. The men went bounding after, hallooing and tumbling, generally disturbing the peace. One by one they would leap or lunge at the careering animal, until a dextrous fellow eventually caught the swine, earning himself the right to butcher and eat it, making him the hero of his messmates.

Some of the soldiers thieved, of course, as did some of the officers. Just a few weeks after Wellington had caused his entire 4th Division to parade before dawn for days as punishment for stealing honeycombs, the 95th's officers, led by Captain Leach, cheerfully plundered the hives around Mata de Lobos or Barba and took delight from shooting and consuming the locals' pigeons. While Leach was aware enough of his and others' infractions to describe the 95th as 'a nefarious corps of poachers', it was during this period on the frontier that the soldiers honed their sense of how much larceny was fair game and how much might bring unhappy consequences for themselves and the battalion. Pinching the odd bird was acceptable, holding up a Spaniard at gunpoint and robbing him was not and would soon enough have brought the provost marshal and his hanging noose in to shatter their mountain idyll. When a party of convalescents, including Robert Fairfoot and Ned Costello, marched up from the south to join the regiment early that year, they were able to tell the others of the draconian punishments being meted out to those caught robbing the Portuguese in the Army's rear.

While some of the riflemen tested the limits of Colonel Beckwith's tolerance for petty crime, there was a serious military purpose to their presence. The French had soon detected the outposts in Barba del Puerco. Across the gorge, and behind the ridge facing the 95th's station, was San Felices, a small village where a French infantry brigade had made its headquarters.

The French commander, General Claude-François Ferey, was one of those hard-fighting warriors who personified all that was best about the imperial officer corps. Ferey had been campaigning for most of his thirty-nine years: he had gone through the revolutionary ferment, rising from the ranks, and his service record as a brigade commander included Marengo and Austerlitz, two of Napoleon's most brilliant battles. Ferey's pickets occupied forward positions very close to the bridge at Barba. Their reports suggested the British force was very small. He also knew that the riflemen picketed at the bridge had evolved the same cheerful modus vivendi with their French partners as had existed down at Almaraz a few months earlier.

There was great uncertainty in the French command about whether Craufurd's line of outposts was at all supported. For an aggressive general like Ferey, the fact that there was a small number of defenders, apparently unsupported, offered the tempting prospect of a *coup de main* attack to take the bridge, seize some prisoners and test the general effectiveness of the British outpost line. The friendly relations that existed between sentries would simply allow him to get his storming party close enough to pounce with virtually no warning.

Early in the evening of 19 March, O'Hare's company took over the task of manning the outlying picket. Two men would stand sentry just by the British-held end of the bridge. Fifty yards to their rear, sheltering among the rocks on the steep hillside, were Sergeant Tuttle Betts and a further dozen troops. The remainder of the 3rd Company, about forty men, for it was at little over half strength due to sickness, would take turns standing guard and sleeping in a little chapel a couple of hundred yards further back. If there was a real emergency, the other three companies, under Beckwith's command, were billeted in Barba itself, about twenty or thirty minutes away to the rear. It was a system that kept most men dry and warm, but one that could only work if the company on duty at the bridge maintained its vigilance – even those who slept were fully clothed, rifles by their sides, ready to respond to any alarm.

As O'Hare did his rounds, shortly after dusk, he was accompanied by Simmons, since it was O'Hare's job to teach the boy something about pickets, supports and all the other arcane business of manning outposts. Such was Simmons's desire to please his captain that he crawled across the bridge so that he could make some brief observations on the French side. With this, the young subaltern retired to a tent near the chapel at about 9 p.m. O'Hare, who had 'been taken unwell', retired to a bed in Barba del Puerco itself. The company's two lieutenants, Mercer and Coane, took turns visiting the pickets.

It was raining heavily, with gusts of icy wind causing those on duty to shiver in their greatcoats or crouch under heavy cloaks, counting the minutes until their relief by fresh sentries. But while most of O'Hare's company slept, Ferey was leading storming parties of his men up the steep mountain paths out of San Felices and towards the bridge of Barba del Puerco.

Ferey had picked his soldiers carefully. A storming party of about two hundred from the elite companies of several battalions would be responsible for seizing the bridge. A larger group would form up beside the bridge once the attack began, so that they could fire at any British supports that came to the assistance of the outlying picket. The general knew that his men were undertaking a difficult mission, at night, over narrow mountain paths. He promised them a double ration of food and wine if they succeeded.

At about 11.30 p.m., the French stormers crept up to the eastern end of the bridge. As the supporting party made its way over the rocks to form a firing line to the left side, there was a kerfuffle of men stumbling in the darkness. Ferey felt sure the British had heard.

The leading French *tirailleurs* and *carabiniers*, the picked soldiers of the 32ème *Léger* or light infantry, hastened across the bridge. Two riflemen posted at the British end, Moore and McCann, heard footsteps and shouted a challenge.

In seconds the stormers were past Moore and McCann. The alarm was shouted at last, and shots rang out. Moments later Sergeant Betts's party, including Fairfoot, was desperately trying to defend itself. Lieutenant Mercer, the officer on duty, quickly began shouting an alarm, sending Lieutenant Coane to fetch those slumbering in the chapel to spring to their arms and follow him to the bridge. Costello was among the men who stumbled out into the darkness.

'Be quick, men, and load as you go to the brow of the hill!' one of the officers shouted, as the riflemen rushed towards the firing.

Down at the bridge, dozens of French were across; Moore, McCann, Fairfoot and others had been disarmed and collared. The remainder of the sergeant's picket had fled higher up the British side of the hill and were crouched behind rocks, trying to pick off the French with rifle fire. Shooting in the darkness, the men were little more than twenty or thirty yards apart in places. As Sergeant Betts shouted orders to his men, a musket ball smashed into his jaw, leaving a bloody mess as he crumpled to the ground. Mercer and a first party of reinforcements joined them.

Simmons was up just in time to see Mercer take a shot through the forehead and drop dead at his feet. One rifleman leapt out of his cover: shouting 'Revenge the death of Mr Mercer!' he ran down the slope until he reached a French officer, and in one deft movement swung his rifle to the Frenchman's head and blew it off. As the officer dropped, there was a cacophony of firing, and the rifleman fell dead too. With Mercer's death, Simmons was in command of the men trying to hold their ground. Lieutenant Coane had rushed off to get their captain.

In the terror of this close-quarter fighting, men loaded and fired like demons. Private Green, in combat for the first time, forgot his ramrod and fired it and the ball it had pushed home through the body of a French grenadier who was charging him. Costello wrote, 'I felt an indescribable thrill, for never before had I been under the fire of a French musket.'

For a moment the moonlight shone through the scudding clouds and several riflemen were able to find the most excellent mark: the white crossbelts that the French soldiers wore across their greatcoats. 'X' marked the spot for their firing. The 95th's shots began opening holes in the ranks of Ferey's storming party and their commander faced the choice of trying to fight further up the slope, to clear the riflemen from their firing positions, or to give up the game and retreat across the bridge. He chose to fight. The French officers tried to urge their men onwards, into the 'well nourished fire' of the British skirmishers. Ferey's drummers started beating the *pas de charge*, the repetitive signal heard above the din of battle that communicated one idea: forward.

O'Hare appeared and joined in the general turmoil, bellowing out for all his men to hear it: 'We will never retire. Here we will stand. They shall not pass but over my body.'

The firing, drumming and shouting had been going on for half an hour when the first of Beckwith's reinforcements appeared. One company had been sent to cover a flank – two others came to the top of the feature that overlooked the bridge. Riflemen loaded their weapons and joined in the general mêlée. With each flash of a Frenchman's firing musket briefly illuminating their targets, Beckwith could see enough through the murk to detect signs that the French attack had faltered, with the officers capering about, beating the backs of their soldiers with the flats of their swords, trying to get them to quit their cover and move up the slope. It was time to use the close-quarters weapon issued to each of his riflemen: a bayonet that was so large and fearsome-looking that they called it a sword.

Orders were given swiftly; there was the sound of metal on metal as the blades were slotted onto the muzzles of each Baker rifle, and then a great cheer. One of the subalterns who was part of the reinforcements Beckwith brought up recorded: 'Our swords were soon fixed and giving the war cheer we closed on the foe sending them helter skelter into the gorge and down the pass as far as their legs could carry them.'

Many of the French turned and began fleeing across the bridge. Moore and McCann were bundled over too, as prisoners – but Fairfoot and one or two others seized their moment to break free and throw themselves into cover.

As Beckwith led his chargers down the difficult slope towards the bridge, they became mixed with the more steadfast remnants of the French, who were still trying to defend themselves. The adjutant fought hand to hand with a couple of enemy soldiers, before being delivered by a rifleman's timely bayonet thrust into one of them.

Little more than an hour after the first shots were fired, the last parties of French ran back across the bridge and the riflemen began collecting their prisoners. The colonel and several men collared one young conscript, who, terrified, remained clutching his musket. As Beckwith started to cross-examine him, the Frenchman pulled the trigger and, with an almighty flash and bang, sent a ball through Beckwith's shako.

A rifle was levelled instantly at the Frenchman's temple, but Beckwith, whose head was singed but intact, checked the rifleman who was about to pull the trigger: 'Let him alone; I daresay the boy has a mother.' The colonel ordered the French conscript to be disarmed and sent to the rear.

The fighting at Barba del Puerco was over by 1.30 a.m. on 20 March. It had cost the Rifles one officer and eight men killed, as well as fifteen wounded, and two prisoners – Moore and McCann had been spirited back to the French lines. Seeing few bodies on the ground the next morning, the riflemen convinced themselves that the French had suffered heavily and carried back many of their casualties. Ferey's dispatch reported the losses: twelve dead and thirteen wounded. Three Frenchmen were also taken prisoner.

In the great scheme of the wars sweeping Europe, the fighting at Barba del Puerco was little more than a minor affair of the outposts. But for many of the men who had set sail on 25 May 1809, it was their first real test.

A certain guilty self-justification showed through, as some officers reflected upon why Ferey had made the attempt. Had the drunken carousing of the 95th's officers alienated the locals to such an extent that they had spied for the French? Several suspected the village priest, who had shown a surly disdain for these goings-on. One officer speculated that the padre must have told Ferey 'that the English officers in his village were in the habit of getting blind drunk every night and that he only had to march over at midnight to secure them almost without resistance'.

Simmons, though, had nothing to feel guilty about. He glowed in the days afterwards with all the self-assurance of a man who had confronted mortal danger for the first time and done his duty, writing that 'after this night I was considered a soldier fit to face the devil in any shape'. From that day on, O'Hare's attitude to Simmons changed profoundly, for the young subaltern had passed the only test his captain really cared about. 'My captain', Simmons breathlessly wrote home to his parents, 'was pleased to say my conduct had given him the greatest satisfaction.' Nobody knew how long the campaign would last – in fact many expected that the French would bring overwhelming numbers into Portugal soon afterwards – but at least these companies of the Rifles had shown what they were made of.

Those officers who remained at Shorncliffe camp with the 2nd and 3rd battalions were delighted at the news that filtered back in letters and official dispatches. One wrote of Barba del Puerco: 'we . . . looked upon it as no inconsiderable addition to our regimental feather . . . with something less than half their number they had beaten off six hundred of the elite of the French Army'.

This little battle had also tested Craufurd's line of observation posts and shown the wisdom of his calculations. Craufurd circulated an ecstatic order to his battalions, relaying Wellington's pleasure in the outcome. But Craufurd also wanted to thumb his nose at those who had doubted what a Rifle regiment might achieve on service:

The action reflects honour on Lieutenant Colonel Beckwith and the Regiment, inasmuch that it was of a sort that Rifle Men of other armies would shun. In other Armies the Rifle is considered ill calculated for close action with an enemy armed with Musket and Bayonet, but the 95th Regiment has proved that the Rifle in the hands of a British soldier is a fully efficient weapon to enable him to defeat the French in the closest fight.

This was a key point for apostles of the new light weapons and tactics. Those light soldiers that Craufurd had seen during his European campaigns would not have been expected to stand their ground against storm troops, particularly if armed with an esoteric weapon like the rifle, one that was seen by some officers and theorists as slow to load and difficult to use. At Barba, the riflemen had shown they could load as fast as any musketman and withstand a close assault too.

In the days after Barba, Craufurd exploited his new standing with Wellington to the fullest extent possible. He pursuaded the Commander of Forces to place more troops under his command: a troop of guns (meaning six pieces) of the Royal Horse Artillery, two battalions of Portuguese light infantry, more cavalry. With these reinforcements Craufurd converted the Light Brigade into a Light Division. He formed two brigades: the 1st or Right Brigade would consist of half of the 95th (known as Right Wing of the battalion) and the 43rd Light Infantry; the 2nd or Left Brigade would have the Left Wing of the 95th as well as the 52nd Light Infantry. The Portuguese battalions would either work together as their own brigade, or one battalion would be attached to each of the British brigades.

The losses of Barba del Puerco and, more significantly, of Guadiana fever and the many long marches of previous months caused Beckwith to change the structure of his battalion too. Two companies, the 9th and 10th, were disbanded. Some officers and NCOs (generally older, worn-out men) were sent home to recruit, and their rank and file were placed under the captains that were staying in the Peninsula. Right Wing and Left Wing would thus consist of four companies each.

Having built up his little military empire and proved his outpost line, Craufurd also began to lobby Wellington for more exciting missions – some escapades that might show him and his battalions to advantage. The brigadier moved some of his red-coated light infantry companies forward a little, closer to the Coa, and began sending schemes to Headquarters for various raids into no man's land. He hoped to cut off some French foraging parties, some of which moved about in groups of hundreds of men, and take them prisoner.

Spring comes late in the Beira uplands: those who subsist on that high plateau must often wait until May for the incessant rains of winter to give way to its flowerings. As the seasons changed, so the number of French troops moving about the plateau grew. One of Napoleon's most able marshals, Michel Ney, arrived with his 6th

Corps to encircle the nearby Spanish fortress of Ciudad Rodrigo. The French intended to take it by regular approaches: trenches and breaching batteries, leading eventually to a storm. With many thousands of troops now supporting this operation, the meagre resources of the frontier were soon picked bare, and Ney's foraging parties began going out in wider circles. Since Spanish guerrillas patrolled the hills, murdering French stragglers without ceremony, they could not scavenge supplies in small groups.

Wellington batted away a series of proposed operations by Craufurd. Eventually, though, the brigadier set off regardless, and on 11 July, Craufurd led a mixed force of Rifles, light infantry and cavalry to surprise a French foraging party of about two hundred infantry and a few dozen cavalry.

This little combat, at a place called Barquilla, was mismanaged by Craufurd. He held the infantry back and tried to defeat the French with cavalry alone. The enemy formed square and saw off repeated attacks. The British cavalry limped home, having lost several men, and the French party made it back to Ciudad Rodrigo, its commander receiving the *Légion d'honneur* for his stubborn resistance.

Resentment of Craufurd simmered once again in his battalions. One of his own staff commented, 'Craufurd cruelly tried to cut up a handful of brave men, and they thrashed him.' Many of the party considered that sending several hundred cavalry against the French had been a sort of sadistic experiment on Craufurd's part – to see whether such a small group of infantry could defend themselves effectively against cavalry. They also speculated whether their commander was seeking such engagements purely to buttress his own reputation. But Marshal Ney was not the man to meddle with if you just wanted a few glorious mentions in dispatches: the affair at Barquilla would prove a portent of a far more costly humiliation for Craufurd, little over a fortnight later.

FIVE

The Coa

July 1810

The 95th's pickets greeted first light, that 24 July, with the heartfelt relief of men who have endured a sleepless and rain-sodden night. Their duty was a difficult one, for they knew that Marshal Ney's 6th Corps lay just in front of them. The snoozing men behind depended entirely on their outlying sentinels for their safety. For several days, the Light Division had been manoeuvring about the plateau between the Coa and Agueda rivers, often glimpsing the French and firing into their forward scouts. Ney had taken Ciudad Rodrigo by assault and, having secured this fortress, everybody now expected him to move into Portugal.

Craufurd had posted his division so that it might cover the withdrawal of some supplies from Almeida. These wagons would have to be taken from the Portuguese stronghold, which would be Ney's next target, two and a half miles down the road. Craufurd's battalions ran from north, just by the walls of the fortress, to south, where they were close to the only line of withdrawal across that difficult obstacle. From top to bottom they went: 43rd, closest to Almeida; 3rd (Portuguese) *Cacadores*; 1st *Cacadores*; 52nd. These Portuguese were clad in brown uniforms and had been trained to perform the same skirmishing tactics as the division's British troops. They were also being equiped with the Baker rifle, although there never proved enough for all of these rangers to have one. Apart from the sprinkling of British officers who led them, the *Cacadores* were generally stocky, black-haired, olive-skinned and enjoyed their own amusements. In bivouacs they would laugh and halloo into the night, gambling over cards, and they returned the suspicious glances of Craufurd's British soldiers with interest.

The Rifles covered the front of this line of battalions: the 1st

Company manned the outlying picket in the northern half, the 2nd Company (Leach's) the southern. Behind them, close in to the main resting place, was a second line of lookouts, the inlying picket in the northern part of the line, which was manned by O'Hare's 3rd Company. The remainder of the battalion was sleeping, but fully clothed as usual, just behind their pickets, ready to act in support. These men slumbered under their greatcoats or blankets in a warren of little enclosures, bounded by stone walls, where the locals grew their grapes, apples and olives.

As the sun began to warm the air, the ground returned a little of the night's downpour to the atmosphere in a heavy mist that hung thickest in the hollows. Craufurd's pickets stoked their fires and got going with a morning brew. Some riflemen came around with dry cartridges in case the rain had spoiled those in the sentries' pouches. In the main part of the Rifles' bivouac the reveille bugles had sounded, and captains were beginning to form their companies, calling out the muster roll.

All of these telltale sounds travelled through the mist to the French scouts who were working their way across the upland. Marshal Ney had prepared himself for a tough contest. The spearhead of his force was made up of the *Tirailleurs de Siège*, light infantry picked from several regiments, who had formed into a special battalion weeks before, while Ney was attacking the fortress of Rodrigo. They would move forward with cavalry on their flanks and columns of infantry some distance behind.

With the morning mist burning off, the riflemen on picket began to realise the magnitude of their crisis. One of the 95th's subalterns noted: 'As the morning fog cleared away we observed the extensive plains in our front covered with the French Army as far as the eye could reach.' The alarm was given and roll-call broken off in the main bivouac, as men packed away their gear, took up their arms and began lining the stone walls of the orchards and vineyards where they had slept.

Ney was moving with twenty-five thousand troops on the four thousand or so of Craufurd's Light Division. The crackling of musketry between the leading *voltigeurs* and the rifle picket announced that the action was beginning. For weeks, the better-informed men of Wellington's army had been worrying about the risks of keeping the Light Division east of the Coa. Major Charles Napier, a clever officer attached to Craufurd's staff, had written in his journal on 2 July: 'If the enemy was enterprising we should be cut to pieces . . . we shall be attacked some morning and lose many men.' On 16 July, disturbed that they had still not withdrawn, he wrote: 'Why do we not get on the other side of the Coa? . . . our safety has certainly been owing to the enemy's ignorance of our true situation.' Wellington himself had echoed these views, with orders to Craufurd not to risk a battle with the rest of the British Army across the Coa and therefore unable to support him.

As the French brigades marched forward that morning of 24 July, drums beating, Craufurd had one more chance. It would still take time – perhaps even an hour or two – for Ney to bring up the columns of his main force and shake them into their battle line, ready for the assault. All the time the drums sent their repetitive signal – a refrain the riflemen nicknamed 'Old Trousers'. This could allow the Light Division to get away – for even the 43rd, furthest from the bridge, were not much more than two miles from it. Craufurd decided to stand. He sent his aide-de-camp, Major Napier, around the battalion commanders, telling them they must hold their ground while some wagons of artillery ammunition and other supplies were taken across the bridge.

Seeing hundreds of French skirmishers moving up through the rocky terrain, the outlying pickets began running back towards their supports – some were cut off, the French bagging their first prisoners. O'Hare's company was formed up, rifles rested on stone walls, ready to give covering fire to the pickets running towards them. As they caught sight of the first Frenchmen, bobbing and ducking among the trees and drystone walls, they started finding their targets, leading them, squeezing the trigger and watching them drop with a yelp or a slap of metal on flesh. But these *tirailleurs* were no recruits. They moved with a mutual confidence born of years of campaigning, timing their dash from one bit of cover to another during moments when they calculated their enemy would be reloading. Some were good shots too: Lieutenant Coane, falling wounded with a ball in his guts, was sent to the rear.

This contest between light troops had been going on for an hour when the main assault columns closed up and began their evolution into attack formation. Simmons observed: 'The enemy's infantry formed line and, with an innumerable multitude of skirmishers, attacked us fiercely; we repulsed them; they came on again, yelling with drums beating, frequently with the drummers leading, often in front of the line, French officers like mountebanks running forward and placing their hats on their swords and capering about like madmen.'

A company or two of Rifles, totalling perhaps 120 men, would stand no hope of defending themselves against whole battalions of French, each one four times their number. Ney's men had been able to get some of the cannon up too, and they were beginning to belch fire. O'Hare knew that his boys would be slaughtered or overwhelmed if they did not fall back. He ordered half his company, Lieutenant Coane's platoon (under Simmons now), to move to a new defensive line, while Lieutenant Johnston's covered them.

Craufurd's line could defend itself better for as long as its flanks were anchored; the left or northern one on Almeida fortress, with its heavy artillery, the right on the Coa gorge. As the Rifles were pushed back, though, the French commanders could see a gap opening on the British left. Some squadrons of the *3ième Hussards* saw their moment and rode around the riflemen, turning the Light Division's flank.

The moment soldiers realised they had been outflanked, there was every risk of panic. A cry of 'The French cavalry are upon us!' went up around O'Hare's company. They were running now, desperate to save themselves, glancing over their shoulders, gasping for breath as the cantering hussars got closer. The riflemen were trying to reach a line of the 43rd that had formed up, ready to cover them. But with little more than a hundred yards to go, O'Hare's men lost their unequal contest with horses. The hussars were among them.

A slashing of cavalry sabres had begun, the crunch of metal on bone making itself heard above the general shouting, shooting and jingle of saddlery. 'A fellow brandished his sword in the air, and was about to bring it down upon my head,' Simmons wrote. 'I dropped mine seeing it was useless to make resistance. He saw I was an officer and did not cut me.' O'Hare's men were starting to surrender.

The officer commanding the three companies of the 43rd, watching all this, knew he could not easily order a volley. That might kill as many British as it would the enemy hussars. But he decided, after a moment's agony, that there was nothing to be lost. His men fired – not a bludgeon volley like some line fellows might, but a discharge in which his soldiers tried to put their training to good use and aim carefully at a target.

With balls flying into the mêlée, the hussars were momentarily stunned. Captain Vogt, one of their squadron commanders, fell dead from the saddle. Should they attempt a charge on the 43rd or fall back? Simmons and some of the other riflemen decided they had not surrendered after all, and taking advantage of the confusion, ran for the 43rd's line. The volley had not altogether discriminated between friend and foe – Private Charity, for example, somehow made it back with Simmons despite two fearsome sabre wounds and one of the 43rd's balls rattling around in him.

Some Portuguese gunners in the fortress who'd seen the fighting had realised the dangers of Craufurd's flank being turned and opened up with their heavy guns. They mistook the darkly dressed riflemen for enemy so the balls, alas, killed without discriminating between the French and the 95th.

At its northern end, Craufurd's line was crumbling. But it was being assaulted at its other extreme too, by none other than General Ferey and his brigade, who gave the 52nd a heavy fight.

The 43rd and 95th being driven back, all order was beginning to vanish – men of the two battalions and different companies became mixed as they jogged along. One of the Portuguese battalions started to disintegrate, hundreds of its troops deciding to save themselves by running back to the bridge. As these fugitives reached the defile, they pushed past the last few wagons of ammunition, causing a general jam.

Breathless, their mouths bone-dry through the biting of cartridges and hours of exertion, the riflemen dragged themselves across one stone wall after another. The French followed up determinedly: 'They sent their light infantry in abundance like swarms of bees and they were regularly relieved by fresh troops so that our poor devils not only laboured under the disadvantage of numbers but fresh men, who hunted us down the mountains like deer.'

The fighting had been going on for hours, as men of the 95th and 43rd stumbled towards the bridge. A couple of knolls stood overlooking the crossing, with the rocky ground sloping steeply down to it. The road from Almeida needed to zigzag to negotiate this last tricky drop down to the span. From this vantage point, Lieutenant Colonel Beckwith could see that the battle had reached a crisis. The bridge was clogged with wagons and men, while the French were just a few hundred yards from it. The 43rd and companies of 95th that were with it were best positioned to hold the heights as these last men crossed, but to his horror, Beckwith realised that the the 52nd was still fighting far out to the front, evidently having received no order to withdraw, and was about to be cut off. Beckwith saw Major Napier nearby and ordered him to get through to the 52nd and tell Colonel Barclay to fall back to the bridge without a moment's delay.

Private Costello was among those scrambling back towards the bridge when he took a bullet under the right knee. Another rifleman answered his cries for help, picked up Costello and staggered forward with the wounded man piggyback. Crack! Another ball – it smashed its way through the Good Samaritan's arm and into Costello's thigh. Both men went down. Costello's saviour was now unable to carry him, for one arm hung bloody and useless at his side. Both of them staggered on, getting the help of some other riflemen.

With the elements of the Light Division that remained on the eastern bank of the Coa having contracted their line from one a couple of miles long at the start of the business to one of a few hundred yards, the French companies that pursued them began firing to much greater effect. Leach explains it in a letter home: 'Now the fire began (as you may naturally fancy) to be cursedly hot from the French because the nearer we drew to the bridge, the more we concentrated and from behind every wall and rock they directed their fire at the bridge and its vicinity.'

The French forced back the troops on top of the knolls overlooking the bridge, and once their shooters were lining that vital ground, the predicament of the defenders became truly desperate. Balls were whistling about the ears of the riflemen, ricocheting dementedly off rocks, whining into the air. Every now and then there'd be the slap of a bullet hitting flesh and the cry of another man going down. Two of Leach's subalterns, brothers called Harry and Tom Smith, sank moments apart, both with leg wounds. Lieutenant Pratt fell, a ball having gone straight through his neck, splashing blood all over the rocks. Many of the riflemen had been firing for hours and could not reply: they had run out of ammunition. If the French wheeled a couple of guns up to the ridge, the British would be massacred.

Sensing the danger, Major Charles MacLeod of the 43rd rode his horse up the steep slope, its hooves somehow planting themselves between the big stones, and called on the men to follow him. About two hundred Green Jackets and redcoats fell in behind, bayonets fixed, determined to drive the French skirmishers off the knolls from which they were doing such slaughter. Second Lieutenant George Simmons was among them, rallying some of the few remaining 3rd Company men with him.

As he was nearing the top of the slope, the men all around him cheering, Simmons felt a hammer blow that sent him crashing into the rocks. 'I could not collect my ideas, and was feeling about my arms and body for a wound until my eye caught the stream of blood rushing through the hole in my trousers, and my leg and thigh appeared so heavy that I could not move it,' he would write. A sergeant of the 43rd stooped over him, tightening a tourniquet around the leg, but as he straightened up, a bullet blew off the top of his head. MacLeod's attack reached its objective, the French driven back for the moment, allowing precious minutes to complete the evacuation. Companies of the 52nd, responding to Major Napier's urgent message, came pelting back through this position, saving themselves from death or capture.

Many of those crossing the bridge were now the walking wounded, or were carried by mates, as Costello had been. A defensive line had been prepared on the western side, anticipating the withdrawal of the last couple of hundred men. Captain Alexander Cameron's men of the 7th or Highland Company of the 95th were crouching behind rocks, ready for anything. Behind them were several rallied companies of the 43rd and some cannon.

As the soldiers carrying the wounded Simmons rushed up the British held side of the gorge, trying to find a surgeon, they ran into Craufurd instead. He ordered them to put the officer down on the hillside and go back. Simmons believed that Craufurd's prejudice against him, stemming from the loss of his personal wagon on the march to Campo Maior, had come into play, and that his brigadier cared not a jot if he bled to death on this godforsaken spot. But the Green Jackets ignored the order, one shouting at Black Bob, 'This is an officer of ours, and we must see him in safety before we leave him.'

With almost everyone across, remnants of the last few companies began scrambling down the rocks, trying to make it down to the bridge in the moments it would take for the French to seize their opportunity, retake the knolls, and start shooting down on them again. 'The French in a second occupied the hill which we left, blazed away at us in crossing and as we ascended the opposite heights made damnable work amongst us,' one of the last across wrote in a letter home.

To his consternation, Captain Leach found a lone artillery officer on the bridge with a tumbril full of ammunition, pleading for help. The riflemen helped push the wagon across to the western side and with that, the Light Division was finally over.

Ferey's men, however, did not intend to leave the matter there, for they had driven their enemy from the field, and success in war demanded that they exploit such an advantage to the full. The *voltigeurs* had worked away throughout the first part of the day in skirmishing; it was now time to employ men of the other elite company in each battalion, the grenadiers. Colonel Jean-Pierre Bechaud called out to the grenadiers of his *66ème Régiment* to rally around him, gathering others from the grenadier company of the *82ème*. Just as the light companies had their role in the scheme of war – to skirmish up ahead of the regiment – so the grenadiers were those you sent for when some desperate feat, a storming, was required.

A cheer and a fusillade went up from the French covering party, as the grenadiers pelted down the rutted road to the Coa bridge. The 95th watched them coming, many of them choosing a target and leading him slowly with their rifle. It was vital, though, not to let fly too soon. As the first Frenchmen made it onto the bridge, muskets held out in front, bayonets fixed, their red grenadiers' epaulettes bouncing up and down on their shoulders, the crackling of rifle fire at last began.

Captain Leach fixed on Captain Ninon, commander of the *82ème*'s grenadier company, tracked him with his rifle as he came onto the bridge, and squeezed the trigger. 'I fired at him myself with my little rifle (which still stands my friend) and cursed my stupidity for missing him, but a running person is not easily hit.'

Each storm had its moment of decision, one at which the moral strength of one side would overcome the other. If the grenadiers kept moving forward, many British troops would run. If the attack faltered under heavy fire, the French officers would have trouble urging any more men to go to a certain death or capture.

Leach fired again and dropped one of the grenadiers. But most of those who'd been engaged that morning had weapons that had become too hot and fouled to fire. Cameron's Scots, though, were fresh, and they kept up a lethal barrage of aimed shots at the head of the French column.

It was the turn of the French grenadiers now to cower behind cover. Colonel Bechaud, shouting, trying to urge them on, made an obvious target for one of the British marksmen: he fired and put a bullet in the Frenchman's chest. Captain Ninon, surrounded by wounded and dying men on the bridge, was unscathed by the hail of balls around him – but he did what even the bravest man must do when he sees the situation is hopeless, and doubled back to his own side of the bridge.

By 4 p.m. the fire was dying down. Everybody knew that the French would not be able to force the crossing. It was not long before an officer appeared with a white flag of truce, calling out to the British side for their agreement to rescue the wounded. Both sides sent down parties to carry off the groaning men who lay mixed up on the bridge and its eastern side. In a few cases, words were exchanged between the two sides as they worked.

The Rifles fell back some way from the bridge and made their bivouac. Many had been fighting for nine hours without interruption and were completely knocked up. Officers and soldiers with barely the energy to speak asked after friends. Half of 3rd Company were on the other side of the Coa, captured, as were quite a few men of the 1st Company. Some soldiers of the 52nd realised that they too had left dozens of men on the wrong side: in their case the result was happier, the men lay low and found their way back west later.

What was clear to everyone, though, was that the Light Division had suffered hundreds of casualties: 333 to be precise. The 95th had accounted for 129 of them, including 12 killed and 54 missing, presumed captured. Among subalterns there had been a shocking toll of wounded – eight were on their way to the rear, where God knows what fate awaited them. O'Hare and Fairfoot had come through unscathed, as had William Brotherwood – one of those men in Leach's company who had slogged all the way back from the outlying picket. The Light Division had at least exacted a heavy price from the enemy, inflicting around five hundred casualties.

On the evening of the 24th and in the days that followed there was deep, hard anger. One subaltern mourned that 'all this blood was shed for no purpose whatsoever'. As they talked it over, they found comfort in the heroism of MacLeod, leading his charge up the hill, or in the cool presence of Beckwith issuing orders when their divisional commander had been absent from the hot side of the Coa. One young officer was adamant: 'But for Colonel Beckwith our whole force would have been sacrificed.' In all of this, they sought to find something redeeming in the defeat of their division by Ney, for a defeat it most certainly was.

The French were delighted with the day's work. General Loison, whose division had struck the main blow, wrote in his official report to

Ney, 'The Combat of the 24th proves to [the British] there is no position the French infantry cannot take and to our soldiers that the English Army is not even as hard to beat as the Spanish and Portuguese.'

Charles Napier, who had delivered several key orders, felt 'the bloody business closed with as much honour for the officers and men as disgrace for Craufurd's generalship'. Napier noted bitterly that Craufurd had almost repeated his feat of Buenos Aires, in having to surrender a British brigade. Others spoke of their close escape from Verdun, the huge French prison where so many British captives languished.

Unsurprisingly, perhaps, those who reacted most bitterly were the officers who had already formed a deep dislike of Craufurd, with his floggings and tantrums. Jonathan Leach wrote home:

He is a damned tyrant and a great blackguard and has proved himself totally unfit to command a company, much less a division . . . I am fully confident that any sergeant in the Army would have brought off the Division in better order, God be praised. If we had not all done something like our duty, I know not but that the Division might have been now on its march to Verdun.

Word of mouth and vitriolic letters like Leach's flew to the four corners of Wellington's Army, and to various quarters in England. The angry young officers of the 95th had no way of knowing it, but Craufurd's harsh regime during the Talavera campaign had already excited adverse comment at the highest levels in London. Wellington had received a letter from Horse Guards, early in 1810, expressing the Commander in Chief's concerns, 'that a very unusual degree of severity is exercised towards the soldiers in the brigades under the command of Brigadier General R. Craufurd'. Among those around Wellington, the dislike of Craufurd was very evident in the days after what became known as the Combat of the Coa. One staff officer hissed, 'I never thought any good was to be expected from any thing of which General R. Craufurd had the direction.'

The Commander of Forces was alive to these views, but he declined to send Craufurd home in disgrace. Wellington reasoned, 'If I am to be hanged for it, I cannot accuse a man who I think has meant well, and whose error is one of judgement, and not of intention.' The choice to keep Craufurd must indeed have been a lonely one. But he reasoned that Craufurd had fire in his belly and knew his profession, whereas most of his generals were timid, and ignoramuses to boot.

Many of those sitting in the comfort of Horse Guards found Wellington's decision incomprehensible. Colonel Torrens, who as Military Secretary was a key figure in the management of senior officers' careers, told his representative in Portugal:

The command of your advanced guard appears to be founded in more ignorance and incapacity than I could possibly have supposed any officer capable of . . . I had a very favourable opinion of Craufurd's talents. But he appears to me to allow the violence of his passions and the impetuosity of his disposition to overthrow the exercise of his judgement.

Craufurd's soldiers did not know about this hair's-breadth escape from ignominy, but they guessed at it in their own way. In the days after the Coa, reports flew about that Craufurd would any moment be replaced by another general. As night fell on 24 July, too many of Craufurd's men were lying caked in blood in field hospitals, or bouncing along in the backs of rough Portuguese ox carts, their lives in the balance. Simmons and Costello were among those unfortunates, beginning their journey into the netherworld of what passed for the Army's system of care for the battlefield wounded.

SIX

Wounded

July–August 1810

The first night for the Coa wounded was as rainy and miserable as anyone could imagine. George Simmons and many of the others found
themselves packed together on the stone flagstones of a little church.
Simmons was deposited next to a man of the 43rd: 'I was on the
ground, very ill from loss of blood; he had been placed on a palliasse of
straw and was dying, but his noble nature would not allow him to die
in peace when he saw an officer so humbled as to be laid near him on
bare stones.' In agony, the soldier moved himself so that Simmons
could share his straw. He did not last the night.

Strange as it may seem, Simmons and the dying man of the 43rd were
among the lucky ones. There were others unable to move, bleeding to
death, out on the hills, wallowing in the downpour. That night the
French soldiers and their camp followers would be tracing the steps of
Craufurd's pickets, searching for fallen soldiers and their plunder. Often
enough, a man who showed any sign of life was dispatched with a blow
to the head as such thieves relieved him of his last earthly possessions.

In the churches or barns where Wellington's few surgeons struggled
to cope with the Coa wounded, there was little to be done by way of
treatment. Bandages might be tied around wounds, or plasters made
from brown sticky paper slapped across less serious lesions. Simmons
knew his surgery, for he had studied it before joining the Army, and he
knew that the heavy loss of blood from his thigh made his case a
doubtful one. He drew a piece of paper and pencil from his jacket and
began scribbling a note to his brother Maud, who was also serving in
Portugal, as an ensign with the 34th. In it, he directed Maud about
how he might best sell his possessions after his death, so as to gain a
few pounds for the education of their other siblings.

To his own surprise, Simmons survived the night, and was transferred the next day to Pinhel, where there were many more wounded.
The surgeons and commissaries who organised the evacuation had few
proper wagons. The roads of the Beira frontier were in any case so
atrocious that only little two-wheelers could negotiate them. Dozens of
local peasants were therefore hired to drive bullock-drawn carts full of
wounded. These wagons were themselves viewed as instruments of torture by many of the soldiers who were obliged to lie across their rude
wooden slats. The vehicles were so crudely made that they lacked a
proper axle; instead, the wheels rotated around a pole and emitted a
head-splitting drone as they went along the roads.

The makeshift hospital in Pinhel was another charnel house, one
even cruder than Simmons's billet of the first night. A sergeant from
one of the regiments nearby, hearing of the sanguinary engagement on
the Coa, allowed his curiosity to get the better of him and peered
inside: 'They were the most shocking spectacle I ever beheld – many
without arms, hands, legs and every other part . . . the cries of them
would pierce the heart of a slave.' When he went back the next morning, many had died.

In this miserable place, some of the 95th's wounded subalterns
found one another and joined forces. Lieutenant Harry Smith, an
active fellow with a grasp of Spanish, was able to make himself understood to the Portuguese. He helped organise a party of wounded who
would be taken over several days down the mountain tracks, to a place
where they could be put in boats on the Mondego River, then cruise
down to the coast where the Navy might be able to evacuate them.

Smith, who had a knack of emerging on top in any situation, was
loaded into a local worthy's sedan chair, hitched between two mules,
while the others would ride in the back of bullock carts. Officers and
men alike were thrown into these conveyances. It cannot be claimed
that the commissioned class received any higher standard of care at this
stage of the journey, except in one particular: each officer, even the pipsqueak subalterns, was assigned a soldier of his company to act as his
servant. The day after the battle Lieutenant Colonel Beckwith sent
these men down to ease the miseries of his young officers. The riflemen
were able to look after their charges in the most basic way, by fetching
water and guarding them as the convoy of sick made its way down
towards the Mondego.

Private Costello, with his two leg wounds, was also one of those being bumped along in the carts. A couple of days out of Pinhel, one of the seriously wounded men who'd been propped up close by slumped across him: 'Foam mixed with blood ran from his mouth which, with his glassy eyes fixed on mine, made me feel very uncomfortable. Being weak and wounded myself, I had no power to move him. Death put an end to his sufferings, and his struggles having ceased, I was able to recover myself a little.' Costello called out to the driver again and again, trying to make himself heard above the din of the wheels. He was convinced the surly old Portuguese had heard him all right, but the shouts were ignored, and Costello endured hours before the dead man was lifted off him.

The journey itself was too much for many. Lieutenant O'Reilly of the 95th died two days after the battle. Not long after that, Lieutenant Pratt, whose neck wound left him in hideous discomfort, had grown angry with a Portuguese who would not help him: his shouting caused the artery in his neck to burst, and he quickly bled to death in front of his anguished friends.

At the end of each day's stage, the men would be left in a barn or some little shrine, with scant chance of a visit from one of the handful of medics who accompanied the convoy. One soldier recorded, 'The surgeons had neither the time nor opportunity to look after us. As a consequence of this neglect, maggots were engendered in the sores, and the bandages, when withdrawn, brought away on them lumps of putrid flesh and maggots.' During the daytime marches, many a dressing slipped off or was clawed away by some delirious man scratching at his wounds. Hordes of flies would then swarm around the wound, laying eggs in the rotting matter.

Six days after the battle, the sick were getting close to the river where they would find more comfortable transport. Many had been disgusted by the Portuguese town officials whom they had encountered on the way. At one point Harry Smith had threatened to hang the local magistrate, if he did not furnish some oxen and drivers to pull the sick wagons. The locals, it can be imagined, did not react well to such usage, and four days after leaving Pinhel, Simmons's servant, Private Short, threatened to kill the driver of his master's cart. Happily, the dispute was resolved without further bloodshed.

The river passage went smoothly enough, the men then being transferred to a naval transport, which sailed them around to Lisbon, where they arrived on 7 August, after a hellish journey of thirteen days. Here, the officers and men went their separate ways. Smith, Simmons and some of the other subalterns limped into the Golden Lion Hotel, an establishment that catered for the British officers going to or from their regiments.

The following day, appalled by the size of the bill at the Golden Lion, Simmons hired himself a room in the Rua de Buenos Ayres. Harry and Tom Smith also decamped, but to another address, the rent a little higher, of course, as befitted young gentlemen of their standing. All of them just wanted to recuperate as fast as possible. None required immediate surgery, although Harry Smith still had a ball lodged in the heel of one foot. It was simply a matter of taking rest, sending your servant out for food, and trying to maintain one's composure as an Englishman, amid the stench of garlic or frying sardines and the incessant shouting of the inhabitants. Simmons wrote home to his father, 'The people are not worthy of notice. I met with great barbarity all the way. They would let you die in the streets before they would assist you.'

Those whose wounds allowed a rapid recovery, and whose spirit remained ardent, did not like to linger at Lisbon, for the outgoings were inevitably greater than those they incurred sleeping under the stars and messing with the other officers of their company. A wound could be turned to your financial advantage, of course, with a visit to the Medical Board resulting in a pension. A lieutenant who had lost an eye or one of his arms could augment his income to the tune of £70 per annum. A great many who were in receipt of such a payment fully intended to return to their regiments.

Those who were seriously wounded but who escaped a lasting disability were entitled to a one-off gratuity of a year's pay. The more gentlemanly sort used this benefit for the purpose for which it was intended and, with their colonel's leave, sailed home for a year's convalescence. However, some of the hardier types with no great expectations, of whom there were many in the 95th, calculated that a man who had been sick in Lisbon for a few months but then rejoined his regiment with a year's pay in his pocket was a man who had made himself a devil of a good bargain.

Soldiers too found themselves parading before the Medical Board, where they might also receive 'blood money' for a wound. For those who'd had limbs amputated or other serious injuries, the board often took the decision to invalid them back to England. They would be put on a ship for Haslar on the Solent; there it would be decided whether they could be sent to an invalids' or veterans' battalion, or were so seriously crippled that they needed to be pensioned off. A man sent out in this way could receive a decent stipend – some got as much as ninepence a day, rather more than they were paid in their regiments, although there, at least, many of the essentials of daily life were found for them. Others, though, were cast out with a few pence a day and considered themselves hard done by.

Among those who had been evacuated, feverish, from the Guadiana, or shot up from the Coa, there was another category of soldier. By the late summer of 1810, it was clear that quite a few – hundreds, certainly – had realised the benefits of lingering about Lisbon. The alternative, after all, was a return to the floggings and grapeshot of regimental service. The wine was cheap in the Portuguese capital and there was always plenty of company around the barracks at Belem, just outside Lisbon, where hundreds of men discharged from general hospital but not yet deemed fit to return to their corps would gather. 'It was a place noted for every species of skulk,' one of the hardier riflemen recorded, 'better known to my fellow soldiers as the "Belem Rangers".'

These skulkers earned the contempt of stout-hearted soldiers, whose privations in hospital left them all the more eager to return to their companies. But those who preferred to parade in Belem, or similar establishments in the interior, eventually numbered thousands. Late in the summer of 1810, Brigadier Craufurd wrote to Wellington estimating that, even in the Light Division, many of the five hundred soldiers from the 43rd, 52nd and 95th who were absent from their battalions and loitering about the Portuguese capital were in fact 'fit to join regiments'.

For the man determined not to leave hospital, there were various tricks. 'Some of the younger soldiers, benefiting by the instruction given to them by old malingerers, caused sores or slight wounds, which under ordinary circumstances, would have healed quickly, to become inflamed and daily worse,' one experienced army surgeon wrote. 'Tongues rubbed against whitewashed walls certainly puzzled us doctors. Fits were common and constantly acted in the barrack yard, lameness was a general complaint, and not a few declared themselves hopelessly paralysed.'

However, the accomplished skulker did not consider it very proper to lie about in hospital, for there they made deductions from your pay, and that was money better spent on gin or Madeira. A man 'awaiting instructions' at Belem Barracks could claim his full six or seven pence day's pay, and spend it with alacrity. Poring over his regimental returns, Wellington eventually noticed that something was amiss. On 23 October, Headquarters issued a General Order:

1. The Commander of the Forces has observed with the greatest concern, the large number of men returned sick in general hospital, compared with the returns received from the medical officers of the number of men actually on their books in the hospitals. 2. The former, at present, is more than double the latter, and it must be owing to some existing abuse.

In short, Wellington had realised that a great many men whose regiments assumed they were in hospital had actually been discharged but were not coming back. It might seem surprising that Headquarters did not tumble to the tricks of the Belem Rangers earlier, but by autumn 1810 it was trying to rein them in. The more artful skulkers had already tried to save themselves from such measures by adopting a shrewder line. Private Billy McNabb of the 95th was one such.

McNabb, a native of Falkirk, was thirty-eight and had been in the Army long enough to lose any dreams of glory. He was also a clever fellow who knew how to work the system. He had sailed from Dover with the 1st Company but had soon discovered that a man of his age could not manage the marches as well as a Costello fifteen years his junior, or indeed risk his life with the same nonchalance. When the Army first set up hospitals in Portugal, there had been no staff, apart from a handful of surgeons or assistant surgeons. These few experts were soon given hundreds of patients to look after. A soldier who could read and write, like McNabb, might ingratiate himself with those in charge and gain a position assisting them. Then he would receive the handsome sum of an additional sixpence a day as a ward orderly. As long as he remained in the good books of his medical masters, they would resist the regiment's attempts to get their man back.

Wellington, however, had got wind of the tricks of men like McNabb. His Army was simply too short of trained soldiers to allow them to hang about the rear, currying favour with the surgeons by day and drinking themselves insensible at night. His General Order directed the hospitals to employ Portuguese civilians in place of the McNabbs, who, it added sternly, 'are to be sent by the first opportunity to their regiments'.

The paths of Privates Costello and McNabb thus crossed bright and early one morning that October. Captain Samuel Mitchell, a tough Scot who had been shot in the arm at the Coa while at the head of his 6th Company, had heard reports of his countryman. Having recovered his health in Lisbon, Mitchell was quite determined that McNabb should join the party returning for service with the 95th. The old soldier insisted his services were indispensable at the hospital, 'so was tied to a bullock cart and amid the jeers of the soldiers, conveyed back to his regiment'. The party set off with McNabb stumbling along, suffering the taunts of Costello and others, much as someone in the pillory might.

For George Simmons, hobbling about on his wounded leg, and Harry Smith, there was still a little time for recuperation and reflection. They sometimes escaped the city's heat by making up a bathing party and dipping in the icy Atlantic waters. Neither man particularly wanted to delay his departure, for Smith had a rare kind of hunger for advancement and Simmons simply could not afford life in Lisbon.

While he was at the Rua de Buenos Ayres, Simmons received a letter from his parents. Brother Maud had sent home reports of the gravity of George's injuries. They had learned too that officers of the 95th were more exposed to danger than those of almost any other regiment in the Army. George tried to allay their fears, writing, 'You make me blush at the idea or observation in the letter, "a dangerous regiment". My dear father, "the more danger the more honour". Never let such weak thoughts enter your head.'

Simmons, like Costello, could not wait to get back to his brothers in arms. They had seen the horrible sights of war all right, but they had reacted in quite the opposite way to McNabb and his ilk. For most of those injured in the 95th did not want to join the ranks of the Rangers. To come through the fire and blood, having conducted yourself in a way that drew the praise of messmates, was just about all that was worth living for. The ironic humour, the softly spoken determination in the face of death: these were the things that drew them back, not the fear of the lash or any desire to please some tyrant like Craufurd.

Had Simmons wanted to give in to his parents' fears, there were some avenues open to him. An exchange of commissions with an officer serving in some quiet corner of England was one route. Of course, he did not consider it for a moment. He had not forgotten his altruistic notion of helping to educate his brothers, and soon enough he'd be finding money from his meagre pay to send home again. But a power-ful new idea now motivated his soldiering, expressed to his father this way: 'I have established my name as a man worthy to rank with the veterans of my regiment, and am esteemed and respected by every brother officer.' Simmons regretted only that his wound had not been suffered in a general action – a battle in which both armies were arrayed under their commanders in chief – for the blood money was usually better under such circumstances. All the more unfortunate for the young subaltern, since a general action was exactly what his com-rades who remained with the 95th were about to experience.

SEVEN

Busaco

September 1810

Early in the morning of 27 September, the *voltigeurs* of the *69ème Régiment* rooted about their baggage. Water was on the boil for their coffee, and some gnawed at stale bread or some morsel of corn left over from their meal of the night before. They had marched deep into Portugal, part of an invasion army of sixty-five thousand under Marshal André Masséna. The 69th belonged to Ney's corps within it, and had already had several brushes with the Light Division.

In the early-morning gloom, they could make out the Sierra de Busaco, which they knew was lined with British troops. The massif lay in front of them, like some great snoozing bear. The feet were anchored on the River Mondego, securing one flank. The ground rose up into a great ridge almost four miles long, and then dropped down somewhat at the neck of the beast, where there was a village called Sula. Not far from Sula was the walled convent of Busaco, but it was on the reverse slope, invisible to the French. The natural dip or neck offered the easiest path for the local road from Moura, at the base of the ridge, up across, through Sula and on to Lisbon. Up beyond this road (to the British left or French right of it) the ground went up again slightly, forming the head of the position. Beyond this crown was a difficult little valley, a gorge almost of a stream called the Milijoso, which secured Wellington's other flank.

Masséna and a party of his staff officers had already been gazing up at this monstrous position, having gone as far forward as Moura in their reconnaissance. One officer with the Imperial Army noted noted:

Their generals could observe all our movements and even count the number of files. Their reserves were hidden on the other side of the mountain. They could concentrate strong masses in less than half an hour, on any attacked point, while the French needed an hour even to get to their outposts, and during that passage would find themselves exposed to grapeshot and musketry from a multitude of skirmishers hidden among the rocks.

There had been a heated discussion the night before about the wisdom of assaulting the Busaco position under such adverse conditions. Masséna dismissed his chief of staff's desire to bypass the ridge, telling him, 'You like manoeuvring, but this is the first time that Wellington seems ready to give battle and I want to profit from the opportunity.' Masséna, like many of the French officers, considered Wellington's tactics so far to have been an unseemly combination of timidity – where his own soldiers' lives were concerned – and ruthlessness, in overseeing the removal of much of the Portuguese rural population, as well as their crops, so that the French would not be able to sustain themselves. If Wellington that day was ready to fight like a man for a change, then Masséna, a tactician considered second only to Napoleon himself in skill and daring, intended to take the bull by the horns.

The noisy arguments between Masséna and his subordinates were quite typical of the French staff's proceedings in the Peninsula. These fellows like Ney, Reynier and Junot owed their advancement to Napoleon's personal patronage. Since the Emperor had been absent from Spain for more than a year and a half, they became quite nervous about suffering some disaster that might result in their fall from grace. Although placed under Masséna's orders, they reserved the right to criticise his decisions while circulating their own version of events through letters to friends in Paris. On the evening of 26 September, however, they were forced into an uncomfortable calculation. Ney and some of the others believed the moment to force the British position had already passed – and there was some justice in this because Wellington had received some late reinforcements – but they had no choice but to fall in with Masséna because the Emperor's orders were unambiguous on the point of his authority. As far as the marshal was concerned, Busaco would offer his one chance of a knockout blow against the British.

Masséna's orders involved throwing two *corps d'armée* into the assault. General Reynier's would take a small track that led up to the peak of the sierra, with the aim of breaking the British line and forcing them to commit their reserves. Marshal Ney would then send his divisions up the road from Moura to Sula and break through at that vital

point. Masséna ordered Ney's 6th Corps to be 'preceded by its skirmishers. Arriving on the mountain's crest it will from in [battle] line.'
A third corps under General Junot would hang back in reserve.

Sub-Lieutenant Marcel of the *voltigeur* or light-infantry company of
the *69ème* formed his men up early that morning, ignorant of
Masséna's precise orders, but quite sure that if there was going to be a
battle, his skirmishers would be leading the way. Marcel had been con-
scripted from his native Aube in 1806 and his rise showed how an
active and intelligent man could climb in the French system. He was
rapidly promoted to corporal and then sergeant, gaining his officer's
commission early in 1810 for his gallantry in the field. For a British soldier, the promotion from recruit to officer in under four years would
have been unthinkable. There were other rewards too: a cross of the
Légion d'honneur did not just make a nice bauble on a soldier's chest,
it also carried a pension. There was no flogging in the French Army.
Instead, the officers would inspire a column that faltered under enemy
fire with slogans, among them: *'L'Empereur recompensera le premier
qu'avancera'* (The Emperor will reward the first to go forward).

Marcel, a tough little man, had every confidence that his *voltigeurs*
could climb the Busaco ridge. They had fought the British at the Coa
and they'd beaten them, just like the Emperor had beaten all the others. The young officer believed that 'happiness, ardour, and love of
glory showed on the face of each soldier: the youngest had three years
of service; what couldn't one do with such men?'

As the attack columns moved up past Masséna, the marshal knew it
was vital that they keep going until they had crowned the heights. If his
men stopped so they might return fire at the British, then all momen-
tum would be lost and the attack would fail. The need to move forward even overrode the fact that marching slowly up the steep slope
while staying in deep columns would make them horribly vulnerable to
British fire. As the *69ème* filed past him, Masséna called out to the
troops: 'No cartridges, go in with the bayonet!'

Plumes of dust were kicked up by the French columns as they
wheeled towards the foot of the ridge. The 95th were able to watch the
whole spectacle, for they were on the mountain's forward slope, having taken up positions to shoot at the French with every plodding step
they took up the forbidding incline. The usual arrangements for com-
bining battalions within the Light Division had been changed this day,
with Beckwith commanding a great force of skirmishers, including his

own 95th, the 1st *Cacadores* of the Portuguese army, light infantry-men, many of whom had also been given the excellent Baker rifle, and some similarly armed King's German Legion men – in all over 1,200 sharpshooters. Beckwith had placed his British riflemen on the left of his line and the rest to the right. Watching the French approaching, the riflemen chose positions among the boulders and firs that littered the steep incline. Few men were held in reserve as supports, since there was no prospect of cavalry being used against them. Further along the ridge, towards the Mondego, there were many more Allied skirmishers from Portuguese battalions or the light companies of British ones wait-ing too. By 5.45 a.m., the leading French scouts were exchanging shots with the British forward posts.

Wellington's position was a very long one, but he had made sure that there were sufficient forces to hold the col at Sula, where he felt sure the French would hit him. The night before he had gone about the ridge, deploying each battalion. The 43rd and 52nd Light Infantry were waiting in Sula, out of view of the French, supported by a couple of guns from the Royal Horse Artillery. To their left and right there were brigades of Portuguese infantry, stiffened with British officers and retrained by them.

As the minutes ticked by that morning, it became apparent that Reynier's attack was going in first, just as Masséna had ordered. These troops clambered up the slope – for in places it is so steep that a heav-ily laden man will have to help himself with his hands – towards the centre of the line, held by General Picton's 3rd Division.

Beckwith's troops could not see the fighting going on in Picton's sec-tor, but they could certainly hear it. Masséna, on the other hand, had positioned himself near a windmill at Moura and could make out the head of Reynier's corps mounting the ridge. The battle was going to plan; it was time to hurl Ney forward.

Loison's division of Ney's corps marched directly up the Sula road. Another division, under General Maucune, followed somewhat behind and veered off to the left, where a Portuguese brigade under the British general Pack awaited them. As soon as the heads of Loison's columns were in range, the Rifles and Portuguese began taking shots at them. They had already seen enough of the French Army in action to know the importance of aiming for the officers first.

General Simon, commanding one of the two brigades now coming towards the Light Division, was out in front, having assumed personal control of the skirmishers. Simon's six battalions were marching behind in tight, long columns, little more than thirty or forty men across the front of each. The French brigade commander's aim was to suppress the Rifles, by making them worry more about preserving themselves than about hitting the dense infantry columns. The Rifles, though, had the benefit of height, as they scampered from rock to rock, moving up the ridge ahead of the French, and so could fire over the heads of the *voltigeurs*, picking their targets with ease. Of course, they could not stop the advance of thousands of Ney's troops – as one 95th officer observed, 'We must give the French their due and say that no men could come up in a more resolute manner.'

With riflemen starting to scurry back over the lip at the top of the ridge, Craufurd could not contain his curiosity. He would dart to the edge, watching the French, hearing the thumping of their drums and shouts of their officers. Then he would rush back again, making sure that the 43rd and 52nd were aligned just right, ready to receive Loison's division with a volley and bayonets when its men came into view at last.

Near the top of the ridge, the French found themselves under devilish fire. Craufurd sent more Portuguese light infantrymen from the 3rd *Cacadores* down to help Beckwith. Several guns firing grapeshot had joined in the British barrage, and were cutting down swaths of men. The colonel of the *6ème Léger* fell to the ground, his head taken clean off by a piece of grape. The French attack was faltering. The officers shouted until they were hoarse, urging the men forward one more time, '*En avant! En avant!*' Simon, who had himself been shot in the face, was close to the Royal Horse Artillery's guns near Sula: he had to silence the battery. With one last effort, a few score of exhausted, blood-spattered troops followed him over the ridge.

The first French had staggered up in front of Craufurd's formed battalions as the last riflemen were running, fast as their legs could carry them, to get behind the red-coated wall. The artillery gunners left their pieces, pelting back too. Simon had got his guns. The shout went around the decimated French companies: the guns were captured! But this triumph was to be short-lived indeed.

'When I saw the head of the French column within about twenty yards of the top of the hill,' wrote Craufurd, 'I turned about to the 43rd and 52nd Regiments and ordered them to charge.' An officer of the 52nd recalled that 'the head of the enemy's column was within a very few yards of [Craufurd], he turned around, came up to the 52nd, and called out, "Now 52nd, revenge the death of Sir John Moore! Charge! Charge! Huzza!" and waving his hat in the air, he was answered by a shout that appalled the enemy and in one instant the brow of the hill bristled with two thousand British bayonets.'

The few French soldiers who had made it to the top never managed to form a firing line, as Masséna had planned. Instead they loosed off a ragged volley at the chargers, but in seconds they were thrown back. Some men were bayoneted, other stumbled, fell and were trodden underfoot. Among those lying wounded on the ridge as the British passed was General Simon himself, who was taken prisoner. The 43rd and 52nd went to the front of the ridge, where they could look down on hundreds of French troops milling about in confusion on the slope. There the British light infantry gave them a thundering volley. The RHA men ran back to their guns and began to serve them again. 'We kept firing and bayoneting till we reached the bottom,' wrote an officer of the 52nd.

Many of the Rifles, left behind and watching this maelstrom, now turned to their right and looked up to where Maucune's brigade was about to suffer the same fate at the hands of Pack's Portuguese. The Scottish general gave the order to advance. Captain Leach of the 95th wrote home, 'I was quite hoarse with cheering and hallooing. Whenever we saw the Portuguese about to charge, who were nearly a mile distant, we all set up a howl which undoubtedly spirited them on.'

Captain Marcel, who had led his men to the top, was a small part of Maucune's brigade. He looked around: where was their support? There was nobody behind the *69ème*, and looking across to his right, Marcel could see Simon's brigade, 'going back down the slope, under a terrible artillery fire and under attack from a column of English of four times its strength [*sic*]; very soon, that same column hit us, and it was our turn to be thrown back.'

For the Light Division men and Pack's Portuguese, weeks of retreating across muddy, execrable roads were being paid back: their blood lust was up. Ney's corps suffered almost 2,500 casualties that day, with Simon's brigade losing the most. Elsewhere, the initial attack by Reynier's corps had met the greatest success: its columns had reached the plateau at the highest point of the ridge and begun to deploy, and only a countercharge by Picton's division had managed to turn the tide.

On the slope in front of Sula it was impossible to say exactly who had lost his life to the 95th, and who to the 52nd or indeed the Portuguese. But it is clear that the six battalions taken forward by Simon suffered terrible casualties among their officers. The *Légion Hanovrienne* had nine of them killed or wounded, including eight of its twelve company commanders. The *26ème Régiment* had twenty-one officer casualties (a little under half of those present with its two battalions). Ferey's brigade, which had tried to follow Simon up the hill, also suffered badly: Colonel Bechaud of the *66ème*, for example, having recovered from his chest wound in July at the Coa, received the same compliment at Busaco. These losses among leaders were the telltale symptom of well-aimed fire.

Busaco, despite this, was a fight in which traditional notions might have seemed, to a British general of conservative cast, to have given Wellington his triumph: devastating volleys at point-blank range and bayonet charges delivered with perfect timing. Even the laurels for successful skirmishing had to be shared between the 95th, Portuguese *Cacadores* and the light companies of various line battalions. The French, though, deduced a general lesson from their officer casualties: that, in the words of one staff officer, 'the English were the only troops who were perfectly practised in the use of small arms, whence their firing was much more accurate than that of any other infantry.' They had become 'the best marksmen in Europe'. That this had come about could be attributed in large part to the training pioneered by the 95th's founders and the growing influence of the system developed before the Peninsular War by General Sir John Moore at Shorncliffe – even the *Cacadores* had fallen under it, for they had been retrained by British officers, including several of the 95th.

If Beckwith and the other officers of the 95th had only a general idea of how well they had picked off the French commanders, they certainly knew that their own losses had been slight: just nine men killed and thirty-two wounded in the battalion. None of the casualties had been officers. Simon's skirmishers had made a great deal of noise and smoke as they came up the mountain, but their effect on the crouching riflemen had been minimal. Concealment was an important factor in this, for the riflemen had become expert in this, whereas other regiments, such as the Portuguese light troops, were less experienced and so suffered more heavily. But there was something else at work here too. Just as the British Army might have its *idées fixes* about the bayonet or flogging, so the French had been blunted in their effectiveness by their generals' received wisdoms about rifles and target shooting.

The French did not want to issue rifles to their men. A small-scale experiment had ended in 1807, the weapons being hard to load and their barrels fouling too easily (since they were of inferior design to the British Baker). The French also considered the rifle a very suspect thing if it just caused the soldier to sit, trying to pick off his enemy at long range, rather than close with him and decide the matter by bayonet. Napoleon's generals understood why such a weapon might be of use in the hands of an American frontiersman, a German forester or even an Englishman, but it would not do for their own people, ruled in war as in so many other matters by Gallic passion. One leading French theorist summed up the aversion to the rifle: 'It was an unsuitable weapon for the French soldier, and would only have suited phlegmatic, patient, assassins.'

Napoleon's light infantry carried instead the *fusil de dragons*, a smoothbore musket slightly shorter than that of the rest of the infantry, and originally designed for mounted troops. As for the whole business of aiming, the French were in something of a muddle. The *fusil* had a fore-sight, a metal blade close to its muzzle, but no back-sight with which to align it. What's more, conscripts like Sub-Lieutenant Marcel's received no training in marksmanship. They pointed at their targets all right, but were self-taught in the business of aiming, that is, adjusting their fire to take account of the distance and movement of their prey. By Busaco some French officers were beginning to appreciate the cost of this neglect.

At the siege of Ciudad Rodrigo just a few months before, one of the more professional French generals present had been staggered by the poor shooting of Ney's infantry. Writing to Paris in order to request an urgent shipment of musket cartridges, he wrote:

The consumption of this munition is quite incredible; it has happened through the inexperience and the negligence of the soldiers, by the carelessness of officers and by the numerous detachments marching with convoys of supplies and munitions. The siege of Rodrigo has seen the consumption of more than nine hundred thousand infantry cartridges solely by skirmishers.

This enormous expenditure of ammunition occurred in one month by light companies whose combined strength did not amount to more than a couple of thousand of Ney's corps. It might be supposed that

Marcel's men and the other *voltigeurs* firing off so many rounds might have become first-rate marksmen, but actually the effect was more haphazard. While some did indeed become good shots, others never grasped the basic principles of adjusting their fire.

Despite these apparently basic limitations, Napoleon's light troops had gained a considerable reputation in the wars of the previous decade. Audacious command and high morale had generally more than compensated for their poor shooting. However, from Busaco onwards, quite a few French officers realised that they were condemmed to fight the British skirmishers at a considerable disadvantage, one that arose from their lack of systematic marksmanship training.

Masséna's defeat came as a profound shock to his people. One eye-witness lamented the army's 'enormous loss of officers'. For the marshal, any hope of hurling the British out of Portugal began to falter. On 28 September, Wellington returned to his old tricks, falling back towards his prepared lines of defence at Torres Vedras. The French could not understand his lack of aggression. Why wasn't he following up his success of the day before? But the British general only liked to give battle on terms of his own choosing. He had succeeded in causing Masséna almost 4,500 casualties and was now inviting an army that had failed to carry the heights of Busaco to come and try its luck against the trenchworks and batteries of Torres Vedras. There Masséna would have to deal with the psychological impact of the Busaco defeat, one staff officer commenting, 'Our heavy losses at Busaco had chilled the ardour of Masséna's lieutenants, and bred ill-will between them and him; so that now all were trying to paralyse his operations, and representing every little hillock to be a new height of Busaco the capture of which would cost copious bloodshed.'

The battle was an enormous relief for Craufurd. He had been despondent after the Combat of the Coa but even he probably did not understand that he had been a whisker away from being sent home. In his official Busaco dispatch, Wellington praised Craufurd for conducting a fighting withdrawal to the Busaco position, 'with great regularity', and for the bayonet charge which had caused the enemy 'immense loss'.

Wellington's Army had performed very well in a general action, the first of its kind since Talavera more than a year before. But whereas the losses at Talavera had been great, this was a more emphatic victory. British officers took pride in throwing back regiments that were veterans of France's fabled triumphs in Italy or central Europe: the fields of Lodi, Marengo and Austerlitz where Napoleon had made his reputation. A company commander of the 95th walked about in the dusk of that September day gathering buttons from the coats of the French dead strewn across the hillside so that he might ascertain their regiments and therefore their pedigree. He was perfectly satisfied with what he found, writing home, 'The 26th, 66th and 82nd are Bridge of Lodi boys, but of the heights of Busaco I daresay they will be less proud.'

EIGHT

The Corporal's Stripes

September 1810–February 1811

It took from 28 September to 10 October for the Rifles to march down through the hilly Portuguese countryside to a little town called Arruda. It was a tortuous journey, attended by the usual hardships and more. Men with sore feet and empty bellies were drenched by daily downpours, one officer noting on the 8th, 'This day's march was about as miserable as I wish to see. Incessant rain all day. We got into a rascally hovel which we contrived to set fire to but soon put it out again.'

During the two-month withdrawal from the frontier, Wellington's soldiers had become used to treating Portuguese property recklessly. It was their commander's intention to fight in the style of Fabius, laying waste to the Portuguese hinterland so that the French would be unable to find food, or indeed people. Orders had been issued by the Portuguese authorities for the evacuation of all inhabitants, if necessary by force, from the path of Masséna's army. Wellington's rearguard daily raided abandoned houses for any food they could find, or indeed for firewood.

When they got to Arruda, the 95th took up a bivouac on a ridge overlooking the town. There they discovered one of the great secrets of the Napoleonic wars: that Wellington had ordered the construction of lines of fortifications stretching twenty-nine miles from the Atlantic coast in the west, in an arc through the hill country of the Peninsula behind Lisbon, to the River Tagus in the east. Arruda was close to the eastern end of this defence, being in a sector where there were twenty-three redoubts armed with ninety-six cannon. The whole programme, involving construction of scores of strongpoints, diversion of streams, emplacement of cannon and drilling of militia, had taken more than one year to accomplish, with a bill of £100,000 for the labour alone, and yet somehow it had remained unknown to the French.

The 95th's task in this scheme was not to man some fort, a task that had been assigned to third-rate troops of the Portuguese militia. The Rifles would remain part of the reserve that would rush to any threatened point and also patrol no man's land in this eastern part of the lines, so as to prevent French penetrations – be they for foraging or surprise attacks.

After such a miserable march, Captain O'Hare's pleasure at finding Second Lieutenant George Simmons in charge of a roaring fire and a laid table can easily be imagined. Simmons had come up from Lisbon with a party of convalescents and quickly commandeered a suitable little house for the officers of his 3rd Company.

It took no time for natural scavengers such as the men of the 95th to start investigating the place in front of their position. 'Never was a town more completely deserted than Arruda,' one officer remarked. 'The inhabitants, dreading the approach of the French, had taken flight to Lisbon, leaving their houses, many of which were magnificently furnished, without a human being in them. The chairs and tables were subsequently carried up to the camp.'

Few riflemen were housed; instead some tents were issued (for the first time since they had arrived in Portugal) to allow them to escape the cold and rain. The soldiers, though, wasted no time in beginning expeditions in Arruda, breaking into houses, where 'many of them had some food in the larder, and a plentiful supply of good wines in the cellar'.

The 95th were guilty of a good deal of vandalism on these missions, since they assumed that Arruda would eventually fall into French hands. Houses were stripped, and ornate furniture was broken up for firewood. 'This was the only instance during the war in which the light division had reason to blush for their conduct,' one veteran later wrote.

Reunited with his messmates, Simmons heard for himself about Busaco and the skirmishes of the retreat from the frontier. He re-acquainted himself with old friends and recounted his experiences in Lisbon.

Simmons was pleased to see Private Robert Fairfoot, for the rifleman, who celebrated his twenty-seventh birthday in Arruda, had become something of a friend and a personal project. During his brief campaigns, Simmons had come to learn the value of a steady soldier.

He had seen the Belem Rangers, and when he and Harry Smith had been placed at the head of a party of eight hundred convalescents for the three-day march from Lisbon to the lines of Torres Vedras, a quarter of these 'heroes' disappeared before they reached their destination.

Fairfoot had gone absent without leave three times while in the Royal Surrey Militia, but on joining the 95th he had at last been able to show his true colours. The 2nd Royal Surreys were ruled by one Major Hudson, 'as great a tyrant as ever disgraced the Army'. The men called him 'Bloody Bob' or 'Wheel 'em again Bob' because of his penchant for the lash and drill respectively. Fairfoot found himself buffeted between the ranks, where he had to drill all day under Hudson's beady eye, and the post of drummer, where his duties included whipping his comrades. Fairfoot's desertions arose from the unhappiness that follows when a man must pick morsels of his comrades' flesh from the knots of his cat, having been forced to flog them all day for no good reason.

Early in the spring of 1809, when the 2nd Royal Surreys found themselves in the south of England as volunteers for the regulars were called for, hundreds had escaped the militia. One of their privates wrote home, 'I have taken the first opportunity and volunteered . . . into what regiment I cared not a straw.' Some 127 of the Royal Surreys went into the 51st (a smart light-infantry regiment) and around 90 joined Fairfoot in the Rifles.

In the 95th, Fairfoot had learnt the difference between parade-ground drill and the life of danger and comradeship in the Rifles. He had shown himself so good a soldier at Barba del Puerco, the Coa and Busaco that he had been marked down for promotion.

The 95th prided itself on giving advancement to deserving, bright men. One of its sergeants, William Weddeburne, had argued in print that the regiment's form of warfare meant that 'frequent opportunities are afforded for the display of personal courage, activity, and intelligence, and, to persons possessed of such qualities, it is a certain road to distinction'. The publication of Weddeburne's text on training light troops was in itself a mark of the unusual position an NCO could achieve in the Rifles. It was evident to any soldier, once in the 95th, that serving in small groups in outposts or patrols rather than in line regiments offered many more opportunities for the deserving soldier to show his mettle, or for a corporal to demonstrate he was fit for further promotion.

As it was, the rank of corporal was a recent introduction to the Army. The printed Monthly Returns forms sent out for the 95th's adjutant to complete had columns marked for 'sergeants', 'buglers' and 'rank and file', but none for corporals. The practice of marking this rank and that of sergeant with stripes on the sleeve was only just beginning. The founders of the 95th had been so pleased with the beneficial effects of giving men these distinctions that they had established a further category – albeit unofficial – between private and corporal, that of 'chosen man'. This was a private being prepared for promotion, who was given extra responsibilities; the officers hoped that these steps would give men something to aspire to, and redress some of the advantages the French had reaped by offering so many rewards to their troops.

The theory of promotions was one thing, but there was a more practical and urgent need for O'Hare to rebuild his company: half of it had been captured at the Coa. Lieutenant Colonel Beckwith had obliged with some transfers of riflemen from other companies, but O'Hare also had to alleviate a shortage of non-commissioned officers. His company had set sail in May 1809 with six sergeants and six corporals. He had since lost two sergeants and three corporals – dead, captured or promoted. One sergeant, Esau Jackson, who'd been given to O'Hare to alleviate matters, soon decided he had seen more than enough of the enemy, and got himself appointed to a comfy sinecure in charge of stores at Belem.

Two weeks after the battalion arrived in Arruda, Fairfoot was promoted to corporal. His pay more than doubled, to one shilling, two and a quarter pence per day. He had been in the Army long enough to know that with that money came added duties and responsibilities. Fairfoot had been an Army child, following his father about, hearing his views about what made a good corporal or a bad one.

In the 95th, a corporal's duties were set out in some texts, like the 'Green Book' written by Colonel Coote Manningham, one of the regiment's founders, and in other pamphlets such as the printed pages of Craufurd's Standing Orders for the Light Division. Reading and writing were essential to the discharge of these duties. Evidently Robert Fairfoot conquered this challenge of literacy, whereas it may well be that his father, with more than twenty-eight years' service as a private soldier, did not. But the 95th's senior officers certainly believed in offering their brighter soldiers the chance to learn.

In each company, there was an orderly sergeant of the day who would be assisted by a corporal, both answering to a duty officer. On the march, their duties ranged from arresting stragglers who had not been issued with tickets by their officers entitling them to fall out, to securing the bivouac. The posting of sentries was equally important on the march or in a place like Arruda.

Colonel Manningham had decreed:

The non-commissioned officer will make the most minute inspection of the men about to be placed as [sentries], and must see both that their arms are in good order, and that the powder in the pan is not wet. The inspection being made, the non-commissioned officer will conduct the sentries to the officer who will also examine them himself; when this is done the non-commissioned officer will march them to their several stations, taking care that the most intelligent men are posted in those stations which require the most circumspection.

The Light Division Standing Orders, as one might expect from Craufurd, took the business of posting sentries to extremes. There were to be outlying and inlying pickets – to prevent the brigade being surprised by the enemy – then there was to be a regimental camp guard (mainly to hinder the riflemen's mischief) and a company guard of one corporal and four privates. If Fairfoot was part of the outlying or inlying picket, camp guard or company guard then the night promised to be one of close attention to duty and little sleep. Given the numbers of different tasks, these could be assigned to NCOs every other day, at a time when their company was light of corporals, and it is clear that a man who was unable to abandon the hard-drinking ways of the private soldier would soon come unstuck – if discovered drunk on duty he would usually be relieved of his stripes. This is what had happened to Sergeant Plunket at Campo Maior a year before, and to many others in the 95th since they had landed. Fairfoot, though, applied himself conscientiously, for he had turned some kind of corner in his life, leaving behind the misery of his militia days. His stripes were never taken from him.

For those who had been broken to the ranks, however, resurrection was possible. If there was ever a moment when Joseph Almond, the Cheshire man who had been busted from corporal in 1808, could have redeemed himself, then Arruda was a propitious one, because of the shortage of NCOs. But while bright enough, and no skulker on the battlefield, Almond's company commander had taken against him, and it proved impossible to regain his former station. He may well have fallen foul of the notion many officers had, that a man in his late thirties who had not learnt to moderate his drinking was, in the words used on discharge papers, 'worn out', 'a bad soldier' or 'dissolute'.

For the illiterate private, there was almost no advancement possible. If, however, he had a good ear, such a man could be appointed as one of the company's two buglers. While at Arruda, William Green was made up to this post by O'Hare, enjoying the better pay. The bugler's bargain, however, was not always a happy one for he, playing that part carried out by the drummers in a line regiment, was responsible for laying the lash onto unfortunate members of his company.

The 95th's stay in Arruda proved pleasant enough, for they drank plenty of plundered wine, lived under canvas and ate well. Four weeks after their arrival, they awoke to discover that the French pickets posted in front of them had disappeared.

Masséna had realised that his men would starve in front of Torres Vedras and that to assault the fortifications was to invite a bloodbath. Every day French troops had to wander further and further away in their foraging expeditions, and with these ever-widening patrols, the number being lost to Portuguese partisans or desertion increased. The Army of Portugal, as Masséna's three corps had been designated, was melting away. Its horses were dying too, or becoming so emaciated that French generals began doubting their ability to draw all the cannon and supply caissons they had brought with them back to Spain, should the order come to quit Portugal. The marshal resolved to pull back to Santarem, a city in a fertile region several marches away from Lisbon and nearer to his sources of supply across the Spanish frontier. There he intended to winter, while awaiting further instructions from Paris.

Craufurd's division was set rapidly on the Army of Portugal's tail, its commander scenting the chance for further distinction. On the second day after they left Arruda, Craufurd spotted a French brigade moving across a plain towards some high ground at a place called Cartaxo. He drew up his division, but before giving any orders for an assault, he berated them for their behaviour on the march there. The text of this harangue has survived, and a quotation will give a flavour of the man in action:

If I ever have any occasion to observe any man of the Brigade pick his road and go round a pool of water instead of marching through it I am fully determined to bring the officer commanding the Company to which that man belongs to a Court Martial. Should the court acquit the officer it shall not deter me from repeating the same ceremony on any other officer again and again . . . I will insist on every soldier marching through water and I will flog any man attempting to avoid it.

Jonathan Leach, always one of Craufurd's harshest critics, commented sarcastically that it was 'a speech well calculated no doubt to make men and officers adore their leader and follow him enthusiastically up the French heights'. As Craufurd deployed his brigades ready to attack the superior French force to their front, Wellington appeared on horseback, 'in time enough to save us from total annihilation'. Seeing that Craufurd had drawn his battalions up in line, with just a single squadron of cavalry in support, Wellington asked him, 'Are you aware, General, that the whole of Junot's corps is close to the advanced body you now see, amounting to, at least, 23,000 men, a large portion of which is cavalry?' The attack was instantly called off, with many men reflecting bitterly on how close their brigadier had again come to destroying them.

The following day, the Light Division stopped just outside Santarem. There was a causeway leading to a bridge across the River Maior ahead of them, and it became clear that the French were prepared to defend it, having wheeled guns up to a position where they could bring a withering flank fire on anyone attempting the crossing. The river thus became the new demarcation line between the forces, for the Light Division was to stop in this area for several weeks, through the worst of the winter weather, while Masséna made up his mind whether to go forward or back.

Craufurd had been making representations to Horse Guards for some time about the need for more troops, and while in Arruda, a further two companies of the 95th (one each from the 2nd and 3rd Battalions) had been made over to him. They had found themselves unable to march to the division's standards, one officer noting, 'The company with which I had just arrived were much distressed to keep pace with the old campaigners – they made a tolerable scramble for a day or two, but by the time they arrived at the lines the greater part had been obliged to be mounted.'

The men of the 1st Battalion had already assumed the air of veterans. Their clothes were rain-washed and ingrained with dirt to the point where they had gone black or brown. Their bodies were lean and sinewy, faces tanned like leather. The spare shirts, brushes and the like which had been hauled up to Talavera had since been jettisoned from

their packs as dead weight. This difference between what they had left
behind and what they had become loomed increasingly large in the
minds of those men who had sailed out in May 1809.

Simmons, who had delighted in the veteran's reputation he had
earned in the battalion, found himself reluctantly recognising that his
ardour to return to service had outstripped his body's powers to heal
itself. He had come down with dysentery – that and his leg wound
meant he could not keep up on the marches. He wrote to his parents,
'Only a little while back I could run miles, always the first to go
through or over anything; judge how my feelings must be hurt at so
serious a difference.'

On surgeons' advice, Simmons returned to Lisbon, a check which he
knew would damage his finances. Lieutenant Harry Smith too discovered that his return to action had been premature. Although his ample
means bought him a mount, he was in acute pain from the ball lodged
in his heel, and resolved to go back to hospital to have it removed.

Those who stayed took over farm buildings and made themselves as
comfortable as they could. In one case, only a sheet draped across a
barn divided the company officers from their men. This provided the
subalterns with a golden opportunity to eavesdrop, since they generally steered clear of their men during the hours of darkness, for all sorts
of unfortunate incidents might befall an officer who charted too close
a course to them when they were drinking. 'The early part of their
evenings was generally spent in witticisms and tales,' one lieutenant
recalled. 'In conclusion, by way of a lullaby, some long-winded fellow
commenced one of those everlasting ditties in which soldiers and
sailors delight so much. They are all to the same tune, and the subject
(if one may judge by the tenor of the first ninety-eight verses!) was battle, murder, or sudden death.'

Captain O'Hare knew well enough that the peace of his company
was best ensured by keeping close tabs on its consumption of alcohol.
His suspicions being aroused one morning by the number of soldiers
who still seemed inebriated, he discovered and smashed a still they had
set up in one of the outhouses. On another occasion, he was woken at
night by the drunken ramblings of Private Tom Crawley, one of
Costello's friends, and decided the man was boozing too much, even by
his own rather liberal standards. Crawley's gin ration was stopped –
under normal circumstances each soldier had his blackjack filled with
the early-evening meal, no mean ration since these cups held half a

pint. 'Had sentence of death been pronounced, it could not have sounded more harsh,' Costello recalled of the moment the quartermaster refused Crawley his grog, explaining it was 'by order of Captain O'Hare'.

Corporal Fairfoot showed himself a reliable helper for O'Hare. He managed that difficult trick of retaining the good opinion of his former messmates, while discharging his new responsibilities fairly. Although an Englishman by parentage and outlook, having lived most of his life in Hampshire, Fairfoot well understood the Irish rankers who made up the company's toughest fighters and hardest drinkers. He had been born in Dublin and spent his childhood there, while his father's regiment was stationed in Ireland, and appreciated all of the complexities of that place.

During these cold, wet, winter days many of the soldiers considered tobacco to be an even more vital comfort than alcohol. The rank and file used clay pipes, which helped them keep their wits about them while on long hours of sentry duty. Officers preferred cigars, consuming them voraciously. Most considered them an essential tool, whether starting one of those hard marching days at 2 a.m. or 3 a.m., or spending time on some rain-swept hillside observing the enemy. 'If a man in England . . . fancies that he really knows the comfort of tobacco in that shape he is very much mistaken,' Jonathan Leach later wrote. 'He must rise, wet to the skin and numb with cold, from the lee side of a tree or hedge where he has been shivering all night under a flood of rain, then let him light his cigar and the warmth which it imparts is incredible.'

These few comforts saw the 95th through the dying days of 1810. On Christmas Day, the officers raced their horses on the flats beside the River Maior. They were tolerably well supplied, because of their proximity to Lisbon, but nobody would have claimed that theirs was a particularly interesting duty.

During the weeks in Arruda and months outside Santarem, the officers tried to relieve the tedious routine of rounds, pickets and commands. Books were in short supply since it was most difficult for a subaltern of Rifles, slogging along on his two feet, often soaked through, to carry some little library with him. A small supply of reading matter was however available, precious volumes carried on captains' baggage mules and passed around freely. There were some of Shakespeare's tragedies, and romantic stuff like Rousseau's *Nouvelle Héloïse*.

Since only a few of the 95th's officers had the education to read novels in French, they sought translations, particularly of plots that were set in Iberia. Lesage's *Gil Blas of Santillane*, both as a novel translated by Tobias Smollett and as a subsequent play written in English, was a great favourite. Its setting in Salamanca and romantic twists and turns amused them greatly. They also liked to identify with the young hero's picaresque adventures as he made his way in the world, starting penniless but eventually arriving at a position of great power and influence. *Don Quixote* was another favourite, neatly satirising the notions of chivalry by which many officers tried to live. References to this novel were so widespread that it was quite common, even among the illiterate rank and file, to refer to broken-down old horses as Rosinante (the Don's steed) and to the objects of their romantic fantasies as Dulcinea.

Some even conceived the idea of acting out the texts they had available: having heard from some French deserters in Arruda that their officers were putting on little skits and plays, the Light Division men decided to do the same. Shakespeare became the basis for the early dramatic fumblings of several subalterns.

Craufurd soon became bored with all this. He also missed his wife and children deeply, frequently succumbing to what he called the 'blue devils'. He wrote to them of his 'miserable position', and his inability to serve their interests while living in this state. He resolved to ask Wellington's leave for a trip home.

The rules of seniority – under which commands were doled out on the basis of time served in rank – had already been violated by Craufurd's appointment. His substantive rank was only colonel: a brigade was properly a major general's post and a division one for a lieutenant general. Wellington had rebuffed Craufurd's legion critics, particularly after the Coa, and worked the military secretarial system judiciously to keep him in position. After receiving several requests for permission to visit home, the general at last wrote to Craufurd, 'I would beg you to reflect whether, considering the situation in which you stand in the Army, it is desirable that you should go home upon leave. Adverting to the number of General Officers senior to you in the Army, it has not been easy to keep you in your command.'

Such language from the aloof and conservative Wellington was highly unusual. Craufurd's response to Wellington's 'begging' was typical: he wrote back expressing the hope that other officers might be satisfied, 'without reducing me to the painful alternative which I have at present to contemplate.' In short, he was ready to resign. Many in the

Army, including senior figures at Horse Guards as well as harassed company commanders, would have been only too pleased if the offer had been accepted – but the secret of Craufurd's hold over Wellington was precisely that the Commander of Forces was a little in awe of this man of such prickly independence and powerful personality.

Early in February, having got his way, Craufurd left Portugal. His timing was as bad in his leave arrangements at it had been on the Coa the previous July, for the Light Division was about to enter a period of frenetic marching and fighting. The Light Brigade and then Division had lived in his dark shadow for the best part of two years and their initial reaction to his departure was relief. Captain Leach noted gleefully in his journal: 'Brigadier General Craufurd has sailed for England. God be praised we have got rid of the Vagabond.'

NINE

Pombal

March–April 1811

On 5 March 1811, a typical sluggy Portuguese dawn brought an end to the outlying picket's night. They were cold and wet during this apparently everlasting Portuguese winter, and through the murk they could just make out the French pickets standing at their usual stations. But as the riflemen of 2nd Company studied those sentries it slowly became clear that they were not moving. One or two intrepid fellows crawled forward and discovered that the French had left behind scarecrows – straw men in greatcoats and shakoes, armed only with broomsticks.

Masséna's withdrawal did not come as a surprise to Lieutenant Colonel Beckwith. For some days, French deserters had been coming in now. Since a couple of weeks before there had been 'constant reports brought in that they cannot remain much longer in their present positions as the soldiery are suffering sad privations'. The day before, on 4 March, two deserters were received by the 95th, who said 'the enemy are burning everything they cannot remove, such as gun carriages, carts etc'.

The earlier accounts had been sufficient to bring Beckwith back from Lisbon. He had gone there to try to recuperate from another bout of the intermittent fever that so many had acquired in the Guadiana. But the colonel rallied himself from his sickbed and travelled back with George Simmons, who hoped he was strong enough at last to keep up with his company. It afforded the young subaltern a chance to foster 'the greatest friendship' with his commanding officer and now patron.

Craufurd's absence meant the Light Division was without a commander. Beckwith was in charge of the Right Brigade, comprising the Right Wing of his own battalion and the 43rd Light Infantry. The two wings served in different brigades, each under one of two majors serving with the 1st/95th.

The riflemen wasted little time in rushing forward into Santarem and were shocked by what they found. Any guilt about their own foraging activities in Arruda the previous autumn was quickly forgotten, for Santarem had been well and truly ransacked. Simmons gave his impressions: 'the few miserable inhabitants, moving skeletons . . . many streets quite impassable with filth and rubbish, with an occasional man, mule or donkey rotting and corrupting and filling the air with pestilential vapours'. Another officer felt it 'looked like a city of the plague, represented by empty dogs and empty houses'.

Masséna had seen his army dwindle from sixty-five thousand when it entered Portugal to just over forty thousand as it left. The difference was accounted for by battle, sickness, desertion, capture and the wrath of the Portuguese militia. He had lost almost six thousand of his fourteen thousand horses, too. The remaining beasts had almost all been necessary to haul back his artillery, scores of surplus wagons being consigned to the flames. His army was ready enough to retreat to Spain, and could still defend itself, but the weeks of starvation had left the French soldiery undisciplined and resentful. As they moved back towards the frontier, many stragglers took the opportunity to visit revenge on the locals. One French officer remarked, 'The labours that beset our soldiers, the obstacles they encountered, the hunger that devoured them, excited the worst feelings in them; their hearts hardened as their bodies weakened; they had no more pity for those they pursued, they accused them of their own faults; they killed them if they put up resistance.'

The 95th, following close behind, may not have suffered quite the same privations, but they were hungry too. The Peninsular Army had become chronically short of cash during the winter. When the Army could not afford the weekly pay parade, it was deferred for one week. As they set off in pursuit of the French, Wellington's soldiers were three months in arrears. The riflemen moved through Santarem with alacrity: they were keen to catch up with some lame Frenchie or a dead one – it didn't matter so long as he was fresh and hadn't been stripped by the locals. They knew that every soldier would be carrying some coin about him, hoarded for the last extreme, hidden in a little belt worn under his shirt or secreted somewhere else about his person.

For two weeks after the French quit Santarem, there were actions of some sort almost every day between the enemy rearguard and the Rifles. Once Marshal Ney and his 6th Corps, the Light Bobs' old enemies from the frontier, took charge of the rearguard, its operations were conducted with great skill. Each day, the lumbering beast of the French Army would turn around and face its pursuers. Sometimes they would engage, sometimes not. Each time the British passed through a Portuguese village, a new outrage would greet them: hundreds of mules deliberately lamed by having their hamstrings cut by the French; Portuguese peasants beside the road, their bellies slit open; a man left to die slowly under a huge boulder placed upon him by several sadistic soldiers. With every sight of this kind, the riflemen felt entitled to deal a little more roughly with any Frenchman they chanced upon.

During the first proper action, at Pombal, on 11 March, two men of O'Hare's company had got into a heated argument over the warm body of a Frenchman one of them had shot. 'Go kill a Frenchman for yourself!' one private had shouted at the other.

Costello and some of the other men had the good fortune to take a French officer's baggage horse. Among the more solvent officers, there was always a ready purchaser for a beast of this kind, and the contents of its bags were soon sold off too. A swift sale of the prize allowed O'Hare to give each man six dollars – a sum in Spanish coin equivalent to a little over a shilling, enough to keep them in wine for several days.

The following day, they had come up with Ney's boys again at Redinha. For many in the 95th, there was an exhilaration about leaving behind the sodden mire of winter quarters and being in action again: 'It was a sunshiny morning, and the red coats and pipeclayed belts and glittering of men's arms in the sun looked beautiful. I felt a pleasure which none but a soldier so placed can feel.' O'Hare, being the senior captain, claimed the post of honour at the head of the column, leading off the attack towards a wooded ridge.

On these occasions the Rifle companies deployed in set-piece fashion. They would come up a road, marching three abreast. When the enemy were sighted they would either be told off in companies, each given their task by the major commanding Right Wing, or would form into column of companies, moving a little closer to their objective in this formation.

Coming closer to the enemy's *voltigeurs*, normally a few hundred yards away, the company commander would give the order to extend, and the bugler relay it with a distinctive call. The files (a pair of men in each case) would then move apart – anything from two to six paces between each file, depending on the nature of the terrain and how numerous their foe. As soon as this advance came close enough to the enemy to fire with effect, the front man in each file would be ordered to stop, the rear man run past him about six paces, drop down, aim at his target and fire. The subaltern or sergeant commanding the section would then call out or blow a whistle and the first rank would get up and rush past those who had just fired, while they reloaded. Within each company, the two halves or platoons might also be stopping and starting in the same way, the whole moving forward with pounding feet, whistle blows and a steady, crackling fire of rifles. Advancing up to the French rearguard, most of the Light Division adopted skirmishing tactics too, for the red-coated battalions – the 43rd and 52nd – had learned to dissolve the rigid lines used by normal battalions when the terrain and tactical situation allowed it. Their men, and the *Cacadores*, were also using the protection of ground and aiming their shots.

It was tough, physical work, particularly if, as at Rehinha, the skirmish followed a march of many miles. Every man also needed to feel complete confidence in his mate – the rear rank man with the front one of each file – since a carelessly aimed shot might easily claim a friend. The same went for the subalterns commanding Left and Right platoons and for the company commanders, one with the other.

At Redinha, Lieutenant Harry Smith was commanding 2nd Company, Captain Leach being ill. His men deployed beside O'Hare's as they worked up towards the French-held ridge line. Smith was eager to prove his worth in this post – few officers in the battalion radiated ambition more intensely. When he moved his company ahead of O'Hare's and suffered a local counter-attack from the French, the old Irish captain did nothing to ease his distress. Smith recorded angrily, 'I sent to my support, O'Hare, to move up to me. The obstinate old Turk would not, and so I was obliged to come back, and had most unnecessarily five or six men wounded.' Perhaps O'Hare had been waiting for an order from his major. Perhaps he just didn't like young subalterns in a hurry.

When, eventually, the two companies pushed through the little town and saw off the French, riflemen soon fell upon their wounded. Costello was disgusted to spy two buglers fighting one another for the right to rob a wounded French officer. One tried to settle the matter by pulling a knife and tearing at the stricken man's shirt so as to find his money belt, but he stabbed the officer in the process. 'It was with difficulty that I restrained myself from shooting the owner of the knife,' wrote Costello, 'but then he told me it was an accident.'

Flushed with battle, three months in arrears of pay, and with little hope of seeing their own supply train as they advanced so rapidly, the riflemen wanted to pillage food and drink as well as coin. They were not inclined to be too generous with their spoils either: any man who held back in action, or went to the rear with a wounded comrade for rather too long, was in danger of being labelled a skulker by his messmates.

That evening Costello and several others cooked up their spoils after the Combat of Redinha. Private Humphrey Allen reappeared and tried to join them, 'but was refused because he had gone out of action with the wounded'. Having sent Allen packing with some choice language, the 3rd Company men chomped away and thought nothing further of the matter until they heard a shot in the distance, followed by a heavy exhange between the two sides' pickets.

Lieutenant Colonel Beckwith raced down to investigate the firing, only to discover Private Allen was the cause of it. On being rebuffed by his mess, he had walked down to the outlying picket, chosen a French sentry and killed him. When Beckwith asked why, Allen replied, 'Why sir, I arnt had nought to eat these two days and thought as how I might find summit in the Frencher's knapsack.'

Two days later, they were in action again, at Cazal Noval. Once again, Ney had made his dispositions wisely. Wearing his dark-blue coat, red hair visible beneath his cocked hat, Ney could be relied upon to appear at the key moment. The troops around him drew new inspiration from this leadership. 'The slightest position offering any advantage was occupied,' Sub-Lieutenant Marcel wrote. 'If there was a gun shot at five in the morning, the Marshal would appear at the post of the sentry who'd fired it; if a man was wounded in the rearguard company of *voltigeurs*, he'd make sure that he wasn't abandoned. "With the redhead we can be calm," said the soldiers.'

It was rather different in the Light Division. Just before Redinha, Wellington had appointed Major General Sir William Erskine as acting commander *vice* Craufurd. Erskine was so short-sighted that some said he could see no further than the head of his horse. Wellington even doubted Erskine's sanity, but felt unable to sack him because of his political connections. Erskine, in theory at least, was a commander of horse, but as Wellington pithily observed, 'He is very blind, which is against him at the head of the cavalry, but very cautious.' The last characteristic seemed to be a faint sort of recommendation. In action at Cazal Noval, he proved not just cautious but quite incapable. The Light Division was checked with ninety-four casualties, including two officers and three soldiers of the 95th killed.

The 95th's dead included the commander of the battalion's Left Wing. He had fallen with a shot through the lungs, and when George Simmons ran to his help, frothing blood was coming from his mouth, a sign the one-time apprentice surgeon knew all too well. 'Major Stewart, as many others have done, asked me if he was mortally wounded,' Simmons jotted in his journal. 'I told him he was. He thanked me, and died the day following.'

It was perfectly obvious to the rank and file that Erskine was a bungler, and they soon began referring to him as 'Ass-skin'. The French, knowing how well Ney brought them away from some difficult situations, considered the British pursuit 'timid' and poorly conducted. Wellington too had drawn conclusions from these affairs and soon began exercising a closer personal supervision of the Light Division, appearing more often at the head of the Army.

With these skirmishes between French rear and British advance guards, many of the riflemen were confronted with the effects of their handiwork for the first time. At the Coa or Busaco, the British had been falling back. But in March 1811 they were advancing and often a rifleman who potted his Frenchman soon stood over him. Rushing forward at Cazal Noval, Ned Costello picked his target: 'My blood was up because he once aimed at me, his ball whizzing close by as I approached, so when I got within fifty yards of him, I fired. I was beside him in an instant. He had fallen in the act of loading, the shot having entered his head . . . A few quick turns of his eyes as they rolled their dying glances on mine turned my whole blood within me. An indescribable uneasiness came over me, and I reproached myself as his destroyer.' The rifleman gave his victim a swig of wine from his canteen, easing his dying moments as he hoped someone might one day do for him.

Costello's feelings were all the more perturbed when he realised that the soldier he had killed was hanging back to try to protect his wounded brother, who lay nearby. When the battle was over, he went back to find them but discovered both Frenchmen, 'naked as they were born, perforated with innumerable wounds, no doubt administered by the Portuguese. I turned back to camp in a very poor humour with myself.'

The following day, the division came up with the French at a small town called Foz de Arouce, through which ran a little river, the Ceira. As the French withdrew, the bridge became choked and it was clear that a small rearguard had been left vulnerable on the wrong side of the river. Wellington spotted the mistake instantly and, dispensing with Erskine, found Beckwith, ordering him to attack.

One of the French regiments, the 39ème, had allowed itself to get caught a little too far from the bridge, and Beckwith sent one wing of his battalion rushing down the slope towards the town. They made their way into the streets, getting between the 39ème and the bridge, opening fire on the Frenchmen to drive home the danger of their situation. The realisation that they might be cut off caused a general panic, hundreds rushing along the Ceira, trying to find a ford to wade through.

Ney, seeing the gravity of the situation, ordered a battalion of the 69ème that was already across the bridge to turn about. One of the officers in that regiment noted that the British were 'pressing us harder than usual'. 'In a moment, our battalion was under arms and beating the charge,' Sub-Lieutenant Marcel recorded. 'The 27ème, in line, fired in two ranks on the Portuguese column that was trying to approach the bridge. It fired with the same calm as at drill. Under the protection of this fire, we marched, bayonets to the fore, with such confidence that the enemy fled.'

The greater than accustomed ardour of the British attack was due to Wellington and Beckwith and the 'Portuguese column' – in fact the 95th. It was quite usual for the French to have difficulty distinguishing between the dark uniforms of the riflemen and the Portuguese *Cacadores*. The loss of the French during this action was about 250, with many drowned in the river. The 39ème's eagle, the standard given to it by the Emperor, was also lost in the Ceira during this action and later recovered, providing the British with a rare trophy.

For the French, 6th Corps' march back to the border had been a textbook operation, despite the final chapter at Foz de Arouce. A fighting withdrawal offered the enemy all kinds of chances to make mischief, and Ney had kept the British in check. One French officer reflected, 'From 5 to 15 March, that is to say in eleven days, [the corps] sped across thirty-three leagues; it did an average of three leagues a day. The Anglo-Portuguese marched in its tracks with their usual timidity: at Pombal, Redinha, at Foz de Arouce, one or two divisions of the 6th Corps sufficed to stop them and paralyse their plans.'

That Wellington had followed cautiously was not in doubt. One officer on his staff wrote home, 'If you ask me whether we might not have done more than we have, I have no hesitation in answering certainly yes, and on several occasions, but it appears to have been throughout the business the plan of Ld W not to risk a man and he clearly has succeeded.' After humbling Masséna at Busaco and in front of Torres Vedras, Wellington had no desire to let him clinch some propaganda victory on the way back to Spain.

But an unadventurous fortnight for the Army as a whole had taken its toll on the 95th, engaged as it was throughout. And while the rank-and-file riflemen shared the French derision for the way the actions had been commanded – blaming Ass-skin – the wider Peninsular Army had learned of the Light Division's almost daily actions and the length of its marches, and was deeply impressed. Wellington had praised the Light Division warmly in his dispatches and on 16 March gave the British regiments of that force a highly unusual reward. Each was asked to nominate a non-commissioned officer for promotion to commissioned status. Sergeant Major Andrew Simpson, who'd sailed with O'Hare's company in May 1809 as a sergeant, was Beckwith's choice and was duly commissioned into the 2nd Foot as an ensign. Wellington might not have been able to pin Legions of Honour to deserving rankers, but some marks of gratitude were at least possible. Even so, it was evident it best served everybody's interest for a newly made ensign like Simpson to be posted away from the regiment where he had served in the ranks.

There had also been a good deal of plunder to keep the riflemen happy and, wonder of wonders, on 21 March, enough coin had turned up to pay the men some of their arrears. The commissaries caught up at last, leading to some regular issues of rations. 'Never let it be said that John Bull cannot fight upon an empty stomach,' Costello remarked. 'If ever a division proved this more than another, it was certainly the Light one for Heaven knows we were light enough at this and other periods.'

The 95th's casualties added up in dribs and drabs through that March. Simmons, who had been fighting almost two years without promotion, began to feel he might have the scent of it. He also feared that his parents would be worrying about him, reading in the *Gazette* the names of those officers of the 95th killed in recent actions. He wrote to his father, 'Our regiment gets terribly cut up. We think nothing of it. Every man glories in doing his duty, and those that survive must be promoted.' O'Hare had drawn conclusions too, notably from Major Stewart's death: there was a vacant majority and he was the regiment's senior captain. Surely he would now have his step unless someone else were to cheat him of Stewart's vacancy, by buying his way over his head or deploying his interest with the Commander in Chief. That would be infamous in the extreme.

The French had not quite been shown out of Portugal yet, though, and that meant more fighting. There remained many marches ahead, too. After Foz de Arouce, the French had suffered something of a slump in morale and discipline, regardless of their pride in Ney's achievements with the rearguard. Masséna had to issue an order of the day reminding them forcefully, 'Pillaging is expressly forbidden, and pillagers will be punished with the full force of the law' – such was the extent of murder and lawlessness, he hung a few of the worst culprits *pour encourager les autres*. But as the marshal tried to bring such matters under tighter control, a heavy fight was getting under way. It was one in which Beckwith and the 95th would face their hardest test to date, being pitted against almost impossible odds.

TEN

Sabugal

April 1811

An eerie sound penetrated the early-morning fog close to the banks of the Coa. One voice would sing out in German, and then a hundred comrades would sing back the next line. It was a manly chorus that might have unnerved some. But the Rifles knew it was the hussars of the German Legion. They had saddled up after a wet, cold night and were reviving their spirits. A song and a smoke was sufficient to restore the German veterans. A big drooping pipe would be lit up and quickly popped beneath a big drooping moustache. With the clumping of hooves and jingle of saddlery, they set off to find a ford across the river.

The Light Division had come up much closer to the frontier, that 3 April, and Wellington issued orders for a large-scale attack on troops of General Reynier's 2nd Corps, whom he believed to be just across the river. The French occupied a long ridge, with the Coa running alongside it. Where the river eventually turned away from this feature, there was a bridge, and a town, Sabugal, with its old castle. Wellington wanted to use some fords higher up the river to begin a combined movement that would see the Light Division strike the French at the one end of the ridge, followed by attacks in their flank and, further down river through Sabugal, cutting off their line of retreat. Having played a careful game throughout the previous month's retreat, the British commander wanted to try a combination that might discomfit Reynier.

With Lieutenant Colonel Beckwith at their head, Right Wing of the 95th marched into one of the fords across the river. In an instant, boots and trousers were immersed in the icy water and, soon enough, they were wading up to their waists. There was a tension in the ranks, a sense that something horrible might await them in the dense fog that obscured the far bank. No professional army would leave a ford so close to its bivouac unguarded, and the riflemen wondered whether a salute of canister might blow their leading ranks to kingdom come or whether some squadrons of *chasseurs à cheval* might burst through the murk and scythe them down.

In the event, the French *bonjour* took the form of a ragged volley of musketry from a few pickets, who instantly took to their heels. As the sopping soldiers emerged from the Coa, their commander, evidently fearing the possibility of cavalry attack, kept them going forward a while in column of companies. Each one, around thirty men across the front and two deep, marched close to the heels of the company in front. If enemy horse appeared, they could quickly close ranks behind the leading company so that the whole would form a compact mass able to resist a charge.

Behind Right Wing 1st/95th (about three hundred men that morning) were the 43rd, and three companies of the 3rd *Cacadores* – generally reckoned the best Portuguese troops, schooled as they had been by Lieutenant Colonel George Elder, a Rifles officer. The ground over which they would have to fight consisted of rolling hills dotted with groves of trees, patches of cultivation and little orchards enclosed by stone walls. This landscape, combined with the weather, meant all sorts of unpleasant surprises might be lurking just ahead of them, but fortunately for Beckwith these uncertainties would also afflict the French commanders.

While the 95th felt their way towards the base of the ridge on the eastern bank of the river, Wellington's carefully drawn plan began to fall apart. The miasma that hung about the Coa that morning led the different British commanders to reach their own personal conclusions about what was required of them. Some of the brigades that were meant to start off before the Light Division, heading for Sabugal itself, had not even moved, their leaders convinced that nothing could be attempted in such a dense fog. General Erskine, meanwhile, had put himself at the head of some cavalry and, almost as soon as the Light Division's infantry left their bivouac, went off on a different path to the one allocated to him in Wellington's plan. Even Beckwith, it must be admitted, for nobody was without fault as the march got under way, had put his brigade across the wrong ford – one that was too close to Reynier's positions. The division was meant to perform a right-angled turn as it crossed by several fords, with Beckwith's brigade forming the inside of this hinge, closest to the Coa, then the division's 2nd Brigade (under Colonel Drummond) in the middle, with the cavalry furthest to the right, or east, moving the greatest distance on the outside of the line as it turned. This way the division would line up to hit the head of Reynier's corps, atop the ridge, with the Coa protecting its left flank and the cavalry its right. Instead of this happening as Wellington wanted, Beckwith's brigade had gone across the river, on its own, too close to the French.

Erskine, who was condemned by one officer of the 95th as a 'short-sighted old ass', was to play no further part in that day's drama. Another disgusted rifleman recorded, 'A brigade of dragoons under Sir William Erskine, who were to have covered our right, went the Lord knows where, but certainly not into the fight, although they started at the same time as we did and had the *music* of our rifles to guide them.'

About half a mile from the ford, the 95th, leading Beckwith's brigade, started moving up the hillside, where they expected to find thousands of Frenchmen. The countryside was dotted with walled enclosures and clumps of chestnut trees. The visibility had improved somewhat, and they could now see a couple of hundred yards in front of them. All of this made a surprise by cavalry less likely, and the 95th's companies began extending up the slope, until the whole of Right Wing formed one long skirmish line.

Among the leading riflemen, feeling their way onto the ridge's flat top, there was still a feeling of tense anticipation. There had been some more French skirmisher fire, but most of them had run off, and whoever lay behind the enemy pickets had most certainly been given the alarm and would be under arms. The vegetation, enclosures and lie of the land meant, though, that they could still not see far ahead; they moved gingerly across country.

Simmons, leading his company, moved up through the chestnut trees and, as the ground dipped a little in front of them, stopped dead. They had come face to face with a French regiment standing in column not twenty yards in front. The officers who caught sight of the first riflemen sent up a shout of '*Vive l'Empereur!*', which was instantly repeated by hundreds of men in the ranks behind, shaking their muskets at the insolent fools who had just appeared to their front. At moments like this, there was only one drill. Simmons and his riflemen turned tail and started running. They flew back towards their supports and the 43rd, bullets whistling about their ears, smacking into the chestnut trunks as they went. The French drums were thumping now and Simmons's men knew they were being pursued. Every now and then, a couple of the riflemen would stop, turn around and pick a target, fire, and move on.

Making a little stand, 'the galling fire of the 95th Rifles at point blank [soon] compelled them to retire,' wrote one subaltern of the 95th, 'but rallying with strong supports the wood again became the scene of sharp work and close firing.' But the French pushed back the Rifles. Beckwith, hearing the firing to his front, deployed the 43rd, ready to receive whatever might appear. As three big French columns arrived in front of them, 'the 43rd formed line giving their fire, we skirmishers rapidly forming up on their left, opening our fire on the advancing columns.' The British realised they were heavily outnumbered – perhaps by a factor of four to one. 'Beckwith, finding himself alone and unsupported, in close action, with only hundreds to oppose the enemy's thousands, at once saw and felt all the danger of his situation,' wrote one officer.

At the front of the French division were the *2ème Léger* or Light Infantry, *4ème Léger* and the *36ème Régiment de Ligne*. They advanced, bayonets to the fore, drums beating the *pas de charge*. Beckwith's men could not stand in front of this phalanx: they started running backwards.

The colonel understood that at such a crisis his own behaviour had to instil confidence. He was able to halt his men and turn them back again towards the enemy, less than a hundred yards away and now looking down at them from uphill. Beckwith manoeuvred his horse up and down as he ordered his line, a prime target for the enemy's sharpshooters if ever there was one, steadying his men and directing their volleys. He knew it was going to be a matter of time until Colonel Drummond's brigade appeared on his right or the attacks by other divisions went in further north – but how long? Another determined French push and they would be fighting with the Coa to their backs. His brigade was about to be crushed.

For some reason, though, the French did not press forward again. Visibility was improving, and even though they could see Beckwith was unsupported, they could not quite believe it. Perhaps the isolated British brigade was trying to gall them into rushing forward into some hideous ambush. However, if the French felt unsure about moving onwards, they knew they could do more to warm the British up a little. Two howitzers were wheeled to their front and started spewing canister – scores of small balls packed into a tin – into the British line. This was bound to make the 43rd suffer and men were soon dropping. An officer of the 95th fell too: Lieutenant Duncan Arbuthnott, his head blown off.

Beckwith could not allow his brigade to be pummelled like this for long. No men, however highly trained, could stand all day under canister from howitzers less than a hundred yards away. Riding forward, he ordered two companies of the 43rd (about 150 or 160 men) to advance behind him, and they set off towards the dark mass of thousands of Frenchmen to their front.

At the very least, Beckwith wanted to stick the French artillerymen with bayonets, but in leading forward this desperate charge, he hoped also that the French might somehow be intimidated into yielding a little ground, so conceding the eminence that commanded the British position. Reynier's three regiments were about to receive just two companies, but they were not ideally deployed. When they had set off towards the British, their commanders had formed them up with caution. Having come forward in columns, they could not now deploy into firing lines because the French battalions were packed too close together and the countryside would not admit it. When the 43rd got close, they were therefore able to fire a volley in their faces, with only a small proportion of the French – those in the leading ranks – able to reply. Having given their fire, the little band of the 43rd, menaced by the French columns, was soon heading back down towards their mates.

Beckwith rallied them and went up again. The result was the same. 'Now my lads, we'll just go back a little if you please,' Beckwith boomed above the firing. Some of the men were running: 'No, no I don't mean that – we are in no hurry – we'll just walk quietly back, and you can give them a shot as you go along.' His voice, though loud, remained utterly calm even when one of the French marksmen finally hit him. The bullet had creased Beckwith's forehead and blood started running down his face. The colonel's soldiers looked up anxiously, only to hear him call out, 'I am no worse; follow me.' When they were back with the main firing line he told them, 'Now, my men, this will do – let us show them our teeth again!'

The French, having been stalled for forty-five minutes, could now see the battlefield well enough to want to bring the fight to its conclusion. Some cavalry was ordered up, to move around and take Beckwith's brigade on its unprotected flank. The infantry columns, meanwhile, stood motionless, their progress checked by the firepower of the 95th, Portuguese and 43rd.

Not for the first time, the riflemen watched enemy officers going out in front of their men, sometimes putting their hats on the ends of their swords, sometimes jumping up and down, waving their arms, exhorting them forward for the honour of their regiment and of France. 'Their officers are certainly very prodigal of life, often exposing themselves ridiculously,' wrote one Rifles officer. Beckwith galloped up behind one group of riflemen to point out one of the senior French officers who had come forward on horseback. 'Shoot that fellow, will you?' he ordered them, knowing that the French would only move forward again if they were inspired by brave commanders. Several riflemen fired and Beckwith watched both the officer and his horse collapse to the ground. 'Alas! you were a noble fellow,' exclaimed the colonel before galloping off. The regiments facing the British brigade in this part of the fight had eighteen officers shot, including two of their three colonels. Another French brigade, consisting of the *17ème Léger* and *70ème* regiments, was now being fed into the battle.

Colonel Drummond, having heard the firing while one mile to the south-east, had begun marching towards the battle. General Erskine sent him an order to stop and not engage himself, but thankfully Drummond ignored it.

While Beckwith's fight had progressed to the point where everyone involved was exhausted, the squally weather opened up a little, allowing a brief window through which both Wellington, across on the western bank of the Coa, and Reynier, before it closed in again, had caught a glimpse of what was happening. Wellington's feelings on seeing that his whole plan had miscarried can easily be imagined. Having observed the mass in front of Beckwith he knew that the pressure on his light troops had to be lessened, so he hastened on the divisions that were meant to cut Reynier's line of withdrawal.

When Drummond's men, principally the 52nd, finally appeared to Beckwith's right, the tide was turned. The two brigades fought their way up the hill to their front. The French rescued one of their howitzers but lost the other to the British charge. The battalions of the *17ème* and *70ème* faced a furious advance. 'The Light Division, under the shout of old Beckwith, rushed on with an impetuosity nothing could resist, for, so checked had we been, our bloods were really up, and we paid off the enemy most awfully,' wrote Harry Smith, adding, 'such a scene of slaughter as there was on one hill would appal a modern soldier.'

Reynier was now engaged in a general withdrawal. A charge by two squadrons of French cavalry onto Drummond's flank helped hold the British up for a while, as did another downpour. The dense sheet of rain dampened down the firing and also allowed the *17ème Léger* and *70ème* to break contact with the British, running back into the gloom.

By the end of the day, Reynier's men had paid a heavy price – suffering casualties of 61 officers and 689 men, as well as having 186 soldiers taken prisoner. Wellington reacted with the unbridled gratitude of a man who had feared he might be presiding over a fiasco, but discovered that everything had turned out better than he could have hoped. He wrote exultingly to a colleague: 'our loss is much less than one would have supposed possible, scarcely two hundred men . . . really these attacks in columns against our lines are very contemptible.' The disparity between the losses was even more dramatic than he imagined, for the British casualties did not exceed 162, and the 95th, for example, had just two men killed. In short, Beckwith's men stood against five times their number and inflicted five times as many casualties.

Something much more subtle than the bludgeon fire of the British line had been demonstrated at Sabugal. Of the five French colonels who led their regiments against the Light Division, two were killed and two were seriously wounded, only one remaining unscathed. There had been heavy casualties among company officers too – all evidence of carefully aimed fire. The British battalions had been handled with the utmost tactical flexibility: at times much of the 43rd had been skirmishing, at others the 95th had formed a firing line on their flank. Beckwith had deployed his shooters in a variety of combinations with the 43rd fighting and manoeuvring in small sub-divisions. His leadership, considered inspirational by everyone who had witnessed it, had shown that soldiers led by an officer who was both expert and humane would follow him to triumph, even in an apparently hopeless situation requiring the greatest steadiness.

On the day of Sabugal, Brigadier Craufurd had been walking the streets of Lisbon. He had just returned from England and had heard rumours of his division's battles in March. He wrote to his wife, insisting he was unrepentant about having taken leave: 'If anything brilliant has been done, it will be to a certain degree mortifying, but I am prepared for it . . . the happiness of having seen you and our dear little ones, after so long a separation, continues, and will continue giving me renewed energy and strength of mind.'

Craufurd's ability to put a brave face on the events of his absence began to crumble when reports started flying about after Sabugal, having taken some days to reach the Portuguese capital. It became obvious that the action had caused considerable éclat, the Light Division and Beckwith having gained a fame from it which March's skirmishing did not provide.

A few days later, when Wellington came to write his official dispatch, a document that would be published in the newspapers, he reflected further on the events at Sabugal. He was certainly not a man given to hyperbole, but it was to be one of the most effusive dispatches he ever composed: 'I consider the action that was fought by the Light Division, by Col. Beckwith's brigade principally, with the whole of the 2d Corps, to be one of the most glorious that British troops were ever engaged in.' As for the leader of the division's Right Brigade, who still technically only held the post of commanding officer of the 1st Battalion, 95th, Wellington wrote, 'It was impossible for any officer to conduct himself with more ability and gallantry than Col. Beckwith.'

This was a bitter pill indeed for Craufurd, for neither he personally, nor the division whilst under his command was ever to receive such words from Wellington. Craufurd could not contain his feelings when he finally admitted to his beloved wife and most intimate confidante that 'it would be stupid to pretend to persuade you that I did not feel any regret that the events, which have taken place in my absence, had not taken place until after my return.'

The Light Division's fame combined with its losses to enhance the prospects for the advancement of its officers. Beckwith was raised from lieutenant colonel to colonel, a step that would eventually remove him from the command of his battalion. On 11 April, Peter O'Hare was also given an in-field promotion, or brevet, to the rank of major. This meant higher pay, and priority in promotion to a major's post once one was vacant. Indeed, the death of Major Stewart in March had created such a gap: the only way that O'Hare could have been thwarted would have been if some officer already in possession of a major's commission (for example, in the 2nd or 3rd Battalion of the 95th) had outmanoeuvred him. But Beckwith appears to have observed a rule that the promotions, wherever possible, should be made within the battalion and on the basis of gallantry or seniority (both in O'Hare's case), rather than allowing an outsider to come in, by purchase or otherwise. This took account of the proud and prickly nature of his battalion's officers and the difficulty that any non-veteran might experience in commanding their loyalty.

Sabugal was O'Hare's last battle at the head of the 3rd Company. He would now serve as a major, commanding one of the two wings into which the battalion had been divided. Had the position been sold, it would have cost someone almost £3,000. But O'Hare had achieved the step through serving his time, hard fighting and being lucky enough to stay alive. In making this promotion, he had managed something so difficult – for the average battalion carried five captains for each major – that even many of the better-connected officers in the Peninsular Army had trouble achieving it.

As for the more privileged class, they had come to look beyond the regiment for their advancement. Duncan Arbuthnott, killed at Sabugal, had been almost the only aristocrat to defy this pattern – for he had continued to serve with his company and had lost his life in doing so, whereas others among the handful of landed types who had sailed with the battalion soon concluded that a staff appointment was a more certain route to promotion. Such a post would locate them closer to men of influence and a little further from the bullets. Lieutenant Harry Smith (from a landed but not titled family) became 'brigade major' or principal staff officer to the commander of the Light Division's Left Brigade at about this time. Captain, the Honourable James Stewart, while technically remaining in command of the 1st Company, actually served in a series of staff appointments after arriving in Portugal. Dudley St Leger Hill had left the 95th in August 1810, gaining two steps in rapid succession by going via the West Indian Rangers to the Portuguese *Cacadores*.

Captain Hercules Pakenham, of the influential Anglo-Irish Longford clan, adopted all of the black arts used by moneyed families to advance an Army career. During his first seven years in the Army, he had changed commission six times in order to boost his rank as quickly as possible. His brother was Colonel Edward Pakenham, the Deputy Adjutant General at Headquarters and, as such, had Wellington's ear. Young Hercules was appointed Assistant Adjutant General, serving in the 3rd Division not long after the 1809 campaign started.

In August 1810 he made the jump to major by buying a commision in the 7th West Indian Regiment. Of course, he never intended to present himself in that poxy, pestilential, Caribbean hellhole where they served. The usual form among richer officers was to buy a step in the West Indian, African or some other garrison regiment, and progress to a more salubrious corps during the one to two years after purchase, before a failure to appear in front of one's commanding officer was deemed bad form. Although Hercules had served several years in the 95th, and was well liked by many of its soldiers, his loyalties were only to himself: he wrote home to his father that April that 'supposing I got into the most desirable Regt. in the service, I should be happy to leave it the moment I could get a step.'

It was possible to buy commissions in the 95th, but the regiment had long harboured a prejudice against such advancement, preferring the principle of seniority. This had led one ambitious officer to abandon it several years earlier with the words: 'As to remaining an English full pay lieutenant for ten or twelve years! not for the universe! . . . rather let me command Esquimauxs [*sic*] than be a subaltern of Rifles forty years old.' Battle losses since the arrival in Portugal two years earlier created more vacancies and therefore promised more rapid advancement, as George Simmons constantly reassured his parents. At the same time, they hardened regimental officers against accepting newcomers and convinced aristocrats that a safer route to advancement could be found elsewhere.

As for the possible consequences of buying rank in the 95th and throwing one's weight around, one need not have looked further than the case of Lieutenant Jonathan Layton. He had sailed with the others in 1809 and served in Leach's company. In Leach's absence, Harry Smith had commanded the company at Pombal and Redinha. On Smith's appointment to the staff, Layton took over, even commanding 2nd Company at Sabugal. Beckwith trusted him to handle the company because Layton was a very tough man, a real 'soldier of fortune'. Layton had no difficulty killing: in fact, he had killed a captain in his own regiment.

When the battalion was about to depart on foreign service in 1808, Layton had argued violently with Captain Brodie Grant, a wealthy officer just twenty-one years old. Layton's company had marched to Harwich the next day to embark, but Grant caught them up. Layton and Grant argued until, pistols being produced, they determined to fight a duel in a nearby field. Grant was killed and Layton went on trial at Chelmsford Assizes, charged with manslaughter. He was eventually acquitted through lack of evidence.

It cannot be said that society knew its own mind on the subject of duelling. The Duke of York tried to use his influence, while at the head of the Army, to stamp it out. A contest of this kind had caused one officer of the 95th to leave the regiment. In Layton's case, however, Colonel Beckwith had turned a blind eye, considering Grant the more blameworthy of the two parties. But Layton's fate was to serve on without the possibility of promotion.

Not long after Sabugal, Captain Jonathan Leach, restored to health, came back to his company and Layton once again resumed his subaltern's duties. The command of 3rd Company, however, had been left vacant by O'Hare's promotion.

By early May, the French were back at the frontier, with the Light Division assuming its old positions on the Beira uplands. An enemy garrison had been left behind the new British lines in Almeida, the Portuguese fortress captured by Masséna the previous year, and Wellington placed himself ready to block any attempt by the marshal to relieve it. The armies were ready to do battle again, and the 95th were once more destined to be centre stage.

ELEVEN

Fuentes d'Onoro

May–June 1811

The journey from Lisbon to the Beira frontier was an arduous one, taking even the most determined traveller more than one week. Being a cross and anxious fellow, it must have seemed to last for ever for Brigadier Robert Craufurd. Those coming the other way brought reports of an imminent general action. Having missed Sabugal and the events of March, he certainly did not intend to be absent. Among the soldiers of the Army, the Light Division was making its name in small battles – affairs of the outposts, advanced guard actions – but home in Old England such fights hardly registered with the public. A distinguished role at a battle like Busaco was another matter. While at home on leave, Craufurd had been satisfied to learn that his family and friends all knew of his part in it, since Lord Wellington's dispatch had featured in the newspapers. Just as blood money was far less likely to be voted for the soldiers in some skirmish like Redinha, so the real baubles or plums served up to senior officers came from the public acclamation gained after victory in a large set-piece battle.

Wellington's Army had taken up a line in front of the Coa, on the upland plateau that marked the frontier. The terrain there was strewn with boulders, ferns and thorns, cultivated only in scattered patches and bounded by deeply carved valleys. There were considerable dangers in fighting with a steep gorge and rushing river to your back, as Craufurd had learned the previous July. In order to allow two possible routes of withdrawal, then, Wellington had extended his divisions across a broad frontage of several miles. A smaller river, the Duas Casas, ran in front of the British position, carving a little valley in which the town of Fuentes d'Onoro sat. To the left of Fuentes, the ground gave its defenders a formidable advantage, a natural rampart

which any attacker would have to assail. The village itself was barricaded and ready for defence. To its right, there were woods around the
river bed and a couple of villages (Pozo Bello and Nava de Haver) on
rising ground behind them which the British also prepared to defend.
The Light Division was being held behind the centre of this position
and slightly to the right as a reserve.

Craufurd appeared near Fuentes early in the morning of 4 May. As he
approached his battalions there was a cry of 'Three cheers for General
Craufurd', and it was answered. 'I found my Division under arms, and
was received with the most hearty appearance of satisfaction on the
countenances of the men and officers, and three cheers from each
Regiment as I passed along its front,' the proud Black Bob told his wife.
Why had these men whom he had so often flogged and insulted
cheered? There was an element of good military form in greeting a
returning commander, no doubt. But the rank and file had tasted life
under General Erskine and it had not been good. They blamed Ass-skin
for their hunger on the various occasions when they had gone without
food or money. They remembered that under similar circumstances in
1809, at least Craufurd had relaxed his own strict rules in allowing
them to kill livestock. More important than that, though, they had the
sense that Craufurd attended keenly to his duty, keeping an ever-vigilant
eye on his outposts, often being near the action, whereas Erskine had
either been present and useless, or lost, as he was in the fog at Sabugal.

Despite the shouted acclamations, the underlying attitude of many
did not change. Among the company officers in particular, Craufurd
was still detested. This did not affect either the brigadier's desire to
grind down those who resisted his orders, or his way of doing things.
So the likes of the 95th's Leach were set to resume their battle of wills
with him soon enough.

On 5 May, Marshal Masséna launched a general attack against
Wellington's long line. Early in the morning, French skirmishers
appeared in the woods to the (British) right of Fuentes, where Right
Wing of the 95th was manning a line of pickets. The riflemen began
their usual work, taking aim from behind trees, firing and reloading.
Their enemy tried to press forward, losing a man here and there, but
the attack was not pushed with real vigour. The riflemen soon discovered why, as a blaring of bugles and a shouting of orders drew them
back towards their supports.

Unseen by them, Masséna had launched his attack by ordering his cavalry to make its way, concealed, through the woods in front of Pozo Bello and Nava de Haver. They succeeded in their aim, mounting up as they emerged from the treeline and surprising the stretched British regiments in that area. Some 3,500 French cavalry drove about a quarter of that number of British horsemen before them and began falling on the infantry.

Faced with this crisis, Wellington sent the Light Division about a mile towards his right flank, supporting his beleaguered division by drawing the enemy off them. He soon made the decision to withdraw his men from Nava de Haver and Pozo Bello, where they had been covering his southern withdrawal route out of the highlands. The British commander was shortening or redeploying his line, at the same time refusing a flank – making it into an 'L' or elbow shape with the village of Fuentes at the bend and with his right drawn back on the higher ground behind.

Early that morning, there were thousands of French horsemen careering about the open scrub as the Light Division formed up. The French dragoons and *chasseurs* were flushed with triumph, but they were also unsupported for the moment by their own infantry. When they charged the redcoats, they were met with volleys of musketry. At moments of extreme danger the British battalions were forming square, presenting a wall of bayonets that horses were too afraid to charge. The 43rd and 52nd moved into this maelstrom and anchored themselves on the plain, giving the threatened regiments a chance to withdraw past them, towards Wellington's main defensive position.

A good cavalry commander – of which the French had plenty – knew he could pretty much make a meal of skirmishers, scattering them into clumps and riding them down at his leisure. In order to avoid this fate with thousands of enemy horses around them, Right Wing of the 95th needed to demonstrate skills of drill and movement that might not shame the Guards, for a few men executing their turn too late or falling behind would soon create an opening for the French cavaliers. As the riflemen emerged from the woods they assembled in column of companies. Moving forward, onto the open plain, they 'formed column at quarter distance, ready to form square at any moment if charged by cavalry'. This 'quarter column' meant having about fifteen feet between the heels of one company and the toes of the one that followed it, transforming them into a mass, easily able to stop and face outwards, presenting a wall of bayonets if charged.

As it happened, Right Wing did not have to form square as it crossed the open ground. It was not moving out to the right like the red-coated Light Division regiments, but making its way to the main British defensive line, where the 1st Division had been formed up to create Wellington's new left flank. The 95th marched close to the British artillery that garnished that ridge. The guns must have deterred the French horsemen, but the Rifles also showed great steadiness and purpose when the enemy's green-clad dragoons did come cantering around them. 'While we were retiring with the order and precision of a common field day, they kept dancing around us, and every instant threatening a charge without daring to execute it,' one officer recalled.

Reaching the main line, the Green Jackets filed between the Guards who formed the mainstay of the 1st Division and lined up behind them. At one point, a couple of riflemen calmly walked forward, past their officers, to try to pick a good concealed sniping position where they might hit one of the officers leading the French forward. When one British commander asked where the riflemen were going, an NCO replied that it was 'for amusement'. One of these riflemen, named Flynn, was a good specimen of the hard-fighting Irish who inspired endless comment among the 95th's officers. Flynn was a good shot and seemed pretty much indifferent whether he was killing a man or something for the pot. At Sabugal, he had been leading a running Frenchman with his rifle and suddenly switched his aim to something scampering in the grass. When one of the subalterns asked him what he was doing, Flynn replied: 'Ah your Honour, we can kill a Frenchman any day but it's not always we can bag a hare for your Honour's supper.'

An hour or two passed and French cannon, having moved up, began to play on the 1st Division, as their infantry tried to turn the British position. The French knew that if they could get around the extreme right of the new British line, they would be able to cut Wellington's regiments off from their only remaining withdrawal route, via the same bridge over the Coa that they had attacked in July 1810. The problem for the French commanders was that they would have to press their attack through a rocky gully, where the Turon, a little stream running parallel with the Coa, ran. Any attack through the Turon would have to be made using skirmishing tactics.

Seeing the danger, Wellington ordered British light infantry to contest the gully. Five companies of the 95th were sent out under Major Peter O'Hare and a couple of light companies of the Guards under

Lieutenant Colonel Hill. They marched about half a mile until they were by the Turon stream, in a boulder-strewn valley, taking up positions in some clumps of trees. But while the Rifles that day had shown a steadiness in close-order marching that would not have disgraced the Guards, the results would be very different when the Guards were required to show their skill as light troops alongside the 95th.

With a chain of French light troops coming towards them, an exchange of fire was soon under way. When the British 1st Dragoons cantered up on the riflemen's left, ready to charge some French horse, there was one of those curious outbreaks of civilised consensus that was peculiar to the Anglo-French Peninsular fight: 'This was the first charge of cavalry most of us had seen and we were all much interested in it. The French skirmishers extended against us seemed to feel the same, and by general consent both parties suspended fire while the affair of the dragoons was going on.'

The crackle of rifles and musketoons then resumed, with both sides standing their ground, using cover while they reloaded. O'Hare's men – something under three hundred of them – were soon given an order to withdraw, since it was becoming apparent that the French frontal attack on the 1st Division would not be pressed home and that the enemy light troops in the Turon had effectively been checked. The Rifles began falling back from tree to tree, firing and loading, front-rank man eyeing his rear-rank man, a rhythmic dance in which every Green Jacket knew his place.

Breaking off the engagement in skirmish order was a difficult undertaking when there were so many French cavalry loitering about. To compound the danger, folds of the ground or trees might conceal the approach of horse until there was no time to react. One officer of the 95th turned around to see that 'a company of the Guards, who did not get out of the wood at the time we retired (from mistake I suppose) were sharply attacked.'

Some squadrons of the *13ème Chasseurs à Cheval*, French light cavalry, came cantering into view, and seeing the Guards were running about in all directions, set spurs to their horses, trumpeters sounding the charge. Lieutenant Colonel Hill's men were unable to form square. Many tried running for it, but the horsemen were soon among them, bringing their sabres down onto the heads and arms of the desperate infantry. The Guards tried to rally into 'hives', small defensive clumps in which the men faced outwards with their bayonets, but it was too late for many. Seventy were killed or wounded, Hill and nineteen others captured and led back to the French lines. Meanwhile, the companies of the 95th engaged that day suffered no fatalities and fewer than a dozen wounded between them.

If the Rifles had been able to skirmish with great success as well as little loss, the last great drama of 5 May was to be a much more sanguinary affair. Since early that morning, the 71st and 79th had been under attack from thousands of Frenchmen in the village of Fuentes d'Onoro itself. The 71st was a Scottish regiment that had been retrained one year before in light-infantry duties; the 79th were Highlanders, the Cameronians, still proudly kilted.

By early afternoon, when the action on the Light Division's flank was petering out, the French were throwing yet another wave of infantry into the village, its defenders having fought doggedly for six or seven hours. 'The town presented a shocking sight,' one observer wrote, 'our Highlanders lay dead in heaps . . . the French grenadiers lay in piles of ten and twenty together.'

The Scots, short of ammunition, were driven from house to house until a few score of the 79th were holding out in a churchyard near the British end of the town, supported by the 71st in nearby houses. Wellington could not afford to lose this critical point, at the elbow of his two defensive lines, and he ordered a counter-attack, sending a brigade of Picton's 3rd Division into action.

They charged into the narrow streets and the French troops, momentarily caught with walls or piles of bodies to their backs, fought desperately with the bayonet. The remnants of the 79th, emerging from their churchyard, set about them with the passion of men bent on revenge, and when their colonel was hit and fell, this anger turned into an unstoppable blood lust. 'Such was the fury of the 79th', wrote a member of Wellington's staff who later went to investigate, 'that they literally destroyed every man they could catch.' In this mayhem, no quarter was given: cornered Frenchmen pleading for their lives were swiftly bayoneted by the Highlanders.

By late afternoon, with the guns falling silent in the village too, some companies of the 95th were sent down to pick their way through the narrow lanes choked with corpses, and post themselves as lookouts on the far side of Fuentes. A few French officers, coming forward with a flag of truce to evacuate the wounded, struck up conversation with the riflemen. Some of the officers recognised one another, for their old foe

General Ferey had been one of those leading his regiments in the desperate fight of that afternoon. Flasks of brandy were passed around and they reflected on that day's terrible cost; how many of their friends and comrades had drunk deep of the 'fountain of honour' at Fuentes d'Onoro. The British had suffered 1,452 casualties and the French 2,192 during the day's slaughter.

Among the Rifle officers gazing at the fallen Camerons and talking to witnesses of the fight, there were some theories about why they had suffered so heavily: 256 casualties. Of course the close-quarters battle had been a desperate affair, but the 71st engaged alongside the Camerons throughout had suffered half the casualties. The 79th had been serving under Wellington for less than one year and still fought by the book: the old book. Most of the Peninsular veteran regiments – as well as the 71st – had adopted the movement and firing tactics of the Light Brigade – 'Sir John Moore's System', so called. But the 79th had been ill equipped for the village fight: instead of dissolving their companies into skirmishers fighting from every window, they had, apparently, tried to keep their men formed up in small groups, firing volleys in sections according to the old drill.

The riflemen posted as pickets found themselves negotiating their way through the dead and dying. The 95th were not indifferent to their suffering, but having marched or doubled many miles that day and fought their own battle, they were dog tired. One of the subalterns, the Scottish lieutenant John Kincaid, chanced upon a Highlander: 'a ball had passed through the back part of the head, from which the brain was oozing, and his only sign of life was a compulsive hiccough every two or three seconds.' Kincaid asked a medic to examine his countryman, and the doctor affirmed the case was hopeless. The lieutenant then 'got a mattress from the nearest house, placed the poor fellow on it, and made use of one corner as a pillow for myself, on which, after the fatigues of the day . . . I slept most soundly. The Highlander died in the course of the night.'

Kincaid's businesslike attitude to passing the night next to this dying man reflected how used the 95th had become to being surrounded by death. It was the currency of much of their daily conversation, be they rankers or officers. Among the latter the topic of sudden death was so common that endless euphemisms were coined to provide a little conversational variety: 'biting the dust', 'entered in today's *Gazette*', 'acquainted with the Grand Secret', 'going across the Styx'.

Those who were unable to deal with the odds in the 95th sought a post elsewhere if they were an officer, or skulked in the hospitals if they belonged to the rank and file. For the most part, though, the veterans who had sailed to Portugal two years earlier embraced their destiny, resigning themselves with a grim fatalism. Reviewing the results of his two months on the march, George Simmons wrote home to Yorkshire just after Fuentes d'Onoro:

Since our advance from Santarem on 6 March, seven of our officers have laid down their lives, and a great number have been wounded. I soon expect to have my lieutenancy. If I live, I shall get a company sooner in this regiment than any other. In six months we see as much service as half the army can boast of in ten years.

The adventurers among the 95th's officers constantly related the risks they ran to their chances of advancement. A little later that summer, doubtless after some maudlin reflection on the events of that year, Simmons told his father, 'It of course makes one gloomy to see so many fine fellows fall round one, but one day or other we must all go. The difference is very immaterial in the long run whether a bullet or the hand of time does your business. This is my way of moralising when I go into a fight.'

Simmons's bargain with danger in the 95th was not quite as he portrayed it to his parents; for while he kept his end of it, the Army was unable to advance him at the speed he expected. George's brother Maud, serving with the 34th Foot, was promoted to lieutenant on 13 March 1811, one year and eleven months after he had joined. Two years on from joining the 95th, George was still a second lieutenant.

Some riflemen had realised that their risks in any single battle were relatively small, skirmishing among the rocks and trees, when compared to those of a line battalion sent shoulder to shoulder into a hail of metal in some hell like Fuentes d'Onoro. The 79th had nine officers wounded in a day there. When a southern detachment of the British Army fought at Albuera later that May, some regiments were completely crushed: the 57th suffering 428 casualties, including two-thirds of its officers killed or wounded in a few hours. Maud Simmons's 34th were at Albuera too, suffering 128 casualties, including three officers killed.

For the average line regiment, though, the odds of being sent into the burning heart of some terrible battle like this were very low. Some served years in the Peninsula without being heavily engaged with the enemy. Since marching towards one's enemy required a moral strength and a resignation to destiny, the Army at large became all the more aware that men in the Light Division were unusual, in that they had to summon up these qualities repeatedly. And within this division, the 95th were called upon most often. Not long after Fuentes d'Onoro, one officer of the 43rd wrote home that his division's 'conduct is spoken of by all the Army in the highest terms, and to be in the Light Division is sufficient to stamp a man as a good soldier'.

The reputation gained by Craufurd's division was not the result of effusive reports in the newspapers – excepting the language used by Wellington himself to describe the battles in his dispatches – but something rather more subtle. Letters home from men like Simmons were read by brothers sitting bored by the fireside and related to cousins or friends. The knowledge of the 95th's deeds and the atmosphere within the regiment rippled outwards by correspondence and word of mouth, through Army families into wider society.

George's brother Maud expressed interest in transferring from the 34th into the 95th. George tried to dissuade him, writing to their parents, 'He is very comfortable in his present [corps], and not half so liable to be exposed to hardships. I have advised him to continue in his regiment.' Maud already knew enough from his Army service to accept the advice. But among the ingénues in Britain or Ireland who thirsted for adventure, attempts to dissuade them by frank accounts of the dangers or of the months spent sleeping in the open only increased their desire to wear the green jacket. George and Maud's teenage sibling Joseph, back home in Yorkshire for the moment, would prove just such a case.

Many young gentlemen set fathers, uncles or military friends of the family investigating whether they might join. At Headquarters, they were sensitive enough to the dangers of this service to try to dissuade one aristocrat from seeking a commission in a Light Division regiment; a staff officer wrote that 'Lord Wellington conceives there he might be treated to more shots than his friends would wish.' Instead, the general recommended that the young peer in question might consider the Fusiliers or Guards. Of course, many of the more humble applicants did not have the benefit of this private advice, nor were there great fortunes at stake if they bit the dust.

Now that the Light Division had won the admiration of the

Peninsular Army and its commander, many of the officers already serving there, having no private funds or connections to fall back upon, became all the more determined to reap some reward for their service and to see off others whom they regarded as having inferior claims to advancement. This, as we shall see, made it increasingly difficult for newly arrived officers to fit in with the old veterans.

It also produced determination in men like Sidney Beckwith to see their best people receive just rewards. For Peter O'Hare, given a brevet in April, Wellington's Fuentes dispatch contained more glorious news. His deeds in fighting off the French in the Turon valley drew a mention from his commander. That, in the formal system observed by Horse Guards, was an endorsement for promotion to the next suitable vacancy. Having gained an acting major's rank in April, O'Hare got Wellington's backing for a substantive post in May. This was a considerable coup, for an officer could soldier on for years with a brevet promotion without any actual change in his situation apart from the pay.

As for Simmons, Beckwith was determined to do something for him too. The commanding officer of the 1st Battalion, 95th, had a duty to make up a quarterly list of officers suitable for promotion, noting as well the number of vacancies open to them. This was relayed to Wellington's military secretary, who in turn would usually gain the general's endorsement on the nod, and the papers made their way to London. Writing several weeks after Fuentes, Beckwith departed from the usual formality of these reports in order to plead the case of Simmons: 'The last named officer, I beg leave in a particular manner to recommend to Lord Wellington's notice. He has been constantly with his company, has been very severely wounded, and his zeal and gallantry have been conspicuous on all occasions.' This was sufficient to win him promotion to lieutenant, at last, in July 1811.

The hot months of June and July were therefore a time of some satisfaction for the officers and men of the 95th. There were marches and the ennui of endless pickets under Craufurd's eagle eye, to be sure. But supplies remained regular, the regiment was operating in familiar territory and many of its members had seen that they could benefit from its reputation as the hardest fighting corps of the Peninsular Army. Nevertheless, those who had spent two years fighting for survival and promotion would not make the easiest bedfellows, as several young men who sought to share in the 95th's glory were about to discover.

TWELVE

The Gentleman Volunteer

June–September 1811

A few weeks after Fuentes d'Onoro, Thomas Sarsfield appeared at the quarters of the 95th. He was an Irishman in his late twenties who had already seen something of the world and encountered various disappointments. Sarsfield was thickset, big across the shoulders, and not particularly tall – all qualities that gave him a rather ungentlemanly appearance.

The spring campaign's losses had caused the 95th to look for more men. Whereas the rank and file could only come out as drafts or in whole additional companies posted from the 2nd and 3rd Battalions, there were few obstacles in the way of a determined young gentleman who travelled out on the Lisbon packet, presenting himself in Portugal. The 95th had actually sought such applications, one officer writing home that May: 'I hope to see a great number of volunteers come out soon . . . I hope many will fancy a green jacket, as our ranks are very thin, having lost a number of brave soldiers.'

Sarsfield was one of several young hopefuls who answered the Rifles' call in the summer of 1811. Before taking the decision to travel to Iberia, another of those volunteers, Thomas Mitchell, considered the simplest expedient and the cheapest, which was to write to the Commander in Chief at Horse Guards in London and ask for a commission. He had drafted the following appeal:

Your memorialist, a native of Scotland, aged 19, is a son of respectable parentage, now dead, and has received a liberal and classical education, qualifying him to fulfill the duties of a Gentleman and a Soldier. That your memorialist desires to enter into the service of his Country in the Army, but has not the immediate means of purchasing a commission nor other expectation of success than through the well known liberality of Your Excellency.

Any person who sent such a letter, bereft of interest, was entering a lottery in which his own life could be sold very cheap. For the recipients of the Commander in Chief's patronage could end up in any regiment, but would most likely be posted to one where the officers were all selling out or dead, due to a posting in some disease-ridden Caribbean graveyard. Mitchell wisely decided not to send the letter. Instead he made his way out to Portugal so that he – not the Commander in Chief – might choose his regiment. Like Sarsfield, Mitchell had heard about the daring 95th and was keen to join it. The only disadvantage to making one's way out like this lay in the lowly status that such recruits were granted, that of 'gentleman volunteer'.

This, then, was what the Scot and the Irishman became, early in the summer of 1811. One officer of the 95th summed up their situation pithily:

A volunteer – be it known to all who know it not – is generally a young man with some pretensions to gentility – and while, with some, those pretensions are so admirably disguised as to be scarcely visible to the naked eye, in others they are conspicuous; but, in either case, they are persons who, being without the necessary influence to obtain a commission at home, get a letter of introduction to the commander of forces in the field.

Mitchell had the very good fortune to discover a distant family connection in the form of Sir Archibald Campbell, an officer commanding a Portuguese brigade in Wellington's Army. Campbell wrote the necessary letter of introduction, which got him admitted to the general's presence, where a short interview usually took place before the young man was dispatched to his regiment. Occasionally, when the candidate failed to impress, he would be told there was no vacancy and packed off home.

John FitzMaurice was yet another of the same species. He had come out a few months before his countryman, Sarsfield, having obtained the necessary letter of introduction from a judge of the Irish circuit. In this way the web of low-level patronage was extended both by the writer of the letter, who earned the gratitude of the young man's family, and by Wellington himself, to whom the author became indebted. In the case of FitzMaurice, his appearance at Headquarters resulted in an invitation to Wellington's dining table.

'Well, what regiment would you like to be attached to?' asked the general.

'The Green Jackets,' was FitzMaurice's reply.

'Why, the uniform isn't very smart!'

FitzMaurice would not be deterred. 'I believe, my Lord, they see a good deal of the enemy.'

Wellington looked across and answered, 'By God they do, and you shall join them.'

Whereas FitzMaurice's induction into the 95th went smoothly, Sarsfield's, alas, would turn into a disaster. Upon their arrival in the regiment, volunteers entered a curious world in which they were neither fish nor fowl. 'While they are treated as gentlemen out of the field, they receive the pay, and do the duty of private soldiers in it,' one officer explained. So FitzMaurice and Sarsfield would have to take their place in the skirmish line in battle, or on sentry when in camp, but would have to retain the manners necessary to get along in the officers' company mess to which they had been attached.

Although FitzMaurice was bereft of good Army connections and therefore ended up as a volunteer, he was from a family of gentry and thus benefited from a sound education and the occasional remittance of cash from home. This made him a convivial enough member of the 3rd Company mess which he joined. More importantly, FitzMaurice had the very good fortune to arrive at the 95th just before its serial fights of that March. The eyes of officers were always upon a volunteer in action, for no question was more important than whether he had pluck or would sneak off at the first whiff of powder. During a skirmish at Freixadas, near the end of March, FitzMaurice had been in such a frenzy of firing that he broke his ramrod while reloading and gashed his hand on it. He continued to fight on, for the wound was a superficial one, but in the process his blood was liberally spread about. Lieutenant Colonel Beckwith, coming away from the engagement, was heard to say, 'That young devil FitzMaurice is covered with blood from head to foot but is fighting like blazes.' The volunteer wisely kept the lightness of his wound to himself and was commissioned shortly afterwards as a second lieutenant. Thomas Mitchell was also fortunate enough to arrive in time for some of that spring's combats.

By the time Sarsfield presented himself, FitzMaurice was already the veteran of half a dozen engagements and an established member of the regiment. It was Sarsfield's bad luck that, following Fuentes d'Onoro, the regiment was taxed by some very long stages (down to Badajoz and back, following an aborted siege of the place), which meant its old hands were vexed by the petty routines of marching, the ill health of the Guadiana plain and the constant presence of Craufurd, but had gone months without a good fight in which to let off steam. Under these conditions, a certain type of 95th man was bound to make mischief.

It became the norm for the veterans to test out the newcomers with some nonsense. When John Kincaid had appeared in the battalion, he had been sent off to catch a pack mule that one of his brother officers swore had broken loose. After careering about the fields for some time in pursuit of the animal, Kincaid brought it back, only to discover that it belonged to someone else entirely, who then reported it as a theft. The new man's reaction to this prank could ensure either his acceptance or a repetition of the teasing.

'Our first and most uncharitable aim was to discover the weak points of every fresh arrival, and to attack him through them,' Kincaid wrote later. 'If he had redeeming qualities, he, of course, came out scathless, but, if not, he was dealt with unmercifully. Poor Tommy [Sarsfield] had none such – he was weak on all sides, and therefore went to the wall.' Kincaid was a leading figure in these proceedings, but others, including Jonathan Leach, when bored, also grew enthusiastic for this form of sport.

Sarsfield, like George Simmons, had a brother in the 34th, but unlike Maud Simmons, Tommy Sarsfield's brother had been killed at Albuera. This might well have ensured a sympathetic reception in the 95th, particularly when added to the fact that Sarsfield had served some time at sea.

The riflemen discovered, though, that any report of the enemy was likely to get this new volunteer overexcited, running about and bellowing the alarm in naval terminology. Since they were actually several miles from their foe, this fun was too good to miss.

Kincaid devised an elaborate charade to show Sarsfield up while amusing one and all. His confederate in all this was William Brotherwood, the Leicestershire soldier in Leach's company known for his wicked sense of humour. Brotherwood was by this time an acting corporal. Sarsfield would be taken out from Atalaya, the Spanish village where they were bivouacked, to a small hill nearby, where pickets were posted to keep a lookout over the rolling groves of oak that cover this part of the country. Brotherwood's job in this, with several riflemen in tow, was to act the part of the French. The corporal and his

Drawn, etched & coloured by J Jones.
London Published as the Act directs Feb 1 1806 by Jn Thos Smith No 36 Newman Street, Oxford Street.

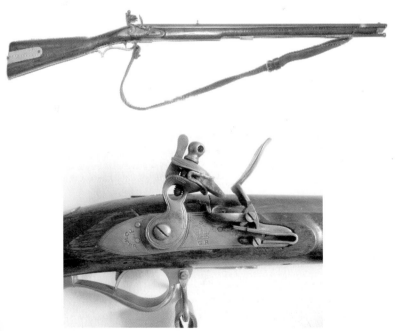

Top: an early illustration of the different firing positions used by riflemen. The need to aim their weapons meant it was much harder for the 95th to stand shoulder to shoulder in the firing line, like normal infantry. *Centre and below*: the Baker rifle was critical to the regiment's success: it combined accuracy with ease of use and robustness in the field.

2 An illustration from Ezekiel Baker's *33 Years Practice and Observation with Rifle Guns* showing how the inventor was just as interested in firing techniques as he was in the design of the rifle itself. Not only is the correct alignment of fore and back sights shown, but the rifleman has also tensed the weapon's sling around his elbow to give a steadier shot.

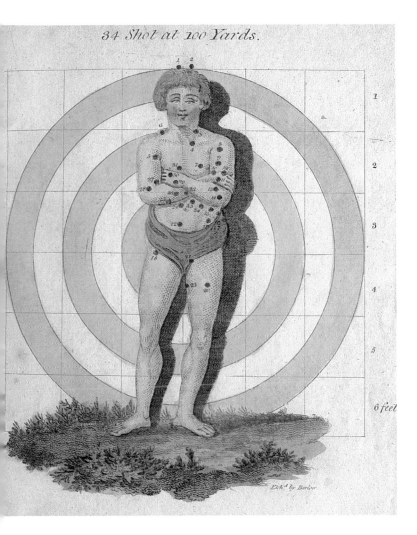

This dramatic depiction shows one of the targets used in the Board of Ordnance trials that selected the Baker rifle.

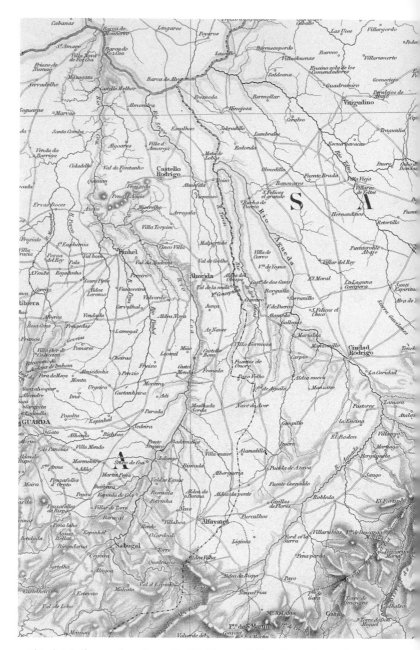

4 This detail of a map from James Wyld's *Maps and Plans* shows the northern Portuguese–Spanish frontier, scene of the Light Division's celebrated exploits from 1809 to 1812. Although Wyld took the credit for publication, most of his maps were surveyed and drawn by Thomas Mitchell, an officer of the 95th, who joined the regiment early in

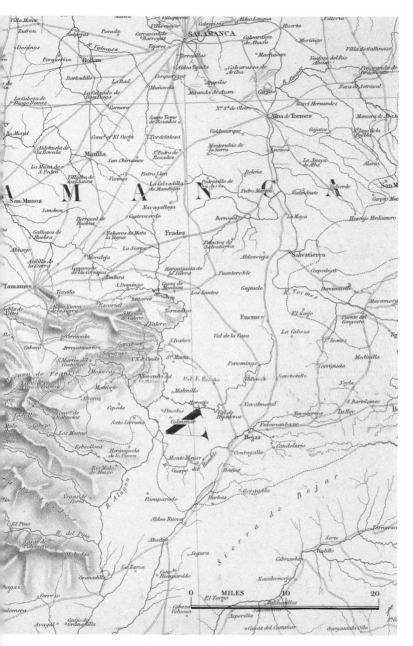

1811 as a 'gentleman volunteer'. The border runs down the centre of the left hand page;
parallel with it are the Coa and Agueda rivers, just across it the walled city of Ciudad
Rodrigo, and near the top of the right hand page is the city of Salamanca.

5 *Top left*: Sidney Beckwith the 1st Battalion's Commanding Officer during the campaign of 1809–11 whose inspired leadership did so much to establish the regiment's reputation. *Top right*: Andrew Barnard initially led the 3rd Battalion of Rifles in Spain, later commanding the 1st, where the self confidence born of family money and an Anglo-Irish pedigree won him Wellington's respect. *Bottom right*: Robert Craufurd pictured in the uniform of the 5th Battalion, 60th Foot, some years before 1809 when he became the 1st/95th's brigadier. *Bottom left*: Alexander Cameron, painted after the Napoleonic wars and showing signs of the sixteen wounds that effectively invalided him out of the service; he commanded the 1st/95th between Beckwith and Barnard.

Top left: Ned Costello painted after leaving the 95th and his service in the Spanish
rlist (civil) War. *Right*: Jonathan Leach, commander of the 2nd Company for almost all
the Peninsular Wars, who personified the 'wild sportsman' officers of the 95th. *Bottom
t*: Harry Smith an instensely ambitious 95th officer who rose to become a successful
ctorian general.

Plan

of the affair at

ALMEIDA,
26ᵗʰ July 1810.

Royal Horse Artillery
Hussars & Lᵗ Dragoons
French

¼ mile
Scale of five inches to an English mile.

AA. First Position.
BB. Second dᵗ covering the passage of the bridge.
CC. Defence of the bridge.

ALMEIDA

From the original drawing by Lᵗ Colonel Bell.

Engraved on Stone by Fr. Kräugert Lond.

7 The Combat of the Coa. French forces moved down from the top (east) of this engraving to the bottom – the legend below the scale indicates that Craufurd's troops have been drawn on in three stages as the battle developed.

men took their fun very seriously, firing their rifles towards Sarsfield and whoever was there with him, so that the Irishman panicked, running back to Atalaya, hallooing and generally sounding the alarm.

On one occasion, Brotherwood picked up Sarsfield's hat, which had fallen off during his escape, made a hole in it with his penknife and presented it to him on his return to the bivouac. Sarsfield seized hold of the trophy and rewarded Brotherwood with a silver dollar. That evening, the old soldier and his messmates were able to laugh at the volunteer's stupidity while drinking away the proceeds.

There was no let-up for Sarsfield when messing with his fellow officers in the evening. One recorded that he had 'the usual sinister cast of the eye worn by common Irish country countenances'. Sarsfield's naval reminiscences, which he presumably calculated might have bought him some credit in the eyes of these grizzled veterans, simply excited their contempt.

This torture could not go on indefinitely without even Sarsfield realising that he was being made a fool of. 'His original good natured simplicity gave way to experience,' wrote one rifleman, 'and he gently informed his tormentors that he kept a clean brace of pistols about him, at any time at their service.' Since neither Kincaid nor the others wished to fight a duel, the bullying at last ended, and Sarsfield, due to the shortage of officers, prevailed, gaining his commission in the regiment. Although the elaborate charades at his expense stopped, the young Irish second lieutenant was never really accepted by officers or men – the old lags like Brotherwood and Kincaid agreeing that he was the type of excitable knave who should be banished from the Rifles.

George Simmons drew his own lessons from the affair, for he was concerned at what might happen to his brother Joseph, who was talking freely about coming out to the 34th or 95th, and had also, briefly, run away to sea. Lieutenant Simmons wrote home: 'Some forward young fellows give themselves great airs and get themselves offended, which will never happen if a young man conducts himself as a gentleman and does not give way to chattering and nonsense.' The desire to impress could be the undoing of a man: Simmons instructed his parents that when Joseph did eventually sail out, he should, 'not be showing his agility in climbing about the ship or using sea phrases, as such proceedings would make the officers have a bad opinion of him.' In short, the saga of the 95th's volunteers demonstrated that the only way to proceed was to measure language and behaviour carefully, be alive to teasing, and wait for some opportunity to prove your mettle in battle, for nothing else would gain the veterans' respect.

Passing muster with those who had been fighting for two years was a challenge that would also afflict those already serving in the regiment who had gained rank but never been near gunfire. There were many such officers in the 2nd and 3rd Battalions, some of whom had merrily spent the last two years' campaigning in Shorncliffe, the clifftop camp relinquished by the 1st Battalion on 25 May 1809. 'General Murray who commands the garrison . . . is very fond of shew and parade,' Second Lieutenant James Gairdner wrote to his father, after experiencing numerous field days that summer near the garrison. Gairdner had been born in America and his family had considerable property in Atlanta. It had been intimated to him that he would be sent on service as soon as possible, and he took his preparation seriously, if at times misguidedly, writing home at one point, 'I am learning dancing every day for it would never do for an officer not to be able to dance. I have been learning drawing, in which I think I have greatly improved.' It was not until early 1812 that he made his debut in the field, and the battalion's hardened officers would get the measure of the callow Gairdner.

The regiment's life during the late summer of 1811 consisted of much marching and countermarching along the frontier. Shortly after Fuentès d'Onoro, the French garrison left behind Allied lines in Almeida had broken out at the dead of night, its commander succeeding in getting most of his men through the British lines and back to French ones. This gave one and all another chance to excoriate General Erskine, widely held responsible for the fiasco, one officer commenting bitterly that Erskine was, 'the laughing stock of the whole army, and particularly of the Light Division'.

Craufurd, back in the saddle as the division's commander, was a man who needed activity and the scent of battle if he was to keep the blue devils at bay and stop himself becoming a bully to his subordinates. His promotion to major general, early in June, did nothing to mollify him. During the marches of June, July and August, he reverted to type, punishing his men for any deviation from Standing Orders, issuing more of them to cover various contingencies, and generally keeping an iron grip on his command.

Some of the newcomers were utterly shocked by what they saw. Ensign William Hay joined the 52nd that summer only to witness the following 'act of diabolical tyranny' during one march. The division was moving through a ford, with Craufurd watching from his horse not far away. 'The general, from his position on the bridge, observed two or three of the 95th take some water in their hands to cool their parched mouths,' wrote Hay. 'Instantly the halt was sounded, the brigade ordered to retrace their steps, the whole division formed into hollow square, and these unfortunate men paraded, stripped, and flogged. Such scenes, alas! were of almost daily occurrence, and disgusted me beyond measure.' Hay took the earliest opportunity to transfer to another regiment.

With Craufurd back to his usual form, his many enemies among the regimental officers were soon seething against him. 'Order upon orders of the most damnable nature were issued . . . by General Craufurd, the whole evidently compiled for no other reason than that of annoying the officers of his Division,' wrote Leach in his journal at the end of July, exclaiming, 'Oh! That such a scoundrel should have it in his power to exercise his tyrannical disposition for years with impunity.'

Thus far, Craufurd had been shielded from his enemies at Horse Guards by Wellington. In the late summer and early autumn of 1811, though, their relationship, hitherto professionally correct, began to break down. Matters took a turn for the worse when the French, after weeks of manoeuvre, finally succeeded in catching Picton's division unsupported on the border and attacked it on 25 September at El Bodon.

Wellington immediately sent orders to several nearby divisions to concentrate in support of Picton, as his 3rd Division performed a fighting withdrawal under heavy enemy pressure. Craufurd chose to spend the night where he was, marching towards the main army early the following day. By the time the Light Division appeared, Picton had won laurels for his performance in steering his troops out of a tight situation, the danger having passed.

Seeing Craufurd approaching on horseback, Wellington called out, 'I am glad to see you safe, Craufurd.' Black Bob replied, 'Oh! I was in no danger, I assure you,' which drew the response from Wellington, 'But I *was*, from your conduct.' Craufurd turned and cantered off, but not before saying to one of his aides in a stage whisper, 'He is damned crusty today.'

As the weather chilled and leaves fell, the armies prepared to go into winter quarters once more. Craufurd and Wellington were set to clash again on matters of supply and the troops' sufferings, as they took up cantonments in the barren border highlands. These hardships were to be intense, sufficiently harsh to raise a spectre that had so far barely troubled the Light Division: desertion to the enemy.

THIRTEEN

Deserters

October–December 1811

On 1 October 1811 the Right Wing of the 1st Battalion, 95th, marched into Aldea Velha, a little village just on the Spanish side of the frontier. Their arrival was attended by all of the usual barking of dogs, peering of children and gruff salutations. The men were footsore, having marched hundreds of miles in a few months. Dozens were sick again, the consequence of their recent brief return to the Guadiana and of the many agues that bedevilled those who went months at a time sleeping in the open.

That day was attended with some relief, though. Lord Wellington had decreed that the Army should enter winter quarters. In short, no further fighting was anticipated for the rest of the year. The Light Division, though, would be cast in its usual role as sentinel for the Army as a whole, keeping a wary eye on the French just a few miles away. Aldea Velha was close to the fighting grounds of the previous months, Fuentes d'Onoro and El Bodon. It was familiar territory; the men knew the itinerant wine and tobacco sellers and felt the Spanish villages were cleaner and a little more salubrious than those a few miles across the border in Portugal.

No sooner had they resigned themselves to the end of the campaign than the Commander of Forces began moving them about every day or two. He aimed to ensure that the Light Bobs could screen the frontier, allowing the remainder of the Army, many miles behind them, a comfortable repose.

With each of these changes, the arrangements of the Rifle companies were upset, and the soldiers would find themselves starting over again. The normal form of creating cantonments involved setting the soldiers about the local woods with axes and billhooks to cut down branches.

These were shaped and lashed together to produce rude dwellings, each of which sheltered a handful of men. The huts would be arranged in company lines with latrine trenches dug nearby and a cooking place too. As the burning sun of the late summer gave way to autumn with its perpetual murk, steady rains and, eventually, heavy frosts, efforts were made to get the troops into more permanent accommodation. This was arranged by the Light Division's assistant quartermaster general, who would issue chits billeting troops on local villagers. These poor Spanish or Portuguese were not paid, but if they were canny, they could soon find ways of extracting money for providing food and drink or washing and mending clothes.

Officers were entitled to a slightly higher standard of accommodation, but in the impoverished villages of the uplands, this still might not amount to anything more than a single-storey dwelling, usually full of smoke from the open fire, with a couple of subalterns sharing a small room. The company messes were sadly depleted during the last months of campaigning and early autumn, due to battle casualties and many of the officers succumbing to agues, fevers and fluxes. Some took to their beds in the upland villages, succumbing as much to melancholy and boredom as to the actual symptoms of their complaint. Others retired to Lisbon or even Britain to recover their health. Quite of few of the 95th's companies had come under the charge of a lieutenant, with perhaps one second lieutenant and a volunteer completing the mess.

All of this sickness and leave allowed George Simmons, for example, to command the 5th Company for several months from October, despite being a newly made lieutenant, and to receive an acting captain's pay for his trouble. It also resulted in Major O'Hare often being in acting command of the battalion. Colonel Beckwith had gone home to England, having come down with bouts of Guadiana fever near the end of the preceding campaign.

Neither O'Hare, nor the hardier types like Leach or Kincaid who remained in the mountains, were ready to let the misery of their situation overwhelm them. In each village where they went, they would soon discover the smoky bothy that passed for a *cantina*, and bring it alive each night with songs and dances. 'A Spanish peasant girl has an address about her which I have never met with in the same class of any other country,' wrote one of them, 'and she at once enters into society with an ease and confidence of one who has been accustomed to it all her life.' They would while away their afternoons and evenings drinking the wine of Duero or Rueda, dancing boleros, fandangos and waltzes. Holding their black-eyed Spanish girls close during these assemblies, they parted at the end of the evening with a friendly good-bye. Sometimes they would pay a few local musicians to provide the music; on other occasions Willie Johnston would saw away on his fiddle or the officers would sing lustily into the night.

There were other amusements too – shooting wildfowl or coursing hares on the surrounding uplands, for example. Some of the officers also kept menageries in their quarters. It became quite normal to see colourful characters like Leach or Johnston strolling down the lanes with a pet wolf, badger or some other beast on a lead. Others also began getting plays together, determined to stage some productions a little more ambitious than those of the previous winter.

An important change in the equilibirum of the 95th occurred on 21 August, when half of the 3rd Battalion – four companies comprising its Right Wing, under the command of Lieutenant Colonel Andrew Barnard – joined the Light Division. These men had been fighting in southern Spain with another expeditionary force, and had been blood-ed during the Battle of Barossa early in 1811, drawing widespread praise for their conduct. Barnard, the son of an Anglo-Irish family that was both wealthy and politically well connected, was unusual in that he quickly impressed the 95th despite being a latecomer to the regi-ment. Although Barnard was senior to O'Hare, in command of the 1st Battalion, Army and regimental protocol dictated that he could not immediately take command of it. However, the colonel would eventu-ally emerge as the man with the unusual skills needed to fill the void left by Beckwith.

General Craufurd kept them busy these days with marches, firing practice and manoeuvring. The floggings and harangues went on too. As October passed, Craufurd was becoming increasingly concerned with the supply shortage in his remote station. The Army had estab-lished depots on the coast, and in some inland towns too, and its com-missaries were charged with bringing the food up by wagon or river to places where it could be transferred to the Light Division's own train of mules. The constant shortages of hard money, combined with the difficulties of sending victuals to the end of this long supply chain, lead to considerable crimping by the commissaries and hardship in the 95th.

'We suffered dreadfully through want, and I underwent more privations than at any other place in Spain, except Dough Boy Hill,' wrote Costello, comparing the dying months of 1811 to the miserable autumn of his first campaign. 'We had to make up for the deficiency of bread with roasted or boiled chestnuts . . . we eventually had to make an incursion deep into the mountains, to press the *alcaldes* of the different villages to supply us.' These 'incursions' took the form of a company or two of riflemen presenting themselves to the mayor, or *alcalde*, asking him to hand over a certain quantity of food, issuing him with a receipt, to be redeemed at a later date by the Commissary General, and marching off with their gains. Since the locals had considerable experience of these pieces of paper – finding that they were generally worthless when issued by their own or the French Army – these foraging trips soon turned into ill-tempered affairs in which the peasants tried to conceal as much of their food as possible.

One evening, returning from an inspection of the outposts, General Craufurd rode straight into a scene of near-riot in one village. A Spanish woman was pursuing a corporal and private of the 95th, shouting to all and sundry that they were thieves. Craufurd apprehended the men, discovering that they had been driven by hunger to steal bread. His prejudice against the 95th once more came into play, as he told the riflemen that their regiment 'committed more crimes than the whole of the British Army'. The corporal was broken to the ranks and awarded 150 lashes, the other man 200. They were duly paraded for punishment the next day.

Craufurd told the assembled soldiers, 'You think because you are riflemen, and more exposed to the enemy's fire than other regiments, that you are to rob the inhabitants with impunity, but while I command you, you shall not.' He turned to the broken corporal and ordered him 'Strip, sir!' As he was bound and readied for punishment, the soldier looked across imploringly:

'General Craufurd, I hope you will forgive me.'

'No sir, your crime is too great.'

With a sickening crack, the first lash was laid on. The corporal called out to Craufurd that they had been together in Buenos Aires in 1807: 'I shared my last biscuit with you. You then told me you would never forget my kindness to you. It is now in your power, sir, for you know we have been short of rations for some time.'

The general halted the punishment and then, his voice trembling with emotion, asked, 'Why does a brave soldier like you commit these crimes?' He turned around and left, trying to escape the 95th's gaze before his composure broke down completely.

Craufurd's spirits had sunk very low in his lousy billet. He wrote home to Fanny, 'I am labouring under a fit of the blue devils.' They had discussed plans for her to spend the winter with him in Portugal, but these had been abandoned as impractical, with him telling her at last, 'This . . . disposes a person who is separated from all he loves to uncomfortable feelings and reflections.'

For some of the soldiers enduring hunger, continued hard marches and barbarous punishments, the autumn gloom brought them to a crisis. Private Joseph Almond was one such. He had been in the 95th for more than eleven years, ever since it was founded, and in the Army for more than seventeen. He had campaigned around the world – Almond need not prove his courage to any man – and twice he had been busted back from corporal. As a soldier again, he had to put up with all the petty tribulations, from extra duties to being short-changed on rations. In sum, Almond was worn out. He was reaching his late thirties, and driving his body through the endless marches was becoming harder and harder for him. The veterans often tried to keep themselves going by easing their aches with booze and tobacco. Quite a few of the broken-down older non-commissioned officers had been sent home 'to recruit' when the 9th and 10th Companies had been dissolved a year before. Such avenues were generally closed to the ranker, however.

Almond had taken advantage of the paymaster, using him as a bank to pay for his comforts and running up a small debt of nine shillings in the process. That, though, would be set against pay arrears, so he still had £40 or £50 due to him. If anything happened to Almond, that money would go to his mother back in Chester, for like most of the rankers, he was not married. Really, he had nothing to show for his life: neither wife, children nor any kind of rank. It was clear to him as it was to all of them that a French ball or some fever could put paid to this execrable existence at any moment.

Private Almond did not have the option of retiring on leave to Lisbon or even Britain to recover his health, as many of the officers had done. Headquarters was putting the squeeze on skulkers in the hospitals again, with a new order to send NCOs who had got themselves comfy jobs there, like Esau Jackson, back to their regiments. In any case, Almond was not a coward and could not allow himself to be taunted as such by his messmates – he had taken his part in all the fights. A different idea had entered his mind: desertion.

The Light Division had little experience of desertion until that autumn. Three men had absconded from the 1st/95th within a year of its landing: one found his way back sheepishly to the regiment; another, it was widely believed, died serving the French. A private of the 43rd had tried desertion back in the summer of 1810 when the regiment was on outpost duty on the frontier. He was caught and sentenced to death for his trouble. Another fellow, John Davy of the 52nd, had headed off not long after that, living off the land for almost a year before he was discovered and arrested. Davy was sentenced to death by firing squad, a singular punishment reserved for deserters, since even murderers got the noose. There had been quite a few Germans from the Brunswick Jagers executed after that – such was their propensity for desertion that they were turned out of the Light Division after a few weeks.

It was a risky business, no doubt. But when the British outposts were only a rifle shot from the French ones, it might be attempted rather more safely than before. The Light Division had been positioned close to the French-held fortress of Ciudad Rodrigo, and this very proximity gauranteed that if they headed in the right direction they would find Johnny François quickly enough. The riflemen knew quite well that some soldiers had made it across to the French side and now served Napoleon.

At the Coa bridge, in July 1810, just after the fighting, the Rifles had an unsettling experience. One of the party sent forward by the French to help clear the wounded had looked up and taunted them in the clearest Irish brogue: 'Well, Rifles, you will remember the 24th of July. We came to muster you this morning.' A soldier of the 95th replied, 'We have thinned your ranks pretty well, and if we had been allowed to keep on firing we should have thinned them a little more.' The Irishman told them that he much preferred the French service to the British, which he had deserted some time before, and then helped carry off one of his new comrades. 'If he had stayed until the time had expired, he would doubtless have had a ball from some of our rifles for his pert language,' one of O'Hare's men later remarked.

So all of them knew that desertion was possible and all of them had also heard enough about the French service to know that its officers looked after the men and were forbidden to flog them. The case of Allan Cummings may also have persuaded them that they might just get away with it, even if caught. Cummings, one of several Scottish brothers in the battalion, was a talented musician in the regimental band who had decamped while the Rifles were in the lines of Torres Vedras. He had signed up with the French, impressing them in turn with his bandsman's skills, but eventually quit their ranks too, ending up back in the custody of the 95th and facing the death penalty. Colonel Beckwith was so determined not to lose his talents that he appealed to Headquarters and saved Cummings from the firing squad.

It was evident that the best opportunity for desertion arose when the armies were close to each other. This had been the case when Cummings went and so it was on 28 October 1811 when William MacFarlane of Captain Cameron's Highland Company deserted. Some days passed without him being brought back a prisoner, which set others thinking.

On 17 November, Almond decided to take his chance. He slipped away from the cantonments at Atalaya and struck out through the oak forest towards the French lines. A little more than a fortnight later, another 1st Battalion man, Malcolm McInnes, also of the Highland Company, followed MacFarlane and Almond. He'd been a soldier almost as long as Almond and had been in jail in England for desertion a few years back. The little Scot had been a popular messmate and a good fighter, but he too had had enough. Five days after McInnes, Miles Hodgson sneaked away too. The 1st Battalion entered returns for two deserters in November and three in December 1811. A few others from the 95th's other contingents, the 52nd and the 43rd, went too.

This desertion from what had emerged as the crack regiments of the Peninsular Army was deeply unsettling to both Wellington and Craufurd. In virtually any other army of the epoch, a few low brutes stealing away would have been regarded as entirely unexceptional. But it vexed the British generals who were not at all used to it, and it brought open conflict between Wellington and Craufurd.

Craufurd had been concerned for some time about the clothing, rations and accommodation of his division. In mid-December, he wrote to the Commander of Forces setting out his views, and implied his division would have to be withdrawn from the frontier unless these problems were addressed as a matter of urgency.

Wellington, who had spent years perfecting the supply system of his Army, took these complaints as a personal affront. He had done everything possible to chivvy the Government for ready money; he had established depots, and even sent agents to North Africa to buy mules with which to supply troops in the mountains. Furthermore, many at Headquarters saw the complaints as the result of Black Bob's depressed and volatile mental state. One of his own Light Division staff even described Craufurd's letter to Wellington as 'one of his mad freaks'.

It was a measure of the tension between the men that Wellington used one of Craufurd's few friends, the Adjutant General at Headquarters, to craft a reply on 19 December, expressing scepticism that there was any excuse for the desertions:

The Commander of the Forces is much concerned to learn from your letter of the 17th inst. that any of the troops under your command should have deserted to the enemy, and that you attribute this desertion to the *real* distress the men are suffering from want of clothing, great coats and blankets, and to their being frequently very badly fed.

Wellington informed Craufurd that he would ride over the following morning and inspect the division in person.

Before it was light on 20 December, Wellington set off on horseback from the poor little Portuguese village of Frenada, where he had made his HQ. He rode down across the southern part of the Fuentes d'Onoro battlefield and then many miles on to a plain near Fuente Guinaldo, on the Spanish side of the frontier, where he had told Craufurd to expect him at 11 a.m. Wellington was quite sure that Craufurd was exaggerating the matter and had threatened to send the Light Division to the rear if he discovered any signs of real want among them.

Finding the division assembled in open ground and awaiting his review, Wellington began to ride down the ranks of its regiments, stopping occasionally to question a man or his officer. At this moment, Craufurd appeared, somewhat flustered and also on horseback. Wellington, with a smile on his face, called out to him, 'Craufurd, you are late.' Furious, Craufurd replied, 'No, my Lord; you are before your time. My watch is to be depended on.' Wellington affected ignorance of his bad humour and told him cheerfully, 'I never saw the Light Division look better or more ready for service. March back to your quarters; I shall soon require you in the field.'

Wellington rode back to Frenada, evidently having satisfied himself that Craufurd was guilty of his usual stuff and nonsense. As he went, though, a germ of uncertainty arose in his mind. If the system of supply had not failed the Light Division, then why were men deserting? It was, he readily conceded, a most unusual state of affairs. He felt sure that those who had gone must be habitual recidivists.

The following day, the Adjutant General addressed a further letter to Craufurd on Wellington's behalf. 'The commanding officers of these battalions', he wrote, were to report, 'whether any of these men who deserted had committed any crime, or were in confinement previous to their desertion, and whether they were men of good or bad character.'

The reports on Almond and McInnes would certainly have revealed previous misdemeanours – the usual soldier's stuff of boozing and lost stripes in the first case and a prior desertion in the second. Evidently this was enough to convince Wellington that the matter was closed, and that Craufurd was guilty yet again of a 'mad freak'.

This simply sent Black Bob him into a deeper despondency, for he felt he had forfeited the regard of his great Army patron. Craufurd wrote home, 'I cannot say that Lord Wellington and I are quite so cordial as we used to be. He was nettled at a report which I made of the wants of the Division.'

When Wellington told Craufurd that he would soon need the Light Division, it had been because he was meditating a siege of Ciudad Rodrigo. His base in Portugal would not feel truly secure until all of the key border fortresses were in Allied hands. Those on his side of the frontier – Almeida and Elvas – were in the possession of their Portuguese masters, but on the Spanish side Rodrigo and Badajoz, further south, were still in the grasp of the French. The British general knew that the coming campaign would require him to take both of these places: this was a necessary preliminary to pushing a British Army deep into Spain so that, eventually, the French invaders might be evicted.

Early in January 1812, Wellington's orders for the siege of Ciudad Rodrigo were sent out to the different parts of his Army. The Light and other divisions abandoned their cantonments and marched through thick snow to cross the oak forests of the borderland and head for the fortress. The British plan was very well calculated, for it involved battering the fortress into submission, or storming it, before the French could unite their forces in western Spain and come to the garrison's rescue. Siege operations could be the most difficult in war, for to storm some great wall bristling with cannon and muskets required troops of the most ardent spirit. The British had already tried and failed to take Badajoz in 1811. This time, it was vital that everything went to plan.

Setting off on this new campaign in the middle of frigid winter, Craufurd wrote home to his wife. He was glad for the activity, for he wanted to give up the command of the Light Division, and felt the best time to do it would be after a successful operation. He told her, 'I expect in a few months, very few, to be with you and to have done with this sort of life.' In an attempt to reassure his wife, he told her, 'You need not be alarmed, for [a siege] is the least dangerous of all operations, particularly for those of higher rank.'

FOURTEEN

The Storm of Ciudad Rodrigo

January 1812

Not long after dark, Lieutenant Colonel Colborne led his column forward. They had spent the afternoon of that 8 January hidden from view behind a hill called the Greater Teson. It was a miserable business having to hang around in this piercing wind, shuffling feet in the snow, trying to keep warm, but this band of killers could not go to work until after sunset. The Teson mount shielded them from Ciudad Rodrigo, which it also overlooked, making it the most obvious place from which to batter the walls. There was an obstacle, though, to digging trenches on this ground, and Colborne had been sent to deal with it. The French, having approached by this same angle when they took Rodrigo in 1810, did not intend to lose the city through the same weakness in its defences. They had created the Redoubt of San Francisco, a makeshift fort outside the city's formal defences, near the summit of the ridge that could sweep the Teson with fire. Three pieces of artillery had been placed in the redoubt for this purpose. Colborne had been given the mission of storming San Francisco so that regular approaches might begin.

A night attack was often a risky business, so Colborne tried to prepare it as carefully as he could. Just before dusk, an officer of the 95th had been sent to lie on the crown of the Teson ridge and to remain there as a guide to the stormers, so they did not lose their way. He had also prearranged signals for the assault. Just under four hundred men had been assigned to the task – two companies each from the 43rd, 52nd and 95th. They had marched several hours before resting up, about noon, obscured by the hill from the gaze of the French garrison. It had been bitterly cold during the hours that they waited, the men crouching under their greatcoats, gnawing on a biscuit or smoking pipes. Now that the attack was being launched, they had a further nine hundred yards or so to make their approach.

Corporal Robert Fairfoot had joined the party. His company was not one of those told off for the task, but somehow he had managed to get himself along. Like many of the others, he had grown bored in winter quarters and was anxious for a fight. Captain Crampton and his 8th Company of the 1st/95th were in the lead, his riflemen walking briskly behind him, the breath from their mouths billowing in the cold night air. Coming onto the flat top of the Teson, ahead and slightly to their right they could see Rodrigo silhouetted in the dark, the spire of its cathedral towering over the defences of the city itself. Directly ahead, the San Francisco – a glacis or earthen rampart had been thrown up around the stone-faced gun emplacements and firing points. The cries of the townsfolk, barking of dogs and thumping of feet filled their straining ears.

Closer now – not much more than fifty yards – and Colborne said to Crampton, 'Double-quick!' Word was passed and the men began jogging along. The footfalls became louder, as did the rattling of canteens, rifle slings and pouches. The shout of '*Qui vive?*' came soon enough from one of the French sentries, but in the seconds that it took between the call and some shots ringing out, four of Colborne's companies had thrown themselves up against the glacis. They presented their weapons, and an awesome fire of almost three hundred British firelocks erupted, sweeping the redoubt's roof just twenty or thirty yards away. Fairfoot and the others reloaded, firing repeatedly.

Most of the seventy or eighty men inside kept their heads down, knowing they would soon be taken off by the hail of bullets ripping the night air. On a prearranged signal – a shout of 'England and Saint George!' – two companies carrying ladders, one each from the 43rd and 52nd, rushed forward, placed them up against the redoubt's walls and began climbing. One or two grenades were lobbed over the walls by the terrified defenders, but most fled to the guard house, where they surrendered a little later. A good few French stragglers were bayoneted. The storm had been a complete success.

Craufurd and some other officers were watching from elsewhere on the ridge. Lieutenant Colonel Barnard, standing a little distance away, was so thrilled that he started jumping up and down, cheering. The general, not quite seeing who it was, snapped, 'What's that drunken man doing?' Moments later the first French prisoners were brought back to the Light Division's main position. They had been comprehensively robbed – even of their clothing – and a naked French colonel was presented to Craufurd. 'Yer honour, I'll lend him my greatcoat if ye'll allow me,' said Tom Crawley. Craufurd thanked him: 'You are a very good rifleman, let him have it.' Colborne, a relative newcomer to the 52nd, had made a brilliant debut as commanding officer. The 95th had been infused with some fresh blood too and they were keen to make their mark in the siege operations which would now begin in earnest.

Fairfoot returned to his company, as the digging of siege trenches began in earnest, right on top of the Teson ridge. This drew fire from the garrison's heavy guns and each day now became a slugging match between the two sides' gunners, the working parties of infantry toiling away at night to shore up or advance the trenches. The eventual aim would be to progress them down the forward slope of the Greater Teson and onto the Little Teson, a smaller feature between it and the walls. Here the Royal Artillery would be able to blast away at the town's walls from little more than two hundred yards, hammering them down bit by bit with twenty-four-pound and eighteen-pound shot. Once breached, storming parties would be formed to rush through the openings and take Rodrigo.

All of this lay ahead of the riflemen, though, as they congregated about their tin pots brewing up some hot tea on the morning of 9 January. O'Hare's old company, the 3rd, in which Fairfoot and Costello still served, had been placed under the command of Captain John Uniacke. Like O'Hare, Uniacke was an Irishman, but while O'Hare was famed for ugliness and ripe age, Uniacke enjoyed his men's renown for his handsome looks and athletic prowess. He was no son of the Ascendancy gentry, though – on the contrary, his family circumstances were among the most desperate of any officer in the regiment. A Catholic from Cloyne in County Cork, Uniacke carried the hopes of his entire family on his broad shoulders. His mother had long been a widow, and her survival and that of John's eight siblings depended on his remittances from the Peninsula. He had sailed with the others in May 1809. After a turn with the 3rd Battalion he was promoted to captain back in the 1st – the extra pay allowed him to send home anything up to £100 each year. If Uniacke thirsted for advancement, it was only so that his mother might have food on the table and his brothers and sisters some sort of education.

The contrast between Uniacke and Second Lieutenant James Gairdner was also pronounced. When that young subaltern eventually reached the battalion, on 13 January, he exhibited the whey face, soft hands and general demeanour of a know-nothing. Uniacke had been serving in the Peninsula for two and a half years, but his new second lieutenant – for it was to the 3rd Company that the Johnny Newcome was sent – had joined the 95th in August 1810 and spent the next eighteen months sitting it out in Shorncliffe, polishing up his dancing, drawing and mathematics. Gairdner was wealthy, too, if not fabulously so: his family enjoyed considerable material success in Atlanta, Georgia. They straddled the Atlantic: while James's aunt and her branch remained in England, his father carried on his business in America without difficulty. Georgia was one of the states least enthused by the Revolution of 1775; the family politics were liberal and generally supportive of reconciliation between the brother peoples.

Each night working parties had to dig away in the shallow topsoil of the Teson, completing the first parallel in the days following the capture of the San Francisco redoubt. The defenders used many cannon to fire on these working parties, so the whole business was conducted at night: the clanking of picks and shovels was interrupted by the cracks of the heavy guns and the whump of the heavy mortars, lofting explosive shells into the air over the British excavators. Having established their own batteries on the Teson, Wellington's gunners would fire back by day, trying to aim their shells through the narrow embrasures in the walls used by the enemy for firing. A bull's eye was a shot that smacked the French cannon right on the mouth, hurling it from its carriage or rendering it useless in some other way; less fortunate hits would eliminate some of the gunners serving these pieces.

For the French garrison of about two thousand men, any initial confidence about the outcome of the siege began to falter. Their engineers knew that Rodrigo was not nearly as strong as Almeida, just across the border, or many of the other fortresses in Spain. Its walls were not thick enough and their layout was poorly thought out. At the corner nearest the Teson ridges, the walls curved virtually through a right angle, leaving it vulnerable to assault: this arrangement made it harder for them to concentrate their fire in its defence, but easier for the enemy. A purpose-built place of war laid out during the eighteenth century would be hexagonal or even octagonal, with bastions on each of the points, allowing each stretch of wall to be swept by flanking fire from two such strongpoints. Often a further element of defence was added in front of the *enciente* or main wall, particularly if the bastions were far enough apart for any firing by the defenders to become less effective at the mid-point between them. In such instances, a triangular strongpoint called a ravelin was added in front of the main wall. It stood like a little island in the ditch around the fortress, giving more opportunities to fire at any attacker, creating yet more lethal intersections with the bastions' fields of fire. The walls and strongpoints were all surrounded by a great embankment. Anyone approaching such a place would walk up a grassy slope which fell away vertically in front of them, about fifty or sixty feet before the main wall. This outer defensive skin both protected the base of the fortress's wall from besiegers' artillery batteries, and created a deep ditch or obstacle for any storming parties trying to rush in.

The men defending Ciudad Rodrigo were a mixed bunch – one battalion each of the *34ème Léger* and *113ème Régiment*. Their officers were generally professional, as throughout the French service, but the men were a combination of conscripts from France, Italy and Holland. Their world had shrunk in the preceding months because the approach of the Allied armies, and patrols of an Allied hireling, local guerrilla leader Don Julian Sanchez, meant they could hardly wander beyond the walls without fear of capture. Falling into the hands of the Spanish irregulars could mean a slow, ghastly end. A couple of months before, the French governor of Rodrigo had been carried off by one of Don Julian's parties and presented as a prisoner at Wellington's dinner table. This close blockade meant it was difficult to get supplies in and people out. So it was that Joseph Almond and the other British deserters had ended up inside the fortress.

Almond, Mills and Hodgson had all been inducted into the French Army. It would evidently have made sense to move them on to some place further away from their former comrades, for everyone could imagine what might happen to them if they were captured – but it had not been possible. In all likelihood their commander was reluctant to let any man go once he had clapped hands on him, such were the vagaries of getting new drafts from France. Almond had traded his old life in the 95th for one in the French Army: reveille became the *diane*; grog gave way to brandy; and the Baker rifle once in his hands was replaced by the *fusil de dragon*.

Outside, the Light Division took its turn with the working parties again on 12 and 13 January, returning to camp to lie up after their dangerous task. Wellington and his chief engineer resolved to advance a communication trench down the forward slope of the Greater Teson and establish a second parallel, or attack trench, on the Little Teson, much closer to the walls.

In his race to take the town before the enemy could concentrate against him, Wellington needed to batter breaches in the walls closest to the Teson ridges as quickly as possible. This had started from the higher feature, although it was obvious that the British guns would do much greater damage if they battered from just 200 or 250 yards. There were some difficulties too: as the breaching progressed, with great slabs of wall being undermined by shot and crumbling away, the French engineers started to send out parties each night to repair the damage a little.

It was decided to order some riflemen down one night to see if they could answer fire with fire, picking off the French gunners with carefully aimed shots and stopping the engineers repairing the breaches. It would be a dangerous task, for the shooters would be lying on the rampart that partly protected the wall itself from fire and created a great ditch twenty or so feet deep between the two verticals, which any stormers would have to negotiate before trying to enter the gaps made in the walls. Lying here would be dangerous work, for the riflemen would be only thirty or forty feet away from the French, who would be bound to hurl all manner of fire against them.

The task of furnishing this sniping party fell to Captain Uniacke, and he decided to expose his new second lieutenant to a whiff of powder. Gairdner, another officer and thirty men were sent down to their position at about 8 p.m. They lay on the glacis or sloping rampart surrounding the fort on a freezing January night, waiting for French spotters or engineers to show themselves, each firing of rifles being answered with musketry, grapeshot and hand grenades. At all times the riflemen had to keep their wits about them, for the defenders might sally out and try to catch them with the bayonet.

After several hours of this duty, with the edge of the sky showing its first glimmer of dawn off behind Rodrigo, over the Sierra de Gata, the riflemen scurried away, defying the French to give them a few parting shots as they worked their stiff legs for the trot back over the Teson to safety.

Gairdner's baptism of fire had been a success, and a shrewd experiment on Uniacke's part. The young subaltern wrote proudly to his father: 'This was the first time I ever was in action, it was a responsible situation and a dangerous one, however we got off very well for I had only three of my picquet wounded.' The injuries attested to the seriousness of the business, and the veterans of 3rd Company returned that dawn with the knowledge that their new officer could be relied upon in action. It would seem that he passed a second trial when Captain Jonathan Leach tested the new boy's gullibility by telling him – confidentially, of course – that the city was going to be stormed by troops of the Royal Wagon Train supported by the *mounted* 14th Light Dragoons. This outrageously silly report did not travel far: Gairdner thus established himself as brave and no dupe, in contrast to Sarsfield.

The British batteries fired with great effect from the new positions on 18 and 19 January, and this, combined with the continuous barrage over several days from the Greater Teson behind, was sufficient to produce two breaches in the wall that were considered practicable for an assault, on the evening of 19 January.

Wellington wanted to ensure success by using picked troops to mount the attacks. General Picton's 3rd Division would be given the task of storming the main breach and Craufurd's men the lesser one, both of the targets being on the north-eastern side of the defences, about two hundred yards apart.

Everything was prepared for that night's desperate service. When expecting a storm, the defenders would pile loaded muskets and bombs so that one man might fire with the effect of many in those crucial moments as the enemy came into view. The batteries would then open up too, spewing grapeshot into the ditch before the walls, as the attackers tried to put their ladders up to the breaches and get through. There would be some other surprises too, for the defenders often set mines in the places where they thought stormers might gather. The defenders in such cases had many advantages, for after days of breaching fire, there could be no mystery about where the main attack would come. The French had discovered during their many sieges in Spain that such attacks were often a desperate business. It was a matter of nerve, and whose broke first. The attackers had to keep going somehow, with death all around, and scale ladders while they were fired at, bayoneted and bludgeoned. If the assault looked as if it might succeed, however, the defenders' spirit often faltered, for they knew that the chances of being taken prisoner by the maddened survivors of a storming party were slim.

Craufurd and Picton did not intend to throw their divisions forwards in the usual order of companies and battalions or the customary lines or columns. Instead, Major General John Vandeleur, recently appointed as a brigade commander under Craufurd, would prosecute the initial assault: a covering party of four companies of riflemen would line the rampart near the walls to keep down the defenders' heads; 160 Portuguese *Cacadores* would go forward with ladders and hay bags to throw in the ditch; a Forlorn Hope (as the leading party, commonly considered the most dangerous task, was known), under a subaltern, would then enter the ditch, placing the ladders that would allow others down into it and up the breaches on the other side; the storming party of three hundred volunteers under a major would then attempt to take the breaches. Throughout these proceedings, Craufurd would hold some companies of the 52nd and the 95th under his own hand as a sort of immediate reserve, and Lieutenant Colonel Andrew Barnard (of the 95th) would keep a further back-up, of the 43rd, 95th and 1st *Cacadores*. All of this, of course, would happen under cover of darkness.

The heroism required to prosecute this business meant that in any successful assault, the commanders of the Forlorn Hope and storming party expected promotion. There were many volunteers for these posts in the Light Division. Even officers who were next in line for promotion often volunteered, for fear of being seen as presumptuous or complacent in the eyes of their peers. In this spirit Lieutenant Harry Smith of the 95th went to Craufurd and asked his permission to lead the Forlorn Hope. Craufurd, wisely, would not hear of it, telling him, 'Why, you cannot go; you, a Major of Brigade, a senior Lieutenant, you are sure to get a Company. No, I must give it to a younger officer.' He chose instead Gurwood of the 52nd for this task, and Major George Napier, of the same regiment, to command the storming party. Other officers would accompany them as volunteers, one commenting, 'While the subaltern commanding the forlorn hope may look for death or a company, and the field officer commanding the stormers an additional step by brevet, to the other officers who volunteer on that desperate service, no hope is held out – no reward given.'

For the rank and file the same applied, but when Gurwood and Napier came to the Light Division's camp looking for volunteers, they were overwhelmed. Corporal Fairfoot stepped forward for the Forlorn Hope. Having been in action at the San Francisco redoubt eleven days before, he had no need to prove himself. Costello, the Irish private of the 3rd Company, was another volunteer, bound for the storming party. The 95th's detachment in that latter group would be led by Captain Mitchell, accompanied by Lieutenants Johnston and Kincaid – all three of them Scotsmen with fierce fighting reputations. 'The advantage of being on a storming party', Kincaid opined later with his trademark irony, 'is generally considered as giving prior claim to be *put out of pain*, for they receive the first fire, which is generally the best.' Kincaid had recently taken over the command of the 7th or Highland Company, its long-time chief Alexander Cameron having been promoted to major at last, in command of the Right Wing of the 1st Battalion, who would provide the covering fire for the assault.

The rank and file knew that joining would earn the respect of their comrades – and the chance of plunder. 'This was a momentous occasion in the life of a soldier, and so we considered it,' Costello recorded. 'The entire company gathered round our little party, each pressing us to have a sup from his canteen. We shook hands with friendly sincerity, and speculated on whether we would outlive the assault. If truth must be told, we also speculated on the chances of plunder in the town.'

At 7 p.m. the storming columns moved down through one of the city's suburbs to a point about three hundred yards from the lesser breach. They would wait there until a rocket was fired, giving them and Picton's boys the signal. Their advance had almost certainly been spotted by the French officer who served high up in the cathedral tower as a lookout. Riflemen in the covering party were leading the way. Craufurd came up with them, annoyed that they were not moving faster, and accused them of lacking courage – 'Move on, will you, 95th? or we will get some who will!'

The sense of anticipation had reached a high pitch among the stormers, some trying to dissipate it with a last-minute bout of activity and chatter. Harry Smith sent Lieutenant George Simmons to bring up some ladders. Making his way through the darkness to bring them, Simmons was intercepted by Craufurd. The general asked the young lieutenant why he had brought short ladders rather than long ones, Simmons replying that he had only done what the engineers had told him to do. Craufurd told him, 'Go back, sir, and get others; I am astonished at such stupidity.'

Captain Uniacke and Lieutenant John FitzMaurice looked up at the defences, looming ahead of them in the darkness. They were meant to be part of the covering party, but like many of the Light Division officers, both could barely wait to rush in and get the business over with. The two Irishmen shared the loss of a father young in life. Uniacke turned to his lieutenant, 'Look there, Fitz, what would our mothers say, if they saw what was preparing for us?' FitzMaurice replied, 'Far better they should not,' before pointing out that Uniacke had put on an expensive new jacket – 'But what extravagance to put on a new pelisse for a night such as this!' The captain replied, 'I shall be all the better worth taking.' He had a point, for every man – defender or stormer – imagined what he might gain on a night like this: plunder; a handsome new pelisse; a glorious reputation; or just the chance to avoid an ignominious death.

Craufurd pushed his way through to the head of the column, and on finding a little higher ground he called out to his division: 'Soldiers! the eyes of your country are upon you. Be steady, be cool, be firm in the assault. The town must be yours this night.' The rocket was up, the leading parties began trotting forward.

Whatever the garrison may or may not have seen, most of the approach was made before the eruption of fire that they all dreaded. At last, with the column moving up the first obstacle, less than fifty feet from the walls themselves, a French sentry called out and then the cacophony began. Hundreds of muskets opened up from the walls, and cannon too. Riflemen from the covering party were firing back from the embankment surrounding the walls as the stormers moved up to the lip of this great rampart. The first men began dropping down into the ditch.

Craufurd, who was standing atop the feature, was hit by a bullet which went through his arm and one of his lungs, then lodged in his spine. The general was hurled over by the force of the impact and rolled down into the darkness. Believing the wound to be mortal, Craufurd asked the captain to tell his beloved wife he was 'quite sure they would meet in heaven'.

Down in the ditch in front of the breaches there was a mayhem of wounded men, screaming out in pain, officers calling on others to follow them and soldiers taking potshots at the French above them. Lieutenant Kincaid got himself to the foot of a ladder: 'I mounted with a ferocious intent, carrying a sword in one hand and a pistol in the other; but, when I got up, I found nobody to fight except two of our own men, who were already laid dead across the top of the ladder.' In the confusion he had stormed not the main wall, but an outlying ravelin unconnected to it.

At the breach itself Gurwood was making his way up one of the ladders when he was either thrown or knocked off by one of the defenders, falling back to the ground with a thump, winded. Lieutenant Willie Johnston of the Rifles was soon up in his stead and so, as if from nowhere, was Captain Uniacke, who had rushed forward of his own accord and joined the stormers. Some cheers had gone up in the Great Breach and the Light Division men feared Picton's were beating them to it.

Looking up in the murk, they could see the mouth of a cannon facing down and across the breach. Doubtless it was double-charged with canister and the French were just waiting their moment to cut down the storming party. But some soldiers scrambled up the jagged rocks at the edge of the breach and emerged in the top of the wall just beside the cannon's mouth. One of the 95th brought the butt of his rifle down like an axe across the head of the French gunner and the danger to the men on the ladders was removed. Men now quickly fanned out along the walls and the defence began to crumble.

In this chaos of shouting and shooting, one of the French engineers touched a match to the fuse on a mine. As Harry Smith and John Uniacke ran along the ramparts with soldiers not far behind, it blew up with massive force. 'I shall never forget the concussion when it struck me, throwing me back many feet into a lot of charged fuses of shells,' wrote Smith. 'My cocked hat was blown away, my clothes all singed.' Uniacke was not so fortunate: he staggered back, charred black, with one of his arms hanging only by threads of skin. As he was led away by comrades, Uniacke murmured, 'Remember, I was the first.'

Soldiers poured into the town, often refusing quarter. Some of the 'French', throwing down their muskets, called out that they were only poor Italians. But according to Kincaid, 'Our men had, somehow, imbibed a horrible antipathy to the Italians, and every appeal they made in that name was instantly answered with "You're Italians are you? then, damn you, here's a shot for you"; and the action instantly followed the word.'

Those who had survived the breaches were flushed with the joy of being alive: 'When the battle is over, and crowned with victory, he finds himself elevated for a while into the regions of absolute bliss.' The Forlorn Hope and storming party volunteers 'broke into different squads, which went in different directions and entered different streets according to the fancy of their leaders.'

Costello stripped some French soldiers of their money and an officer of his watch. He and his party then found their way into the house of a Spanish doctor, who was hiding with his pretty young niece, fully expecting the sack of Rodrigo to conform to all the horrors of medieval warfare, whereby those inside a stormed town forfeited their lives and property. 'Like himself, she was shivering with fear,' according to Costello. 'This we soon dispelled, and were rewarded with a good supper crowned by a bowl of excellent punch which, at the time, seemed to compensate us for all the sufferings we had endured in the trenches during the siege.' Elsewhere, the sources of liquor were soon discovered and gallons of the stuff rapidly thrown down the stormers' necks.

In Rodrigo's ancient plaza, the jubilant soldiery gathered in mobs, cheering and firing into windows. The alcohol was taking its effect now, and a general riot seemed imminent. 'If I had not seen it, I never could have supposed that British soldiers would become so wild and furious,' wrote a young officer of the 43rd. As the firing at nothing in particular built up, one private of the 43rd dropped dead, a bullet through his head.

Major Alexander Cameron, who'd been commanding the covering party of riflemen, arrived with Lieutenant Colonel Barnard and tried to check the collapse in order. 'What, sir, are you firing at?' Cameron bellowed at one rifleman, who shouted back at him, 'I don't know sir! I am firing because everybody else is.' Cameron and Barnard looked about them at the debris on the streets, each seizing a broken musket which they used to beat their soldiers into some kind of order.

The search for plunder was not confined to the soldiery. Lieutenant FitzMaurice helped himself to the governor's silver snuffbox. Lieutenant Gurwood, having been overtaken by keener men in the breach, was determined to recover the situation. 'Gurwood's a sharp fellow,' noted Harry Smith in admiration of a glory seeker equal to himself, 'and he cut off in search of the Governor, and brought his sword to the Duke, and Lord Fitzroy Somerset buckled it on him in the breach. Gurwood made the most of it.'

Some 1,360 unwounded French troops were taken prisoner, along with 500 or so injured men. A little over 1,100 British and Portuguese troops were casualties during the entire siege, about one-fifth of the total being killed.

It did not take much time for the parties of stormers to recognise one or two familiar faces skulking in the dark alleys of Rodrigo that night. A Cummins or a Hodgson was soon spotted by his messmates, no matter the French uniforms that they wore as disguise – or doffed, depending on what they thought offered the better hope of escape. Lucky not to get a ball on the spot, these men were quickly clapped under arrest and into the hands of the provost marshal.

There was one exception, though. Joseph Almond had managed to slip out in the chaos following the storm. He scrambled down the steep slope leading away from Rodrigo. Hurling himself headlong into the black night, he tried to get his bearings for Salamanca, from whence the French reinforcing column would arrive. He ran and ran, puffing and panting, knowing that he could expect little mercy if he fell into the hands of his old comrades.

FIFTEEN

The Reckoning

January–March 1812

The sack of Rodrigo lasted one intense night. Brandy flowed in the gutters and troops moved from one house to another, turning everything upside down in their desperate search for plunder. The following day, one private of the 95th recollected, 'We marched over the bridge dressed in all variety of clothes imaginable. Some had jack-boots on, others wore frock coats, or had epaulettes, and some had monkeys on their shoulders.' The mood was buoyant: many had gained materially by the victory and the butcher's bill had not been so high.

For those not hardened to war, of course, the sights and sounds of Rodrigo on 20 January aroused feelings of turmoil. Young James Gairdner told his father, 'I walked around the ramparts that morning at daybreak and never saw such a shocking sight in my life, there lay Frenchman and Englishman dead and dying in every direction, stript and mangled shockingly.'

In small billets in San Francisco or Santa Cruz, outside the walls, there were men in their death agonies. Neither General Craufurd nor Captain Uniacke was to survive his wounds. Craufurd, to the last, murmured his love for his wife. For Uniacke, unmarried, slow death must have been accompanied by anxiety about how his mother, Eliza, would look after her other children. Both men were laid to rest on 25 January.

Craufurd and Uniacke received the military obsequies appropriate to their rank: a slow march, pall-bearers, soldiers with reversed arms at the graveside. In Craufurd's case, the ceremony was grander, of course – thousands of men of the 5th Division were paraded to line the route. The general's coffin was borne by sergeant majors from each of the Light Division's battalions, and behind it walked his friends, Sir

Charles Stewart, the Adjutant General at Headquarters and his aides-de-camp, followed by Lord Wellington and the Army's other generals and staff. Some soldiers had cut a niche at the foot of the breach in Rodrigo's walls and it was into this space that Craufurd was to be interred. After the reading of a short funeral service, ashes to ashes and dust to dust, the general's coffin was lowered. A volley of musketry saluted him, followed by another salvo, much louder, from a battery of cannon on ramparts overlooking the ceremony.

The soldiers dispersed afterwards, some Light Division men marching straight through a great slushy puddle as they went – at least one observer detected a kind of silent tribute to their fallen general in this. Wellington's words home marked Craufurd's passing in a correct, formal tone, lamenting him as an 'ornament to his profession'. In their letters and thoughts, the British staff reflected on the passing of a man whose services they had valued but who had been almost impossible to deal with. 'He is a man of a very extraordinary temper and disposition, it will be difficult to find a person qualified to replace him in the command of the advance,' FitzRoy Somerset had written, businesslike, shortly before Craufurd's death. William Napier, who served under Craufurd as a major in the 43rd, later wrote of his character: 'At one time he was all fire and intelligence, a master-spirit in war; at another, as if possessed by the demon, he would madly rush from blunder to blunder, raging in folly.'

Uniacke's farewell, by contrast, was more of a wake. His honour guard was formed of several dozen men of the 3rd Company, and the funeral dirge was played by the band of the 1st Battalion. They marched from their quarters to Gallegos, a nearby Spanish village, where a resting place had been prepared in the little churchyard. Finding a grave in consecrated ground had required Corporal Fairfoot, who'd won his spurs as a fighter in two storms that month, to show a rare kind of tact. At first, the priest at Gallegos had refused to allow the burial, claiming it would be an outrage to inter a heretic in his place. Fairfoot assured the priest that Uniacke was Irish, thereby hinting at his Catholicism. The corporal transmitted his message without exposing the dissimulation required of Uniacke in life, an evasion made necessary by the British laws against Papists holding commissions.

Many of Uniacke's lads had been boozing ever since the storm. 'The men, who had obtained plenty of money at Rodrigo, got drinking,' wrote Costello, 'and while conveying the body to the grave, they stumbled under the weight of the coffin. The lid had not been nailed down so out rolled the mangled remains of our brave captain.' This profane incident did not shock men so inured to death. Instead, they slung their officer back into his box, resumed their journey, then buried him, before returning to their camp for many a toast to Uniacke's memory and much late-night talk of his courage.

Harry Smith, recuperating from his own wounds, remembered the last thing the captain had said to him before the storm on the 19th, a reminder that, as senior lieutenant, Smith would probably be a captain by morning. 'Little, poor fellow, did he think he was to make the vacancy,' wrote Smith. That was the essence of their business, a highly risky game in which the advancement the officers craved could often be gained only at the expense of comrades. As for Uniacke's mother Eliza, her situation became quite miserable, and she ended up petitioning for charity, seeking a Royal Bounty or pension to make up for the lost remittances from her dead son.

For some days after the storm, the British troops made new discoveries of deserters in Rodrigo. There had been around two dozen turncoats serving the French garrison there, sixteen of whom were now prisoners. Some were doubtless killed during the siege or storm, and Almond at least had escaped. One of the five men of the 1st/95th who'd deserted the previous autumn, William MacFarlane, having entered Rodrigo before the others, was apparently able to escape with the last French relief column the previous November and to soldier on as a turncoat. As far as his former messmates knew, though, he might well have been slung into a mass grave with the other dead.

On 12 February the captured deserters were marched into a makeshift military courtroom, a hall in the village of Nava de Haver, a place familiar enough to the Light Division men as it was very near where they'd fought on 5 May the previous year. In a garrison, courts martial might have several members, particularly when hearing a capital case. In the field, though, a major general sat in judgement as the president and a captain, the deputy judge advocate, put the case for the prosecution. The men were entitled to speak in their own defence, but much of the first day was taken up with the lengthy reading of charges detailing when they had deserted and the circumstances of their capture.

For those among the prisoners who still dared to hope, there was the consolation that even serious cases of desertion were only punished in England by transportation for life to some dingy Australian colony. As for killing your fellow soldiers, why, Murphy of the 95th had been sentenced to six months' incarceration for that just before the siege. On the other hand, there had been evidence aplenty in the execution of the Brunswick deserters and some others during the previous two years that Lord Wellington was determined to make a severe example of any men who deserted in the face of the enemy – and those fellows had not even served the French.

When asked why they had all pleaded not guilty, the soldiers spoke of the privations of the previous autumn. They argued they had been driven to desertion by hunger and suffering.

General Kempt gave his verdict on 13 February, the business having lasted a day and a half from beginning to end. 'The court having considered the evidence adduced on the prosecution against the prisoners, together with what they have severally offered in their defence, are of opinion that they are guilty of the charge preferred against them,' the official verdict read, 'and do thereby sentence them, the prisoners [all named] to be shot to death, at such time and place as his Excellency the Commander of Forces may be pleased to direct. Which sentence has been confirmed by his Excellency the Commander of the Forces.' It was to become quite evident that Wellington wanted examples made of these men.

Confirmed or not, there was still time for some last intercession by the men's commanding officers. Miles Hodgson of the 95th was among those saved from the firing squad by his superiors, presumably because of the notion that he had been a good soldier in most respects prior to his desertion. Hearing of this in their bivouac, the injustice was not lost on the riflemen, some of whom blamed Hodgson for persuading McInnes of the Highland Company to desert in the first place.

It was not that the others held McInnes entirely innocent in the matter – rather that they would have preferred to see Hodgson share his punishment. As they discussed the condemned men's fate around the campfire, everyone was pretty much agreed that they would get what was due to them. Some held that the deserters had fought twice as well as any Frenchers and that they had even called out in English as the storm began, 'Now here comes the Light Division; let us give it them, the rascals!'

McInnes and nine others were duly taken to a clearing in the upland forest one week after their sentence was passed. In order that the lesson not be lost on their comrades, the Light Division was paraded to witness the punishment, and the firing party made up from contingents of its battalions. Each of the prisoners would be shot by members of his own regiment. 'They soon after appeared, poor wretches, moving towards the square, with faces pale and wan, and all with the dejection such a situation is calculated to produce,' one witness remembered. The provost marshal and Lieutenant Harry Smith, as major of brigade, supervised proceedings.

Graves had been dug for the prisoners, each being stopped in front of his own last resting place. They then kneeled with their backs to the grave and facing their old regiments. Blindfolds were fastened and they were 'left for a few moments to their own reflections or prayers, the Provost Marshal proceeded to the firing party'. At the order, the firing squad levelled its weapons and fired.

The smoke from the volley cleared to reveal two men still upright. One, a rifleman, was wounded. The other, Cameron of the Royal Horse Artillery, was untouched, for in a piece of sad incompetence, the provost marshal had forgotten to include members of his regiment in the firing squad.

Harry Smith recalled what happened next: '"Oh, Mr Smith, put me out of my misery," called the wounded rifleman, and I literally ordered the firing party, when reloaded, to run up and shoot the poor wretches. It was an awful scene.' The provost marshal walked up and finished off each man with a shot to the head.

The regiments of the Light Division filed away from the execution ground. They had seen plenty of death in battle, but there was something deeply disturbing about what they had just witnessed. Quarter Master William Surtees wrote:

I cannot describe the uncomfortable feelings this spectacle produced in my mind – nay, not only there, but in my body also – for I felt sick at heart; a sort of loathing ensued; and from the recollection of what I then suffered, I could not easily be persuaded to witness such another scene, if I had the option of staying away.

Following the execution of its former members, the Light Division was soon under way again, marching south for an appointment with another siege. Badajoz, the last remaining border fortress still in French hands, was their objective, Wellington having resolved to take it as quickly as possible so that he might press on with the campaign of 1812, deeper into Spain. The 95th and its brother regiments faced a series of marches, down through the Sierra d'Estrella mountains to the plains of Alemtejo (where they had suffered such sickness before) and across the Guadiana into Spain.

The columns moving south were commanded under improvised arrangements. Craufurd was dead, Colborne of the 52nd seriously wounded. Others accompanied the column in a state of fragile health, either through wounds or sickness, drifting in and out of their posts as each bout of delirium subsided or rose. Among these officers were: Colonel Beckwith, who had returned from England, in theory to resume command of the 1st Brigade, though in fact he was never well enough to do so; Major General John Vandeleur, the 2nd Brigade chief who now coveted the command of the entire division but had also been wounded at Rodrigo; and Major O'Hare, the commanding officer of the 1st Battalion of the Rifles, who had been laid low by a series of fevers. So it was a time of acting commands throughout: lieutenants led companies; Cameron, a brevet major but technically still a captain, commanded the 1st/95th; majors from the 43rd and 52nd ran the brigades; and Lieutenant Colonel Barnard, having arrived less than a year before, was in charge of the entire Light Division.

It was in this atmosphere, in which nobody exactly felt confident of his place, that a grubby prisoner was taken swiftly down the division's march route and delivered to its provost. Shortly after the previous executions, Joseph Almond had been captured by a patrol of Spanish guerrillas while trying to make his way through to Salamanca. The forests and byways between Rodrigo and that city were intensively patrolled by Don Julian's men, who were always on the lookout for Spanish collaborators or spies carrying messages. Anyone who seemed out of place soon attracted their attention.

Almond's former comrades were quickly aware of his capture because he had to join their daily marches, manacled, at the rear of the column. February's executions had, for many of the men, righted the wrong caused by the deserters' defection to the French – accounts had been settled. Quite a few of them had been disgusted by the spectacle of the firing squads too. So when it came to Almond, there was a general feeling that they did not want to see another capital trial.

Since the division was marching, it was not possible to convene even the semblance of a general court martial, as had been done the previous month. Instead, the recuperating General Vandeleur would act as president and his staff officer or major of brigade, Harry Smith, would be given the prosecuting role of acting deputy advocate general. The 'court' was convened in Castello Branco on 4 March and its proceedings would last but an hour or two. Almond, like the others, pleaded not guilty on the grounds of the sufferings he had faced the previous November.

Smith and Vandeleur did what they believed Headquarters expected of them:

The Court having duly considered the evidence on the part of the prosecution, as well as what the Prisoner has stated in his defence, are of the opinion that he is Guilty of the crime laid to his charge, and do therefore sentence him the Prisoner Joseph Allman [sic] to be shot to death at such time and place as His Excellency the Commander of the Forces may deem fit.

'The fate of this man excited much commiseration,' according to Costello. 'Because of his previous good character, and the fact that he had marched as a prisoner for many days, it was commonly thought he would be pardoned.' Everybody had learnt the lesson that they were intended to learn from February's firing squad. Surely someone would step forward and say a few good words for Almond, saving him as Hodgson had been saved – but who? At the time of his desertion, his company had been under the command of George Simmons, a junior lieutenant. As for O'Hare or Cameron, they were hard men all right, but they lacked the connections to feel confident about putting their heads above the parapet in such a situation. Only someone with the stature of a Beckwith could have saved Almond, and he was confined to a sickbed.

On 9 March, the division halted in Castello de Vide, a little hillside spa town in the northern part of Alemtejo Province. Almond's execution had been fixed by the court martial for the next day. Costello found himself, with several comrades, guarding the prisoner. They were playing cards and chatting among themselves when the provost arrived. There was to be no pardon: the sentence would be carried out the following morning at ten.

Almond sent for the 5th Company pay sergeant and asked for his arrears. Indeed, the prisoner was insistent on the point that the execution could not be carried out until these several pounds had been received. These were made over, one of the guards being sent out to buy some good wine with it. What remained was signed over to Almond's mother. The prisoner then noticed that one of his keepers had worn-out shoes, so he swapped his own with him, saying, 'They will last me as long as I shall require them.'

The following morning, 10 March, the Light Division was drawn up as ordered, to witness another execution. A muffled drum was beaten and the band played the Dead March as the prisoner was led out. It was raining a typical, damnable Portuguese winter's rain, and the grave that had been dug for Almond was soon waterlogged. The prisoner marched up, looked into it and said, 'Although a watery one, I shall sleep sound enough in it.' He seemed completely composed, showing no signs of fear either in his step or in the timbre of his voice.

Almond knelt and declined the blindfold with the words, 'There is no occasion, I shall not flinch.' The provost, embarrassed, explained that these were the rules. As the firing party made ready, he called out to his guards of the previous night, giving each of them a word and a farewell. 'As I nodded to him in return,' wrote Costello, 'I fancied it was to a dead man. And in two minutes, he was no more. The intrepid and cool manner in which he met his fate drew forth a general feeling of admiration.' The blindfold went on at last, rifles were presented at their mark, and the damp stillness was shattered by a volley. Almond tipped back into his grave and sploshed into the muddy water like a sack of butcher's scraps.

SIXTEEN

Badajoz

March–April 1812

The French gun captain peering down the barrel of his great beast of a cannon could see enemy soldiers running across a trench, on the ridge five hundred yards or so from his position. Several nights before, the enemy had thrown up this earthen defence on the gentle rise overlooking Badajoz's eastern wall. It was the first parallel of their siege works. Every day the gun captain and his company had been hurling heavy shot at it, trying from their platform on the city's massive walls to flatten the insolent work of men with shovels. He watched the running figures, three of them. You could not lead running soldiers with a massive great gun in the way you did with a rifle. Instead you aimed for your target – the trench – and if you caught some member of the working parties in the process, then *ça ira*! But an experienced gun captain using the mental mechanism honed by years of practice and thousands of shots could judge very precisely the time required for the flight of his ball to a known range, add to it the moment's delay of the powder burning from the touch hole through to the main charge and subtract from this the instant it would take running men to cover a given distance. The gun went off with an almighty thump.

Private Costello was aware of the whoosh of air just behind him and the splash of something on his jacket. He jumped down into the trench and turned around, 'and beheld the body of Brooks, headless, but quivering with life for a few seconds before it fell . . . the shot had smashed and carried away the whole of his head. My jacket was bespattered with the brains.' Costello and Tom Treacy had made it, James Brooks had not. Another man who had sailed in May 1809 with the 3rd Company was dead. Brooks was one of the many captured on the Coa in July 1810, but he had managed to escape the French. In the days before his death, he had told Costello several times that he had dreamt of a headless corpse.

The siege of Badajoz was already proving something harder fought and more desperate for the Rifles than their action at Rodrigo three months earlier. There were three times the number of French in Badajoz for one thing – and it was thrice the fortress for another, having thicker walls, deeper ditches, the works.

On 22 March, the day after Brooks was killed, another party of riflemen was sent forward on a hazardous duty. Some French guns across the Guadiana River to their north had been playing havoc on Wellington's first parallel. That trench ran atop the San Miguel ridge from north to south and the French on the other side of the river were able to send flanking shots right along it. The riflemen got themselves settled and waited in cover for daybreak.

As it became lighter, they chose their targets. The sentry walking along the walls, appearing now and then in the gun embrasures. The gunner preparing one of the twenty-four-pounders for the day's work ahead. Once the word was given, the 95th began picking off anyone who showed himself near the guns. It was long-range shooting – two hundred or more yards – much further than Gairdner and his party had been firing at Rodrigo. But with careful adjustment for distance, they soon began claiming victims, one officer noting, 'This had the desired effect; and the field pieces were withdrawn into the fort, after some of the gunners had bitten the dust.'

There were several more missions like this in the following days. Moving close to the city's walls under cover of darkness, riflemen would dig pits for themselves and wait for dawn when any Frenchman on the ramparts was fair game. They tried to concentrate on the gun crews and this led the enemy to close up the embrasures in front of the cannon with planks or gabbions until just before the moment of firing. One French officer tried to counter the sniping by waving his hat on a stick to draw British fire and then having a party of picked shots try to kill the marksmen. This contest went on for a whole day before the French officer himself dropped, believed to be killed by a ball from the 95th. Lieutenant Simmons, who commanded such a party, wrote in his journal, 'I was so delighted with the good practice I was making against Johnny that I kept it up from daylight till dark with forty as prime fellows who ever pulled a trigger.'

There was another obstacle to the British plans: a strong redoubt on the San Miguel ridge called La Picurina. The task of storming it was set for the evening of 25 March and given to a brigade of the 3rd Division, but all manner of volunteers went along.

Robert Fairfoot was one of them. He'd developed a thirst for action that, on that very day, got him promoted to sergeant. Evidently there was no need for him to go. If Fairfoot kept volunteering, he'd soon be a dead sergeant. But why should a man who'd just been made up hold back and let others take the risk? That was the way they saw it. William Brotherwood, Kincaid's old confederate in the bating of Tommy Sarsfield, went too. Four months before, he'd been promoted to corporal and, like Fairfoot, he was not a man to rest on his laurels.

The storm of the Picurina was a desperate business – much less easy than the San Francisco redoubt on 8 January – for the defenders had been able to pour fire on the British as they struggled to break in to the fort, killing or wounding half of the five hundred attackers. The surviving stormers returned to their camps in the early hours to regale their expectant messmates with the horrific tale of that night's storm.

Sergeant Fairfoot and Corporal Brotherwood both survived. The latter, already well known to his fellow riflemen as a wag, furnished those who had not been there with a good yarn about how the Green Jacket put the redcoat in his place. Some of the 3rd Division stormers, knowing the Picurina business to be theirs, were evidently furious at the arrival of the Rifles 'volunteers'. One of them had shouted at the riflemen to place their ladders and get out of the way. 'Damn your eyes!' Brotherwood had bellowed back above the din. 'Do you think we Light Division fetch ladders for such chaps as you to climb up? Follow us.' That was putting the lobsters down, and it was repeated among many of the 95th.

The desperate business of grinding down the city's defences continued from one day to the next, the incessant banging of cannon filling the waking hours, giving way at night to mortars with their distinctive double bangs. There was an almost febrile air of anticipation among the British troops. Some regretted holding back at Rodrigo; the losses had not been so great and the stormers got drunk for a month on the proceeds. Others wanted to get Badajoz over with. Some officers may have thought a coming war with Russia might shorten the Iberian conflict. Alexander Cameron read in a letter from a friend in England that 'the Russian army is 400 thousand strong on the frontiers . . . war commences, Boney will have too much to do to think of the Peninsula.'

It was in this atmosphere that a party of hospital convalescents marched up to the 95th's bivouac one morning. Major O'Hare, back in good health, was in acting command of the battalion and greeted the returnees, including Sergeant Esau Jackson, who'd spent almost two years as an orderly at Belem. 'We anticipated a scene,' said Costello, 'we were not deceived.'

O'Hare spotted his man: 'Is that you, Mr Sergeant Jackson? And pray where, in God's name, have you been for the past two years? The company have seen a little fighting during that period.'

Jackson, aware no doubt that the eyes of all were now trained on him, replied, 'The doctors wouldn't allow me to leave the hospital, sir.'

O'Hare looked hard at him, 'I'm sorry for that, because all I can do is give you the choice of a court martial for absenting yourself from duty without leave, or I can have your stripes taken off.'

Jackson knew he had no choice but to surrender the sash around his waist and the stripes on his shoulder, the symbols of his rank. O'Hare turned and said loud enough for all his soldiers to hear, 'By God, I will not have these brave fellows commanded by skulkers.' Corporal George Ballard, another 3rd Company man, was promoted in his stead.

Had Jackson's desire for redemption exceeded his zeal for self-preservation, he could have volunteered for the storming party. Many of those who went were soldiers who chanced their lives because they were desperate to gain resurrection in the eyes of their comrades. Private Thomas Mayberry was one of those readying himself for the moment when men were called to assault Badajoz. Mayberry, too, had been a sergeant once, but he had been broken and flogged back in England for defrauding his company's paybooks in order to pay off gambling debts. 'Mayberry was held in contempt by his fellow soldiers, and ill thought of by the officers,' according to one private. He was fed up with the taunts and abuse of messmates and superiors alike – it was not a life he wanted to carry on living.

Private James Burke was another determined to volunteer. He had been on the Forlorn Hope at Rodrigo with Fairfoot, but had neither that man's intellect nor Mayberry's contrition. Burke, an illiterate labourer from Kilkenny, personified the hard-fighting, fatalistic Irish in the 95th's ranks. He was, in the damning words of one of his officers, 'one of those wild untamable animals that, the moment the place was carried, would run to every species of excess'. In short, Burke was bound to volunteer because he had learned it was the best way to get the fight of his life, with a fuck and the devil of a good drink at the end of it.

Among the officers, too, there were many who wanted to put themselves forward. The chances of promotion were one factor, but like the men, many of them had become convinced of the doctrine, 'The more the danger, the more the honour.'

All of this meant that when the volunteers were finally called for, 'so great was the rage for passports to eternity in our battalion, on that occasion, that even the officers' servants insisted on taking their place in the ranks; and I was obliged to leave my baggage in charge of a man who had been wounded some days before.'

On 5 April, Wellington's engineers told him that their battering of the two bastions at the south-east corner of the defences, Santa Maria and La Trinidad, had shattered them to the point where they were vulnerable to assault. Fearing the approach of a relieving French column, he gave orders for the attack, but at the last minute, concerned about the height of the rampart in front of those broken works, he postponed it for twenty-four hours. The extra time would allow the gunners to pound away, to see if they could do anything to blow away this rampart in order to make the job a little easier.

The postponement of the assault meant that the picked men waited throughout 6 April, knowing their trial would come that night. Sergeant Fairfoot, having volunteered for his fourth storm in as many months, would be part of the Forlorn Hope – so would Private Burke and Ned Costello. Major O'Hare had been given the command of the storming party, to be made up of three hundred men. Esau Jackson was not among the volunteers.

Such was the zeal to take part that some curious deals had been done between Colonel Barnard and the officers of his division. Lieutenant Willie Johnston would not be put off, so a task had been invented for him, in command of a 'rope party' to advance with the Forlorn Hope and pull down some defences the French had erected on top of the breach. The command of that Forlorn Hope was ultimately given to Lieutenant Horatio Harvest of the 43rd on the basis of seniority alone – precisely the nonsensical solution rejected by Craufurd in January. 'He insisted on his right as going as senior lieutenant; so over-scrupulous was he that his permitting a junior officer to occupy this post might be construed to the detriment of his honour,' one officer of the

95th wrote years later, evidently still angry. 'He went, and . . . by his too refined sense of honour deprived another officer, probably, of that promotion which would have been the consequence of going on this duty had he survived.'

The volunteers were excused normal duties on the 6th. 'I went to the river and had a good bathe,' wrote Bugler Green, who joined Fairfoot in the Forlorn Hope. 'I thought I would have a clean skin whether killed or wounded.' It was a sunny day, one in which the soldiers were able to lie about and reflect on the trials ahead. One subaltern of the 43rd chanced upon Horatio Harvest, sitting on a bank, sucking an orange. 'My mind is made up. I am sure to be killed,' said Harvest, without apparent emotion.

This lull before the storm played very badly with Lieutenant Thomas Bell. He had joined the 1st/95th in February, just after Rodrigo, with two other subalterns sent out from England to replace casualties. Bell was an old acquaintance of George Simmons, having served with him in the Lincolnshire Militia – they volunteered into the 95th on the same day back in April 1809. Bell had sat the war out in Shorncliffe so far. Although he had no experience of fighting whatsoever, he arrived in the regiment with a more senior rank than a hardened warrior like John Kincaid.

Sympathetic voices would have told Bell that he would have every chance to prove himself soon, just as Gairdner had quickly shown his mettle at Rodrigo. But the gallows humour and fatalistic resignation of the 95th's soldiers only made Bell more anxious. As the siege of Badajoz wore on, Bell's feelings of turmoil grew unbearable.

The day also gave way to some uncomfortable meditations for O'Hare. He had been wounded before, in south America, but had somehow gone through the current Peninsular campaign with only one slight wound (at Fuentes). Did that give him the mysterious aura of a survivor, or had he already pushed his luck too far?

At around 8 p.m. the stormers fell in, prior to being given a last-minute pep talk by their officers. Lieutenant Bell chose this moment to complain of feeling sick, and to abandon his men, heading back towards his tent. A double allowance of grog was doled out to each soldier, to numb them for the business ahead. O'Hare was ill at ease. Captain Jones, of the 52nd, asked him, 'Well O'Hare what do you think of tonight's work?'

'I don't know, tonight, I think, will be my last,' said O'Hare.

'Tut tut man! I have the same sort of feeling, but I keep it down with a drop of this.' Jones handed O'Hare his calabash and the old Irish major took a good draught of brandy. The Light Division stormers had formed up in some quarries about a third of a mile from the Santa Maria breach. They waited a while longer, for they were not due to move forward until 10 p.m. One more chance to peer into the gloom and talk over the objective.

The Santa Maria and Trinidad bastions had their tops shattered by the incessant artillery fire. The sloped stonework bases remained intact, having been protected – such was the design of a fortress – by the earthen rampart around it. Heavy damage to the bastions, though, meant that the batteries located in them at the start of the siege had been largely disabled. Great chunks of the wall stretching about 150 yards between these two targets had also collapsed under the bombardment, being only partially screened by the ravelin that sat between the two bastions and the edge of the great ditch in front of them.

For the stormers, the line of assault would take them almost due north from the quarry for about four hundred yards until the gentle rise of the surrounding escarpment began. Another fifty or sixty yards would bring them to the top of that feature, where the ground fell away vertically in front of them, dropping about twenty feet to the floor of the ditch. There was every chance that a man jumping down into it would break his legs, so ladders and haybags would be used to help them down. The Light Division men would then have to bear slightly left and travel another ten or twenty yards, circumventing the ravelin (lest they assault it by mistake in the chaos, as Kincaid had at Rodrigo) in order to get their ladders onto the wall of the Santa Maria bastion itself. The Trinidad bastion would be attacked by stormers from the 4th Division. Simultaneously, Picton's 3rd Division would approach the medieval castle walls at Badajoz's north-east corner and escalade them with long ladders. The 5th Division would make a diversionary attack on the western side of the town.

General Phillipon, the governor, had made elaborate precautions to turn Wellington's planned attacks into a bloody fiasco. Where sections of the main *enciente* or wall had collapsed between the bastions, a retrenchment had been thrown up, a makeshift wall made from piled-up debris to form a new obstacle right behind the old one. Along this breach and on the bastions, *chevaux de frises* – wooden frames with sword blades and bayonets attached – formed a prickly last line of defence. The engineers had partly flooded the ditch between the wall and outer rampart; calculating where the troops would have to go to avoid the water, they placed mines and planks with nails driven through. The men atop the ramparts would have piles of loaded muskets, grenades and stones to throw down.

The stormers moved up, with a couple of hundred riflemen of Right Wing who would provide a covering fire. O'Hare caught sight of George Simmons, the subaltern he had tutored, now one of the battalion's most experienced officers. The men shook hands, and as he turned to part, the major told Simmons: 'A lieutenant colonel or cold meat in a few hours.'

Shortly before 10 p.m., the four companies of the 95th's Right Wing, under the command of Major Alexander Cameron, began trotting forward. They were going to line the protective slope around the walls, to provide a covering fire for the stormers. Some British cannon had kept up a fire of blanks in order to deceive the garrison, but as the riflemen crawled into position on top of the escarpment, many felt sure they could see the defenders watching them and doing nothing. Both sides were holding their fire.

The rope party and Forlorn Hope came forward too now, dozens of men trotting up the incline, many carrying ladders or haybags in order to break the fall into the ditch ahead. As they came to the top of the slope, silhouetted against the sky, a couple of carcasses were thrown down by the defenders, burning with a furious intensity and illuminating walls and men alike with an unearthly flickering pink light.

'Instantly a volley of grape-shot, canister, and small arms poured in among us as we stood on the glacis about thirty yards from the walls,' one officer recalled. Men dropped all around as Cameron's riflemen tried to answer the French fire. 'What a sight! The enemy crowding the ramparts, with the French soldiers standing on the parapets . . . a tremendous firing now opened on us and for a moment we were stationary.'

'I was in the act of throwing my bag when a ball went through the thick part of my thigh, and having my bugle in my left hand, it entered my left wrist and I dropped,' wrote William Green. 'When it entered my wrist, it was more like a six-pounder than a musket ball! It smashed the bone and cut the guides, and the blood was pouring from both wounds, I began to feel very faint.'

Sergeant Fairfoot heard Green's cries and asked him, 'Bill, are you wounded?' He gave Green his flask, which still held some rum, and bid him, 'Drink it, but I cannot assist to carry you out of the reach of shot.' Fairfoot knew the attack would instantly falter if they stopped to help the wounded.

Some men endured the first moments of this hail of fire lying flat, and as it slackened a little, the first ladders were tipped down into the ditch where some intrepid stormers, including Ned Costello, climbed onto them. Almost as soon as he was down, Costello was flattened by the body of another who'd been shot on the ladder behind him. The group in the ditch built to a few score. They were floundering about, discovering the water, several feet deep in places they had not expected, treading on rusty nails, flinching with the impact of splinters and mines that lacerated their flesh.

Many men were falling among the covering party and reserves gathered on the rampart, even though they had not been designated for the initial assault. Second Lieutenant James Gairdner fell on this slope, pierced in a breath by musket or canister balls in his right leg, left arm and through his chin.

Those in the ditch were looking about, confused, unable to gain their bearings or see the way ahead clearly. The Forlorn Hope commander, Lieutenant Harvest, was dead. Willie Johnston, the rope party commander, had fallen seriously wounded. It was down to the NCOs or anyone with a commanding manner to try to organise the men. Sergeant Fairfoot went forward and there was a sickening crack as the musket ball hit the peak of his cap, going through it into his left temple. He dropped like a felled tree. In this hellish chaos, just like at Rodrigo, some men assaulted the ravelin in error.

Seeing Private Mayberry had already taken several wounds, one of the officers told him to go back and find himself the dressing station. 'No going to the rear for me,' Mayberry shouted back, 'I'll restore myself to my comrades' opinion or make a finish of myself altogether.' He fell dead moments later.

Some time had passed, perhaps as much as forty minutes, before Major O'Hare and one or two other officers got enough men together in the ditch to place ladders against the correct walls and prosecute the final phase of the assault. O'Hare got onto one of the ladders and began to climb. A musket shot to the chest stopped him, and he dropped back to the ground. Costello went up the ladders too, only to get a blow from a musket butt or some such that sent him crashing down to the bottom again. Cooke of the 43rd tried his chances: 'Within a yard of the top, a blow deprived me of sensation and I fell. I recollect a soldier pulling me out of the water, where so many men had drowned.'

One solitary rifleman managed to get to the top of the ladders and was trying to get under the *chevaux de frises*, when several Frenchmen set about him: 'Another man of ours (resolved to win or die) thrust himself beneath the chained sword blades, and there suffered the enemy to dash his brains out with the ends of their muskets.'

Those who had fallen, winded or wounded, like Costello and Cooke, now lay among piles of bodies, beaten. 'I had lost all the frenzy of courage that had first possessed me and felt weak, my spirit prostrate,' wrote Costello.

Among the dead and wounded bodies around me, I endeavoured to screen myself from the enemy's shot. While I lay in this position, the fire continued to blaze over me in all its horrors, accompanied by screams, groans and shouts, the crashing of stones and the falling of timbers. For the first time in many years, I uttered something like a prayer.

Many of them, looking up at the flashes of musketry or grenades briefly lighting the dark walls and the devils who stood on top of them, recorded these grim sights and sounds as their last, as their blood pumped away into this filthy ditch and they drifted into their last sleep.

In that desperate battle of wills that was a storm, the defenders knew they were winning. 'French troops were standing upon the walls taunting and inviting our men to come up and try again,' wrote one British officer. The French called down in their broken English, 'Why don't you come into Badajoz?' They were not just savouring their triumph; it was also a way to persuade the British with any fight left in them to get up off the ground and show themselves, so they could pour another volley onto them.

At the rear of the division, down near the quarries, a handful of bandsmen were collecting the wounded and helping them back to a dressing station, where the surgeons laboured in a candlelit tent. Bugler Green peered in to find a terrifying scene of bones being sawed, discarded limbs and anguished screaming.

I stepped up to the doctor; he saw the blood trickling down my leg, and tore off a piece of my trousers to get at the wound, which left my leg and part of my thigh bare. He then made his finger and thumb meet in the hole the ball had made, and said, 'The ball is out, my lad!' He put in some lint and covered the wound with some strapping.

Two or three hours after the initial attack, successive waves were still moving forward. All sense of the original grouping of storming party, reserve, and so on had been lost now, and it was just a matter of some intrepid or indeed foolish officer putting himself at the head of whoever wanted to follow. These men dropped down into the ditch, where they found hundreds of dead or dying comrades:

In the awful charnel pit we were then traversing to reach the foot of the breach, the only sounds that disturbed the night were the moans of the dying with the occasional screech from others suffering under acute agony . . . it was a heart-rending moment to be obliged to leave such appeals unheeded.

Half a mile away, near the city's castle, men of the 3rd Division had moved up to the walls. They faced a forty-foot climb, as these were far higher than those of the more modern defences on the Light Division's side. Here too men of different regiments became mingled and confused as the defenders poured fire on them. One gentleman volunteer noted in a letter home:

The men were not so eager to go up the ladders as I expected them to be . . . I went up the ladder and half way up I called out 'Here is the 94th!' and was glad to see the men begin to mount. In a short time they were all up and formed on a road just over the wall.

Picton's attack was succeeding.

The small group of officers that marked the Light Division's makeshift HQ stood disconsolately near the outer defensive rampart. The slaughter had gone on a good four hours before they had broken off their attack. Just then, Major FitzRoy Somerset, Wellington's military secretary, popped out of the darkness and accosted Captain Harry Smith. Where was Colonel Barnard? Lord Wellington wanted the Light and 4th Divisions to resume their attack. 'The devil!' said Smith in reply. 'Why, we have had enough; we are all knocked to pieces.' Somerset was adamant: 'I dare say, but you must try again.' Smith smiled and replied, 'If we could not succeed with two whole fresh and unscathed Divisions, we are likely to make a poor show of it now. But we will try again with all our might.'

Before the order could be passed, a ripple of shouts began spreading through the British ranks – 'Blood and Wounds! the 3rd Division are in!' – and as the rumour strengthened, the French fire slackened, for the defenders knew their enemies were now behind them and it was time to *sauve qui peut*. Badajoz had fallen.

SEVENTEEN

The Disgrace

April 1812

Major Cameron walked slowly and deliberately up and down the ranks of riflemen. The four companies under his command had been formed up on top of Badajoz's defensive rampart once the French firing stopped. It was about 4 a.m., and the men could hear gunshots and women's screams occasionally rising above the constant moaning of the hundreds of wounded still lying just below them in the ditch. Cameron fixed them with his grey eyes; the flashes of gunfire and flames licking around buildings behind them occasionally lit up the Celtic pallor of his countenance. He knew they were itching to join the plunder. 'If any man leaves the ranks,' he shouted, 'I shall have him put to death on the spot.'

Down inside the town's streets, the cement that held discipline together in Wellington's Army was crumbling. Ned Costello, wounded, had dragged himself in once he heard the town had fallen. In the streets mobs of stormers mixed together, shooting locks open with their rifles and breaking into houses to see what they might find.

Some soldiers came running down the street, manhandling a French prisoner. Costello stopped them. The rifleman, caked with blood, powder and filth, stared into the Frenchman's eyes, snapped back the hammer on his weapon and levelled it at the prisoner's head. None of the other lads was going to stop him. The prisoner dropped to the ground, sobbing and pleading for mercy: 'The rifle dropped from my hand. I felt ashamed.'

The Frenchman joined his new-found saviour as he prowled about. 'We now looked around for a house where we could obtain refreshment and, if truth must be told, a little money, for wounded though I was, I had made up my mind to gain by our victory,' Costello later wrote.

A small gang, 'who by this time were tolerably drunk', broke into a prosperous-looking home to find the *patrone* quivering with fear. After threatening him, he revealed something up to 150 dollars which the men divided, and answered their demands for more drink. Costello and the others had found their spot for the night, but were soon obliged to defend it at the point of the bayonet against some Portuguese troops who tried to evict them. Eventually the prowling soldiers discovered their terrified host's greatest hidden treasure, his two young daughters and wife. Costello alluded later to the 'frightful scenes that followed'.

Two or three hours into the sack and the mob had consumed enough alcohol to be well and truly steaming. The rapes began, some women violated repeatedly to the point of insensibility. And there were Spanish inhabitants murdered when the soldiers thought they were not handing over their money, their booze or their women.

Elsewhere in the town, the stormers of the 94th stood in ranks, still in perfect order. 'I hear our soldiers in some instances behaved very ill – I only saw two and stopped them both,' George Hennell, the volunteer who had led them up the ladders, wrote home. Had the officers marched their men out of the city at that moment, as the sun's first rays broke into the dull Estremaduran sky over the San Miguel ridge, it is possible that all manner of catastrophes might have been averted. But the officers understood something very well: their men had laboured under shot and shell for two weeks and run the most terrible risks in the storm. A few kind mentions of the regiment in His Lordship's dispatch weren't worth a damn to them. They expected a reward. They had earned a reward. The officers commanding the 94th called out to their soldiers that they were free to fall out for two hours' plunder.

Over on the escarpment in front of the Santa Marta breach, four companies of the 95th were still standing under arms. No man had dared risk death by moving during the hours they had stayed there. Was Cameron determined to protect the regiment's good name at any cost? Or was he simply trying to ensure that the bravest men, those selected for the storming parties, got what they deserved: the right to a few hours' plunder on their own? Cameron looked at his watch. It was getting light. He called out to his soldiers: 'Now, my men, you may fall out and enjoy yourselves for the remainder of the day, but I expect to see you all in camp at the usual roll-call in the evening!'

During the daylight hours of 7 April thousands more troops flooded into Badajoz. In places, officers were knocked to the ground when they tried to stop the outrages. For the most part, though, they did not try. Some, among them Captain Harry Smith, attempted to rescue women from the mayhem. Smith emerged with two young ladies from one of the city's better families. One of them, Juana Dolores de Leon, was fourteen years old. The rescue changed Smith's life for ever. He later wrote:

Never was one so honoured and distinguished as I have been by the possession of this dear child (for she was little more than a child at this moment), one with a sense of honour no knight ever exceeded in the most romantic days of chivalry, an understanding superior to her years, a masculine mind with a force of character no consideration could turn from her own just sense of rectitude, and all encased in a frame of Nature's fairest and most delicate moulding, the figure of an angel, with an eye of light and an expression which then inspired me with a maddening love.

Juana remained under Smith's protection in the months after the siege and they eventually married.

Another young officer who went to gaze at Badajoz that afternoon came away only with bitter reflections: 'Every atom of furniture was broken and mattresses ripped open in search of treasure. One street was strewed with articles, knee deep. A convent was in flames and the poor nuns in dishabille, striving to burrow themselves into some place of security.'

Elsewhere some of the surviving Light Division officers were hurrying desperately to save the lives of their friends lying strewn across the area before the breaches where their men had struggled vainly for hours to break in to the fortress. Daylight had revealed several hundred bodies packing the area immediately in front of the two demolished bastions. Some of these men, drained of blood, were just clinging to life. Scavengers were already flitting amongst them, taking their boots or trousers, rifling pockets.

Lieutenant Colonel Barnard and several other officers went about, trying to find those with a beating heart and then organise their evacuation to the surgeons' tents. Quarter Master Surtees found his friend Lieutenant Cary with a bullet wound to the head,

stripped completely naked, save a flannel waistcoat which he bore next to his skin. I had him taken up and placed upon a shutter, (he still breathed a little, though was quite insensible) and carried him to the camp. A sergeant and some men, whom we had pressed to carry him, were so drunk that they let him fall from their shoulders, and his body fell with great force to the ground.

Cary did not survive his wound. Amazingly, Sergeant Fairfoot, who had a bullet lodged in his forehead, came through the surgery to extract it. He was taken to a makeshift hospital, as were young officers like James Gairdner and John FitzMaurice, who had also survived their wounds.

Among those dead in the breach was Peter O'Hare. He'd been stripped and his naked torso showed the holes made by several musket balls. When his personal effects were, by the usual custom, sold off to his brother officers, they amounted to a little over twenty pounds and five shillings. O'Hare's property at home was more substantial, some six hundred pounds' worth, which was duly passed on to his widow Mary and daughter Marianne. His rise in the Army had been remarkable for a man of such humble origins, but in the end it relied upon incessant campaigning, the very thing that finally did for him.

Captain Jeremiah Crampton of the 8th Company had joined O'Hare's storming party, just as he had put himself forward at Rodrigo, and was taken away on 7 April severely wounded. He would probably have preferred O'Hare's end at the foot of the breach, for poor Crampton was to suffer a lingering agony of several months in dark hospital quarters before succumbing to an infection.

In an army with so many brothers serving, it was inevitable that the breach would produce some heart-rending scenes. One Rifles officer was asked by a distraught Guards major to take a lock of hair from his dead brother who lay before them so that he might send it to their mother. Having kept himself composed in the heat of battle, this exhausted man was unable to contain his emotions any longer.

Lieutenant Maud Simmons, hearing of the carnage, came to search for his brother. It was quite common for false reports to fly about after a battle and Maud was distraught when one rifleman told him that his brother had been mortally wounded in the breach before expiring in his tent. Rushing to find the corpse, Maud discovered George lying on his blanket, deep in sleep. Such was his relief, that Maud slumped to the ground, sobbing. George took his brother in his arms and told him, 'My brave fellow, you ought to laugh. I am sound and untouched.'

George Hennell, the young volunteer, took a walk across the battle-field to the surgeons' tents. There they were working like possessed men to save life, while much of the Army carried on with the sack of the city. 'I have seen limbs amputated on the field, the dead lying in heaps like rats after a hunt, some thrown in a ditch,' Hennell wrote home. 'I have seen them afterwards putrid. This horrible scene I have contemplated over and over again.'

He went back towards the town, to see drunken soldiers emerging from the city to talk over their experiences and compare plunder, just feet away from their comrades in the breaches. Hennell was perplexed: 'The want of reflection in numbers of the men surprised me. They were singing and swearing and talking of having a damned narrow escape while their comrades lay around them in heaps dead.' Hennell's bewilderment at the lack of compassion among the soldiers was that of the ingénue, for it was his first time in action, just as Rodrigo had been Gairdner's. But veterans too had been shocked by the soldiers' behaviour after Badajoz. Quarter Master Surtees believed many of the riflemen had been brutalised by their three years of campaigning: 'They had . . . become quite reckless about life from so long an exposure to death.'

Hearing the commotion, Wellington had gone into the town himself on the afternoon of 7 April. Some drunken soldiers, seeing him, raised a glass, calling out, 'Old Boy! will you drink!' Returning to his bivouac, the general penned a furious General Order: 'It is now full time that the plunder of Badajoz should cease . . . the Commander of Forces has ordered the Provost Marshal into the town, and he has orders to execute any men he may find in the act of plunder, after he shall arrive there.' He ordered Brigadier Powers and his Portuguese in with fixed bayonets to reassert order. Major Cameron's hope that the 95th would return in time for the evening roll-call on 7 April had proved a pious one: 'in place of the usual tattoo report of all present, it was all absent'.

Some men quit the town that night – there was little left worth stealing in any case. They set about plundering the baggage of their own Army, a disciplinary nadir for the British in the Peninsula. Quarter Master Surtees awoke on the 8th to find that 'they stole no less than eight horses and mules belonging to my battalion, and took them to the other divisions, where they sold them as animals captured from the enemy. I lost on this occasion an excellent little mule, worth at least £20, and for which of course I never obtained a farthing.'

By that morning, Wellington was in a cold rage. Powers' Portuguese were joining the plunder instead of stopping it. It was time to start hanging the scum. 'The provost marshal erected a gallows, and proceeded to suspend a few of the delinquents, which very quickly cleared the town of the remainder,' wrote Kincaid. A further General Order was circulated to the Army, commanding that the muster rolls be read every hour as the marauders came in – for with each missed roll their crime of absence was compounded.

Those few officers of the 95th, like George Simmons, who had emerged from the proceedings without a scratch, now gathered some reliable NCOs and soldiers around them and proceeded to round up their companies. 'Coercion was necessary on many occasions (with men who had never behaved ill before) and obliged to be resorted to,' wrote Simmons. 'The men were made to throw away a quantity of things, and to prevent them secreting any of the articles, their packs were examined, and the plunder that had not been made away with was collected into heaps and burnt.'

Overall, the Light Division had 919 men killed or wounded in the storm of Badajoz, out of total Allied casualties that night of 3,713. The losses for the siege as a whole brought that to more than 4,600.

There was a good deal of anger among the surviving Light Division officers who felt that hundreds of lives had been thrown away on an ill-considered venture. They did not believe it humanly possible for men to have conquered the obstacles set in their way by the French. 'The defences on the tops of the breaches ought to have been cleared away by our batteries before the assault commenced,' according to one. They blamed Wellington and his engineers for the failure to think through their plan, or to order light guns to be wheeled forward with the stormers to blast the blades of the *chevaux de frises* out of the way.

For officers of the Rifles, the anger at the slaughter and the sorrow of loss soon turned to consideration of the vacancies that had opened as a result. Gairdner wrote from his sickbed to his father: 'I was before this last action sixth from the top of the Second Lieutenants, and there being seven vacancies by deaths I shall of course get my first lieutenancy.' Another officer put it even more crudely: 'This regimental havoc will give me promotion.'

There would be one more vacant lieutenancy arising in the regiment from the horrific night of 6 April. It belonged to Thomas Bell. Major Cameron discovered him skulking in his tent the day after the storm. James Gairdner told his father what happened:

One Thomas B— has been kicked out of the regiment for cowardice. On the evening of the sixth when the regiment fell in to march to the attack, this said gentleman, who was moments before skipping about very merrily, pretended to be very ill and he actually lay in his tent the whole night. The next morning Major Cameron, the commanding officer, sent word to him that he might either resign his commission or stand an inquiry into his conduct, he chose the former, and was I think let off a great deal too easily. Such pitiful scoundrels ought to be shot, and ought not to disgrace the army by entering it.

EIGHTEEN

The Salamanca Campaign

May–December 1812

The battalion that marched in stages back to the northern Portuguese frontier was a shadow of the one that had embarked three years before. Wellington was keen to have the men away from Badajoz as soon as possible, back into some sort of daily regimen. Major Cameron, who marched at the head of the column, was the man who would have to impose it on the 1st/95th. He and Captain McDearmid were the only two of the thirteen more senior officers who'd arrived in Portugal who were now left fit to march. There were four other captains lying wounded or sick and a couple more who'd got themselves staff jobs. But the leaders were simply not there to maintain the 1st/95th as an eight-company battalion.

There were huge gaps among the ranks too. Behind Cameron now marched 492 privates and NCOs, compared with the 1,093 who had come ashore in 1809. In many cases – several dozen – the men would be out of hospital and marched up the regiment as soon as their legs could carry them. Quite a few arrived in dribs and drabs at Ituero, the Spanish village where the battalion quartered during June. But down in Lisbon and elsewhere medical boards processed soldiers like Bugler Green and invalided them home as unfit for further service. Until Badajoz the number of 1st Battalion men who had departed the Peninsula in this way did not amount to more than four dozen, but by the late summer of 1812, taking in the human wrecks of that siege, the medical boards doubled the total of those sent home. Some would find their way into veteran, invalid or garrison battalions, others would be pensioned off on ninepence or a shilling a day.

For those who had survived Badajoz, the storm became a bloody, horrible watershed in their experience. Thereafter, men were divided according to whether or not they had been there. Had he somehow escaped Cameron's wrath, Lieutenant Bell could never have survived the veterans' taunts for his skulking. Badajoz became the yardstick when trying to describe the intensity of enemy fire. Such was the melancholy pall cast over the regiment after the siege that a couple of men committed suicide and quite a few fell into deep depression. For this reason there was a subtle and unmistakable change in the conduct of quite a few old sweats in the battalion. Having been to the gates of hell, and proven themselves in the most terrible situation, they wanted to survive to tell the tale.

Among the officers who disappeared after the siege to recover his health was Colonel Sidney Beckwith. He was destined never to return to the Peninsula. Having gained major general's rank, Beckwith was sent to America, an arduous service lacking any of the kudos of fighting the French. Wellington would no doubt have liked to keep him in the Peninsula, but he could not shield him indefinitely from the consequences of his promotion, Army rules dictating that a newly made general had to be available to command a brigade in any place the Horse Guards hierarchy dictated. Although Beckwith would retain a close interest in the welfare of his old corps and its men, his ability had carried him to a level where he could no longer lead them in battle. Following O'Hare's death, Cameron was the acting commanding officer. A mention in Wellington's Badajoz dispatch would mean brevet promotion to lieutenant colonel for him, and O'Hare's death a step in his substantive post to major.

Cameron was born and grew up in Lochaber on the west coast of Scotland, the eighth son in an important clan family. The Camerons had covered their bets during the 1745 Jacobite rising, serving both the Army and the Pretender. These days, though, perhaps by way of compensating for earlier deeds, their loyalty was intense, the Camerons having discovered that the monarchy was always grateful for the tough troops they could skim from their impoverished tenantry. Although of landed stock, Alexander Cameron had himself joined the regular Army as a volunteer, fighting with the 92nd Highlanders in Egypt. His relatives had kept too tight a grip on the family funds for him to advance himself by purchase and he had succeeded to the acting command of the battalion at what his promotion-hungry peers would have considered the ripe old age of thirty-four.

There was a dense web of Scottish patronage woven in the early nineteenth-century Army. Beckwith's predecessor as commanding officer, Sir William Stewart, had been a key figure in the formation of the 95th. He had promoted his officers in such a way as to ensure that the battalion that landed in 1809 had seven Scots among its dozen captains and majors. Stewart was a man of intense passions and strongly held views. He wanted tough recruits, and well knew that they could be found in the Highlands and across the Irish Sea. In the early days of the 95th, there had been intense recruiting among Scottish militia regiments and the poor peasantry. As a young subaltern during the early days of the regiment, Cameron was chosen to march a great party of Scots down from Lochaber. Stewart granted them the special privilege of forming the Highland Company, which paraded with bagpipes, whereas the nationalities mixed together in other parts of the regiment.

Later, during 1804–6, the 95th's officers looked more to Ireland for fresh men. Stewart believed they made excellent private soldiers, 'perhaps from being less spoiled and more hardy than British soldiers, better calculated for active light troops'. This generation of Hibernian recruits had, in their turn, been overtaken early in 1809 by a large number (like Fairfoot and Brotherwood) from English militia regiments. But the legacy of building the 95th on a bedrock of Scots remained: they were heavily represented among the more senior ranks, both commissioned and non-commissioned.

The Highland or 7th Company had survived Stewart's passing, and indeed the vicissitudes of the Peninsular campaign. It was still strong enough to take part in the coming march into Spain that everyone expected as they waited at Ituero. Now Cameron enlisted the help of his fellow Scot John Kincaid as adjutant, the lieutenant having served as acting commander of the Highland Company for several months before. The new adjutant was certainly grateful for this prestigious post, and there was evidently a high regard between the two men, for he later wrote of Cameron: 'As a *friend*, his heart was in the right place, and, as a *soldier*, his right place was at the head of a regiment in the face of the enemy. I never saw an officer feel more at home in such a situation, nor do I know any one who could fill it better.'

Cameron resolved that the battalion would have to dissolve two of its companies in order to keep the six that would remain in the field up to reasonable numbers. The axe would fall on the 3rd and 4th. Without doubt the 3rd, previously O'Hare's and Uniacke's, had been among the hardest fighting if not the toughest in the regiment. It had been at the centre of the Barba del Puerco action and in every important fight since. At Ciudad Rodrigo, four officers had messed together: Uniacke, Tom Smith (Harry's brother), FitzMaurice and Gairdner. Now Smith dined alone as acting commander of 3rd Company, Uniacke being dead and the other two subalterns casualties of Badajoz. One officer simply could not perform the duties previously given to four. The company's men would now be scattered about the remains of the battalion.

James Gairdner, newly promoted lieutenant, would go to the 2nd Company once he recovered his health, under that wild sportsman Jonathan Leach; Sergeant Fairfoot, rejoining after he recuperated from his head wound, to the 8th Company. Ned Costello, another 3rd Company veteran, also went to Leach's 2nd Company, where fellow stormer and regimental character Corporal William Brotherwood was also serving. Costello rejoined in mid-June, by which time the battalion was in motion again. Having taken Rodrigo and Badajoz, Wellington was striking into Spain, seeking to take the fight to the French.

McDearmid, the commander of the 4th Company, was sent home, in theory to recruit, as was Second Lieutenant Tommy Sarsfield. The one-time volunteer had not disgraced himself like Thomas Bell, but Cameron and Kincaid wanted rid of him in any case. The 95th had been so short of subalterns that it had commissioned Sarsfield – but everyone wanted rid of him. Kincaid damned him, saying his only mistake 'was in his choice of profession'. Colonel Beckwith wrote to Cameron that Sarsfield was 'not suited to our *specie of troop*'.

It was a matter of recruiting at home 'in theory', because the 9th and 10th Company cadres, posted back more than a year before, had performed poorly in providing the battalion with fresh drafts. Some eighty-eight men sent out from England during 1812 were to be the only replacements of this type during several years of campaigning. Bereft of a man of Stewart or Beckwith's rank and force of character directing matters in England, the junior officers presiding over the regimental depot achieved little. What's more, the effective collapse of four companies into a single depot one would help frustrate officers like George Simmons who had believed that the terrible risks they took would be rewarded by 'a company in five years'. The battalion's casualties meant three fewer captains' posts to aspire to.

In trying to make up its losses, the Army resorted at last to a desperate expedient that had been contemplated for some time: it recruited Spaniards from the border country. Initially there had been hopes of finding twelve men per company. The experiment was racked with difficulty from the start, only being attempted in some battalions (including the 95th) and then bedevilled with problems. Since many of the men whom the local authorities clapped hold of were more or less pressed into service against their will, and since local Spanish commanders claimed many of the choice specimens for their own regiments, a great many of these new recruits deserted the British service as soon as they could. It might also be surmised that it was a rare kind of *campesino* who could adapt to the brutal codes – both official and those self-imposed strictures of the soldiers' messes – that governed Wellington's Army. Lazarro Blanco, though, was to prove one of the survivors. He found himself in Leach's 2nd Company and soon impressed Costello both with his courage in the field and his facility for foul Spanish oaths. Blanco joined the others in the trials of the late summer of 1812.

That June and July was a period of intense marching for the Light Division. They struck out hundreds of miles into the open country of Castile and Leon, marching up through Salamanca, north-east to the River Duero. Having gone all the way there, they doubled back down towards Salamanca as Wellington sought to fight the French on the most advantageous terms, but failed to find them. This slogging was conducted across parched plains in baking midsummer heat. In order to achieve as much as possible before the sun was at its zenith, reveille was sounded earlier and earlier, with many 'nights' ending rudely with a blaring of bugles at 1 a.m. Throughout these movements the Light Division's prowess in marching and manoeuvre was noted by other regiments. An account of their routine by one of the 95th's company commanders is worth quoting at length both for its detail and its colour:

The march was commenced with precisely the same regularity as would be observed by a regiment or regiments moving into or out of a garrison town; the bands playing, the light infantry with arms sloped, and those of the riflemen slung over the shoulder, the exact wheeling distances of the sections preserved and perfect silence observed. After having proceeded a short distance in this manner, the word of command, 'March at Ease' was given by the general at the head of the leading battalion, and this was passed quickly on to the rear from company to company . . . the soldiers now carried their arms in the manner most convenient, – some slung them over their shoulders (most of them, indeed preferred this mode as the least fatiguing), others sloped them, and many trailed them, and they constantly changed from the right hand or right shoulder to the left. Whilst some lighted their black pipes, others sung or amused their comrades with stories and jests, as is usual on those occasions. Although allowed to prosecute their march in this easy and unrestrained manner, a heavy penalty, nevertheless, awaited the man who quitted the ranks without permission.

At the end of the march, the battalion would arrive in its bivoauc for the night:

The alarm post or place of general assembly having been pointed out to every one, the men were dismissed; the arms were piled, the cooking immediately commenced, and all further parades dispensed with for the day, except a roll-call about sunset.

During all of this wearing out of shoe leather, Wellington had been trying to bring his enemy, Marshal Auguste Marmont, to battle; he, meanwhile, wanted to turn the tables by exploiting the French Army's skill at manoeuvre. On 18 July, there was a sharp little skirmish at a place called Castrillo. This engagement did not figure greatly in the story of 1812, nor indeed did the 95th have much to do in it, but it is worth mentioning as it showed the vicissitudes of life on campaign.

The two armies had been marching in parallel across the open country when one of the French divisions turned onto the British line of march and attacked. The British had fallen back for miles across the countryside before Wellington prepared a stand and checked them. During this rush, Lieutenant George Simmons had been obliged to abandon a pack mule. He had begun his campaigns three years earlier on foot, largely to save money, but by July 1812 he had acquired both a riding animal and one for his baggage. The second had received a kick from a stallion, keeled over and died, and Simmons's servant had not had time to take off all its saddles. Simmons was only grateful that he had not been carrying the company pay-chest on his person, for he was liable for any losses under such circumstances. He had, in any case, lost skins containing a hundred pints of the local wine, sundry other baggage and the mule itself, all to the value of around a hundred dollars. This was pretty much exactly the sum – £20 in English money – that he had been hoping to remit to his father as one of his twice-yearly contributions to his siblings' education.

'All these misfortunes coming at once played the devil with me,' Simmons wrote home; but with the calm of a man who had come unscathed through Badajoz, 'I took up my pipe and thought to myself that things might have been worse . . . the life of a soldier is well calculated to make a man bear up against misfortunes.'

As the same engagement came to an end, the British cavalry charged some Frenchmen, driving them off. A trooper of the 14th Light Dragoons captured a French cavalier on his mount in this fight and, seeing the 95th, rode over, wishing to cash in his prize forthwith. He chanced upon Private Costello, his countryman from Queen's County, and greeted him cordially. Lieutenant Gairdner was standing nearby and was soon drawn into the conversation, as he was able to translate the Frenchman's plaintive cries. The French dragoon insisted that he would never have been captured if he'd been as well mounted as his Hibernian captor. The trooper turned to Gairdner and said, 'Than by Jasus Sir, tell him if he had the best horse in France, I would bring him prisoner if he stood to fight me.' The riflemen all had a good laugh at this Irish bravado. Then it was down to business. What would your Honour give me for his horse? Gairdner, knowing the trooper's time was short and the Army was going through one of its periods of short pay, struck an excellent bargain, buying the beast for five dollars, or little more than one pound. Pocketing his cash, the trooper started rooting through the Frenchman's valise, eventually drawing out a pair of cavalryman's strong trousers, which he threw to Costello, gratis. It was only fair to share one's good fortune. Gairdner had picked up a cheap packhorse and the Irish trooper galloped off with enough for several bottles of wine.

Simmons's loss, or indeed that of the French dragoon, happened in the same affair as Gairdner's or Costello's gain. It was all as arbitrary as the flight of bullets, or so it often seemed to them – this sense was summed up in the much-used phrase, 'the fortunes of war'. It was the way that soldiers rationalised the inexplicable workings of fate and their own powerlessness in the face of them.

The fortunes of war also decreed that the 1st/95th played almost no part in the events of 22 July 1812. Posted on Wellington's left flank, they observed a little light skirmishing around the middle of the day and were formed up to pursue the flying French as light faltered towards the end of it. In the intervening hours, the fate of Spain had been decided by Wellington's crushing defeat of Marmont on the battlefield of Salamanca. It was later celebrated as the defeat of forty thousand men in forty minutes, and while not exactly conforming to this propagandistic hyperbole, Wellington's battle marked his emergence as an offensive commander and one of the great captains of the age. 'Our division, very much to our annoyance, came in for a very slender portion of this day's glory,' wrote a grumpy Kincaid.

With this French defeat, the wrecks of Marmont's army streamed away from the frontier, pursued by the British, uncovering Madrid. After a march of a couple of hundred miles, Wellington's Army entered the Spanish capital on 12 August to scenes of hysterical rejoicing. When the British commander left at the end of the month to continue his pursuit of the French Army, the Light Division was among those that remained behind to guard Madrid.

Once in Madrid, the men of the 95th felt they had reached civilisation again. 'The public buildings are really splendid,' one Rifles officer wrote in his journal, 'no abominable dunghills in every direction, like Lisbon.' More importantly for most of them, there were the women: this interlude was first and foremost a chance to gaze upon well-dressed, cultured, beautiful women. At dances in Gallegos and Ituera a man made do with what was available. For those long starved of female company, the frumpy maidens, occasionally mustachioed, of the Spanish peasantry had sufficed and even proven the stuff of many a romantic fantasy, for a soldier quickly learns to make do under such circumstances. In Madrid, it was a different story entirely.

The *guapas* were best observed at about 7 p.m. strolling on the Calle Mayor or in the pleasure gardens near the Retiro:

It is here the stranger may examine, with advantage, the costume, style and gait of the Spanish ladies. Their dress is composed of a mantilla or veil, gracefully thrown back over the head; a long-waisted satin body; black silk petticoats fringed from the knee downwards; white silk stockings with open clocks; and kid shoes of white or black.

At public dances twice a week in the assembly rooms of the Calle de Baños and El Principe, they could actually hold hands with these beauties and quadrille or waltz with them. The officers' pleasure at taking in these sights and sounds was soon tempered by a sense of their own poverty. A fine meal could be had in Madrid, but it would cost you six shillings. The Army was desperately short of coin again and pay was six months in arrears.

The mortification of one well trained in dancing, like James Gairdner, can easily be imagined. He wrote in his journal, 'I have been very unwell, add to that I never had money for the army has never been worse paid than since we have been here, so that I have not had much pleasure to boast of having enjoyed the capital of Spain.' He sent to his family for some cash to rectify matters. Those who could not fall back on family help were reduced to all kinds of expedients. One captain of the 95th recorded, 'I sold some silver spoons and a watch to raise the wind.'

George Simmons, serious-minded and dedicated to his family as ever, managed in the few months after his losses of July to scrape together £22 6s 7d to send home. The money was first sent to a banking house in Lisbon who produced a bill which came back to Simmons. He then posted it home, his family cashing it with an English money dealer who, along with the issuing house in Lisbon, skimmed off his cut. Simmons, always ready to stand *in loco parentis*, had decided that his brother Joseph was at risk. Having come to the Peninsula as a volunteer in Maud's regiment, the 34th, Joseph had been commissioned into the 23rd Fusiliers, a fashionable corps in which a young boy from Beverley could fall in with all sorts of moneyed blades with extravagant habits. To add to George's concerns, Joseph had fallen ill and been placed in hospital in Salamanca.

Knowing that this would be the best way for Joseph to avoid mounting debts or the kind of disaster that had befallen Tommy Sarsfield, George Simmons arranged to have his younger brother transferred to the 95th. There he could instruct him, protect him from muttering his youthful opinions aloud, and indeed from that type of older officer who delighted in torturing young subalterns with their tricks. The mentor principle had worked very well for all brothers in the regiment: the Smiths, Coxes, Coanes and Travers among them.

Many officers also found themselves enjoying the largesse of those who could afford to give generous hospitality, like Lieutenant Samuel Hobkirk of the 43rd. He had an allowance of £700 a year but was rumoured to spend £1,000 on his uniforms and campaign comforts. Hobkirk threw a party in Madrid which provided many a comrade with a night's lavish entertainment. The 95th did not have a figure to compare with Hobkirk, in terms of spreading money about, but its most recently joined subaltern, Lord Charles Spencer, a callow youth of eighteen, was at least able to subsidise his mess.

The officers in Madrid also took to organising their own entertainments so that they might extend some hospitality to the youth and beauty of the city. Light Division theatricals had begun in the Torres Vedras winter of 1810. There had been further performances during the winter quarters of 1811–12. In Madrid, they were able to find a proper theatre to put on two plays: *The Revenge* and *The Mayor of Garrett*. These performances were acted by young, high-spirited officers such as Freer, Havelock, Hennell and Hobkirk of the 43rd (the last bankrolling the production, as might be expected) and the newly arrived Spencer and Gairdner of the 95th. Their Madrid efforts were a great success, netting such a large profit from the curious, paying Spanish public that the officers were able to donate $250 to the city's poor.

This happy interlude was destined to be short-lived. Wellington's push to the north-east had been checked at the fortress of Burgos. He had known that the Light and 4th Divisions could not be asked to storm again, after the recent horrors of Badajoz, and had therefore left them near Madrid. However, his attempts to take the citadel with other troops resulted in a number of costly rebuffs and he realised he would have to march all the way back to the Portuguese frontier in order to avoid defeat at the hands of the French armies now massing against him.

The British Army quit Madrid on 31 October, their departure arousing the ire and contempt of the *Madrileños*. Being left to their fate among the French dashed the hopes of many Spanish. Men shouted insults at the marching redcoats and the young women, so delightful at weekly dances, hissed accusations of cowardice and effeminacy. 'I was truly glad to get away from this unfortunate place,' one officer wrote in his journal. 'We could not do the people any good and pity is at best (under the circumstances) a sorry way of showing good wishes.'

Marching down towards the border, they went in long stages in order to stay ahead of the French; they were frequently drenched by chilly autumn downpours and generally grumbled at their reversal of fortunes. The talk after the order 'March at Ease' often took a darker tone on this journey, as one Light Division officer vividly described in a letter:

The conversation among the men is interspersed with the most horrid oaths declaring what they will do with the fellow they lay hands on. What they intend to get in plunder, hoping they will stand a chance that they may split two at once. Then someone more expert at low wit than his companions draws a ludicrous picture of a Frenchman with a bayonet stuck in him or something of the kind . . . as they grow tired they begin to swear at the country and the inhabitants. As they get more so, at soldiering and commissaries and when they are nearly exhausted there is little said except now and then a faint dispute about the distance &c. But when they arrive, if they can get wine, all their troubles are instantly forgotten and songs and hoarse laughs resound through the place.

As the marches continued into November, the supply of booze – that essential lubricant for Wellington's Army – began to break down, along with that of all other rations. The commissaries simply could not cope with the sudden reappearance of the main Army in the impoverished borderlands, for they had been buying much locally in more prosperous parts of Spain during the late campaigns. The hard marching had taken its toll in every sense. Lieutenant George Simmons, for example, had been obliged to put his sick brother Joseph on his pack mule and, having bought no new horse to replace the one lost in July, was himself walking. He had worn through the bottoms of his shoes, and as for many of his riflemen, each squelch into the mire brought his bare sole into contact with muddy road. By 16 November, matters were assuming a desperate aspect, Simmons noting in his journal: 'Most of us walking barefooted, my shoes having no bottoms, as well as my friends'; my legs and feet much frost-bitten; could hardly crawl.'

It was under these trying conditions that the Craufurd system proved itself once again: its Standing Orders provided a means of regulating the marches and determining what to do with men who couldn't keep up. For Wellington's Army had begun to disintegrate: the failure to issue rations had combined with the weather and long marches, meaning that around five thousand British and Portuguese soldiers, straggling behind the divisions, were listed as missing. The Light Division remained one of the least affected by this phenomenon, which in others saw one in six or one in seven soldiers going absent without leave. The French picked up about two thousand of these men, while others eventually returned to their colours.

The French were still there, nipping at their bloody heels. Even a British Army in what the soldiers of the previous generation would have called a 'flight forward' could not outstrip the advanced guard of a French Army, so practised were Napoleon's men in the business of marching, living off the land and pursuing an advantage.

On 17 November, the French caught up, falling upon the British rearguard (formed of course by the Light Division), as the Army made its way across the foaming waters of the Huebra at a place called San Munoz. Crossing a difficult obstacle like this river inevitably caused a blockage. 'The road was covered with carcasses of all descriptions, and at every deep slough we found horses, mules, donkeys and bullocks mingled together, some dead, others dying, all mingled with baggage,' wrote Simmons. Taking advantage of the exhaustion and congestion that morning, advanced French patrols of dragoons attacked the British waiting in the oak forests to cross the river.

The 95th's baggage train fell into French hands at one point, a company of Rifles attacking through the trees to drive off the plundering dragoons. General Sir Edward Paget, the Army's second in command, was captured during these chaotic events. The French forces arriving on the heights overlooking the Huebra and held by the Light Division began to build up to the critical point where a determined attack would be launched. Fortunately for the British, the crossing was continuing apace.

When the Rifles finally quit the heights and began marching down the slope leading to the ford, the French were able to give them a heavy fire of musketry and cannon. 'It is impossible to conceive of anything more regular than the march of the Light Division from the heights to the river and across it although the whole time under a heavy cannonade,' wrote Leach in his journal. 'No troops at a field day ever preserved their formation in better order.'

Their order might have been good, but they were suffering. Knowing that the enemy cavalry infested the woods, Cameron had no choice but to form the battalion in column for the crossing. This allowed the French gunners an unusual opportunity to make good practice on the 95th, in tight ranks instead of its usual skirmish order, 'which was fun for them but death to us'. Several soldiers were struck down by the shot as the column finally plunged, chest-high, into the icy waters.

Once across, the Light Division deployed with its usual alacrity. A French column was seen heading down to the left of the fords, clearly with the idea of trying to force a passage. Cameron sent the Highland and 1st Companies out to the water's edge as skirmishers to kill some of them, while the other four companies remained formed in line some way back from the bank, ready to charge with fixed swords any French who attempted an assault. Some companies of the 52nd joined in the skirmishing.

As the crackling fire continued, most of the British felt themselves safe for the first time that day. But George Simmons looked around. Where was his brother Joseph, whom he'd last seen on the other side, slumped across his mule? He asked others. Simmons realised he had been left behind. He hurled himself into the water and began sloshing his way up the enemy slope, bullets whistling around him, finally finding Joseph in one of the oak groves. He dodged the parties of French dragoons in the trees and hurried back to safety. The incessant downpour of recent days had resumed again now, and to add to their general misery, the light was failing too. Simmons wrapped his brother in his own cloak, fearing from his shivering and pallid countenance that he might not survive until morning.

Gathering themselves together in the dark woods overlooking their bank of the Huebra, the company messes faced a bleak night. The cavalry action of earlier that day had claimed many officers' baggage – James Gairdner, for example, had lost his pack horse and, with it, all his belongings except a boat cloak he had earlier confided to his captain, Jonathan Leach. The wheel of fortune had thus turned full circle: the beast bought at such a knockdown price not so far away in July had now been reclaimed by its former owners, the imperial cavalry. Gairdner fumed, accusing his servant of negligence in allowing it to happen.

Leach, Gairdner and Spencer tried kindling a fire but found it extremely difficult, for the wood was green and the downpour continuous. Someone nearby had slaughtered one of the draught animals, a bullock, and great slabs of bloody meat were soon parcelled out. But how to cook it? Each time they thought they had a blaze going, the wind shook the trees, showering them and extinguishing the flames.

'About midnight, in spite of the elements and green wood, my jolly subalterns and myself contrived to make a fire of some sort,' wrote Leach in his journal. 'We instantly began toasting on sharp pointed sticks pieces of the newly slain bullock. Swallowing the meat was out of the question but we continued grinding with our teeth this delicious morsel without salt or bread. We stretched ourselves on the ground in our cloaks wet to the skin as near as possible to this apology for a fire.'

The following morning, they awoke to the news that there would be no issue of provisions whatsoever that day. Those who wanted to have some breakfast could try cooking the acorns that lay about them in the embers of their fire. Charles Spencer, distraught at the prospect, burst into tears. The old sweats of Leach's company, far from having contempt for this sprig of the aristocracy, rushed to offer him morsels of their last biscuits. Leach himself settled for some grilled acorns washed down with a glass of rum.

With rumbling stomachs and bleeding feet they marched on that day, towards the familiar post of Ciudad Rodrigo. By that evening the quartermasters managed finally to bring some stale biscuits up to the regiment. The soldiers were desperate by this point, having gone seventy-two hours without any real food, and the officers, fearing a riot, posted 'sentries with fixed bayonets placed around the piles while commissaries and Quarter Masters of regiments divided the biscuit'. Each man got to fill his blackjack with a ration of rum, too, and this most basic meal 'soon appeared to set everything right again', according to Leach. Viewed from the ranks, the experience of the retreat had been a bitter one – the kind that rendered many soldiers miserable enough to resign themselves to death. Private Costello commented, 'Some men, from the privations they endured, wished to be shot, and exposed themselves in action for that purpose.'

The following day, the Light Division marched into the pasture that surrounded Ciudad Rodrigo. The Army's crisis, like the campaign of 1812, was over. Three days' ration of biscuit was issued to every man. Wellington's Army was about to enter its winter quarters yet again. It should have been a time of peaceful reflection, but for many officers of the 95th it was to be a winter of intrigue and bad feeling.

NINETEEN

The Regimental Mess

December 1812–May 1813

A banging of hammers, sawing of wood and hallooing of names filled the crisp air of Alemada. The little border village had become home once more to the 1st Battalion, 95th, and a barn had been commandeered as an officers' mess. For the first time since landing in 1809, these gentlemen would be dining together instead of in the twos, threes or fours of their respective company arrangements. Hands were clapped, that 1 December, on some riflemen carpenters, and two great brick chimneys were built in the improvised dining hall: 'Fire places of no small dimensions were made by our soldiers of the most uncouth and gigantic description, into which we heaped an abundance of ilex or Spanish oak.' Each company mess pooled its cutlery, pots and pans and great dining tables were knocked together too. 'Having ransacked the canteens of each company for knives, forks, spoons, &c., and purchased wine glasses and tumblers nearby, nothing was now wanting but a mess room and some good Douro wine.'

Settling down to a few months without constant marching and fighting would afford the officers a chance to get to know one another, for many serving in different wings of the battalion were on little more than nodding acquaintance and plenty of new men had arrived during the preceding campaign. Faces were windburned and uniforms tattered, leaving them looking 'a most ruffian-like class of fellows'. But the optimists among the company, like Leach, believed an atmosphere of brotherly companionship would soon be cemented by some communal singing around the supper table.

Lieutenant Gairdner, who had carried on happily enough in Leach's company mess, was not so sure. He would have preferred to keep out of Colonel Cameron's way. Several days before, near Rodrigo,

Gairdner had had an altercation with his colonel which showed how easily such proud gentlemen could fall out – and all over apparent trifles. Gairdner had just received a £27 bill from his family and was keen to go into town to cash it so that he might replace the personal belongings he had lost with the baggage at Munoz. It was a matter of some urgency, since he did not even have a razor or a spare shirt with which to maintain an officer-like appearance. Cameron, in Gairdner's words, 'after a great deal of needless and ungentlemanly blustering, gave me leave. I had not gone one hundred yards towards the town when the adjutant came and told me that it was the colonel's order that I should go on command with the sick.' The matter of who should take charge of the little parties of feverish stragglers, so that they did not commit robberies along the road, was one regulated by a strict rota, and Gairdner was quite sure that it was not his turn.

Gairdner remonstrated with Cameron that the honour belonged to Lieutenant MacNamara, but he could not refuse his colonel's order. Cameron told him: 'You may think it a hard case and may be it is, but if you think so, do the duty first and make your complaint afterwards.' The young lieutenant could not refuse a direct order and sloped off to find the sick party. Gairdner's feelings were deeply hurt and he fumed in his journal: 'I cursed the service in which a low-lifed brute can with impunity annoy an officer, even though he does not fail in one point of his duty, merely because he has a command. That Cameron dislikes me I know, but of his reasons for doing so I am perfectly ignorant.'

The following day, another young lieutenant was sent to take over the sick and tried to soothe Gairdner, telling him that Cameron had made an innocent mistake, not realising that he had called Gairdner out of his turn. But through glances or tone of voice the colonel and his aggrieved American lieutenant communicated their dislike for each other. The day before they marched into Alemada, Gairdner was 2nd Company's duty officer and he felt the commanding officer hovering about him throughout the march, noting in his journal, 'Col. Cameron . . . took every opportunity of finding fault with me and with the Company because I commanded it today – dirty low-lifed work!'

For a few days, Gairdner felt pleasantly surprised by the new arrangements in the officers' mess. When Captain Jeremiah Crampton died (of the injuries sustained at Badajoz), Gairdner had bought his rifle; he now joined Leach in various hunting expeditions on the Beira moorlands, some partridge and other luckless beasts falling into his bag. 'Between field sports by day and harmony and conviviality at night in our banditti-like mess house, we certainly do contrive not only to kill time but to make it pass very happily,' wrote Leach. Their conversation ranged from unhappiness with the angry General Order that Wellington had published on 28 November, venting his fury on the Army for its straggling, to sad regrets about having to leave new-found friends in Madrid. 'Up to this period Lord Wellington had been adored by the army,' according to Kincaid. However, 'as his censure, on this occasion, was not strictly confined to the guilty, it afforded a handle to disappointed persons, and excited a feeling against him, on the part of individuals which has probably never since been obliterated.'

There were other subjects too, relating to Britain's interests in the wider world. The officers were all aware of Napoleon's march into Russia and heartily wished every disaster possible on the Corsican upstart. The newspapers reaching them early in December seemed to answer these hopes. For some months these same papers had also charted a new and most curious conflict: one between Britain and the United States. Congress had declared war in June 1812, having become aggrieved at Britain's attempts to shut it out of European trade and to press its citizens as sailors. While the American armies had suffered some reverses, their small fleet managed to humble the Royal Navy in a number of frigate actions.

For James Gairdner, who had been born and raised in Georgia, this new war provoked some anxiety, not least because the reinforcement of the British Canadian garrison might require the dispatch of some riflemen. Gairdner's father would eventually write to him that he would have no option but resignation if the 95th received orders for America. Few in Britain felt much enthusiasm for this new war and in general those who tried to justify it belonged to a certain class of high Tory who supported the ministry right or wrong. These were the same sort of fellows who aped George III's horror at the idea of any Catholic emancipation in Ireland.

As the winter wore on, the initial mess conversation about leaving Madrid or Wellington's intemperate General Order gave way to a more sensitive kind of discussion, lubricated by many bottles of Douro, concerning the divisions within the English-speaking nation itself: between Englishman and American, Protestant and Catholic. Among these prickly, dangerous fellows, these were tricky subjects. Things were made all the more difficult by the fact that certain Scottish officers took the Tory part in these debates, doing so with the apparent backing of Colonel Cameron.

Lieutenant Willie Johnston, having returned from his Badajoz sick leave with his right arm shattered, became a leading light in these proceedings. According to John Kincaid, Johnston was 'the most ultra of all ultra-Tories . . . many of his warmest friends were Irish, but as a nation he held them cheap, and made no secret of his opinions'. Kincaid's prejudices had shown themselves too, for example in his treatment of Sarsfield, whom he described as having 'the usual sinister cast of the eye worn by common Irish country countenances'. In an attempt to pacify the Irish and buy off those who might otherwise be tempted to repeat the rising of 1798, the ministry scattered patronage liberally about the island. Commissions in the Army were part of this effort, and evidently the Sarsfields of this world were considered by some to be far too vulgar to act the part of gentleman, rightful holder of the King's Commission. The Scots, by contrast, had atoned for their own 1745 rebellion with such zealous military service to George III that many officers from north of the Tweed considered themselves to be loyalists par excellence. Had an O'Hare or a Uniacke overheard the Irish disparaged by Johnston or Kincaid, there is no telling what the result might have been, but they were both dead, and MacDiarmid, the other Irish captain in the battalion, had been packed off home that summer with Sarsfield.

Just before Christmas, Johnston was appointed to the captaincy left vacant by Crampton's death. There was nothing outrageous in this, for Johnston was high on the seniority list of lieutenants and had shown himself as brave as any man, having volunteered for both Rodrigo and Badajoz. Along with Kincaid's nomination to the adjutancy, however, this decision served to convince certain observers that Cameron conformed to Dr Johnson's stereotype of the Scot, as one who would advance his people ahead of others. This left lasting rancour, John FitzMaurice's son noting years later that his father's 'prejudice against the Scots was caused by what he considered the injustice of a Scotch colonel . . . who never lost an opportunity of favouring his own countrymen at the expense of English and Irish officers'.

It was just as well for the regiment that FitzMaurice remained on sick leave until early 1813, for he was the type who might easily have called out some Scot who gave a little too freely of his views about the

Irish and their base qualities. But he was not there, for most of the winter at least, and any young Irish subaltern who considered settling matters with a Johnston or a Kincaid would have had to consider his position very carefully. To get away with duelling, one needed a powerful patron, just as Beckwith had saved Jonathan Layton from the consequences of killing Captain Grant in 1808. But a captain called out by a subaltern might, in the words of another Rifles officer, 'take advantage of his superior rank, not only to decline giving me that satisfaction, but report me, thus destroying my prospects for life'.

Gairdner thus felt himself oppressed and alone, resorting to writing his misery in code – to stop others reading it – in his journal: 'Although the regimental mess has been the means of our living much better than we could have done by companies, I am sorry to observe that the conduct of our Commandant and a few of his adherents is tending to establish *parties* and foment discord in the battalion.' He tried to steer clear of his enemies, spending hours striding across the moors, joining in hunting trips and finding a quiet corner to write poetry.

From the middle of December, Captain Leach was among those channelling their energies into some more constructive direction. The performances in Madrid had whetted the appetites of many for theatricals, but had also established a standard of production that would be rather hard to match for men who now scurried about a blasted moorland, living in hovels. Leach jotted in his journal, 'We are now busily employed in considering where we shall find a building that may answer for a theatre . . . dresses and scenery will be rather a puzzler.' Frequent gatherings were convened either in the 95th's quarters or those of the 43rd, who were their partners in the venture. Eventually, an old chapel in the Spanish village of Gallegos was found, the mayor giving his permission for its conversion into a theatre. Soldier carpenters were pressed into action once more, casting began, and there was much copying out by hand of lines from *The Rivals*.

There was no question of getting locals to play the female parts, which instead went to wan subalterns, one Rifle officer commenting, 'Lieutenant Gore and Lord Charles Spencer who are both good looking, very young and by no means badly dressed might have passed for fine handsome women.' Assuming his familiar role as banker, the fabulously rich Samuel Hobkirk of the 43rd snapped up the plum part of Mrs Malaprop. His military career was also being advanced by cash that December with the purchase of a captaincy.

When *The Rivals* was finally staged, Wellington and his senior staff were counted among the audience:

At one very nervous period of the play where a certain worthy amongst the actors had forgotten his part, and everyone felt awkward about it, the Marquis of Wellington rose up and began clapping his hands and crying Bravo! This not only restored instant confidence but the part was recollected and the play went off much to the satisfaction of all parties.

Jonathan Leach looked across the theatre admiringly at his chief. Of course, he had seen the general in action many times in the field and knew him to be a skilful commander. There had been much debate about the peer's qualities and limitations following his angry General Order in November, but whatever rancour Leach might have felt a few weeks before, gazing upon his hero in the half-light of Gallegos's little auditorium, he forgave him:

This is the right sort of man to be at the head of an Army. Whether in the field near the enemy or in winter quarters during the temporary inactivity of his Army he is all alive and up to anything. He gives no trouble to us whatever and knows perfectly well that the more the officers and soldiers enjoy themselves during winter, the more heartily will they embark in the operations of the forthcoming campaign.

With theatrical preparations continuing into the Christmas season, there was much riding about the uplands to receive hospitality at the messes of other Light Division regiments. On 25 December, the Rifles were hosts, staging a cockfight for the amusement of their brother officers. Major General Karl von Alten, who had been in command of the Light Division since the summer, also invited various officers to enjoy his food and wine. 'He is equally delightful at the festive board as at the head of his Division in the field. I spent several very pleasant evenings at his table,' wrote one captain. Alten was an officer of the Hanoverian service which, maintaining its close historic connection with George III, had furnished his army with brigades of German Legion troops and many fine officers.

The new commander of the Light Division was the kind of man who was punctilious about the regulation of outposts, usually at the hottest part of the action, and easy in his manners. In short, he was professional without being overly gifted or assuming any airs and graces. This suited Wellington perfectly, for he liked to keep his hand closely upon his troops but had been obliged to tread carefully with his light regiments in Craufurd's time. Alten, if anything, was a little too timid in defence of his prerogative, for during November's Huebra engagement, Major General Erskine (in command of a cavalry brigade) had at one point tried to give orders to the 95th to cover his withdrawal. Alten's attempts to assert his authority were rather weak, and it took the arrival of Wellington in person to countermand Erskine's order. This, though, was a failing that his Lordship could live with more easily than Craufurd's overweening pride. In future, Wellington was to take a closer personal role in commanding his advanced guard.

That winter, the riflemen saw quite a bit of their Commander of Forces, since his headquarters was just a few miles away in Frenada. Every couple of days, Wellington hunted across the moorland. A blaring of horns and barking of hounds signalled the arrival of his party, consisting usually of the finely mounted sons of the aristocracy on his staff.

A sportsman like Leach would have liked nothing more than to join in such fun, but he did not have the money. 'Lord Wellington's fox hounds often met within reach of our cantonments, but such was the miserable state of our horses that the staff-men only could avail themselves of it,' he wrote. The Rifle officers would look at their bony nags and call them Rosinantes. A fellow on the staff was expected to keep two or three horses to ride on, because he was about delivering orders day and night, and he therefore received extra allowances for forage. In truth, though, it was not simply a matter of a few shillings' stipend here or there, since the young bloods would think nothing of spending a lieutenant's annual pay on a horse and its upkeep.

Even the slowest-witted Rifles officers, seeing their well-bred comrades disappear to the staff, had concluded that such a post offered a far better opportunity for advancement than fighting with the 95th. George Simmons was wise enough to have grasped this early on, and his parents, learning these facts of military life from his letters, had begun their own efforts to help. Being straightforward Yorkshire folk, and bereft of any great interest, they had begun their campaign with the local Member of Parliament. George wrote back to them, touched by their efforts but clearly considering the case hopeless: 'I am too well hackneyed in the ways of the world to for a moment imagine that a Member of Parliament would give me anything, or, in other words, ask for a company for a perfect stranger who had not given him the least assistance.' Simmons's father had evidently seen Harry Smith's rise as a pattern for his own son, but George had to disabuse him that he could even aspire to such a thing: 'You make me laugh with the idea of an aide-de-camp being the high road to a Brigade-major's situation. Aides-de-camp are generally chosen by general officers through relationship or family connections or friends. My ideas of the world since I became a soldier are quite changed.'

Simmons was perfectly right, for he predicted Lord Charles Spencer's departure from the regiment several months in advance. That officer exploited a family connection to get onto Major General Sir William Stewart's staff, after serving around a year with the 95th.

The technique of using the dashing and dangerous 95th as a stepping stone into a somewhat safer and better-remunerated staff job was sufficiently well known to those officers without connections to generate some resentment. It was generally felt that one year's regimental service was the bare minimum, Leach noting:

If there is one school worse than another for a youngster, on his first obtaining a commission, it is that of being placed, *instanter*, on the staff as an aide-de-camp, before he has done duty with his regiment for a year or two. If a sprig of aristocracy assumes any airs with his regimental companions, he pretty quickly learns a useful lesson – and finds *that* system will not do.

Cameron, always comfortable in the role of curmudgeon, felt strongly that young subalterns needed whipping into shape – indeed, this may have been the sole basis of his antipathy to Gairdner. During the final weeks of 1812, Cameron tried to obtain the recall of Second Lieutenant Thomas Mitchell, whose regimental career had lasted a bare three months in 1811 before secondment to the Quarter Master General's staff. Mitchell, ironically, was a young man who had come into the Army almost bereft of interest, volunteering like Cameron himself had done long before. This, though, brought no sympathy whatsoever and Cameron had written angrily to Headquarters: '2nd Lieut Mitchell being a young officer and entirely unacquainted with his duty as a Regimental Officer, I have to beg that his Excellency the Commander of the Forces will be pleased to order him to join his Regt forthwith, being deficient in subaltern officers.' In order to ram home his point, Cameron recalled Mitchell's servant, a private rifleman, to the regiment.

Mitchell, however, had proven himself an exquisite map-maker and the staff needed his services. Cameron soon found he had bitten off more than he could chew. The Quarter Master General himself wrote to Wellington that Cameron's actions in castigating Mitchell and recalling his servant 'appeared to me such a measure of harshness and irregularity that I wrote to M General Alten intending to lay the whole matter before the Commander of the Forces'. Little could the commanding officer of the 1st/95th have imagined that in trying to exercise his rights over a penniless pipsqueak barely in his twenties, he would end up having to explain himself to General Alten and Lord Wellington. Cameron stood his ground, though, falling back, as military pedants were apt to do, on regulations, insisting that Second Lieutenants were too junior to be attached to the staff. Mitchell sheepishly returned, doubtless further improving the brittle dinner-table atmosphere in Alemada. The matter did not rest there: a new QMG arrived, someone in whom Wellington had complete trust, and a few weeks after he had appeared in his regiment, Mitchell packed his bags once more and rode back to Frenada.

In a number of small ways, then, Cameron's character and the limitations of his command became known to those in charge of the Army. All of this must have been extremely vexing for him, since he was a man who believed in solving problems, as far as he was able, inside the regimental family. For example, when Private George Stratton was caught by Don Julian's guerrillas trying to make his way to the French lines, having robbed some of his comrades, Cameron resolved to deal with the matter himself. The battalion was marched out to witness the punishment of four hundred lashes, and Cameron told him: 'I ought to have had you tried by General Court Martial – in which case you should have been shot – but the high character the regiment has borne in the army prevents me from having it mentioned in General Orders that a man of the Rifles could be guilty of the heinous crime of desertion.' The case of Almond and the others one year before appears to have taught the officers that execution would not operate in the deterrent manner that Wellington had hoped and that it was best to resolve these matters in ways that would not make it into the newspapers at home.

Cameron, for all his clumsiness in dealing with brother officers, understood the soldier's mentality well, and told the assembled regiment, 'If his own company shall be answerable for his good behaviour, I shall forgive him.' Nobody spoke up for Stratton. The soldiers were happy enough as the buglers started laying on the lash. After all, someone who stole from his messmates ranked second only to a skulker in their book of villains. After sixty or seventy strokes, though, one of the men did call out, a private called Robinson whom Cameron said was as bad as Stratton. Reluctantly, the colonel halted the punishment.

Stratton's desertion was almost a singular event that winter. The Spanish drafted in to the 95th earlier that year, on the other hand, proved rather more prone to it. The Spanish experiment was tried in several of Wellington's regiments, the 1st/95th's quota being forty-six men. Most of these deserted during the last few months of 1812, the battalion's monthly return for 25th November containing a rather tart annotation next to the figure of nine for soldiers who deserted: 'Only one is a native of Great Britain.'

For the most part, it was not a winter to rival the previous one for privations. The men had been given arrears of pay shortly after going into winter quarters, enabling them to buy drink, tobacco and some other comforts. There was a better supply system in place too, bringing up each man's daily pound of beef with biscuit and rum to boot.

Wellington was keen for his Army to be re-equipped during this winter, for its clothes had fallen apart during 1812's tough fights and marches. The 95th's quartermaster was able to buy some dark-green cloth in Lisbon, which tailors ran up into new trousers and jackets for those needing them. 'Green having become the least conspicuous colour in the regiment,' wrote Costello, 'it was amusing to see our fellows strutting about as proud as peacocks among the Spanish peasant girls.'

The soldiers also had their dances and assemblies. This was their fourth winter away from home, and during the long stay in Alemada some became smitten with local girls. Many might have thought it wiser not to have a woman trailing around with the regimental baggage, but they had been through such horrors in their campaigns that they wanted to live for the moment. A few dozen men in the 95th took Spanish or Portuguese wives, although these unions were rarely consecrated in church, for the men were mostly heretics in local eyes. But enough impoverished families were sufficiently content to see their daughters fall in with a British soldier, who would take some sort of financial care of them, that these arrangements did not cause scandal. Some of these women would march with the regiment, playing the sort of roles – washing, mending and peddling drink or smoking fodder – that regimental wives embarked on service might have done, before Beckwith banned them in May 1809.

In all the boozing, smoking and easy living of those months, the Light Division lost some of its fighting edge. One officer of the 95th wrote to a friend in London, 'We have acted some plays . . . with various success, we have got drunk with constant success.'

Early in 1813, with the prospect of a further campaign against the French in the offing, General Alten began a programme of marches, firing practice and field days designed to bring his division back up to scratch. Matters were made more difficult for him by the replacement of Lieutenant Colonel Andrew Barnard in command of the 1st Brigade by Major General James Kempt. The 2nd Brigade remained for the time being under General John Vandeleur, who had proven a tough and effective officer, earning the affectionate nickname Old Vans from his men.

Barnard had enjoyed nearly a year in acting command of the 1st Brigade (and indeed of the whole Light Division at Badajoz), a mark of the faith Lord Wellington placed in him. Eventually, though, those who ran the Army at Horse Guards insisted on a general holding substantive rank taking over the command. Barnard took the setback philosophically, and began plotting how he might make his promotion to full colonel permanent. He devoured political news and pleaded in his letters home for more papers and caricatures to help pass the hours in his billets. In the meantime, he knew he was about to return to regimental soldiering, taking over command of the 1st Battalion of Rifles just before the start of the new campaign. Cameron would be pushed aside as acting commanding officer, just as Barnard himself had been displaced from the next rung up the military ladder by Kempt's arrival.

Barnard had not yet taken over when the long winter lay-off and changes in command made themselves felt on 8 April, as the 1st Brigade was put through its paces. 'We had a brigade field day this day on the plain between this and Espeja, the movements were done very badly indeed,' one officer of the 95th wrote.

With its mixture of men hardened almost to the point of villainy with others who had campaigned too much, the battalion would not be easy to command in the forthcoming campaign. In his last weeks as commanding officer, Cameron took an opportunity to pack off several older men in the battalion who were simply too broken down to keep up with another season's tough marching. Ten were sent away early in 1813, most to the 13th Royal Veteran Battalion, where they could at least still live with some dignity, wearing a red coat and having all the essentials of life found for them. Had the supply of fresh recruits been better, there can be little doubt that the expedient of invaliding men home in this way would have been used much more widely, for those unable to keep up with a regiment were frequently the source of all sorts of difficulties.

Some tough weeks of training lay ahead for everyone. George Simmons broke off a message to his parents on 30 April with the words: 'I must end my letter, as the company are already mustering at my door for target practice. I shall pass the remainder of the day in proving the abilities of my men in hitting a mark in order to do justice to our enemies when we meet with them.' When the brigade held another field day on 8 May, its performance was much improved. There was still time for some further preparation before Lord Wellington reviewed the Light Division on 17 May.

Around the 95th's dinner table, a lively conversation about the next campaign followed the end of each day's training. They knew from the English newspapers that Napoleon, having suffered a complete disaster in Russia, which of course delighted them, was preparing to fight in Germany. The wiser ones anticipated some weakening of the French Army in Spain in order to succour the Emperor in the north. However, each report of a movement by some French division across the frontier was considered highly unreliable. Officers would offer up the latest theory with an '*on dit*' or 'it is said' in order to distance themselves somewhat from it: '*on dit* a corps of fifty thousand Russian auxiliaries is daily expected to disembark at Lisbon'. Percolating absurd reports and obvious ones down to their essence, one captain wrote to England, 'Rumour says that we are about to retrace our steps and that we shall not stop until we have driven the French out of Spain . . . however I am totally in the dark upon the points which enable us beings of an inferior description to form any opinion at all.'

They did know one thing, though, and that was that the long winter's repose would soon be over. Every soldier or officer, appreciating the comforts he would require on the marches ahead, set about finding them. 'We now only require that the canteens of each Company's mess should be well supplied before we begin the campaign with tea and sugar, a pigskin full of wine – a keg of spirits – lots of segars – and some spare horse shoes and nails to be carried with us in case of losing a shoe on the march,' wrote Leach.

The division which assembled for Wellington that 17 May had been

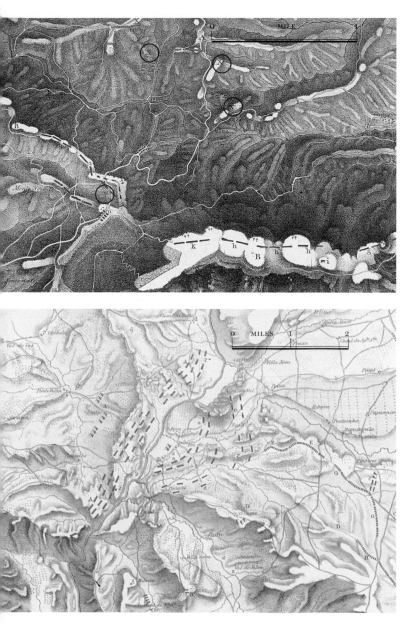

Top: Busaco. Units of Ney's 6th *corps d'armée* are marked 'X'; the Light Division, near
[a]la, is 'm'; and Pack's (Portuguese) Brigade 'k'. *Bottom*: Foz d'Arouce, the most success-
[fu]l of the Light Division's combats against Ney's rearguard leaving Portugal. The initial
[Li]ght Division march is marked 'D' and its attack 'd'.

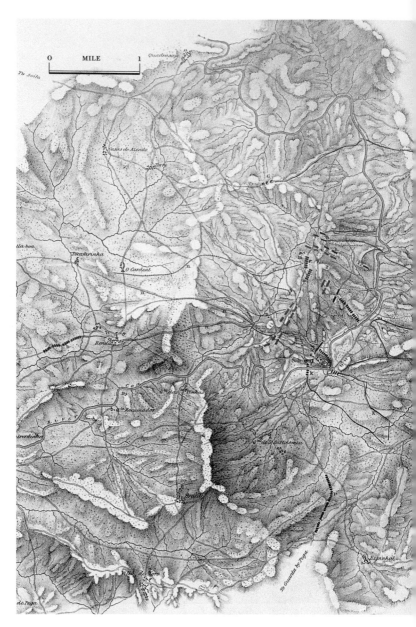

9 Sabugal. The Light Division's attack formations are marked 'h', upper right. The 3rd and 5th Division attacks, 'i' and 'k' respectively, were elements of Wellington's plan that went into effect far later than planned, leaving the Light Division dangerously exposed.

Above: a fine view of Ciudad Rodrigo just after the siege, done in watercolour by
Lieutenant Thomas Mitchell of the 95th. Two brother officers stand in the foreground; the
right-hand breach in the walls was assaulted by the 3rd Division and the left by the Light
Division. *Bottom*: the Great Breach at Badajoz, painted by Atkinson who, unlike Mitchell,
was not present.

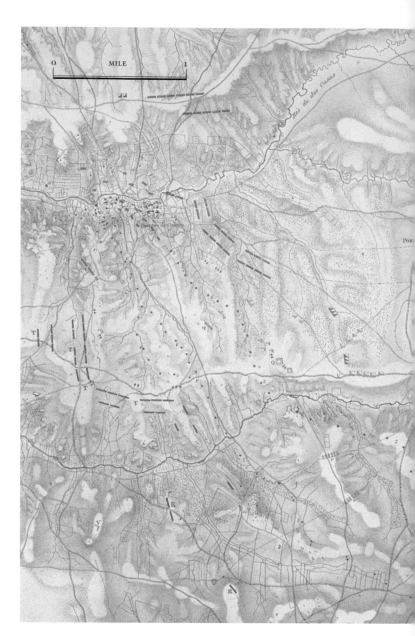

11 Mitchell's view of Fuentes d'Onoro. 'Q' shows the Light Division covering the withdrawal of the 7th Division, which took up new positions at 'R'. Once Wellington had pulled back his right flank, the 1st and Light Divisions occupied positions at 'T'. It was from there that Guards and 95th skirmishers went into the Turon valley.

, Vitoria. The Light Division's attacks are marked 'D', Barnard's Brigade being the left-
nd one which found its way around the hairpin bend in the Zadorra river. Wellington's
and design can be seen with the arrival of the flanking columns, 'F' (3rd and 7th
visions). The main French defensive line, 'B', was pushed pack as the British broke their
ntre at Arinez.

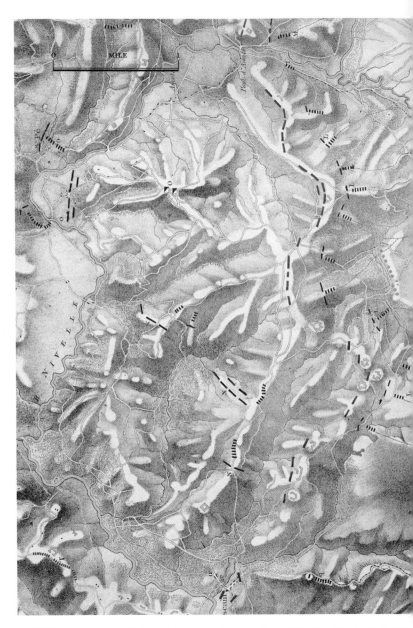

13 Wellington breaches the French Pyrenean defensive line at Nivelle with attacks by the 3rd, 4th, 7th and Light Divisions, marked 'L'. They fought through their initial objective to positions marked 'N'.

Top: a later portrayal by Simkin of the 95th fighting in the Pyrenees. Already, a certain
mythologising of events shows through, for example with the pristine uniforms. *Bottom*:
the Battle of the Nive, showing Arcangues and Bassussary, scene of several Light Division
fights in November and December 1813.

15 *Top: Morning at Waterloo* by Aylward: Kincaid, Simmons and Barnard were probably all witnesses to this scene as riflemen offered a morning brew to the passing Wellington. *Bottom*: the fierce fighting in La Haye Sainte involved mostly riflemen of the King's German Legion but also, just behind the wall pictured here, Leach's companies of the 1st/95th.

made up to more than 5,400 men by drafts and the acquisition of a further Portuguese regiment. In battle, the general dressed informally, but
when reviewing his troops he adopted his red coat, riband of the Bath
and numerous other decorations. His staff, following behind, were
equally splendidly attired. As the general rode down lines of troops he
knew that the Light Division was composed largely of the veterans of
four or five campaigns. This spectacle, accompanied by the music of
the division's bands, was reserved only for its participants. One officer
of the 43rd wrote home, 'Such a review in England would have been
attended by crowds and here, tho' in great measure their prosperity
depends upon it and there are several towns within 2 or 3 miles, not a
single Spaniard or Portuguese came as a spectator.' There was indeed a
vital Spanish stake in what was going on, for within days, Wellington
would fling the Light Division and the rest of his army at the French
with the aim of finally breaking their hold over Iberia.

Andrew Barnard had taken over as the commander of the 1st/95th.
He was thirsting for the step to colonel, but this fact, far from distract-
ing him from the command of the battalion, made him bring to it a
drive and energy that had been conspicuously lacking under Cameron.
Barnard also did his best to restore harmony, dispensing, for example,
with Kincaid's services as adjudant. The new commanding officer was
searching for any opportunity to demonstrate his skills, an impulse
that would launch the Rifles into their last great adventure of the
Peninsular War.

TWENTY

Vitoria

May–June 1813

The scene which greeted the marchers on 23 May 1813 was familiar enough. It was the same bit of godforsaken ridge overlooking the Huebra where they had reached their lowest ebb in the driving rain the previous November. It was very different now, though. The sun was shining and every man's countenance had that well-fed look. 'We encamped today in a most heavenly May morning with a very luxuriant vegetation all around on the very identical spot where the Light Division passed the dreary dismal night of 17th November last,' wrote one officer.

Many of the riflemen felt glad to be campaigning again. There would be privations of course, but the months on the Beira frontier had dragged terribly. They did not see the point in sitting about while the job of kicking Johnny François out of Spain remained to be done. They trusted their luck in battle and hoped that the coming campaign would deliver plenty of plunder as well as some hard fighting.

The Light Division made its way down the slope to the Huebra ford, a long snake of marching men that stretched for a mile. At the rear were dozens of mules and other pack animals, the Portuguese boys who looked after the officers' personal beasts of burden, and the 'wives' who had been acquired that winter. Riding at the head of the 43rd, Lieutenant Colonel William Napier, refreshed by a leave in London, found it hard to believe that the campaign of 1813 would see the French thrown out of Spain. They had already been trying for years and there were plenty of naysayers in England who felt that Wellington had been too cautious a general. Napier turned to one of his friends in the 95th and said, 'Well, here we go again. We shall go so far and then have our arses kicked and come back again.'

Wellington's successes had been such, though, that the ministry had poured additional troops into his army. The war band marching forward that May consisted of 81,000 troops, over 52,000 of whom were British, the remainder Portuguese.

Once this force was striking out to the north-east, heading for the French defensive line on the Duero, the Rifles were able to catch sight of the various battalions who were old campaigners and those who were the Johnny Newcomes. The 95th had become soldiers for whom personal appearance or regulation dress counted far less than prowess in combat. They were very struck, therefore, to see the two smart brigades of cavalry sent out to Wellington shortly before the campaign: one of hussars, three fine regiments of more than five hundred sabres each, the men resplendent in their pelisses and tall hats; the other new brigade of heavy Household Cavalry. The hussars had not seen any action since early 1809, when they had covered the retreat to Corunna skilfully. As for the Blues and Life Guards of the Household Cavalry, they had not campaigned for fifteen years. The contempt of the old sweats for these parade-ground soldiers showed itself in Leach's private journal:

We cannot allow these gentry who have during the last five years been luxuriating in London to come under the head of 'old Peninsular soldiers' nor can we either consider the Dandy Hussar Regiments just arrived from campaigning at Brighton, Hampton Court, Weymouth and those places ever since the month of *January 1809* (a period of four years and four months) to be entitled 'old Peninsular men'. I dare venture nevertheless to prognosticate that any of us who may be so fated as to live to revisit England and to see the termination of this protracted war in the Peninsula [will] *hear* these gentry newly arrived talk louder and with greater self-sufficiency than the troops who have been through the whole business.

The Army moved ahead in three great columns, forcing back the French in a great movement across the north of Spain towards the Ebro and the Pyrenean frontier. Three times the French, trying desperately to regroup their forces, attempted to block the British on a river line in their path, but three times the right of the French line was turned by Wellington, sending his men through inhospitable mountain country which many had thought impracticable for an advance. During one of these outflanking movements the hussars distinguished themselves in a combat with the enemy rearguard and this was enough to silence most of the Light Bobs. As for the Household regiments, they continued to excite the contempt and, it must be said, the envy of the veterans, if for no other reason than because of the absurdly well-fed appearance of their huge mounts, the average Rifles officer having become used to his $40 nag with its scrawny neck and sagging back.

On 7 June, in Palencia, matters reached the point of open abuse. Here, the Household Cavalry enjoyed the acclamations and cheering of the liberated populace so much that they held up the rest of the Army. 'The Household Troops', wrote George Hennell of the 43rd, 'paraded the streets such as they did Piccadilly for they went up one, down another, up again, so whether it was a mistake or not I do not know, but this I know, they kept our baggage an hour in the streets and we were waiting for breakfast all the time very impatiently.'

The Army of 1813 was very different to that of 1809. It was not just that the *soi-disant* elite had finally deigned to join the fray, but the doctrines of using light troops and riflemen extensively for every type of demanding task had gained supremacy. When Craufurd disembarked his brigade four years before, his reinforcement meant the Army had two battalions of riflemen (the 1st of the 95th as well as the 5th/60th) and two of light infantry. The reinforcements sought by Wellington over the years meant that in May 1813, it had three battalions of 95th, three of foreign riflemen, six battalions of light infantry, and eleven of Portuguese *Cacadores* (most of whom carried rifles). Although Wellington remained a military conservative in many respects, his experience in command of the 95th since the Baltic expedition of 1807 and Portuguese campaign of 1808 had convinced him of the intrepidity and fighting qualities of such forces.

With its phalanxes of light troops (infantry and cavalry) the British Army moved across northern Spain with unparalleled speed. The French had derided them, in the spring of 1811 and at other times, for timidity or slowness, but by mid-June 1813 they were being pursued back, harassed all the way, to a defensive line which would mark their final chance to hold any part of Iberia.

On 18 June, the Light Division, having outmarched the French stragglers, emerged into a deeply incised valley – a gorge almost – called San Millan. The terrain nearly formed a 'Y', with the British and French on the converging forks. A small river, the Boveda, was bridged just after the valleys' junction. As the first men at the head of the British column came over a rise and saw San Millan and the Boveda, they realised that several French battalions were standing about near the village without having posted pickets or seeming at all on their mettle. Wellington, wrote one company commander, 'suddenly appeared amongst us and directed the first and third battalions of the 95th riflemen instantly to make an attack on the French infantry brigade which was in Millan and who, to judge from appearances did not dream that that a British soldier was within a day's march of them'.

Four companies trotted up the road and began extending into skirmish order. The alarm had been given among the French now and they tried to get some of their battalions moving while others sent out skirmishers to meet the British. The French began firing ineffectively, but the Rifle company commanders knew their business well enough to ignore them and keep pressing forward until they were very close: 'The 1st Batt 95th extended over their flanks within pistol shot of them, rattling away as fast as they could.' Two Rifle companies kept going for the French centre and one around each flank. The French, seeing riflemen streaming past them on the slopes of the hills on each side, began running, fearing their retreat would be cut off. George Simmons, who had been with the 7th Company – turning one of the French flanks – watched his brother Joseph in action for the first time and saw that he acquitted himself well.

There was panic now in the narrow main street of San Millan, drivers fleeing their wagons and men running back through the village and out its other side. There the French commander managed to form one battalion in line, ready to check the advance of the British skirmishers as they issued from the San Millan. The British would get a crashing volley of musketry and that would buy him time to try to turn the situation. For the French general Antoine-Louis Maucune knew something that the riflemen jogging through San Millan did not: that his division's second brigade was somewhere further back on the same road, cut off by the British surprise attack.

Wellington had by now ridden into the village – with the very spearhead of his Army – and was no further than a couple of hundred yards from that one formed French battalion. One of the 95th's captains recorded, 'Lord Wellington ordered four of the companies of our first battalion to attack.' The riflemen came running towards the French firing line, dropping to one knee or to a prone position to squeeze off a shot now and then, but hardly slackening their pace. A few hundred skirmishers were not meant to be able to drive off a similar number of men in a formed line, but the French were already shaken and as the

95th came straight towards them, their volleys, aimed at men who were partially dispersed with some in cover, had no appreciable effect. The 95th maintained its progress and the French ranks broke and began fleeing before the British bayonets connected.

The riflemen did not let up, even as they reached Val Puesta, the next village along the road. Many enemy soldiers, winded or bewildered, were now running off in all directions or giving themselves up. In the next little hamlet, Villa Nueva, the bugles sounded the recall and Colonel Barnard rallied his men before they dispersed too far. By this time they could hear the heavy firing behind them that announced that Vandeleur's 2nd or Left Brigade of the Light Division had discovered Maucune's lagging formation, and was giving it the same treatment. There the French troops had the choice of fighting to the death or fleeing up the steep hillsides: most opted for the latter course, leaving *fourgons* and *caissons* behind them.

Some three hundred French prisoners were taken, along with many wagons and baggage animals. The Rifles and some Portuguese *Cacadores* soon set about breaking open the trunks and boxes, helping themselves to the plunder. The 43rd, who had been left behind by the rapidity of the attack, were miffed to miss out on the spoils: 'Our men became outrageous, swearing they were never employed when there was anything to be got by it.'

On occasions like this, it was first come, first served for food, drink and anything else easily portable in the baggage. The victorious regiments, however, would auction the animals, wagons and other large items, with the prize money being divided among the soldiers. The sale took place two days later, with those officers who still had a little money in their pockets able to pick up various bargains. There had been many ladies' dresses in the baggage, intended presumably as gifts for the French officers' sweethearts or mothers and now destined to serve the same purpose for the British: 'They were purchased by some of the officers either as *momentos* of the fight . . . or very possibly intended as presents to their fair friends in England should the *purchasers* be fated to *survive* [emphasis in original].'

As for Lord Wellington, he was already preoccupied that day with formulating a battle plan for a general action against the French on the plain of Vitoria. He intended to fall upon the combined armies of King Joseph, Napoleon's brother, the following day, 21 June.

At daybreak on the 21st the Light Division marched almost due

north through a narrow gorge, emerging into an open valley surrounded by peaks. They followed the line of the River Zadorra for about two
miles, keeping to its left bank, and then allowed the curve of the river
and hill spur they were marching along to bring them around until they
were facing due east. The entire French deployment of 57,000 troops
was laid out in front of them. To the Rifles' right, on a great ridge
called the Heights of Puebla, action had already been joined by General
Hill's 2nd Division and one of Spanish troops. Smoke, musket fire,
drumbeats and perhaps even the odd bagpipe announced that the battle for this lofty eminence had begun an hour or two earlier. It was
Wellington's aim to draw off French reserves to Puebla while he hit
them in the centre and on the other flank.

Looking from the riflemen's vantage point, the centre of the French
deployment was an impressive array of infantry and cannon in two
lines. Not all of it was visible, since there were vineyards, orchards and
undulations of the ground. On the British left of this position, the
Zadorra snaked around the plain, along the flanks of the main French
deployment. A right-angled bend in this stream meant that it marked
not only the front of the enemy position (where the Rifles were) but its
right flank too. Further to the British left of that stream were the mountains that marked the northern limit of the Vitoria plain, through
which were several passes. Wellington had sent other columns on a
wide-flanking march through the valleys, with the idea that they
should burst out of these defiles, into the French flank and rear.

Downhill in front of the 95th was a small village, Villodas, and its
bridge across the Zadorra. This would be the objective for the Light
Division's 1st Brigade, but Wellington did not want to throw them forward too soon. He was just by the 1st Battalion of Rifles, looking now
and then up and to his right, then over to the left, squinting into the
distance for any sign that his columns were coming through the mountains. The French would have to be hit at several key points simultaneously, or the British general's men would be defeated in turn.

One officer of the 43rd looked down at Villodas, seeing its defenders, and said, 'I do not like the idea of forcing the bridge. How the
grape will rattle around us!' Others thought the Rifles would soon be
able to pick off the French gunners. Second Lieutenant Hennell looked
along the line to see how the soldiers were dealing with this waiting
game and was struck by their calm: 'More jokes pass then than at a
halt on a wet day and when we move forward every officer is more on

the alert than usual. The men wipe their pans and see that the flint and steel are right as coolly as you would go shooting sparrows.'

Seeing the British on the high ground behind Villodas, the local French commander did not intend to sit passively. He sent some companies of *voltigeurs* across the bridge and into the village, from where they opened fire. Since French balls began whistling around the ears of Wellington and his staff, Colonel Barnard led several companies of riflemen down to flush them out. Half an hour later the little French sally was over and they retired back across the stream.

Wellington looked off to the left again and asked Lieutenant Simmons whether he could see anything. Simmons replied, 'Yes my Lord, I see smoke and dust in that direction.' It was time. Wellington looked across to the Rifles' commanding officer and said, 'All right; get along Barnard.'

Riflemen moved down towards the old bridge but then, in one of those chances of war, Barnard met a local peasant who told them that a crossing further up the Zadorra was unguarded. The Rifles' commander had been itching for a chance to distinguish himself and it could not have been offered more plainly to him. Barnard and his riflemen followed their guide to the left, up the river bank, as the slope became steeper and steeper. This little path, clinging to the craggy rock face, led them around the right-angled bend in the river and over one of the little bridges at a village appropriately named Tres Puentes. There, the riflemen, followed by the 43rd, crossed unopposed and went up a great hillock, the site of an ancient earthwork, from where they could see a few dozen French light roops by Tres Puentes' main crossing, and Picton's 3rd Division coming down from the north towards it. There were just a few French *voltigeurs* and dragoons guarding this point and Barnard resolved instantly to attack them with rifle fire, driving them away. A few dozen rounds sufficed to throw back the enemy. The Rifles' unexpected appearance in this quarter earned them a few cannon shot from British guns on the opposite bank, and several men were cut down by their own side's artillery before the firing could be halted. 'The 3rd Division, at a run, crossed the bridge of Trespuentes, cheering but unopposed.' Barnard's gamble in bypassing the bridge at Villodas had succeeded beautifully. Realising they might soon be cut off by British troops who were almost behind them, the French defenders quit that point on the river bank, allowing the Light Division's 2nd Brigade to cross at Villodas unopposed.

With much of the Light and 3rd Divisions now across the river and somewhat to the rear of the foremost French line, the rest of this advanced defensive cordon had to fall back. These enemy redeployments gave the Rifles half an hour of calm, which made everyone a little uneasy, in case a counter-attack was about to be launched. Soon enough, though, it was the British who were moving forward again, onto a tree-covered knoll about half a mile east of the Villodas bridge. Behind this feature was a village called Arinez, which the French were barricading and preparing to defend.

On emerging from the trees on top of the knoll of Arinez, the 43rd and 95th were, for the first time, visible to a great many French defenders. An ear-splitting barrage of cannon began. The first rounds roared overhead and then others started skipping across the ground, smashing whoever got in the way. One British officer estimated that they had come under the fire of thirty pieces. The 43rd were quickly ordered to lie down. They could see, though, that quite a bit of the firing was coming from some artillery in and around Arinez itself. To their left one of Picton's brigades began to form up, ready to assault the village. 'During the few minutes that we stopped there,' wrote Kincaid, 'while a brigade of the 3rd division was deploying into line, two of our companies lost two officers and thirty men, chiefly from the fire of artillery.'

Into this maelstrom rode Wellington, placing himself in great danger. The battle had reached a decisive moment and the British commander knew that if the French could be driven out of Arinez, their centre would be broken. 'I heard a voice behind me, which I knew to be Lord Wellington's,' wrote Kincaid, 'calling out, in a tone of reproof, "Look to keeping your men together, sir."'

Leach's company was one of those pinned under this heavy fire. Lieutenant Gairdner, Corporal Brotherwood and Private Costello were all serving in it. Gairdner was one of those who soon became a casualty. Costello was hit too: 'A grape or round shot struck my pouch with such violence that I was hurled several yards along the ground. From this sudden shock, I imagined myself mortally wounded but, on being picked up, I found the only damage I had sustained was to my pouch, which was nearly torn off.' Private Miles Hodgson, the pardoned Rodrigo deserter, ran up to help Costello, only to get a bullet in the face. Leach's company, and the 6th Company under Lieutenant FitzMaurice, went charging down the hill towards Arinez.

The walls and hedges on the village's outskirts were now lined with

French defenders. Wellington rode across the short distance to Picton's men where he personally formed up the 88th, the Connaught Rangers, for the advance. With a beating of drums, they marched forward in line, presented their pieces only thirty or forty yards from the enemy and game them a thumping volley, a cheer and the bayonet. The French fled back through the village. One battery of guns which had been firing in support of them was quickly limbered up by its commander, for in his trade losing your cannon was the ultimate disgrace. At this moment the artillery men got help: a counter-attack by the French infantry briefly reclaimed the village, allowing this battery to pull out. Seeing the track that the horses towing the cannon were taking, Lieutenant FitzMaurice called his men to follow him and raced across an open field to intercept them.

On arriving near the guns, FitzMaurice was running at a cracking pace. He shouted to his company, urging them forward, only to make the uncomfortable discovery that just a couple had managed to keep up with him as he ran. The Irish lieutenant threw himself onwards nevertheless, the French gunners and drivers defending themselves with whatever came to hand. There was a short, sharp, close-range fight in which a pistol was discharged almost in FitzMaurice's face, the ball going through his shako. Soon he and another rifleman had shot one of the draught horses and were cutting the traces that connected it to the howitzer it was pulling. The lieutenant and four riflemen had captured the first French gun of the day, but certainly not the last.

As the 2nd Company burst into Arinez, Costello caught sight of Lazarro Blanco sticking a straggler with his bayonet. The Spanish private plunged the blade in manically, taking out the sufferings of his country on this unfortunate Frenchman, cursing him all the time in the most profane and abusive language.

With their enemy streaming back from Arinez, the Light and 3rd Divisions followed up. There was still heavy firing, but the French Army was disintegrating. Its battalions had broken into clumps of men running across the countryside, heading east. Near the city of Vitoria, hundreds of wagons, containing the treasures plundered by the French during their five-year occupation, fell into British hands.

Wellington had scored an emphatic triumph. The French Army lost 151 artillery pieces – all but one of those weapons that they had brought to the field. Many of the British soldiers felt a determined cavalry pursuit would have annihilated the disordered wreck of Joseph's army. No such movement by the horse soldiers materialised and one Rifle officer noted, 'It was impossible to deny ourselves the satisfaction of cursing them all, because a portion of them had not been there at such a critical moment.' The Household Cavalry regiments were sent into Vitoria to stop the Allied army plundering it, Hennell of the 43rd being unable to resist a dig at these court soldiers, writing home, 'I do not know what good they did, if any I am sure you would hear of it.'

As for the Light Division, they felt they had more than earned the rewards that might be earned from plundering the French baggage. Their role in assuring the passage of the Zadorra and attacking Arinez had been the most important part of any general action they had enjoyed since Busaco almost three years before. Some soldiers, though, were to be rewarded beyond their wildest dreams, for among the chests and cases were millions of gold doubloons and silver dollars.

'I observed a Spanish muleteer in the French service carrying a small but exceedingly heavy portmanteau towards the town,' wrote Costello. 'I compelled him lay it down, which he did, but only after I had given him a few whacks with my rifle.' These saddlebags contained a breath-taking sum – perhaps as much as £1,000 in Spanish coin. A couple of troopers of the 10th Hussars, seeing Costello staggering along with this load, soon tried to divide it with him. 'Retiring three or four paces, I brought [my rifle] to my shoulder and swore I would shoot dead the first man to place his hands upon my treasure.' This persuaded the cavalry to look elsewhere. Costello clapped hands on a mule to carry the bags and headed back to find his company.

One other rifleman was rumoured to have taken £3,000 in coin. He had the added good fortune of a wife following with the regimental baggage. They sewed their gains into a mule saddle, which she kept closely under her supervision, the couple later depositing their money at a bank in Dover. Costello knew there was nobody he could trust in this way. Instead he signed over £300 to the regimental paymaster, who was happy to acquire the coin in order to settle his many accounts and issue a receipt in return. Some the private also loaned to officers. The remainder he and Tom Bandle, a messmate whom he had taken into his confidence, guarded. Bandle had sailed with Costello in the 3rd Company, back in 1809, and upon its demise had also been transferred into Leach's – they had a long history of fighting and drinking together. He was a little weasel of a man who, in return for a small cut, helped Costello guard the cash. Most of it was to go on ensuring he and his company lived well and were adequately lubricated during the coming months.

Most soldiers did not of course reap quite such rewards, but that did not stop them searching hard. Costello himself put it charmingly: 'Even if our fellows had been inclined to be honest, their good fortune would not allow them.'

The 95th's officers did not benefit in quite the same way. Simmons recorded, 'I lay down by the fire in a French officer's cloak, which one of the men gave me; he had that day shot its wearer.' Leach dropped down in his company's bivouac, exhausted. 'The soldiers of my company brought me a large loaf of excellent French bread, some Swiss cheese, cognac brandy and excellent wine they had found in some French general's covered wagon.' The men, in sharing their bounty with delicacies for their officers, ensured that they remained free to roam that night. Leach jotted in his journal, 'Our soldiers did nothing the whole night but eat, drink and smoke, talk over our glorious successes and occassionally steal away from camp to look for plunder which it must be allowed was very excusable.'

Around the 2nd Company campfires there was much discussion about what had happened to them that day and who had been absent from roll-call. Private Dan Kelly piped up, 'Don't drink all the wine boys, until we hear something about our absent messmates. Do any of you know where Jack Connor is?'

'He was shot through the body when we took the first gun in the little village near the main road,' was the reply.

Bob Roberts spoke next, asking, 'Where is Will John?'

'A ball passed through his head,' said another. 'I saw him fall.'

Tom Treacy then joined in: 'Musha, boys! Is there any hope of poor Jemmy Copely getting over his wounds?'

'Poor Copely, both his legs were knocked off by a round shot.'

Treacy looked down bitterly. 'By Jasus, they have kilt half our mess. But never mind boys, fill a tot, fill a tot. May I be damned but here's luck . . . Poor Jemmy Copely! Poor Jemmy! They have drilled him well with balls before, damn them, now they have finished him. The best comrade I ever had, or ever will have.' As Treacy said these last words, a tear streaked down his blackened face.

In the days following Vitoria, the Rifles fell in with the French rearguard several times. After the great affair of 21 June, these fights piqued their superstitions, one officer summing it up: 'After surviving a great day, I always felt I had a right to live to tell the story; and I, therefore did not find the ensuing three days' fighting half as pleasant as they otherwise would have been.'

Just as the riflemen had begun to think more about their own survival, so their propensity for plunder had grown, as their brigade set off in pursuit of a remnant of the old Army of Portugal. On 29 June in a village called Caseda, quite a few riflemen joined in a stripping of firewood and farm produce so vigorous that it crossed the thin line between foraging and plunder. Wellington got one of his staff to write an angry letter to the commander of the Light Division, exclaiming, 'This renewed report of disorder committed by soldiers of your division has much dissatisfied the Commander of the Forces, his excellency being of the opinion that such continued irregularity shows evident relaxation of discipline both regimental and divisional.'

The following day, following Headquarters' complaints, Lieutenant Simmons was put in command of a party of riflemen collecting firewood when General Picton rode up, declaring that the logs had been assigned by the staff to his own 3rd Division. The 95th knew well enough that in former times a feud had built up between Craufurd, in his role of irresistible force, and Picton, acting the part of immovable object. On this occasion, Picton shouted at Simmons to drop the wood, telling him, 'It is a damned concern to have to follow [the Light Division]. You sweep everything before you.' General Alten arrived on the scene at this moment, saving the fuel for his own division.

While the soldiers doubtless revelled in the image of the Light Division as peerless scavengers or *banditti*, it posed no small problem for Lieutenant Colonel Barnard in his command of the Rifles. The last thing he wanted was for the banditry of his wilder soldiers to tarnish the laurels he had won on 21 June. Although some were now beginning to prophesy the end of Bonaparte's rule, he knew that he would have to use both the carrot and the stick to combat the disorderly tendencies of his men.

At least nobody doubted the Light Division's marching prowess as it found itself heading in the direction of the River Bidassoa, Spain's border with France, early in July. General Kempt had been deeply struck by the quality of soldiers under his command, telling Barnard one day on the march, 'By God I never saw fellows march so well and in such weather and roads too. I will order the Commissary to issue them a double allowance of spirits tonight.' The Pyrenees loomed ahead of them. French forces remained isolated in two Spanish fortresses: Pampluna inland, at the base of those mountains, and on the coast at San Sebastian. Wellington did not intend to advance into France itself until those places were reduced, and sieges, as he had discovered, could be a tedious and bloody business.

The smoky hovels of the Portuguese frontier were behind them. They knew enough about the French losses against the mighty coalition ranged against Napoleon in Germany to begin hoping that the final battle was under way. The French, though, were determined to exact a high price in blood in the mountain ranges of their southern border.

TWENTY-ONE

The Nivelle

July–November 1813

The Pyrenean mountain air echoed to the sounds of picks, shovels and cursing throughout that late summer of 1813. Local workmen, the National Guard and the army proper had all been pressed into service, creating a line of outposts along the peaks of the western Pyrenees.

Following Vitoria and the collapse of Joseph's Kingdom of Spain, Napoleon had sacked his brother ignominiously and appointed Marshal Jean de Dieu Soult to reorganise his southern armies. The marshal drew thousands of men into his scheme to turn the mountainous frontier into a solid defensive wall. Dozens of redoubts had been built, usually on heights. These were garnished with artillery pieces, heaved up the slopes with ropes, block and tackle. Once emplaced, these guns were positioned to sweep any likely approach with fire. The strongpoints were sited to allow each to support its neighbours, with others further back to allow a defence in depth.

Less than a month after Vitoria, the Light Division men marched within view of these fortifications and were duly impressed. They knew that if they were called upon to storm the forts, it would be warm work, for a soldier lumbering slowly up a mountainside would be exposed to enemy fire for far longer than those who had broken the French line at San Millan or taken Arinez. One officer of the 43rd wrote home, 'By throwing up redoubts on the heights one regiment may hold up an entire army.'

There were obvious parallels with the lines of Torres Vedras, which the pick of Napoleon's generals had not even dared to attack. Perhaps the French saw it as a chance to inflict a Busaco on Wellington too. Attacking this system, though, was a bigger prospect than that ridge in Portugal, for the Bidassoa defence line stretched for forty miles south-east, from the Bay of Biscay into the high mountains. Marshal Soult predicted that his enemy would suffer 25,000 casualties breaking the line. He issued patriotic edicts, exhorting his men to prevent the English setting foot on the 'sacred soil of France'.

Wellington's concerns were first and foremost to find his own defensive positions in this mountainous terrain, for he felt it likely that Soult would try some attacks to relieve the French garrisons left behind inside Spain at Pampluna and San Sebastian. Once these places had been reduced by the Allies, Wellington would have to attack the Bidassoa line.

It became readily apparent as the Army adjusted to its new fighting ground that this work would belong largely to the infantry. Many positions could only be reached by shepherds' tracks, making them impassable to limbered guns, and the steep slopes were too tricky for mounted troops. 'Our cavalry therefore and I understand a considerable part of our artillery', wrote Captain Leach, never missing his chance for a put-down, 'are living in clover in different towns as snug and as far from the possibility of surprise by the enemy as if they were in England.'

British generals soon discovered other qualities to this new arena of war. The Pyrenees could only be crossed by certain passes and the ridges or mountains separating those could make it very hard to move troops to a threatened sector, if the enemy were able to gain a local surprise. Just as movement along the British or French defensive lines could be very tricky, so too were communications.

The Pyrenean battlefield was therefore one in which every commander would have to be on his mettle. It was unfortunate, then, for the Light Division that the idiocies of the Army hierarchy deprived it of General Vandeleur, the respected commander of its 2nd Brigade at this time. He was replaced by Major General John Skerrett, to whom the brigade major, Captain Harry Smith of the 95th, instantly took exception. 'My new General,' wrote Smith, 'I soon discovered, was by nature a gallant Grenadier, and no Light Troop officer.' Smith termed him gallant because Skerrett's personal courage was never in doubt. But for the 95th it was almost an insult to call someone a grenadier, for they used that term to evoke a picture of pipeclay, parade-ground formalism and pedantry which belonged firmly in the previous century.

The Light Division was fortunate at this time in having some exceptional commanding officers and these men did much to adapt its tactics during this final phase of the Peninsular War. Colonel John Colborne, recovered from his Ciudad Rodrigo wounds, was back at the head of the 52nd (often conspiring with Harry Smith to do things their own way rather than Skerrett's), and Andrew Barnard enjoyed a high reputation after his shrewd handling of the 1st/95th at Vitoria.

Barnard had that inner confidence, arising from education, wealth and political connections, that Alexander Cameron had clearly lacked when in command of the battalion. At forty, Barnard was no youngster, and had entered the 95th only three years earlier after a long career in the line infantry. The Rifles officers were very hard to impress, being convinced they knew their business best, but Barnard succeeded by becoming an enthusiastic apostle of light troops and the rifle. As a representative of a significant Anglo-Irish family, he also had a familiar relationship with Wellington (often the prickliest of customers), which in turn made him the kind of advocate the regiment needed.

Late in July, Soult attacked in the direction of Pampluna, surprising British brigades in several places and forcing Wellington back. After the initial setbacks, the British commander rallied his divisions and began pressing in on the French. Following days of hard fighting, with both sides having little food, Marshal Soult resolved to head back into France by a different route to the pass he had entered by. He turned his forces northwards and sent them towards a village called Yanzi.

The Light Division had not been involved in the early stages of this, but was sent to try to intercept the French withdrawal. The last two days of July and 1 August were thus ones of hideous marching for General Alten's men. The retreat of an enemy down a narrow mountain valley could not be overtaken and intercepted by moving along an equally easy path: it required the Light Division to haul themselves up precipitous ridges and across deep valleys in what was still high summer. In short, the terrain forced the pursuers to work twice as hard as the pursued. This was to prove a death march for several Light Division soldiers, who succumbed to exhaustion, dying by the sides of dusty shepherds' tracks.

After an infernally hot march of thirty miles across the peaks, scouts sighted the French at Yanzi, and Alten urged his 1st Brigade to make one last effort to reach them. They came upon the French in faltering light, across a river, and evidently just as hungry and exhausted as they were. Some of the riflemen began shooting – and it was very easy shooting, for the French were hemmed in by a rock face, crowded along the banks of a fast-flowing mountain river. There was utter panic in their ranks: litters bearing injured soldiers were dropped by their porters; men were trampled underfoot; others, tipped into the river by the scrum, disappeared under its waters. It was every man for himself, one Rifles officer being shocked to observe that some French dragoons 'actually flogged the infantry with their sabres to drive them before the rearguard'. 'Happily, and to the honour of the British soldiers,' wrote Costello, 'many of our men, knowing that the French suffered from what they had themselves endured, declined firing, and called out to the others to spare them, as it was little better than murder.'

The following day, after hundreds of French prisoners were taken, their divisions were escorted through the pass of Vera, back onto their side of the border. The Rifles were involved in a brief but sharp skirmish to retake one of the heights dominating the Spanish side of that gateway. This mountain, the Santa Barbera, became their home for some weeks.

A quiet interlude for the Light Division then followed as Wellington and Soult's attention switched to the coast, where the besieged imperial garrison in San Sebastian was holding out stubbornly. The British meanwhile advanced their batteries and trenches around the fortresses, just as they had at Rodrigo and Badajoz.

On 20 August, an appeal reached the Light Division for 250 volunteers to take part in a storming party. This was to prove an interesting test of the men's moral state and the degree to which the wounds of Badajoz had healed. When faced with the possible storms of some redoubts in Salamanca, in June 1812 (ten weeks after Badajoz), the Light Division's officers had been obliged to nominate men, since it was clear there would be virtually no volunteering. Thirteen months later there had been some change, but for the great majority of those survivors who had sailed in May 1809, there was no desire to go, or need to prove themselves.

Sergeant Robert Fairfoot, having volunteered four times in 1812 for these desperate duties, did not go to San Sebastian, the livid crater on his forehead testifying to the closeness of his brush with death at Badajoz. It was only in one or two cases, such as that 'wild untamable animal' Private James Burke – who saw the chance for rape and plunder – that there was a strong desire to repeat the Badajoz experience. With officers it was a little different, the requirement of honour dictating that they aspire in principle at least to this most dangerous of duties. As George Simmons wrote, 'It is a melancholy thing to be a junior lieutenant in such times as these, because the senior claims the first offer. Whenever a party is detached upon such an occasion, our boys are so proud of it that, according to seniority, they would not think of letting it pass them.' In truth, though, neither of the officers who went from the 95th were original members of the battalion.

The division's stay at Vera allowed dozens of officers to sit down to dinner together on 25 August, celebrated as the 95th's founding day. The feast took place in a field, with trenches cut to form benches and the ground itself forming a natural table. The bands played, songs were sung and vast quantities of wine drunk.

Those last days of the summer of 1813 were marked by the frequent echoing of the battering guns at San Sebastian through the peaks. Everyone was aware that, for the time being, the outcome of the siege would determine when they would move forward, attacking the Bidassoa line of defences that stared them in the face. Marshal Soult, though, was determined to try one last effort in favour of the besieged garrison, just as he had at Pampluna in July. A series of battles thus raged on the lower Bidassoa, close to the sea, at the end of August. One French division, having struck into Spain and finding its line of retreat blocked, was forced to attempt a different route back to safety: it approached the Vera pass late on 31 August.

General Skerrett had left two companies of Rifles, under Captain Cadoux of the 2nd Battalion, down at the bridge to secure it, and it was against these hundred or so defenders that General Lubin-Martin Vandermaesen flung thousands of troops on the night of 31 August. The French, several battalions of whom approached the bridge through driving rain at 2 a.m., knew that the defenders were all that stood between them and captivity. The riflemen, however, managed to hold their positions in barricaded houses at the bridgehead as Vandermaesen led his men in one attack after another.

The gunfire woke the remainder of the Light Division, who were on higher ground. Despite the remonstrations of his staff, General Skerrett refused to send any reinforcement to the bridge. The chance to cut off thousands of French was lost, along with the Rifle company commander and sixteen of his men. The French finally forced their way across, but paid a heavy price of around two hundred troops, including Vandermaesen himself, who was at the head of his troops when shot dead by a British rifleman. This affair caused lasting rancour between the Rifles and Skerrett, whom they blamed for utter incompetence in failing to reinforce Cadoux.

The battles of July and August had taught Marshal Soult a lesson too. His experience of the British Army during the Peninsular War had been limited before the late summer of 1813. But when fighting it in the Pyrenees, he was deeply shocked by the effect that accurate rifle and skirmisher fire had in blunting the success of his attacks. The quality of the British marksmen – not just the 95th, for such weapons and tactics had been adopted in various parts of the Army by this point – had shown Soult that his divisions would be decapitated almost as soon as their officers tried to lead them into battle. Soult told the Minister of War in Paris about the British light troops:

They are expressly told to fire first at officers and in particular commanders and generals . . . this way of making war and harming the enemy is most disadvantageous to us; the losses in officers that we have suffered are so heavy, that in two battles they are usually all out of action . . . you will understand that if we start having these losses again, it will be very difficult to be able to replace the officers.

Soult's lesson in the new ways of war was not over yet, though. Just as the Light Division had pioneered new levels of marksmanship, so its style of movement under fire would prove an important ingredient in the battle for the Bidassoa line. The French in San Sebastian had finally surrendered on 8 September, after weeks of heroic resistance. Wellington was now ready to breach Soult's defences and enter France. This would require some preparation, and on 7 October the Light Division was given a mission vital to the opening of the Vera pass. They would have to storm some of the French lines at the mouth of this natural gateway, positions that dominated Santa Barbera, their resting place of the previous weeks.

Early in the morning the Light Division columns began moving out of Vera and up the slopes to the left of the feature towering above them, La Rhune. Right Brigade, including the 1st and 3rd of the 95th, the 43rd and some Portuguese rangers, all under Kempt, would attack a ridge on the right of La Rhune. Left Brigade, appropriately enough, would hit, to the left of them, a stone-built redoubt called Saint Benoit which dominated the narrow road up into the pass. Colonel Colborne had taken over acting command of this brigade, Skerrett having gone away sick.

The layout of the French defences assumed that an attacker would try to force them in the formed columns or battle lines of regular tactics, for the French officers thought that it was only by standing shoulder to shoulder with his comrades that a soldier could maintain the courage to storm such a strongpoint. Those who skirmished and hid among the rocks would surely never want to quit these safe places once the metal was flying – or so they reasoned.

Kempt's attack, however, was ordered almost entirely in skirmish order. Having climbed a couple of thousand feet to a point close to the French trenches, the British troops were rested so they could regain their breath. The 3rd Battalion of Rifles, accompanied by some of the 1st and Portuguese, then went forward to hit the French trenches, swords fixed to their rifles. The Rifles officers knew it was important not to allow their men to get into a shooting match with the well-entrenched defenders. One observer described their advance:

The 95th moved regularly (I do not mean in a line) up the hill within fifty yards of the top without firing and then, by way of breathing, gave them a volley, loaded and advanced to the top, the support close behind them. The French did not attempt to defend it but moved to their left, not without music, in quick time.

With the French soldiers fleeing, the attackers quickly used their newly won position to get around the flanks of some trenches behind it. Their mission was complete and the loss trifling. Hennell of the 43rd had watched it all with pride and admiration – his own battalion had been in reserve and was not even required to fight. In a letter home, he told his brothers, 'I firmly believe there are no better troops in the world than the 95th. They take things so coolly and deliberately and seem to know their business so well. You have no idea with what glee we saw them and how readily we fell in to advance.'

Across to the left, Colborne led the 2nd Battalion of Rifles and his own 52nd Light Infantry to a tougher objective. Like Kempt, Colborne intended to make his attack with skirmishers, using his red-coated regiment as their support or reserve. But the French in the Saint Benoit redoubt did not behave entirely as expected. Like the other defenders, they fired off some ineffective volleys which all went too high – having not been trained properly in shooting, they did not realise that those aiming down at attackers from a lofty height need to shoot much lower than feels natural, aiming almost at the feet. Colborne's attack was upset, though, by the actions of the fort's commander, who led a party of his men out of the redoubt to charge the riflemen as they reloaded. This they did with some success, bayoneting some and getting close enough (perhaps ten or twenty feet) to hit others with their fire. The 2nd Battalion of Rifles was repulsed with dozens of casualties. Colborne had no choice but to order forward his own battalion (the 52nd) and the Saint Benoit was then carried.

Colborne went to reconnoitre ahead, accompanied only by Captain Smith and a handful of riflemen. To their consternation, a battalion of three hundred French light infantry appeared, right in front of them, moving up the valley towards their position. 'The only way was to put a brave face on the matter,' Colborne said later, 'so I went up to them, desiring them to surrender.' This extraordinary bluff worked. The colonel ordered the French to deposit their arms in a pile, in case they realised just who ought to be taking whom prisoner, while someone was sent with all haste to bring up some more troops. And with this gamble, the battle was effectively over for the Light Division.

The troops found themselves encamped on the wind-blasted Rhune mountain for the next few weeks, as the seasons turned and they contemplated getting to grips with the next belt of French defences. 'We remained a whole month idle spectators of their preparations, and dearly longing for the day that should afford us an opportunity of penetrating into the more hospitable-looking low country beyond them,' wrote Kincaid, 'for the weather had become excessively cold and our camp stood exposed to the utmost fury of the almost nightly tempest.'

Once in the Pyrenees, the Rifles found themselves again in close quarters with the French outposts. After the hard marching of previous weeks, six men of the 1st Battalion took the opportunity to desert during late September and October. This sort of loss had not happened since Almond and the others decamped two years before. However, this time there were no executions, even when men were repeatedly caught trying to flee. One soldier of the 3rd Battalion, 95th, for example, was sentenced to be transported for life after being court-martialled for attempting desertion three times in the space of a few weeks.

With the weather deteriorating, officers were urged to keep a close eye on the men, in case others were tempted to flee the hardships of their mountain station. Riflemen of the 1st Battalion had bivouacked by a small hermitage near the summit of La Rhune, others having slightly more sheltered spots lower down its slopes. They had tents, unlike in previous campaigns, issued just before they left winter quarters; the mules that had spent four years carrying the useless cast-iron camp kettles around Iberia were at last given a load that might be of some value to the regiment. While these get-ups kept the men alive on the top of this mountain, they did not make them comfortable. Leach wrote in his journal: 'Whether in or outside our tents, whether asleep or awake we were never dry, never warm nor comfortable. Our chief employment was when not on picket to cut out all kinds of trenches and drains to endeavour to turn the springs of water which sprung up inside and outside our canvas habitation.'

Finding some slightly sheltered spot to get out of the wind, they would read letters from home – sometimes even newspapers enclosed by relatives – and learn of the Emperor Napoleon's worsening fortunes in Germany. Lieutenant John FitzMaurice got one from a family friend which, referring to Bonaparte's difficult situation at the end of August, continued, 'The successes in Germany are most exhilarating. The Tyrant seems almost hemmed in, and his personal escape very doubtful . . . All this promises at least a speedy peace upon the terms of Bonaparte falling within the Rhine, the Alps and the Pyrenees, or possibly a revolution and the extinction of this scourge of the human race.'

For many officers, the sense of resignation to the apparently endless nature of the Peninsular conflict had given way, since Vitoria, to an anxiety about what might happen after Napoleon fell. They all expected the Army to contract in such a case: third and perhaps even second battalions would go – maybe the 95th would disappear altogether, as previous regiments bearing this number had thirty years earlier, after the American wars and again in 1796. A young sub or captain might then be cast out with half-pay, or worse. One officer of the 43rd told his family in a letter, 'Peace is now I think fairly beyond doubt and it is likely to be speedy and soon. The half-pay monster is staring some of us lieutenants in the face again. However, I heartily wish for it.' These concerns, along with a desire to know whether Wellington's Army or some other would have the honour of penetrating deep into France first, fuelled a great thirst for information. One Light Division officer, expressing thanks for a month-old copy of *The Times*, told his family the soldiers were 'gaping for news like trout on a summer evening'.

Many of the officers thought that the arrival of heavy frosts and snows would freeze the armies into winter quarters somewhere along the Pyrenean chain. George Simmons had experienced enough of campaigning and being truly wet and cold to yearn for a trip home. 'I have been thinking of visiting you this winter after the campaign is over and we go into winter quarters . . . I could have leave when I chose,' he told his parents. The only obstacle was money. While he felt he might afford the passage on a packet boat, he realised he only owned what he was wearing: 'There is another consideration – plain clothes, which are very expensive, and I have nothing but military attire, which would make people gaze at me as upon a dancing bear.'

Simmons's plans, alas, were arrested, and his curiosity about how the English public might react to the sight of a fighting Green Jacket on their streets was not to be satisfied. Early in November it became apparent that Wellington was preparing to force the Bidassoa line proper. For the Light Division, this would mean assaulting the slightly smaller mountain in front of theirs – named La Petite Rhune, appropriately enough – and its system of defences.

Wellington had walked along the forward slope of La Rhune with Colborne, Kempt and Alten, studying the French works on the opposite mountain. In forcing Soult's entire system of fortifications, this was where he intended to open the ball, with the Light Division in its usual post of honour. To their front was a series of entrenchments on top of La Petite Rhune. The 43rd would be attacking this point. Slightly to the left and rear of that objective was another stone-built redoubt, the Mouiz fort, mounting several cannon, which Wellington wanted attacked by Colborne using the 52nd, 1st/95th, 3rd/95th and some Portuguese.

'These fellows think themselves invulnerable,' said Wellington as he studied the French lines in front, 'but I will beat them out and with great ease.' Colborne looked at his objective, protected in several places by precipitous rock faces, and replied: 'That we shall beat them when your Lordship attacks, I have not doubt, but for the ease –'

Wellington cut him short, telling Colborne that the French would be assailed in many places simultaneously and did not have the men to defend all of their battlements. The British commander told Alten to move his division down into the valley between the two Rhune peaks during the hours of darkness, 'so as to rush La Petite Rhune as day dawned, it would be of vast importance and save great loss'.

At 2 a.m. on 10 November, the Light Bobs were duly served up with the earliest of breakfasts and began filing down to the low ground at the base of their objective. The brigadiers, fearing the enemy would be alarmed, were terrified of some man firing off his musket by accident or losing his way. Both types of misfortune actually happened, rattling everyone's nerves. 'That this was an anxious, I might say awful moment may well be believed,' wrote Leach. Somehow the French did not respond, and as the sun appeared across the peaks to the east, everyone was in their start positions. The 1st/95th and the rest of their column had to pick their way up a precipice in order to emerge on the flank of the French defences.

Just after 6 a.m. the report of three cannon shots from a British battery echoed around the peaks: it was the signal for a general attack to commence. Within fifteen or twenty minutes all of the trenchworks in front of the Mouiz fort had been taken at the point of the bayonet. 'We moved forward under a heavy fire from the enemy's works without ever exchanging a shot until we got up to them and scaled the walls,' wrote Simmons, 'then the work of death commenced.'

While younger officers in the 95th usually carried rifles in battle, it was unusual for them to use the blades fixed to their barrels. Although shooting could just about be reconciled with the status of a gentleman, bayoneting was another matter entirely. Lieutenant FitzMaurice, seeing a Frenchman impaled by Second Lieutenant James Church, one of the rougher Irish soldiers of fortune who had recently joined the 95th, asked him something along the lines of 'How could you?' Church looked around, the crackle of gunfire echoing about him, and replied: 'Eh, but Fitz, just see how easy it slips in!'

Storming into the positions, the riflemen found the French tents were still up and food on the boil in some of the positions. Leach looked around from this vantage point: 'It is impossible to picture oneself anything finer than the general advance of the Army . . . as far as the eye could reach almost soon became one sheet of fire and smoke and of an infernal fire of light troops with frequent volleys of musquetry as the lines approached one another.'

Across on the main part of La Petite Rhune, the 43rd's assault was beginning. Six of the regiments' companies went forward in extended order, four remaining formed in reserve. The redcoats ploughed through the first French defensive position before coming up against more serious resistance. It turned into a vicious close-range fight. 'One of our officers gallantly jumped into the second fort,' according to an officer of the 43rd. 'A French soldier thrust a bayonet through his neckerchief, transfixed him to the wall, and fired his piece. This blew away the officer's collar, but he jumped away unhurt.'

Barnard led the 1st Battalion of Rifles across to support the 43rd at this point, and could be seen by its officers urging his men on, and firing a rifle at the French defenders himself. Soult's officers, for their part, did everything they could to incite their companies to continue their resistance. Simmons 'saw some French officers trying every means in their power to make their men remain. One officer was doing prodigies of valour and would not leave the wall; he was shot and came tumbling down.'

At length, the 43rd, supported by Barnard's riflemen, cleared La Petite Rhune and began pursuing the fleeing French down the back side of the mountain towards the sea. Barnard, who was following on horseback with his men, was at this moment shot in the chest, falling back off his horse, onto the rocky ground where several of his officers quickly attended him.

Simmons, not for the first time, put his surgeon's training to use. He unbuttoned Barnard's tunic and examined the wound. Foaming blood was coming from the colonel's mouth and the gaping hole in his chest made a sucking sound – neither augured well. Barnard, fully conscious, looked up at Simmons and asked, 'Simmons, you know my situation. Am I mortally wounded?' The young lieutenant put a couple of fingers into the wound and probed, feeling the bottom lobe of Barnard's left lung.

'Colonel, it is useless to mince the matter; you are dangerously wounded, but not immediately mortally.'

'Be candid,' Barnard answered. 'I am not afraid to die.'

'I am candid.'

Barnard looked away, saying, 'Then I am satisfied.'

The colonel was carried off in a blanket by several riflemen, attended by Simmons as they went.

Elsewhere, Colborne's 52nd had reached the Mouiz fortress, the toughest objective by far. Attempts to rush the walls met with failure, a hail of bullets and grapeshot cutting down dozens of men. They crouched in cover, the cracking and whistling of metal just over their heads. Colborne waited until the attacks around them had succeeded and then called upon the French commander to surrender. For the second time in as many months, his nerve paid off and the defenders marched out and into captivity. By 3 p.m. the fighting in what became known as the Battle of the Nivelle was over.

Some 4,300 French had been killed, wounded or taken prisoner. The officer commanding the French division struck by the Light Division reported that 'a swarm of skirmishers' had made the attack. Wellington's casualties, combined with those of his Portuguese and Spanish allies, came to just below three thousand.

Simmons was asked to stay with Barnard, as the crisis of his wound passed. There had not been too many strokes of good fortune in Simmons's life, and he was quite sure he had to take advantage of fate. He wrote to his parents, telling them that he would not be coming home on leave: 'To gain the friendship of a man of Colonel Barnard's ability, who will next year be a General Officer, will always be of use.' Perhaps, at this late stage, Simmons believed his commanding officer might make him the prize of an ADC's job.

Fate was unkind, however, to Sergeant Robert Fairfoot. He had survived the Pyrenean battles, along with most of his comrades, and was considered such a trusty fellow that he was made the company pay sergeant. Since this job involved collecting large amounts of cash from the paymaster and doling it out to the men, it was a weighty responsibility.

Not long after he received this new duty, Fairfoot awoke, having – if truth be told – drunk a little too much the night before, to discover that he had been robbed of £31. It disgusted him to think that one of his own company was probably the culprit. The sergeant knew he was liable and was soon in a high pitch of anxiety about what to do. He went to Ned Costello and told him what had happened. Costello recorded that his sergeant 'said his credit would be for ever destroyed in the regiment, and he could not endure remaining in the battalion afterwards'. Sergeant Fairfoot had made up his mind to desert.

TWENTY-TWO

The Nive

November–December 1813

It would perhaps have been better if Captain Hobkirk of the 43rd had confined his flamboyance to the stage. But on 23 November the Mrs Malaprop of February's Light Division theatricals opened his mouth and well and truly said the wrong thing. The result this time was not farce but tragedy.

They were skirmishing up towards a little French village called Arcangues in the foothills north of the Pyrenees. It was handsomely made, with a chateau, a tall church spire and woods to both sides. The Light Division's Right Brigade was advancing to take the village and the French were falling back through it. Behind Arcangues the ground rose up to a feature called the Bassussarry ridge where the French had dug some trenches.

Brigadier Kempt sent Hobkirk with two companies of the 43rd into the trees on the left of Arcangues, with the words 'Now mind, you are not to go beyond the wood.' The redcoats moved gingerly forward, 'to the front of the wood, each man to his tree, and kept up a fire upon their trenches. They did not forget to return it but they did little mischief as we were all covered by the trees. The boughs dropped fast around us and the leaves were knocked up by our sides.'

The 43rd could maintain this position for as long as was necessary, for they were in cover and far enough (120 to 150 yards) from the French positions for their fire to be poorly aimed. But then Hobkirk's bugler sounded the advance. The soldiers looked at one another for a moment and then the first men began running out of cover and into the open ground. The banging of French muskets suddenly increased, and the redcoats started dropping. Lieutenant Hennell, running forward, saw Baillie, another subaltern in his company, felled with an

[236]

almighty crack as a bullet smacked into the centre of his forehead.

Having covered about twenty yards, just to a low hedge that offered some slight cover, the companies that had burst out of the wood were pinned down. They lay with their faces pressed to the wet earth, musket balls cracking and ricocheting around them. Looking about, the British officers could see that they had come into a killing ground raked by fire on three sides. A regiment of Frenchmen was loading and firing their pieces – the cacophony was intense. Hennell, who survived these desperate moments, would write, 'I have passed, as you will see, the hottest fire I ever saw, Badajoz not excepted.' The lieutenant shouted to his men to stop firing since, 'for every shot we gave them they sent five or six in return'. He knew they could not just lie there, for the ground afforded them almost no cover – a man lying next to Hennell suddenly had his jaw shot off. Looking off to his right, the officer spotted a small ditch, to which he led his men, crawling on their bellies.

When the bugler finally sounded the retire, the soldiers knew they would have to stand up into this withering fire again to make their escape. But they went all the same, several more men falling. Seeing the retreat commence, the French launched a bayonet charge which captured Hobkirk and a dozen of his men. The remainder rallied in the woods and considered the cost of their little sally: the two companies had suffered seventy-six men killed, wounded or missing.

The 43rd's mistake at Arcangues had resulted primarily from wanting to cut a dash. The battalion's commanding officer told his wife in a letter home, 'Some young sanguine officers who are more vain than good, concluded that with three or four companies they could drive the whole French army before them.'

Hobkirk, perhaps, had fallen victim to the desire to get written up in a dispatch for a daring act, and a great many men had paid for it. There was a feeling among the officers of the Light Division that peace could be close, a sense that changed the atmosphere. Latecomers felt that there might not be much more time to distinguish themselves. Even some of the poorer veterans in the 43rd or 95th realised that further laurels won in combat might be the only way to avoid being put on the half-pay list when the eventual disbandments or amalgamations happened. Others, though, having been through so much, just felt that they did not want to get killed in the last battle of a war whose outcome was becoming a foregone conclusion. Lieutenant George Simmons, for example, remained with the recuperating

Barnard, having decided that he had already shown a great deal of pluck in battle and his advancement now required him to ingratiate himself with a man of influence.

Barnard's convalescence robbed the battalion of his energy and diligence at the very moment that its men faced a new challenge. There was an erosion of discipline on both sides, arising from the feeling of impending peace. Some Light Division officers had received *The Times* of 8 November and read of Napoleon's complete defeat at Leipzig, the greatest battle of this epoch. They showed it to some French officers who had come down to inspect their own pickets, the two parties approaching each other with a friendly wave.

Fraternisation was taking over among the outposts. When the division set up a new line of pickets on top of the Bassussarry ridge (the French having fallen back of their own accord), the enemy placed theirs close by, just thirty or forty yards in front. Officers would approach with a waved newspaper or a flask of alcohol prominently displayed, in order to signal their peaceful intent. It was understood that if one side were ordered to attack the other, the pickets would approach tapping the stocks of their weapons. This meant 'We are in earnest' and the other side would have the choice to fight or retire.

So intimate were these understandings that only the most ardent fire-eater on the British side, or dyed-in-the-wool Jacobin on the other, would violate them. One morning Lieutenant James Gairdner (returned after his Vitoria wound) was with his company's pickets when a French officer was seen approaching far closer than the agreed spot. The American-born officer and Kincaid, who was inspecting the outposts, watched this advance, before Gairdner concluded, 'Well, I won't kill these unfortunate rascals at all events, but shall tell them to go in and join their picket.' Gairdner walked forward to point out the mistake only to be saluted with gunfire. 'The balls all fell near, without touching him,' according to Kincaid, 'and, for the honour of the French army, I was glad to hear afterwards that the officer alluded to was a militia-man.' It was this sort of fellow, having imbibed too much Bonapartist propaganda or just being a raw civilian, who violated the rules adopted by the chivalrous professionals.

Among the rank and file, these arrangements went rather further. A roaring contraband trade grew up, with deals being done almost nightly at the outposts: the French bought cheap but delicious brandy on behalf of *les Goddams* whereas the riflemen provided food and tobacco for Johnny. 'We frequently went into each other's picket houses,' Costello recollected. 'This state of things at our outposts was too subversive of discipline to be tolerated by those in command, and it was only done on the sly, upon a reliance of mutual honour.' In the soldiers' case, this code of behaviour meant keeping the officers in the dark, and Costello himself cheerfully admitted to deceiving Gairdner on these occasions.

Sergeant Robert Fairfoot was able to join in these barters because Costello had managed to stop him deserting. Taking some of his Vitoria windfall, Costello gave Fairfoot £31 to replace the stolen pay. Such were the bonds between old comrades.

Arcangues, just behind the Bassussarry ridge, was turned into a kind of strongpoint during the last week of November and first of December. The chateau, church and surrounding walled enclosures had been barricaded and put into a state of defence by the 43rd and 95th. The officers made their mess in the chateau, where their host was happy to sell them many a fine bottle from the cellars.

Although the French footslogger anticipated the end of the Napoleonic system, there were still plenty, from Marshal Soult downwards, who insisted that they should do their duty in defending the sacred soil of their country. To this end, he was determined to launch an offensive against the new British lines, and it began on 9 December. An attack by General Clausel, leading two divisions onto the Bassussarry ridge and Arcangues, was ordered for the next day.

The night before the French attack there had been heavy, driving rain. It was still coming down early the following morning as the French columns were mustered and moved forwards. Everything was slowing down in the mud, particularly the artillery, which, in places, was sinking up to its axles on the tracks. The French general ordered his men to press on in any case and a first wave of skirmishers was within a hundred yards of the British pickets by 9 a.m.

On the ridge some of the mounted Light Division staff officers were trotting along with their brigadiers. The fighting elsewhere the previous day made them alive to the possibility of an attack and their battalions had been stood to arms in the valley behind them at dawn, but the day was wearing on and nothing seemed imminent. Both brigadiers – Kempt and Colborne – stood their men down. The formed regiments began returning to their billets, the pickets remaining on the ridge, hunched under their coats, trying to stay dry. Colborne's brigade major, Smith, and the divisional staff officer, Charlie Beckwith (another Rifles officer, and nephew of Colonel Sidney Beckwith), were both worried, though. They could see parties of Frenchmen moving about in the woods to their front. 'The enemy are going to attack us,' said Smith. Colborne replied, 'No, they are only going to resume their ordinary posts in our front.' Smith became agitated: 'I prayed him to allow me to order my Brigade under arms. At last he consented.'

Some Frenchers, led by officers, walked right up to some pickets of the 43rd: 'The French soldiers witnessing our civility to their small party, were determined not to be outdone in politeness, and called out to our sentinels, in French and Spanish, to retire.' A few minutes later, at around 9.30 a.m., hundreds of French troops began appearing out of the woods in front of the Bassussarry ridge. The British pickets started firing but could see immediately that they would be driven in. On one part of the ridge, where the Highland Company had made its outposts, fourteen riflemen swiftly fell as prisoners into enemy hands.

Hearing the alarm back in Arcangues, Lieutenant Gairdner was mustered along with the reserve for the outlying picket and ordered by Lieutenant Colonel Gilmour, who was in acting command of the 1st/95th (in Barnard's absence), to go onto the ridge and reinforce the picket. Gairdner discussed this briefly with Hopwood, another subaltern of the 2nd Company, to which they both belonged, and could see no sense to it. If the might of the French Army was falling on their front, there was no point in reinforcing a hopeless situation. Best to withdraw the pickets and fight at Arcangues, where a strong defensive position had been prepared. They looked up to the source of the firing, the ridge, and could see some British soldiers running back. Gilmour was insistent. Gairdner recorded his feelings:

Our company was sent out from the Chateau . . . in order to support the 3rd Batt who were actually *retiring from the ridge when we received the order to occupy it to support them.* This was mentioned to the commandant who however had not sense to comprehend that it was not only useless but dangerous to send one company up to occupy a ridge on which we were not able to communicate right or left. However we were ordered to go.

Gairdner and Hopwood went forward, taking Corporal William Brotherwood and a platoon of men. When they reached the top of the ridge, there were French just a few dozen yards in front and musket balls flying all around. They began moving about, directing their men where to take up firing positions. Corporal Brotherwood was talking to Hopwood when a crack and a puff of red mist signalled that both men had been hit. Gairdner crawled across to them. Brotherwood was twitching and breathing his last. Lieutenant Gairdner reached out and held Hopwood's hand. The back of his skull had been blown away, and Gairdner saw the grey flecks of his brain matter on the wet grass. A single bullet had gone straight through Brotherwood's head before taking off the back of Hopwood's – 'Thus died uselessly two as brave soldiers as ever stepped.'

Costello, with the same party, was firing away like a man possessed, a little way along the ridge: 'We received them with a fierce and deadly fire. They replied with spirit.' Gairdner could see the French battalions forming up now in front of him and beginning their advance, with a beating of drums and the customary cries, '*En avant, en avant Français, vive L'Empereur!*' To their left and right, enemy skirmishers were working around them. The position was quite untenable. Gairdner ordered a retreat back down to Arcangues: 'I certainly never ran quicker in my life.'

Although the remainder of 2nd Company saved itself, a good many men of the outlying picket had been killed or captured. The 2nd Battalion baggage was also taken: a financial loss and a blow to their professional pride. Gairdner, puffing and panting, fell in with the remainder of his company, fuming at what had happened.

The French footsloggers pursued their advantage, coming marching down the slope, inspired by their officers as men began falling to well-aimed British shots. The forward French battalions were able to get right up to the outskirts of the village and throw themselves into a charge, but as the shouting men came forward, fusils and rifles were directed at them from every firing point. One French officer reported: 'Although Clausel . . . got to the base of the church walls . . . the Anglo-Portuguese, in cover, poured a murderous fire on the attackers, while our weapons, soaked with rain gave only mediocre service.' After an hour of this punishment, the French pulled back, carrying their wounded and leaving dozens of dead around the village. The day was decided once again, for the British had been rained upon just as much, by superior skill at arms.

Having taken the ridge, but failed to make any progress into Arcangues, the French wheeled up twelve cannon. This powerful battery would support a general attack on Arcangues by thousands of infantry. It took until midday for the French to place their battery, the gunners sliding and falling many times as they wheeled their pieces through the boggy fields.

Seeing the guns about 350 yards away on the ridge, the British knew that effective artillery fire could cost them dear. The 95th's officers had been trained in a technique for shooting gunners at these extreme ranges: 'Riflemen may be employed also with great success against field artillery . . . keeping up a steady fire, the enemy's guns, if unsupported will soon be obliged to withdraw.' This tactic had been rarely practised, even during the long years of the Peninsular War, and it required a remarkable degree of skill on the part of the shooters, for firing was rarely considered effective – even with rifles – beyond 100 or 150 yards. Some of the soldiers had done it before, though, against the batteries near Badajoz, for example, and the 43rd's men were up for it too.

When the French battery opened up, its shells ripped through the dank air and smacked into the church tower, showering shards of masonry onto the men below. However, the French had fired barely half a dozen times when a hail of bullets began to fall among them. The defenders of Arcangues had to tip their muzzles up at an angle in order for the balls to carry all the way up to the ridgeline. But they could see their balls arcing through the sky and adjusted their shot. The French gunners were soon falling. 'We kept up an incessant discharge of small arms, which so annoyed the French gunners that, during the latter part of the day, they ceased to molest us.' The artillerymen fled back over to the safe side of the ridge. A general French offensive along the line of the River Nive had been defeated with more than four thousand casualties.

From their vantage point near the church, the Rifles could see some of their dead comrades lying on the Bassussarry hill, and at twilight, some French soldiers approached them. These men were saluted with rifle fire, the men of Leach's company being determined to drill any dog who came to plunder Corporal Brotherwood or the others. Eventually a French officer came forward waving a white handkerchief, followed by men with shovels. Assuming them to be a burial party, the riflemen held their fire.

Gairdner looked back on the day's events with considerable anger, noting in his journal, 'Both Hopwood and myself were too aware of the useless danger we were going to meet to have done it without an order . . . Hopwood lost his life through the ignorance of the commanding officer and if Colonel Barnard had commanded this day Hopwood, Brotherwood and the other sufferers from the company this day would have been spared.'

The next day, the Light Division re-established its line of outposts on the ridge. There they were saddened to discover that Hopwood and Brotherwood had been stripped of all their belongings by the 'burial party' and had no more than a sprinkling of earth on them. Among the rank and file there was much close examination of the men and the place where they had fallen, the tale of how one bullet had killed two fine men being told around many a campfire in the following months.

Reports of the action at Arcangues spread quickly in the Army. The capture of the fourteen Highland Company men was an embarrassment to the 95th of a kind it had not experienced since the Coa more than three years before. One officer of the 43rd, finding himself away from the Light Division a few days later, was asked, 'whether we had been surprised on 10 December? When assured to the contrary, he assured us that it was generally supposed to be the case . . . before leaving the main road, the same questions were put to us in another quarter, by an officer who had previously been in our own corps; which will give a faint idea how rapidly evil and malicious reports fly.'

There were those who envied the Light Division's reputation, no doubt, and thought it rather a good tale to spread that they had been humbled. The flying about of these reports, equally, pricked the pride of those who saw themselves as the best soldiers in the Army. Captain Harry Smith later conceded: 'This was nearer a surprise than anything we had ever experienced.' These weasel words, however, were in a public work. The private verdict in Gairdner's journal was quite blunt – the troops on the Bassussarry ridge, including those of a couple of divisions, had been 'taken completely by surprise'. The cost, apart from the killed and wounded, was that forty men from the 1st/95th and 43rd had been taken prisoner, including Second Lieutenant Church – he of the bayonet in the charge up La Petite Rhune.

The lessons of all this were complex – hard enough to digest for those whose own pride was involved. Peace, looming as it was, had unsettled the usual regularity of the Light Division. Some felt they should make a desperate attempt to garner some personal glory before the fighting was over, hence Hobkirk's conduct of 23 November. But for many other veterans the prospect of an end to the fighting had softened their usual vigilance and allowed the outposts to exist on terms with the French that were rather too friendly. It was the atmosphere of bonhomie among the pickets that allowed the British to be surprised. Perhaps it might not have happened under the iron grip of a Craufurd, prowling about the outposts day and night, or perhaps it would have made no difference. Such speculation doubtless filled the long nights of officers drinking and dining in the chateau.

Those officers who had felt Colonel Barnard's absence most keenly during the recent affair were delighted when he reappeared at Arcangues on 24 December, with Simmons in tow. His recovery had been remarkable, considering he had been shot through the chest, with a graze to his lung, the previous month. Despite the efforts of Army surgeons (who bled him prodigiously soon after his wounding), Barnard had been back riding his horse just a fortnight after the injury. He once again became a source of inspiration to officers or soldiers whose spirit might otherwise have been flagging.

Arcangues became remembered by most of them as a place where the division had suffered some costly mishaps, even though its defensive fighting on 10 December had turned back thousands of French troops and was among its most impressive feats of arms. However, the 95th had not yet been through its last great trial of the Peninsular War. This would come in the new year, in the dying days of Bonaparte's empire.

TWENTY-THREE

Tarbes

January–March 1814

The columns that emerged from the little town of Rabastens, just north of Tarbes, on 20 March 1814 were full of confidence. The Light Division marched in the van as usual. Their chief, Lord Wellington, was among them, darting about in his plain coat, taking everything in with his owlish eye. Marshal Soult had suffered a succession of beatings since the beginning of the year and was now falling back on Toulouse.

The 1st Battalion riflemen had been given new suits, their previous ones having more or less fallen to pieces on their backs. Colonel Barnard wanted them to have as soldierly an appearance as possible and had managed to scrounge enough shakoes – the proper regimental headgear – for each man to wear. The 2nd and 3rd Battalions were still making do with forage caps instead of those black felt cylindrical hats. The general sense among the riflemen that their war was nearing its end had hardened into a certainty, for reports coming in the mail told them that the main Allied armies were pushing deep into northern France.

A mile or two up the road, looking up to the left at about midday, Wellington spied some French light troops on the ridge, moving among the gaps between thick clumps of trees. The general quickly ordered the 2nd Battalion of Rifles to fall out and prepare to sweep the enemy *voltigeurs* from the hill. These riflemen moved off from beside the road, extending as they went into the familiar chain, and began walking uphill.

The French general here, Jean Harispe, had a surprise in store for the Rifles. The test he made of them would be almost as tough as Sabugal in April 1811, and like that battle it came about – for the British at least – as something of an accident. Harispe had spent his war in

Catalonia in the east of Spain and was not used to fighting the British
– so it might be said he was not intimidated by them.

Harispe, a French Basque, knew the country around Tarbes inti-
mately, having grown up just a few miles away. Behind the ridge that
Wellington could see, there was a dip and then a further rise. Harispe
had prepared a series of trenches on that piece of rising ground to the
rear. This would allow him to ambush whoever came over the first
ridge with several battalions of his own troops, arrayed on a hillside so
that they could fire over one another's heads.

This unpleasant surprise duly greeted the 2nd Battalion men (num-
bering about four hundred) as they cleared the initial ridge. One of the
Rifle company commanders noted, 'On gaining the summit of the hill
we found a much larger force than was supposed to be there and we
had to sustain a very severe fight against a large force before the
remainder of our corps was sent forward to support.'

The six companies of the 1st Battalion and those of the 3rd Battalion
now moved up the ridge. Costello recalled, 'We went down the road at
the "double". As we passed them, some of our regiments of cavalry
gave us an encouraging huzza.'

Many 2nd Battalion men were now dropping, falling under a withering fire of musketry. 'The whole of their heavy infantry [was] drawn
up on a steep acclivity, near the windmill, which allowed them to have
line behind line, all of which could fire over each other's heads, like the
tiers of guns on a three decker.'

The French officers ordered a charge, seeing just skirmishers in front
of them; they knew unformed men must fall back before a phalanx of
cold steel. Harispe, wrote one Rifles officer, 'having been accustomed
for many years to oppose imperfectly organised Spaniards, probably
did not calculate on so warm a reception'.

This charge drove the 2nd Battalion men back fifty yards or so and
they now found firing positions among some stone-walled vineyards
and orchards. The French battalion commanders were redressing their
ranks and readying their men for another push forward when the 1st
Battalion riflemen came trotting up, dropping into firing positions next
to their 2nd Battalion mates.

The French drums beat Old Trousers again, but these would-be
chargers were discomfited by the 1st Battalion as it began to skirmish
forwards. 'This column was driven back by a rapid advance of the 1st
Batt 95th Rifles and a close fire of a few yards literally mowed down

the French officers at the head of the column with their drummers beating the *"pas de charge"*.'

Lieutenant George Simmons, seeing the French falter and begin to crumble, stood up to lead his men forward, but then, 'a Frenchman took a long shot at me; the ball fractured my right knee pan and knocked me down as if I had been struck with a sledge-hammer'. Colonel Barnard, who commanded this battle of eighteen Rifle companies against a French brigade, had meanwhile sent the 3rd Battalion off to the right to turn the enemy flank. In the centre, 'a heavy tirallade was then kept up in the vineyards between the riflemen and large bodies of French *voltigeurs* which caused loss to us as we had no cover and could not give up any of the ground we had taken'.

With the French falling back through walls and trees, the two sides blazed away in a withering contest of firearms. They were close enough for the Baker rifle's advantages to be negated, the French being able to get aimed shots in over the twenty or thirty yards that separated them. The Rifles officers, leading their men forward, paid a heavy price, eleven becoming casualties. Captain William Cox, 2nd Battalion, got a ball in his left thigh, breaking the femur like a dry branch, and his brother John, still serving with the 1st, was shot in the right leg.

Harispe ordered a general withdrawal of his division, for there were other British formations advancing on his flanks and he needed to disentangle himself. With the enemy streaming back, the British buglers sounded the recall and Barnard's companies formed up in case the French changed their minds and resumed the attack. Wellington rode up to see the 1st Battalion on top of the ridge, telling them, 'Ah, there you are, as usual, just where you should be; not gone too far.'

Barnard found the general and insisted that he should come further, for there had been a great slaughter of the attacking French. Wellington told him, 'Well, Barnard, to please you, I will go, but I require no novel proof of the destructive fire of your Rifles.' The 95th's officers were quite taken aback by the casualties: 'The loss of the enemy from the fire of our Rifles was so great that one could not believe one's eyes. I certainly had never seen the dead lie so thick, nor ever did, except subsequently at Waterloo.'

It is unclear exactly how many men the French lost. Official French returns indicate only around 180 killed and wounded. The Rifles officers, though, were adamant that the numbers had been substantial. Their estimates ranged from asserting that the French suffered as many casualties as the entire number of riflemen engaged (over a thousand) to suggestions that they had suffered double the British losses (those being 111 officers and men, killed and wounded), an estimate not so hard to reconcile with the official French figures. It is quite possible, though, that French casualties may have reached three or even four hundred, Lieutenant James Gairdner commenting in his journal, 'I never saw on any occasion so many men killed by skirmishers as the enemy lost on this occasion.'

Although the French Army was pretty well knocked up by this point in the campaign, the importance of the engagement at Tarbes was that it was the 95th's own battle – a mass employment of Rifles which involved taking an entrenched position by frontal assault and then withstanding a countercharge by enemy assault columns. There had been no partnership with the 43rd or 52nd at Tarbes, as in so many other battles. It thus marked the final emphatic vindication of the 95th's tactics and methods of the Peninsular War.

'On the 20th the Army advanced near Tarbes and we had quite a 95th affair,' Barnard wrote to Cameron, his predecessor as commanding officer.

I assure you the rifles were laid very strait . . . the enemy lost as many men as I think it possible to be knocked over in so short a time – the beauty of the business was that we were formed and ready for another attack in a few minutes. Lord W. saw the whole business and was most pleased with the rapidity with which the corps made its attacks and equally so with the quickness with which they got together when it was over.

Lest this seem too much like the 95th trumpeting its own achievement, it is worth quoting the views of a British officer from another regiment who was attached to the Portuguese army at the time of Tarbes:

I never saw such skirmishers as the 95th, now the Rifle Brigade. They could do the work much better, and with infinitely less loss than any other of our best light troops. They possessed an individual boldness, a mutual understanding, and a quickness of eye, in taking advantage of the ground, which taken together, I never saw equalled.

George Simmons, in agony from his smashed knee, was taken back to Tarbes in a wagon with some other casualties. There, to his delight, he found that his brother Maud had been appointed the town major. Maud soon installed George in the best lodgings at his disposal. The two brothers were to spend weeks together there as Wellington's Army marched towards the last act of the Peninsular War in Toulouse.

They wrote home, George reflecting that the French Army's performance in 1814 had improved somewhat but that 'Every cock ought to fight better upon its own dung hill.' Although Marshal Soult had been able to inspire those who stayed within the ranks to fight well, thousands had deserted from the French Army in expectation of the imminent collapse of the Empire.

The brothers managed to lay in large supplies of excellent Bordeaux at one shilling a bottle and spent the evenings talking over the fate of Europe and of the Simmons clan. George proudly showed off an inscribed gold watch that Colonel Barnard had given him in thanks for his nursing after the Battle of the Nivelle. He was relieved that his own wound would not disqualify him from further service.

Maud Simmons was evidently more reconciled to the end of hostilities, telling his parents that 'peace must shortly bring us together'. George talked of getting back to his regiment and of enlisting in some other country's army if indeed Bonaparte was really done for. His feelings, and the degree to which he accepted the vicissitudes and simple pleasures of a soldier's life, were quite unusual. Captain Leach was speaking for far more when he stated, 'The general and universal feeling . . . was that, for the present we had had enough of campaigning.'

Those days of late March involved the battalion in another reckoning, one infinitely less to its credit than the combat of Tarbes. The facts were as follows: on 18 March several soldiers had entered a French farmer's house near the village of Plaisance. When he refused them drink and cash, an argument began and the farmer struck one of the soldiers. This cuff cost the Frenchman his life, for one of the intruders, flying into a fury, killed him on the spot.

When British officers investigated the complaints of the villagers in Plaisance, they soon determined that the criminals were riflemen. 'We tried every means to find out the villain, but to no purpose,' wrote one officer. Soldiers were paraded and told that they would all suffer if they did not give up the culprit. There was little chance, however, of intimidating the men. Not only were they grizzled veterans who would be loath to rat on a messmate – they all also knew the strict orders against pillaging the French that had been issued by Lord Wellington. If you handed over a man for this crime, it would be as good as putting him on a rope yourself.

Careful consideration of the timing of the murder led some to suspect the 1st Battalion and, indeed, Leach's company. Many of the officers, though, chose to blame the crime on the Portuguese and to turn a page on the whole affair. A collection of a hundred guineas was made for the French farmer's wife; the battalion marched away and the murderer remained undetected. But just as the men of Lieutenant James Gairdner's platoon had deceived him about the degree of their fraternisation and commerce with the enemy the previous autumn, so some of them were now keeping secret the identity of the murderer and his accomplices within 2nd Company's ranks.

TWENTY-FOUR

Castel Sarrazin

April–June 1814

Almost a month had passed since Simmons's wounding at Tarbes when he reached Toulouse. He was still limping heavily, but was fit, in his own view, to rejoin the regiment. There he was able to gaze upon the city's defences, shattered that April in the battle that marked the final chapter in the Peninsular War. The fight, with its thousands killed and maimed, was doubly futile, since a messenger carrying news of Napoleon's abdication reached Marshal Soult just too late to stop it happening. Toulouse was another of those large set pieces in which the 95th's role had not been great.

Simmons pressed on until 20 May, when he reached a town called Castel Sarrazin. There he 'found the officers living in the gayest manner possible. The people extremely kind to us.' Those who had spent years living in rude bivouacs, not knowing whether each day would be their last, found an idyll in Sarrazin. They walked along the banks of the Garonne, escorted the prettiest French girls to dances, lay reading in the long grass and supped fine feasts *à la fourchette*.

The local women were grateful for such chivalrous companions – their own stock of men had been depleted by the long wars, the wine was sublime and the delicacies were cheap. For the soldiers, though, there was an irony in their situation: it was part of the perverse logic of war that whenever they found themselves somewhere truly delightful, they were deep in arrears of pay, in this case nine months. Nevertheless, they somehow contrived to scrape a few pennies together and benefited from much local hospitality.

The change in the lives of these hardened men was so complete that some were quite disorientated by it. Captain Harry Smith described their feelings eloquently:

The feeling of no war, no picquets, no alerts, no apprehension of being turned out, was so novel after six years perpetual and vigilant war, it is impossible to describe the sensation. Still, it was one of momentary anxiety, seeing around us the promptitude, the watchfulness, the readiness with which we could move and be in a state of defence or attack. It was so novel that at first it was positively painful – at least, I can answer for myself in this feeling.

Quite a few of the young men fell hopelessly in love in Sarrazin. It took no more than a nervous introduction, a chaperoned walk by the river and some exchange of pleasantries for their hearts, starved for so long of female company, to soar to the heights of passion. John Kincaid tells us, 'in returning from a ride, I overtook my love and her sister, strolling by the river's side, and, instantly dismounting, I joined in their walk . . . when I looked round, I found her mounted astride on my horse! and with such a pair of legs too!'

The girls being of good family, and their suitors chivalrous gentlemen, few if any of these passions were consummated. But there were towns from Toulouse to Bordeaux with whores enough for those who could not contain themselves amid so much beauty. Leach was convinced that even among the peasantry of the French Basque region, 'I never remember in any country having seen more handsome women collected together . . . their complexions were strikingly and almost universally beautiful.'

The Rifles officers escorted their new-found belles to dances and *fêtes champêtres*, thankful for the recent issue of clothing that had at least stopped them looking like scarecrows. But French ladies, like their warrior husbands, were unused to the dark-green uniforms of the 95th, leading to many misunderstandings and much teasing by officers of other regiments. One subaltern of the 43rd noted gleefully that his friend in the 95th 'was most confoundedly annoyed when the officers of the Rifle corps were taken for Portuguese, which was very often. Then again, the foreigners could not understand their not wearing epaulettes, and they were under the painful necessity of telling the people of every town they went to that they were really officers.'

The other ranks were also able to amuse themselves during these weeks. Costello, who by this time was a corporal, went with another NCO across the River Tarn one evening to join in a feast at the sergeants' mess of a French infantry regiment. The two riflemen walked along lines of their former foes, saluting them before being summoned inside to sit at tables groaning with local produce. Toasts were raised, and 'we did not forget to do justice to the acknowledged merits of John Bull in all matters of this nature, and much good feeling and conviviality followed, with encomiums and compliments being passed on the English.' Only one of their hosts tried to sour the atmosphere with a choice remark about the visitors' fighting qualities, and he was thrown down some stairs by his fellow *sous-officiers* for his trouble. Costello discovered a bond with some of the French soldiers, their shared freemasonry helping to cement good feeling.

Napoleon's defeated legions were not so polite everywhere. The French civilians generally welcomed the British, but following one visit to a dance in Moissac, across the Tarn, Simmons noted, 'The French officers were jealous of the civility shown to us by the people, and requested we would not visit the town any more.' Leach went to watch a review of some of the French regiments and was delighted to spot Marshals Suchet and Soult. The first seemed garrulous; as for the junior officers, they were 'for the most part lively and animated, without the smallest appearance of despondency or disappointment at the late change, or the loss of their imperial master. Marshal Soult alone appeared sullen and dejected.'

As the Rifles battalions waited to discover what would happen to them, Lieutenant Gairdner once more faced the anxiety of being ordered to fight in his native America, where a nasty conflict of raids and inconclusive but bloody engagements continued. Although serving with the 1st Battalion, Gairdner was technically on the strength of the 3rd and it was they who were eventually ordered, along with thousands of Wellington's men, to embark for America. Thankfully, Colonel Barnard was able to retain him with the 1st Battalion, for otherwise he would have felt bound to resign. Gairdner's feelings were further complicated by his infatuation with a local girl in Sarrazin.

On 30 May, when the 1st/95th finally received its order to embark for England, Gairdner was wrenched away from his sweetheart along with all the other Light Division officers who had enjoyed the Elysian fields on the banks of the Garonne. Gairdner wrote in his journal, 'The thought of leaving Castel Sarrazin perhaps never to see it more gives me greater pain than I could have thought possible.' His company commander would later write, 'Great regret was expressed when the order arrived which obliged us to leave our new French acquaintances; some of the fair females of whom had ruined the peace of mind (*pro tempore*) of many of our gallant gay Lotharios.'

The farewells were to prove particularly difficult for those men of the regiment who had acquired Spanish and Portuguese wives. It became clear, with the orders to return to Shorncliffe, that these women would not be allowed to travel back with them. Some tried to make arrangements for their *guapas* to follow on later, others bade them goodbye. In six cases, though, the riflemen chose to desert rather than leave their lovers behind. One of the Scottish Cummings brothers, Joseph, a bugler in the 2nd Company, was among those who disappeared as the dread day approached.

This moment came on 11 June 1814, as the Light Division was marching across southern France for embarkation at Bordeaux. The 95th, 43rd and 52nd lined the streets, presenting arms, as the *Cacadores*, men of the 17th Portuguese Regiment, and wives and followers who had been their companions through thick and thin passed between them. The twenty-one Spaniards who soldiered on in the 1st/95th's ranks, including Lazarro Blanco, who had been in Leach's company since June 1812, were also discharged on this day. British soldiers gave three lusty cheers to their comrades, many of whom marched away in tears. The young boys who had looked after the milk goats and mules for company messes were given the animals as presents. Some of the followers, evidently feeling cheated, stole before they went.

It was only after their departure that some of Costello's mates told him that Blanco, then marching to his home in Spain, was the man who had killed the French farmer in Plaisance two months before. Not only had he got away with murder, but the role of his British or Irish accomplices in the company was to remain a secret for ever, for the reports had made it clear that Blanco did not commit the crime on his own. Another mystery was solved, however, as the battalion prepared to embark: William MacFarlane, a soldier who had deserted the regiment in October 1811, decamped from the French Army and was returned to his old battalion. Three of the five men who deserted during the same period, including Joseph Almond, had been executed. But MacFarlane, who had served Napoleon for as many years as Almond had weeks, escaped with his life.

As for the financial rewards for all those years of bitter fighting, many of the men felt hard done by. Marching into Bordeaux on 14 June, most had nothing more than the coloured clothes they stood up in. It was true that some, like Costello, had secreted away some treasure from Vitoria or some other place of plunder. The great majority had not, though, and all their pay had been spent maintaining a supply of rum and tobacco during countless freezing wet nights on the Beira frontier.

The only medals carried by the rank and file of the 95th were the odd *Légions d'honneur* taken from Frenchmen during their campaigns. This they resented bitterly. For many of the riflemen even a distinction like the little badge bearing the letters 'V.S.' inside a laurel would have been something. These were run up by the 52nd's tailor for men who had survived Badajoz and Rodrigo, the initials standing for 'Valiant Stormer'. For some reason the 43rd and 95th did not get even these distinctions.

In trying to reward these veterans, the hands of Wellington and other officers were tied by the Horse Guards' bureaucracy. Napoleon had proved far better at establishing a scheme of payments and marks of distinction for outstanding soldiers. The Peninsular Army did manage to copy one such French measure: the appointment of deserving men to guard the regimental colours. The British rank of colour sergeant had been introduced to reward distinguished NCOs with an extra nine pennies a day. Robert Fairfoot was an early recipient of this bounty, having been appointed colour sergeant in September 1813.

Among the officers, many had spent rather more than they earned in the Peninsula. One subaltern of the 43rd calculated his net loss at £70, a sum made good in bills dispatched by his parents. For the likes of George Simmons, sending £40 or £50 each year in the other direction, only the most careful husbandry of his resources prevented him from ending his campaign in debt. Simmons and many of the other officers had profited from the fortunes of war, too, having unburdened a good many dead or captured French of medals, trinkets, horses and cash. The wheel of fortune had turned quite a few times during those long years, of course, and most of the old campaigners had also lost horses and mules during their marches, bearing the expense out of their own pockets.

For the real veterans, the group who had sailed out in May 1809, the moment was coming to cash in the pay arrears. Pay parades had been cancelled or deferred so often that many had received considerably less than their due during the five years they had been away. The money owing – hundreds of pounds for a subaltern – would be payable when they got home. There was also the blood money due to many of them for their wounds. Simmons had been seriously wounded twice, Costello twice and Sergeant Fairfoot five times, most severely at Badajoz.

How many, though, had soldiered through like them? The battalion, along with the 2nd Rifles, was carried home on a huge three-decker battleship, the *Ville de Paris*, arriving off Portsmouth on 22 July 1814. They came back as they had left, to three cheers – not from their loved ones, for they had no idea when the battalion would dock or where, but from the yardarms and tops of the *Ville de Paris*, a tribute from the tars to the toughest soldiers of Wellington's army.

Of the forty-seven officers who sailed with the battalion in May 1809, only six were still serving with the Peninsular Army at the end of the campaigns in southern France. Of these, Captain Harry Smith was away on the staff (and sailed at the last minute for America) and his brother Lieutenant Tom Smith was serving in the 2nd Battalion. That left four 1st Battalion officers – Lieutenant Colonel Dugald Gilmour, Major Jonathan Leach, Captain Willie Johnston and Lieutenant George Simmons – of whom two had been back in Britain for leave during the years of fighting. So just two officers returning in July 1814 – Leach and Simmons – had served with the battalion all the way through from May 1809, and even they had both had periods of sick leave in Portugal.

What became, then, of the forty-five officers who were no longer with the 1st Battalion? Fourteen of them had fallen in battle or died of wounds received there, with two more perishing of sickness. Eighteen had been wounded at some stage. These and the other unscathed officers had all gone home at some point during the long conflict. Leach was doubly exceptional in both being there at the end and having escaped wounding in his many fights.

The picture among the disembarking rankers was a little different, because almost none of them had had the option of taking leave in England during the long wars. The 1st Battalion had 1,095 NCOs and soldiers at the time it sailed in May 1809, but the vagaries of Army record-keeping do not allow every single man's fate to be precisely determined. The fact that the Army itself did not know the exact numbers is clear from a note on the monthly returns for March 1814. The acting paymaster had listed twenty-one men as having died on 1 March, a day on which the battalion had no combat losses. That this was a book-keeping exercise becomes clear with the symbol beside each name, one which was explained at the bottom of the ledger with the words, 'those for whom no satisfactory account could be given'. This squaring of the regimental books was a writing off of men last seen in hospitals or disappearing from camp at night; in short, those whose fate was unknown. When multiplied by all the corps in the Peninsular Army, the 95th's twenty-one lost soldiers became an extraordinary 1,837. Wellington's Adjutant General, reporting this vast writing-off of lives to Horse Guards in London, opined that 'it is to be presumed that nearly the whole of these men have died in hospitals'. Given the skill of some soldiers at sloping off after they were discharged from hospital, it is difficult to share his confidence, and it is likely that a significant minority of these men deserted. To return to the riflemen, though, it is possible – leaving aside these twenty-one – to determine pretty much what happened to the rest of the original battalion.

Of the 1,095 who originally went out, about 180 were sent home during the course of the war, with something like 125 of them invalided by a medical board for being too injured or broken down to continue and the others sent home 'to recruit' as the battalion dissolved four of its companies in the field. The 1st/95th had lost seventy-nine prisoners of war and at least twenty-three men had deserted. It is likely that a good few of the men written off on 1 March 1814 had also deserted, which is why the 'at least twenty-three' lost to the battalion in this way was probably more like thirty. The largest portion of the original group, 421, were those who had died in Iberia – about two-thirds in battle and the remainder through sickness. All of this meant that only about a third of those who had sailed with the battalion – roughly 350 – also returned with it.

Having formed the men up on the quayside, Barnard led his battalion to Hilsea Barracks. Many officers took immediate leave. One captain who disappeared off to the capital recorded, 'Here we enjoyed the luxuries of London life for a short time, having three years' pay to receive – one for arrears and two for wounds received.' The men took a sort of communal holiday, marching up the coast to Hythe and Sandgate, 'for seabathing'. Those who had been wounded received in many cases not just the official blood money but also extra grants of anything up to £50 from the Patriotic Fund, set up by citizens grateful to the men who had vanquished the Corsican ogre.

George Simmons, who had sailed home on another ship, made his way immediately to London, where he settled down on the morning of his arrival at Old Slaughter's Coffee House to drink a pot of the fine stuff, have a smoke and peruse the newspapers. Whether the people looked upon the weathered Green Jacket like a 'dancing bear', he did not record. He was able to use some of his back pay to buy some plain clothes and return home to Yorkshire to see his beloved family.

Very few of those who had gone to war in 1809 had left behind wives. The figure may have been as low as one man in twenty among the NCOs and privates. There were, though, a few awkward home-comings to be negotiated. In one case, Ned Costello accompanied a sergeant who went in search of his wife and daughter in Portsmouth. Finding the house at last, they saw several children and another man, clearly her new spouse, in residence: 'My poor friend looked perplexed, his features alternating between doubt and fear.' The woman began sobbing and there was a general expectation that murder might be committed. Costello's comrade, however, had lived through enough to take this reverse phlegmatically. The sergeant told his wife's new husband that 'it is no use our skirmishing about', then extracted a six-pence from him to seal the bargain; he placed a golden guinea in the hands of the daughter he had not seen for five years, turned, and left, retiring to a nearby public house with Costello to drown his sorrows.

Among many of those who had rediscovered their wives in happier circumstances, there was a strong desire to resume some sort of quiet domesticity. Riflemen who had lived for years with hungry bellies and no roof over their heads at last found normality. A few – fifteen or so – decided that they did not intend to take their chances on another campaign and deserted in England during the later part of 1814 and early 1815.

Some, like Sergeant Robert Fairfoot, who had sailed as unmarried men, were struck by the providential nature of their survival, and wanted to settle down and raise families. He did not intend to be back-wards about it: so it was that Fairfoot married Catherine Campbell, a slip of a girl of sixteen, on 2 October 1814. That it had been a rapid courtship is self-evident. There is every reason, though, to suppose that the couple were happily in love. He was a handsome man, despite his scars, and one in receipt of a good deal of pay, evidently well qualified to keep Catherine in some comfort.

The battalion wintered, then, with its members rediscovering the pleasures of peace. Lieutenant John Kincaid disappeared to Scotland for hunting and fishing. James Gairdner planned to take several months' leave to visit America in the summer of 1815, and the battalion was left in the hands of its veterans, with the likes of Jonathan Layton and George Simmons overseeing the companies.

All calculations were upset, however, in April 1815, when news reached the battalion of Napoleon's escape from exile in Elba. Lieutenant Colonel Barnard received orders to prepare the 1st/95th for imminent embarkation. It had been tricky enough leading them through the final year of their campaign in Spain and France – the desertion, looting and sickness had shown that a significant number of soldiers had endured enough campaigning, and wanted only to escape the regiment on terms as advantageous to themselves as possible. Although the Rifles had received hundreds of new recruits since returning the previous summer, Barnard saw fit to use just six out of ten companies, one already on the continent would fall in with another five that he would bring across the Channel. His aim was to concentrate the best men in the small battalion that he was taking on service, and to sprinkle them with a leavening of recruits. In this way, as in the battalion that sailed six years before, the veterans would aim to impress the new men and vice versa. There was a difference, though: many of the old soldiers who embarked in 1815 considered that their survival through so many years of war was little short of miraculous, and were unsettled at being wrenched out of peaceful southern England. For this reason, the campaign that lay ahead would be the 95th's ultimate test.

TWENTY-FIVE

Quatre Bras

April–June 1815

The embarkation at Dover was performed at the same quay as that of 1809. On 25 April 1815, six companies of the 1st Battalion, 95th, were put on board a packet boat, the *Wensley Dale*, to the cheers and acclamation of the townsfolk. The Rifles had already changed quite a bit since returning from France the previous year, and about one soldier in four was new to the battalion.

Leach's 2nd Company was the least altered. It was under the same chief that had embarked it in 1809, and its lieutenants, John Cox, FitzMaurice and Gairdner, were all veterans. The more senior subalterns had pulled rank on the lowly ones when Colonel Barnard had begun to prepare the battalion for its new campaign. Costello and many of the other 2nd Company soldiers remained under Leach too. Sergeant Fairfoot, meanwhile, had gone to the 8th Company, and George Simmons to the 10th. Simmons's brother Joseph had been left behind in the general trampling over the junior men. The Smith family, always able to pull a stroke, had managed to attach Charles, younger brother of Tom and Harry, to make his military debut in Simmons's company as an uncommissioned gentleman volunteer.

That the battalion included many Johnny Raws was simply one of those features of military life that would have to be overcome, just as it had five years before – and never mind that the old sweats were calling them 'recruits' in a derisive tone of voice. The more subtle difference from 1809 was that now, many of the regiment's veterans felt a certain tiredness and even resentment at having all their hopes for a peaceful life thrown over for a new campaign. James Gairdner wrote to his father:

This cursed war has knocked all my plans in the head; I thought a month ago that by this time I should be on my way to see you, but this scoundrel Bonaparte to the astonishment of the world has, as it were, by magic reseated himself without spilling a drop of blood on that throne which cost Europe just twelve months ago so much blood and treasure to pull him down from.

As for those who had hoped to get on with the business of raising a family, their dilemmas were personified by Corporal George Pitt, who brought his wife to Dover docks. Lieutenant Colonel Barnard was determined to stick with Beckwith's 1809 ban on embarking women, and soon found himself in a heated argument with the corporal. 'Sir', cried Corporal Pitt, 'my wife was separated from me when I went to the Peninsular War, I had rather die than be parted from her again.' Barnard was not used to being confronted in such an insolent way and he gave Pitt the choice of leaving his wife behind or embarking her and facing court martial. The corporal chose the latter, for he and Mrs Pitt had no way of knowing whether he would be away for six months or six years, or indeed whether he would ever come home.

The *Wensley Dale* docked in Ostend on 27 April, after a wretched voyage in which many men had been helplessly seasick. Their feelings were further upset when they were paraded on the quay to witness George Pitt's punishment. Barnard had ordered him broken to the ranks and awarded three hundred lashes. The flaying of his back duly began, the buglers laying on their cats nearly a hundred times before George Simmons called out, testifying to Pitt's qualities as a soldier and asking Barnard to spare him further punishment. The colonel agreed to stop it, telling Simmons afterwards that he 'disliked flogging as much as any man', but had been left with no choice because of the flouting of his orders.

The Pitt affair meant the campaign began in poor humour. Among the veterans, there were many who doubted whether they had the fortitude to endure years more suffering. Even Simmons himself, a real fire-eater, wrote home that he must buy a riding horse, for 'my legs will never carry me through a long campaign. After a day's march I am lame. If I get hit again they must promote me or recommend me for Chelsea.'

The surliness of the Belgians did not help matters either. Simmons had noted that on entering Brussels on 12 May, there were 'crowds of natives who were gaping and staring at us. I heard no *Vivas*, they appeared to treat the whole concern very coolly indeed.' There was still a great of sympathy for the Bonapartist cause among Belgians. On 17 May, some riflemen were even attacked by the locals, resulting in a sergeant shooting dead one of the rioters.

All the same, campaigns were best endured by putting a best foot forward and some compensations were soon discovered. Many did not expect the fighting to last long. The 1st Battalion of Rifles would be brigaded under General Kempt, who was known and respected from the Peninsula, as was Picton, their divisional commander. Picton was remembered by some for his feud with Craufurd and his occasional signs of ill grace towards the Light Division. In this new campaign, however, this evidently did not prevent him appreciating the 95th's military qualities.

Food was very cheap, the messes being able to fry up a pound or two of bacon every morning. Drink, likewise, did not strain the pocket, with many soldiers indulging rather too freely, reminding their officers of their duty to limit the consumption of alcohol.

'As the middle of June approached', wrote Kincaid, who had scurried across to Belgium from a shooting party in Scotland, 'we all began to get a little more on the *qui vive*, for we were all aware that Napoleon was about to make a dash at some particular point.' Orders were duly received in Brussels late at night on 15 June to muster the men in the Place Royale at 11.30 p.m. Such were the pleasures of the Belgian metropolis that 'in consequence of the difficulty of assembling the division, it did not march until near four o'clock this morning'. Lieutenant Gairdner was left behind to round up the 95th's stragglers and this party got under way at 8 a.m. on 16 June.

Kempt's brigade was marched down towards Charleroi, south of the forest of Soignes, where there were alarms that the French were present in great numbers. Wellington, 'humbugged' by Napoleon's marches, had been obliged to throw together a disparate body of men to reinforce his Dutch-Belgian allies near an important road junction called Quatre Bras.

At about 2 p.m., the 95th, having marched a hot summer's day, paused just north of the crossroads and began cooking up a meal. As they sat there, the riflemen watched the Black Legion, the Germans under the Duke of Brunswick, march by. Wellington soon appeared and directed the Rifles to move to the south-east of Quatre Bras to occupy a position in some trees on the left flank of his army, maintaining the line of communication to the Prussians who were heavily engaged that day at Ligny. As was often the case in the Peninsula, Wellington gave orders to the commanding officer of the Rifles in person, saying, 'Barnard, these fellows are coming on; you must stop them by throwing yourselves into that wood.'

The 95th marched a little south-east on the Namur road and then turned right, or south, into the fields. Four companies were ordered by Barnard to attack some French light troops to their front. The companies extended among rows of billowing corn, which came up so high they could hardly see over it. Simmons, with the 10th Company, fell under that tough old duellist Jonathan Layton, for the titular commander, Charlie Beckwith, had quickly removed himself to a staff position, just as he had in the Peninsula.

Layton and Simmons directed their men down to a formidable-looking hedgerow not far in front of the French. Some enemy cannon had begun playing on the Allied lines and one of the old riflemen quipped, 'Ah! My boys, you are opening the ball in good style!' Simmons worked his way through the thorny hedge, dropping onto lower ground on the other side and instantly coming under French fire. With the crackle of musketry intensifying, he wondered why his men were holding back. Simmons went back through the thorns and found Sergeant Daniel Underwood, a veteran like himself of O'Hare's old Peninsular 3rd Company. Why was he holding back? Underwood made out it was because of the thorns. 'Why man! You are like a fine lady!' Simmons taunted him. Still he did not go forward. 'I rushed forward and struck him in the centre of the knapsack with my right shoulder, it had the effect of a battering ram, through it he went.'

With his men on the same side of the brambles as their enemy, they opened fire. For the French soldiers at the head of this column, this sudden hail of metal came as a shock. 'We were saluted by a fusillade of extreme violence,' wrote one French colonel, 'it was the English who, hidden in the tall corn, fired onto us. Since, for the moment, we could not see where this firing was coming from, the column faltered somewhat.' Seeing the effect of this murderous rifle fire, Picton threw his formed infantry forward. The kilted Black Watch and Camerons marched on, accompanied by several English or Irish battalions.

The French were thrown back some way, but soon rallied their forces. The thump of hooves announced the imminent arrival of cavalry and the *voltigeurs* at last began to move forward again, answering the 95th's fire with fire. The French fusillade was becoming heavy, and

Layton made his way over to Simmons to confer. As he arrived, a bullet smacked into the company commander's wrist, leaving Layton's hand hanging limply and blood pouring out of the wound. Simmons ripped off Layton's shirtsleeve and began to bind it, advising him to go to the rear and find a surgeon. Layton, one of the few to soldier through the Peninsula without injury, took it personally: he looked in the direction from where the shot had come, telling Simmons, 'You must hit the fellow first.'

Simmons ran forward at a crouch with one of the sergeants to take cover behind a tree stump just in front. The lieutenant readied his rifle, while the sergeant kept his eyes keenly on the spot where they expected the French sharpshooter to appear, so that he might direct the shot. When the Frenchman at last fired, the ball hit Simmons's companion square in the forehead. The sergeant was hurled back several feet and his brains blown out of the back of his head. Simmons turned to see how his men might react to this loss, calling out to them, 'Look at that glorious fellow, our comrade and brother soldier – he now knows the grand secret!'

The Rifles had put themselves in a particularly hot post, for they were under fire from hundreds of French light troops. Costello was hit too, a ball tearing off his trigger finger. Lieutenant Gairdner followed Layton to the rear, having been struck in the leg by a shot – his personal run of bad luck continuing from Badajoz and Vitoria.

With heavy French columns advancing now on the Quatre Bras junction, supported by cavalry, the Rifles would soon have to step aside. Several of their men had been killed in the initial skirmishing; those wounded included Private James Burke, that 'wild untameable animal' of the Peninsular sieges, who would die of the wounds received that day. The 95th took refuge in a wood close to the Namur road and to the flank of the main fighting, which raged between French divisions under Ney and the British infantry led forward not half an hour before by Picton.

Two of the British battalions, including the 42nd Highlanders or Black Watch, had advanced in line into some dead ground south of the Namur road. While this position sheltered them from artillery, it also gave them little time to react to the approach of enemy horse, who were now thrown on them by the French generals. This was the British Army's first real brush with cuirassiers, the heavy cavalry in breastplates that Napoleon usually kept as a personal reserve. These big men came galloping through the smoke; on seeing the Highlanders, they bore down on them. Being caught in a two-deep line, the Scots were hardly able to defend themselves except by firing off a volley as the cuirassiers ploughed through their files, sabreing left and right as they passed: many of them were knocked flying by the flanks of the cuirassiers' big chargers and some were trampled under hoof. The 42nd were then ordered to about-turn, where they gave the French another, slightly more effective volley and then belatedly attempted to form square, as the onslaught continued. Many riflemen witnessed this bloody engagement, which cost the 42nd dear, with some anxiety. At length, the dark falling on the field, the 95th were withdrawn a little to a group of farm buildings, where they lay down for some rest.

On the morning of the 17th, the day began with a satisfying brew of tea and a few pounds of good bacon, but it was destined to be marred by one of those bizarre mishaps of war. Sergeant Fairfoot was standing chatting with his old friend Lieutenant Simmons when the latter decided on a little horseplay. Finding a cuirassier's breastplate and gloves, he began to parade up and down, eliciting hoots and laughter from the men. One French sharpshooter posted nearby, regarding this as a fighting rather than laughing matter, took a shot at Simmons. The ball hit, not its intended target, but Fairfoot's right arm. Doubled over with pain, Fairfoot shouted out, 'Oh Mr Simmons, the game is up with me, for this campaign anyhow.' His resignation turned to anger as Simmons bound the wound. Before heading back to the surgeons with his arm in a sling, Fairfoot loaded his rifle, rested it on Simmons's shoulder, and fired it with his left hand towards his assailant.

The 95th spent the remainder of the 17th covering the rear of Wellington's army as it fell back towards Brussels, taking up its fighting position on the Mont Saint Jean ridge. News had reached the British of the mauling received by Field Marshal Blucher the day before at Ligny. Leach commented, 'The man of candour will not deny, be he ever so determined a fire eater, that the news of this disastrous defeat of our allies was calculated to throw a damp on the prospects of the campaign.'

That night they were all dampened more literally, by a torrential downpour of the kind that the veterans had come to regard as a good omen during their years in Iberia. Barnard was able to find quarters in a small farm building and, perhaps remembering the lieutenant's kindness after his wounding at the Nivelle, invited Simmons to stay with him. Simmons thanked him but replied, 'Sir, if I were to stay here, the Company would have contempt for me, I must go and rough it with them.'

At dawn on the 18th the French Army was revealed to them in the murky light. Fires were started and men stretched stiff, wet limbs. They were soon hard at work, checking their weapons were dry and ready to fire, drinking tea and preparing themselves for the trial that would be Waterloo.

TWENTY-SIX

Waterloo

June 1815 and Afterwards

From early morning on 18 June, the 95th's camp kettles were boiling away outside Barnard's billet. The house was just behind a crossroads on the Mont Saint Jean ridge. As it was one of the pivotal points of the battlefield, the riflemen found themselves serving up hot, sweet tea to every variety of commander from Wellington downwards, as they came to study the ground.

The paved road from Brussels to Genappe extended away downhill to their front. About two hundred yards from the top of the ridge, on the right of the road, was the walled farm of La Haye Sainte. This had been turned into a strongpoint and was occupied by light troops of the German Legion. On the left of the road, halfway between the ridge top and that farm, was an area which had been excavated for gravel, known as the sandpit. It was here that Captain Leach was initially posted with two companies, ready to go forward and skirmish. Just to his rear was another company, which could join them. The 1st/95th's formed reserve, its other three companies, would be posted on the road running from east to west on top of the ridge, behind some hedges. Barnard and his second-in-command, Major Alexander Cameron, would be here too.

Wellington and Napoleon had of course brought vast armies to this field and the 95th's position represented but a stitch or two on the tapestry of deployments. Several artillery batteries were placed on the ridge just in front of Barnard and the 95th's reserve. Picton's infantry battalions were mostly behind them, in an area invisible to the French. Off to the Rifles' right was an infantry division under Karl von Alten, the Light Division's old Peninsular chief. Way off, further to the right and outside their view, was the chateau of

Hougomont which would be defended by the Guards Division.

As for Napoleon, he chose a ridge about five hundred yards in front of Leach's position to site his main concentration of artillery. This wall of eighty guns would be able to hurl a weight of shot at the British centre and left quite unlike anything they had experienced in the Peninsula. During the morning, 'we perceived our adversaries bringing into position, on the heights opposite, gun after gun', Leach wrote, 'intended particularly to salute our division, the farm of La Haye Sainte and the left of Baron Alten's division.' Wellington had ensured that by placing them on the reverse slope of the ridge, much of his infantry would be untouched by that battery, but the 95th and German Legion around Haye Sainte would not have that luxury.

While the French were hauling up caissons full of ammunition and yet more cannon, the 95th distributed cartridges and sent its transport to the rear. Simmons and a party under him went to cut down trees to help build up a barricade on the main road south, near Haye Sainte. This would stop enemy cavalry and horse artillery using this route to rush up to the British position.

At about 1 p.m. the French guns opened the ball, the very first shot from the grand battery taking off a rifleman's head, and scattering its contents about. The eighty guns thundered away for most of that hour, the riflemen lying down in the sandpit or on the ridge, as the shot ripped through the air just above them.

This firing had little effect on Wellington's concealed infantry, and as the familiar drumming and '*Vive l'Empereur*'s of an infantry attack replaced the cacophony of the guns, the three forward companies of the 95th extended out and began skirmishing with their covering *voltigeurs*. The firing checked this screen, but General d'Erlon's columns kept advancing, marching through their light troops, who were still engaged in their private struggle with the 95th.

Captain Duthilt marched forward in the main part of d'Erlon's column. He was a grizzled veteran of twenty-two years who had fought in the first revolutionary campaigns. He looked up towards the ridge, and a little to his left at La Haye Sainte. He was worried by the strength of the defences, the cloying mud, the unusual formation in which they were delivering their attack, and by the fact that the usual cheering and egging on of the conscripts had begun too soon in their progress forwards. 'This rush and enthusiasm were becoming disastrous,' according to Duthilt, 'in that the soldier still had a long march to make before meeting the enemy, and was soon tired out by the difficulty of manoeu-vring on this heavy churned-up soil, which ripped off gaiter straps and even claimed shoes . . . there was soon some disorder in the ranks, above all as soon as the head of the column came within range of enemy fire.' Riflemen, German legionnaires, light companies from Picton's division and cannon all poured death into the head of d'Erlon's corps.

The French, falling into confusion, were still moving forward – at this point, confronted with several thousand infantry, Leach had little choice but to fall back up the slope to his supports on the ridge. Stopping every now and then to turn and fire, the riflemen made their way up and were soon behind the hedge.

The engagement had become hot, and raged across the front. Major Cameron was hit in the neck by one shot, being carried to the rear. Picton too fell, his wound being mortal.

It was at this moment, at around 2 p.m., that the riflemen looking down to their right saw French cuirassiers cantering up to a Hanoverian militia battalion, which was making its way to reinforce the defenders of Haye Sainte. Catching them unawares, the French cav-alry rode down the whole lot. The armoured horsemen set about the infantry with their long sabres, bringing pathetic cries for mercy from the lacerated Germans. No quarter was given, though, and the few bloodied survivors fled back up the slope.

The French were soon coming onto the ridge. It was at this moment that the 1st Battalion of the 95th faced the final crisis, and one of the most severe, of all its years' fighting under Wellington. Seeing the cuirassiers cantering up the slope towards them, and hearing the cries of the sergeant majors who were getting their men into square, many of the riflemen panicked. They had seen what had happened to the 42nd at Quatre Bras and they had witnessed the riding down of the Germans moments before. The power of heavy cavalry *en masse* was not something that even the Peninsular veterans had really seen before. Dozens of them started running.

Rallying the steady men around them, the 95th's officers were able to withstand the cuirassiers. Having arrived on top of the ridge, faced with red-coated walls bristling with bayonets, the French heavies were unable to make any serious impression. Those riflemen who had fled, meanwhile, were running into the woods at the rear of Wellington's position.

A general charge of British cavalry now swept forward, inflicting the same treatment on the leading battalions of d'Erlon's corps as the Germans had suffered not an hour before. The riflemen stood or lay flinching, hoping desperately that they would not be trampled as the Life Guards came thundering past them and down onto the French. With the leading battalions already disordered by their long and trying march towards the ridge, the French were at the mercy of the British horse. In a few moments, two eagles were taken and thousands of enemy infantry were sent streaming back towards their own lines. Captain Duthilt joined in the rout: 'The brigade started retreating, dissolving, ridden through everywhere by this cavalry, and the ground was clogged with dead and wounded.' The old veteran was captured by a British trooper, but his luck soon changed. Some of the British cavalry, enthused by their success, rode down as far as the French battery, where they were duly overwhelmed by a French counter-attack. Duthilt and hundreds of other prisoners from the wrecks of d'Erlon's column were freed.

Once the French cavalry pulled back from the ridge, Leach once more led the three Rifle companies, now somewhat depleted, back to the sandpit and the left of La Haye Sainte. The Rifles then enjoyed a period of comparative calm, while Napoleon prosecuted a huge attack between La Haye Sainte and Hougomont. This the 1st/95th could hear but not see.

By about 4 p.m., pressure was building again in front of La Haye Sainte. The French battery had regained its organisation after the driving off of the British horse, and was lofting dozens of shot at the defenders of the walled farm. Many shells also struck the 27th, the Inniskillings, who had remained in square, close to the crossroads on the ridge top. Fear of further cavalry attack prevented them abandoning the formation, but increased the effect of the roundshot that ploughed through its ranks. In front of the sandpit, French skirmishers too were coming forward again.

Simmons, firing with his men at this new swarm of *voltigeurs*, was felled by a blow to his midriff. He bit the dust and struggled for breath. Blood was pouring out of a wound to his belly. Probing with his fingers, Simmons could feel that a couple of his ribs had been smashed by the ball going in. He had seen enough wounds in his campaigns to know that a ball smashing through the trunk made the outcome most doubtful for him. Four riflemen carried him back up behind the ridge to a little house that was being used as a dressing station.

Finding himself surrounded by dying men, fighting for breath, Simmons was struggling not to lose hope. Then, to his surprise and delight, Sergeant Fairfoot appeared. Having heard his old friend was seriously wounded, with his own right arm still strapped up from its wound of the day before, Fairfoot came to rescue Simmons. 'Oh lift me up, I am suffocating!' cried Simmons in agony. Fairfoot struggled to prop up the lieutenant. Six years they had campaigned together, fighting against the odds from that dark night in Barba del Puerco to Tarbes. Tears began streaming down Fairfoot's cheeks, cutting tracks through the grime of battle. He was not ready to see his old friend die like this.

At last an assistant surgeon began poking around Simmons's insides in what passed for an operation. Fairfoot propped him up, all the time, as the sawbones prodded and pushed with his infernal instruments and Simmons gritted his teeth against the pain. At last the ball was extracted. Moments later a British cavalry officer ran into the surgery and shouted the alarm. The French were attacking again and would be upon them in moments!

Fairfoot helped Simmons, wincing with agony, blood pouring down his side, to his feet. The sergeant spied a French prisoner on a horse and pulled him off it without ceremony. Fairfoot and another tried to help Simmons up, but he passed out and the two men could not manage the dead weight.

The alarms at the aid post had been occasioned by the renewal of a heavy French infantry attack at about 6 p.m. Leach, who was now in charge of the battalion, both Barnard and Cameron having fallen wounded, could do little but watch in horror as the German Legion abandoned La Haye Sainte. After resisting heroically for six hours, the legionnaires had run out of ammunition and taken heavy casualties. They were forced to quit the buildings with dozens of their men strewn about the courtyard, shattered timbers and tiles spread crazily across them.

With the French now in possession of the shattered farm, balls began whistling into the sandpit from its exposed flank, killing several riflemen. A further French infantry attack was also making its way up the ridge to Leach's left. Having both flanks turned, he had no choice but to abandon the position again, taking his survivors back to their supports on the ridge.

Behind them, Fairfoot, desperately agitated, had at last found a cavalry horse for Simmons and was taking him further to the rear. The immediate crisis was over, but neither of them had any great faith that Simmons would survive his wound.

With the light beginning to fail on the field of Waterloo, the tide at last turned. The French capture of La Haye Sainte did not prove decisive. Instead the defeat of the Imperial Guard in the centre, and the arrival of the Prussians on Wellington's left, settled the matter. In that first contest, Colonel John Colborne had covered himself with glory, leading his 52nd forward to complete the Guard's discomfiture. The struggle was over, as was Bonaparte's gamble to regain power.

With his second abdication, the French imperial dream was buried, and Europe began its 'long peace' of almost forty years. The hopes of individual veterans for some tranquillity and relief from the dangers of campaigning were now answered. But the inevitable contraction of the Army posed its own risks to the 95th.

In the days after this epic struggle, church bells rang in England and Wellington wrote a weary victory dispatch. Scattered across the Belgian countryside on smelly mattresses, Barnard, Cameron and Simmons all made their recovery. The short campaign, the Hundred Days, would soon be over. It had not passed well for the 1st/95th.

Barnard had been deeply shocked by what had happened on the ridge. Three days after the battle, he wrote to Cameron:

I regret to say that a *great* number of our men went to the rear without cause after the appearance of the Cuirassiers, there were no less than 100 absentees after the fight and this vexes me very much as it is the first time such a thing has ever happened in the regiment. Kincaid says very few if any quitted the corps after the charge of the cavalry. Many of those that went to the rear were men that I little expected to have heard of in that situation.

It may be deduced from the fact that many of these men were evidently veterans that the incidents involving Corporal Pitt at Dover and Sergeant Underwood at Quatre Bras were in some sense portents. There were too many in the battalion who had fought more than they felt anyone could reasonably be expected to fight and resented being wrenched from what they thought would be a peaceful life back in England. For that reason, the short Belgian campaign had proven the severest moral test of the battalion.

Simmons, Fairfoot and Leach had all come through. Their devotion to one another and their ability to resign themselves to whatever fate the battlefield held for them had allowed them to end their campaigns with heads held high.

The losses of the 1st/95th in the battle were not great – amounting to around 21 men killed and 124 injured. The 27th, by way of contrast, suffered 478 casualties (of whom 105 were slain) – well over half of the men who came into action. They had been close to the 95th (actually slightly further from the French), standing in square, with enemy cannon balls ploughing great lanes through their ranks. With its open fields, reserves of French heavy cavalry and artillery, Waterloo had not been a good place for the 95th to demonstrate the superiority of rifle power over mass or bayonets. Many thousands of Green Jackets would have been needed for that. However, the comparatively slight losses at least showed yet again that troops who fought in this way were far less vulnerable, even when standing under the fire of Napoleon's huge battery for an entire day.

It seems that Wellington and other British generals were unaware that a significant proportion of Barnard's battalion had fled. This was to become an unmentionable subject in the regiment, which had long shown sensitivity about its reputation. Had the Duke ever become aware of it, he would probably have been philosophical, given the Rifles' previous service. He was, after all, the general who said that *all* soldiers ran away sometimes, it was just a matter of how quickly they came back.

With Napoleon's second abdication, the campaigns of the 1st Battalion of the 95th came to an end. The months after Waterloo saw the battalion reconstitute itself. For a couple of days after the great battle, those skulkers who had fled at the sight of Boney's cuirassiers returned to the abuse and scorn of their messmates. The journey of the sick and wounded was often a longer one. Corporal Costello, Lieutenant Gairdner and Sergeant Fairfoot, wounded at Quatre Bras, all returned after a brief recuperation. George Simmons took longer, as befitted a man drilled in the guts at Waterloo.

They were all back in the ranks before the battalion left Paris in the bitter cold of that December of 1815. It was not the happy idyll of Castel Sarrazin and the previous summer. Instead there was plenty of grumbling. Certain reports of Waterloo in the newspapers highlighted the role of the Scottish regiments in Picton's division. This nettled some officers like Leach, who felt that those from north of the Tweed were always making great claims for their own valour and ignoring those of others.

The award of a Waterloo medal caused some other latent tensions to break into the open. Peninsular men were livid that their own long sufferings had not yet been recognised with any badge or distinction, whereas dozens of Johnny Newcomes could wear the Waterloo medal. Some of the old soldiers taunted the younger men, calling them 'recruits' long after the battle, ripping off their Waterloo medals.

Wellington tried to repay some of his debt to the 95th by insisting that they be taken out of the 'line': from 1816 they would no longer be part of the sequence of numbered infantry regiments, but were known instead as the Rifle Brigade. This distinction honoured the riflemen, but also saved their skills for the Army. In times of peace there would soon be disbandments, and there was evident agreement in Horse Guards that the 95th Rifles must be saved from the fate of two regiments previously given that number: one was broken up at the end of the American wars, along with many other higher-numbered corps.

The 5th Battalion of the 60th, the mercenary corps that predated the Rifles and also served in the Peninsula, did not escape the disbandments. With its passing, it might be said that the Army finally abandoned the eighteenth-century notion that the rifleman was a born woodsman, best recruited from Germany or Switzerland. Britain and Ireland would henceforth be quite capable of furnishing the raw material for its rifle corps.

Even the formation of the Rifle Brigade, however, did not completely protect it: the 3rd Battalion was wound up a couple of years later. This event helped to ensure that George Simmons, who had written to his parents in 1810 that a man could get his company in five years in the Rifles, did not achieve that goal until nineteen years after he entered the regiment – despite all the suffering that attended his service.

In the meantime, the 1st Battalion returned home in November 1818, losing many veterans before being sent first to Scotland and then Ireland to protect the ministry from the anger of the mob. Although these were simply the exigencies of the service, none of the old sweats could pretend that keeping rioting Celts in check was a particularly pleasing occupation.

Ned Costello was among those invalided out of the regiment – aged thirty-one, he was awarded the miserly sum of sixpence a day. He later married, but finding the money insufficient to keep him, he ended up volunteering to fight in a British Legion which took part in the Spanish civil war in 1835. Costello's previous services qualified him for the rank of lieutenant in this mercenary force, and he returned to England in 1836. A year and a half later, Costello's difficulties in maintaining his wife and seven children finally came to an end with his appointment as a Yeoman warder at the Tower of London.

Many of the private soldiers who had served with Costello were a good deal less fortunate. Several succumbed to drink, becoming penniless drifters, begging beside the roads. Tom Plunket, the man who killed the French general during the Corunna campaign and was held up by his colonel as a 'pattern for the battalion', was sighted years later selling matches on the streets of London. In his case, the best efforts of that old commanding officer to obtain him a good pension failed to save the old soldier from alcoholism.

George Baller was another veteran of O'Hare's company whose fate gives some insight into the pitiful circumstances into which many of the old 95th men fell. Baller was one of the hard core of the regiment, having been given the skulker Esau Jackson's stripes outside the walls of Badajoz in 1812. He was invalided out in 1816, while the regiment was still in France, aged just twenty-eight. Baller had attained the status of colour sergeant but could not carry on due to the severity of his five wounds. One month after his discharge Baller was awarded a pension of ninepence per day by the board at Chelsea. Once married, Baller found himself too sick to work, with a pension too small to provide for his children. He ended up making a desperate appeal to the Chelsea board for more money in 1819. Baller's exact fate is unknown, but it is clear that despite the most exemplary record, and testimonials from Andrew Barnard, he lived what remained of his life in grinding poverty and great physical pain.

As the years of the 95th's great Peninsular fights receded, so those who were still fit and serving in the regiment found themselves living, as they had before the war, according to the petty routines of a peacetime army. For an officer like Jonathan Leach, who personified the 'wild sportsman' of those campaigning days, this was all too much. 'I feel no particular penchant for passing the remainder of my days in marching off guards, going grand rounds and visiting rounds and performing other dull, monotonous and uninteresting duties of the kind, on which great stress is laid, and to which vast importance is attached, in various stiff-starched garrisons,' he wrote. Leach resigned from the Army with the rank of lieutenant colonel to pursue other business.

Those with less wealth did not have this option. While serving on in the Rifle Brigade, Robert Fairfoot committed himself to raising a family, his wife Catherine bearing four children between 1817 and 1823. He named his son Joseph George Fairfoot, thus commemorating his father and his closest friend. Fairfoot eventually joined Simmons in the commissioned class, being made quartermaster in 1825. He had been a model soldier and was long overdue his reward. Andrew Barnard, writing to recommend the promotion, stated, 'I cannot give a stronger proof of his merit than the anxiety that *all* the officers who command the Battalion to which he belongs feel for him.'

Simmons was destined to raise a family too, although he did not marry until 1836, by which time he had reached the ripe old age of fifty. The poorer officer's life was not conducive to romance, involving as it did periods of unaccompanied service which might go on for years at a time. Several, including John Kincaid, never married.

In the years after Waterloo, the admiration for the 95th that permeated the old Peninsular Army spread pretty much throughout the service. In line regiments, an officer who survived the Peninsula might have considered himself lucky to have participated in a couple of general engagements and a lesser affair or two. The average soldier in any of the usual regiments simply did not have a turn at the centre of the action any more often than that. Even George Simmons's brother Maud, of the 34th Foot, was in just four major actions, despite serving throughout the war. The Light Division, though, was usually first on the field and last off, as its men boasted. This meant that many years later, when a general-service medal was finally awarded for the Iberian campaigns, the metal clasps across its ribbon numbered two or maybe three for the average veteran, but twelve for Leach and eight for Simmons. Had Fairfoot lived long enough to get the wretched thing, his medal would have had nine.

The odyssey of the Rifles was therefore one of immense hardship and tough fighting, even by the harsh standards of the rest of Wellington's Army. This left a passionate bond between its men. Simmons wrote to his parents, while recuperating after Waterloo, that he owed his life to Fairfoot, who 'if I can do him a service may always command me; his character as a soldier stands with the first in the regiment'. The experience of campaigning with the 95th was so intense that it burned through the distinctions of rank and status that constrained so much of nineteenth-century society.

The great treasure of the Rifles' experiences was hoarded by the British military caste for some time. It was inevitable, though, that the wider public would eventually come to learn the soldiers' story, and that the 95th would become a legend.

TWENTY-SEVEN

The Legend is Born

Although many individual Rifle veterans remained in obscurity, or indeed poverty, the regiment was to make a dramatic mark. As Simmons and Fairfoot aged in the role of lowly regimental officer, other veterans of the 1st/95th were scaling the heights of the Army. Sidney Beckwith, Andrew Barnard and Harry Smith all became generals. In fact, among those officers who sailed with the battalion in May 1809 and survived the wars, there were to be seven generals, although some, like Alexander Cameron, achieved the rank through seniority but did not serve actively in it. The 43rd and 52nd similarly produced many of the generals who would command Queen Victoria's armies in India and elsewhere in the Empire; the three regiments of the old Light Division in aggregate provided the backbone of the Army's staff throughout the mid-nineteenth century.

With the promotion of so many ex-Light Division officers into senior positions, the survival of the special Peninsular system of fighting and discipline was assured. The success of the tactics developed at Shorncliffe and then used to devastating effect in Iberia was enshrined in the issue of a new drill manual for the entire Army in 1824.

Major General Sir Henry Torrens's book *Field Exercise and Evolutions of the Army* finally laid the 1792 Rules and Regulations to rest. Torrens extended the subtle skirmishing used by the Light Division to the Army as a whole, stipulating that a battalion in line could space its men, 'at any distance, either by single or double files'. This gave official sanction to the breakdown of the old linear tactics (which had in fact been comprehensively subverted in the Peninsula) in which the deployment of a compact, regulated line was deemed vital. Torrens also gave instructions on skirmishing that could be traced directly back through the 95th's training manuals, such as Sergeant Weddeburne's, to the original rules for riflemen published in 1798. In the pivoting of companies or the formation of squares, the light-infantry drills also became the order of the day.

If the Torrens rules contained a powerful dose of Light Division tactics, then it cannot be said that these new principles triumphed unchallenged. Quite a few officers emerged from the Napoleonic wars with the conviction that the bayonet was the key to success. This, after all, had seemed to be the lesson of Waterloo. To many observers, particularly those who had not been present at Wellington's battles, the image of the impassive British line awaiting the shouting French, giving them the close-range volley and then the bayonet, seemed like the expression of a stoic national character, and this was an age in which such notions were extremely powerful.

A heated debate got under way about whether this blade was the arbiter of the battlefield. Lieutenant Colonel John Mitchell, a veteran of the Peninsular War, scorned what he saw as a myth, that the red-coats had charged across the fields of Spain impaling their enemies:

The bayonet may, in truth, be termed the grand mystifier of modern tactics . . . that in some scrambling attack of works or villages, a soldier may have been killed or wounded with a bayonet is possible; but to suppose that soldiers ever rushed into close combat, armed only with bayonets, is an absurdity; it never happened and can never happen.

Mitchell's point was that an attack delivered in this way rarely connected with the enemy – either it faltered, or it resulted in that foe running away before they were skewered. The colonel argued that in every French attempt to break through the British line, Wellington's men had galled them with long-range skirmisher fire before delivering a thumping close-range volley, which meant the enemy 'halted in order to fire . . . and got into confusion'.

French theorists drew the opposite lesson from these contests, and developed a preoccupation with delivering an unstoppable bayonet charge. The musings of French generals on this subject led to the final obscenity of sending men on bayonet attacks in the First World War without any ammunition, so that they would be *unable* to halt and return fire, having no choice but to continue their onward rush or die where they stood. Colonel Mitchell would have had none of this nonsense, believing that attempts to charge were far too unpredictable in their consequences, and that instead, while some improvements in marksmanship had been made, the infantry as a whole needed to reach a much higher standard in it.

There were quite a few officers who took issue with Mitchell's thesis in the columns of the *United Service Journal*. The intensity of military conservatism and the vehemence of some of the arguments can be judged by this passage:

It is discipline, which is nothing but each man, shoulder-to-shoulder, depending upon a whole, instead of himself alone, that has raised our ragamuffins to an equality . . . with more able bodied individuals; and it is this that has enabled civilised nations, with their very scum, first reduced to order and mechanical obedience, to overcome and conquer the boldest, bravest, and most athletic barbarians that ever dwelt on the face of the earth [the French].

The author of this vitriol, who signed himself only as W.D.B., added, 'Each soldier is, comparatively speaking, but a sixpenny knife: therefore to make the soldier of infantry depend upon himself is the destruction, the pulling to pieces of the machine.'

W.D.B.'s attitude, with its emphasis on rigid linear tactics and contempt for the ordinary soldier, flew in the face of everything the Rifles had demonstrated in their campaigns. It was hardly surprising, then, that John Kincaid was one of the Rifles officers who joined these debates in the *Journal*, giving Colonel Mitchell some supporting fire. The veterans of the old 95th would do much in their writings to try to give the lie to such repugnant ideas.

Jonathan Leach, never one to mince words, wrote, 'Our corps gained the reputation, which it wrung from friends and foes, not by aping the drill of grenadiers, but by its activity and intelligence at the outposts; by being able to cope with, in all situations, the most experienced and best trained light troops which the continent of Europe could produce; and by the deadly application of the rifle in action.' Holding up to scorn the image of the grenadier, like some clockwork automaton, Leach insisted that the rifleman was a universal soldier able to undertake all duties from skirmishing behind rocks to standing in the firing line or storming a fortress like Ciudad Rodrigo or Badajoz – the business reserved for those parade-ground soldiers in the eighteenth-century conception of warfare. In such bloody storms, Leach boasted, the 95th 'proved itself equally efficient in the form of grenadiers'.

Wellington managed to synthesise the opposed views expressed in these debates. He did indeed appreciate the value of well-trained riflemen as well as light infantry, although he sought to differentiate these special troops from the common or garden line. As far as those regiments were concerned, the Iron Duke readily accepted that the British recruit was 'scum' who had to be kept in his place by fierce discipline.

The 95th's officers considered these questions during their later years with humanity and realism. The rifleman was not some component in a machine, let alone a 'sixpenny knife', but a *man* who had to be motivated, praised, even kept amused. They gave much thought to the psychology of battle, Kincaid for example arguing that skirmishing soldiers needed to be kept moving in order to stop them dwelling on the dangers they faced under fire. In this way it was actually easier to fight in skirmish order, since the men did not have that sickening feeling of powerlessness that came from standing in packed ranks while enemy gunners knocked over your comrades with roundshot.

Distinctions between different types of soldiers, of the kind Wellington and many other senior officers believed in, were an important part of military psychology before the Peninsular campaigns and were to prove so again after them, but while the regiments were fighting hard against a shared enemy it was apparent that the different categories had rather more in common than was supposed. Before the Peninsula, many of the 95th's enthusiasts had believed that the regiment would only be really effective when firing at long range – even over 250 yards. There had been concern that the rifleman's slower rate of fire might make him unable to defend himself in a close-range fight.

In battle, though, the rifleman was rarely able to engage targets at very long range. On one of the occasions when he did, the action at Arcangues in December 1813, the 43rd with its smooth-bore light-infantry muskets joined in the fusillade at some enemy artillery 350 to 400 yards away with equal effect. At Barba del Puerco, early in 1810, the Rifles had shown themselves able to stand against greatly superior numbers in a close-range fight – circumstances which the pre-war orthodoxies suggested would spell deep trouble for them.

Similarly, the use of a great proportion of a regiment, sometimes the entire corps, in extended or skirmish order, might before the wars have been regarded as the preserve of the 95th, but these tactics were practised so successfully by the other regiments of the Light Division that they were spread to the entire infantry in Torrens's 1824 regulations. The rifleman's mission of picking off leaders – which proved highly effective in the campaigns against the French – was clearly not invented by the 95th, and had also spread pretty extensively through the Army by the end of the Peninsular War.

Because of the constant cross-fertilisation between Light Division corps like the 43rd and 95th, many issues in the emergence of light-infantry tactics became blurred. Many could claim paternity of the Light Division's success: Colonel Rottenburg for laying out the original ideas on skirmishing; Colonels Stewart and Manningham for founding the 95th and inculcating new ideas on discipline and promotion; Colonel Kenneth MacKenzie of the 52nd and General Sir John Moore for spreading those to the red-coated 43rd and 52nd while developing new drills for them too; Craufurd for his emphasis on vigilance in the outposts as well as his scheme of marching; Colonel Beckwith of the Rifles for being the most successful tactical commander of the Light Division and providing his superb model of leadership at Sabugal; Barnard for maintaining this high standard of command during years when much of the battalion was sick of fighting and longed for peace. In the years after the wars, partisans for Moore and Craufurd in particular would claim one or other to have been the key architect, but no single figure can be given all the glory.

Although there was much gradual evolution and cribbing of others' ideas in the way that a recognisably modern British soldier emerged from Wellington's campaigns, it is worth recording that certain honours must be reserved for the 95th. Their uniqueness derived from several factors. The emphasis on marksmanship training or skill at arms made them the Army's best shots and showed the future shape of warfare in engagements such as Sabugal or Tarbes, demonstrating that firepower would prevail over mass. Their dark clothes, emphasis on using cover while skirmishing and on concealment in their observation positions were novel and, as an unwanted by-product, often resulted (for example at the Coa, Ciudad Rodrigo and Vitoria) in the thoroughly modern phenomenon of the 95th being accidentally engaged by its own side. And although credit can be given to the 5th/60th Rifles for many innovations, this mercenary battalion was almost always split in penny packets and therefore unable to demonstrate, as the 95th did, the power of riflemen *en masse*. In deploying whole battalions of these special troops (or even eighteen companies together, at Tarbes), the

95th was able to show that even powerful fortifications such as the French works in the Pyrenees did not require the old linear tactics, but could be taken by skirmishers in a frontal assault.

The 95th's French opponents were often confused about which regiment was aiming such deadly fire at them. But they ended the Peninsular War convinced that the British were the 'best marksmen in Europe'. During the Revolutionary wars, the French had pioneered the mass use of skirmishers and attempted, with their poor marksmanship, to decapitate the enemy by killing his officers. This tactic was turned back on them to devastating effect by British riflemen in the Peninsula, Marshal Soult complaining in 1813, 'This way of making war and harming the enemy is most disadvantageous to us.' Those British officers who had come through the wars and wanted to advocate this form of warfare had no access to the French Army's internal records of officer casualties. If they had, they would have seen that rifle fire stripped out the French regimental officers at Busaco, Sabugal and the Bridge of Vera, paralysing their forces.

Many of these notions about what made the 95th special have been formed with the benefit of two centuries' hindsight. In the decades after Wellington's campaigns, professional debates, particularly about the bayonet, raged over the port at the United Service Club and in the pages of its *Journal*. It was hardly surprising that a wider national interest in these battles and in the exploits of one or two regiments in particular should arise. The public thirst for knowledge about these subjects focused not on dry technical stuff about floating pivots or marksmanship training but on the place of the wars in British history and experience.

In 1828, William Napier began publishing his *History of the War in the Peninsula and in the South of France* – a six-volume series that he only completed in 1840. As a veteran of the 43rd Light Infantry, it was inevitable that Napier would have much to say about the Light Division's fights. But he had even more to say about the character his troops had shown in action. He wrote of the British infantryman: 'The whole world cannot produce a nobler specimen of military bearing.' Napier managed to turn the epic fights into a page-turner, and the prejudices exhibited in his prose simply enhanced its appeal. In places, he was unashamedly populist: 'Napoleon's troops fought in bright fields where every helmet caught some beams of glory, but the British soldier conquered under the cold shade of aristocracy; no honours awaited his daring; no dispatch gave his name to the applauses of his countrymen, his life of danger and hardship was uncheered by hope, his death unnoticed.'

Fired up by such eulogies, the public would want to hear more from these unsung heroes. Memoirs had started appearing, and many extolled the valour of the Rifles. Major Blakiston's, for example, published in 1829, noted, 'I never saw such skirmishers as the 95th.'

The stage was set for the Rifles to tell their own story. John Kincaid led off in 1830 with *Adventures in the Rifle Brigade*. While many such books had a print run of only two or three hundred copies, Kincaid's is thought to have been double or treble this figure. Not to be outdone, in 1831, Jonathan Leach, the only officer of the 1st Battalion to have gone uninjured all the way through the events of 1809–14, followed with his *Rough Sketches*. The books sold out almost immediately. Kincaid followed up with *Random Shots from a Rifleman* in 1835. In 1838 the publishers issued a second edition of Kincaid's *Adventures* and Leach wrote three more books.

Kincaid and Leach adopted a similar style: laconic, picaresque, heroic in an understated way. Consciously or not, they pandered to their public and its preconceptions about the British character in adversity. They are stirring accounts and the evergreen nature of their appeal is such that it is easy to buy reprints even today. Their philosophy of soldiering neatly dovetailed with the requirements of the market; there were many anecdotes about officers and ordinary riflemen. While avoiding any personal trumpet-blowing of the kind favoured by French diarists, they did not refrain from hyperbole in describing the feats of Wellington's Army in general or the Light Division in particular. One wrote that 'there, perhaps, never was, nor ever again will be, such a war brigade'.

In the Kincaid and Leach accounts there was hardly a mention of the flogging that punctuated their marches, and none at all of incidents such as the resignation of the cowardly Lieutenant Bell after Badajoz or the flight of a hundred or so men at the battle of Waterloo. Some other indiscretions, such as the large-scale larceny on the campaigns or the bullying of Second Lieutenant Sarsfield, were briefly recounted, but presented as humorous episodes. The memoirs did discuss the execution of the Ciudad Rodrigo deserters, presenting it as a tough but justified measure, but kept from the reader how many other riflemen deserters had escaped this draconian fate.

The memoir writers were perhaps most guilty of selective memory or indeed hagiography in their treatment of General Robert Craufurd. Both Leach and Kincaid, it is true, acknowledged his unpopularity in a coded way. Neither, however, was willing to share the intense hatred felt for him during the campaigns with their readers. Indeed Leach – one of the general's bitterest critics – seemed to reverse some of his views in the most perverse way. In 1809 in his (unpublished) journal he had castigated Craufurd for issuing the 'most *tyrannical* and *oppressive standing orders* that were ever compiled by a British officer'; but in one of his books of 1835 the same orders were described as 'most excellent, and extremely well calculated to ensure regularity on the march'.

It is evident that Craufurd grew in the estimation of many Light Division veterans after he had fallen in battle, and Kincaid explicitly said so. This revisionism stemmed in part from negative experiences under other generals, particularly the hopeless Erskine. It seems, however, that the attitudes to their long-dead chief expressed in print were coloured to a great extent by the fact that Craufurd had ascended into a sort of pantheon of national martyrs of the anti-Bonaparte struggle, along with the likes of Sir John Moore and even Nelson. Craufurd had many political friends who saw to it that his reputation was extolled in print, as did Moore. Besmirching his name might have led a Leach or Kincaid into all sorts of difficulties, ranging from a lawsuit from some relative to a duel.

The lionisation of Craufurd took a further turn with the publication of two memoirs from the ranks: Edward Costello's in 1841 and Benjamin Harris's in 1848. Both men expressed warm approbation for Black Bob – but both did so with the assistance of gentlemanly ghost writers. Harris, an illiterate, was written up by a former officer in the 52nd and stated, 'I don't think the world ever saw a more perfect soldier than General Craufurd.' Notwithstanding that Harris only served alongside his hero for a few weeks in late 1808 and early 1809, his book was full of anecdote and had a lasting appeal.

Costello at least benefited from being one of those who had gone all the way through from 1809. His memoirs, initially published in a magazine, managed an honesty unmatched in almost all other accounts of the Peninsular War. He freely described the soldiers' thieving along with their bravery in battle and contempt for skulkers, and he even dealt frankly with the rapes and other crimes committed after the fall of Badajoz.

Leaving aside Costello's honourable exception, the memoirs, particularly of officers, generally eschewed the sordid or cowardly and extolled the heroic. As one 95th author joined another in print there was a sort of upward spiral of praise for the regiment, with the most effusive panegyrics often coming from those who had been in other corps. Major General Bell, who had served in the 34th alongside George Simmons's brother Maud, and may well have been influenced by discussions with him, described the 95th, for example, as 'the most celebrated old fighting corps in the Army or perhaps the world'. By the 1860s, when most of the Peninsular veterans had died, the laudatory parameters for these works had been set – the 95th had achieved legendary status. That said, it is quite possible that the numbers of copies of all of the 95th memoirs put together circulating in, say, 1865 did not exceed twenty thousand.

It took another twenty-five or thirty years, until the end of the nineteenth century, with the Wellingtonian generation long buried, the price of books falling and literacy burgeoning, for the popular appeal of the Rifles' story really to show itself.

'A remarkable revival of curiosity in the events of the time of Napoleon has lately arisen,' wrote one author in a magazine article presenting the reminiscences of an old Rifles man, 'and there is a romance and interest in the wars of those times which attach to none of the more recent contests.'

The 'romance' derived from several factors. Napier had already shrewdly identified that the public ignorance of the Peninsular Army's years of privation and suffering at the time of the campaigns created a kind of national debt to the veterans. What better way to discharge it than to patronise their writings? In the case of the Light Division or 95th men, the sense of indebtedness was even stronger because they had fought so often and regularly performed their duty against dreadful odds. There was something too about the rifleman's personal sovereignty – deciding when to fire or when to drop into cover before getting up and charging forward again – that seems to have appealed to British sensibilities.

Kincaid's *Adventures* were reprinted in 1900 and 1909. George Simmons's journals and letters were 'discovered', edited and printed in 1899. Harry Smith's memoir was finally published too, having hitherto only existed as a manuscript for circulation within the family. Sir Charles Oman meanwhile fed the interest by publishing the massive and authoritative *A History of the Peninsular War*, starting in 1902. The growing secondary literature emphasised glory and self-sacrifice, holding Wellington's Army up as mythic warriors, examples to a nationalistic Britain at the peak of its powers.

The 95th's specific role in this publishing phenomenon grew out of the popular appeal of their saga. These were not the memoirs of cannon fodder, packed into their red-coated ranks awaiting death, but of spirited individuals who, by slaying a senior French officer or storming a post, somehow made a difference to the tide of history.

Inevitably, as the essence of these first-hand accounts was boiled down by writers or historians who were not present, certain episodes were glossed over or mythologised. Costello, for example, bore an early share of the responsibility for promulgating a widely held view that the men of the 95th were rarely flogged and had somehow escaped the system of brutality that typified the eighteenth-century Army. The early twentieth-century authors often took this rosy picture at face value. As we have seen, though, the desire of the officers who founded the 95th that their men should be spared the lash was to prove no more than a noble aspiration, particularly under Craufurd. But it is also only fair to the general to point out that even regimental officers of the 95th such as Beckwith, Barnard, Cameron and O'Hare, as well as lowly fellows like Lieutenant James Gairdner, all ordered riflemen flogged. In short, riflemen got no special treatment in this regard.

While the 95th were not spared the stick, they were offered various carrots by way of incentive. Some of these, such as the pillage of French convoys, were regarded as the reward due to enterprising fellows in the advance guard. In other respects, though, the acknowledgement of the Rifles officers – particularly Colonel Beckwith – that bathing, football, coursing and races could all make a soldier's life enjoyable, marked a radical new departure for the Army. Beckwith's approach in this regard was complemented by a reduction to the minimum of the drills repeated endlessly in other regiments. Many redcoats, for example, practised the 'manual exercise' of loading their musket ad nauseam on the drill square but almost never actually fired a cartridge. The 95th, on the other hand, maintained its high standards of marksmanship by constant target practice, even when they were just a few miles from enemy outposts. The fun and games helped build regimental and company spirit and, as Leach and others explicitly pointed out, meant the soldiers were ready to follow Beckwith into hell when the time came.

They also helped maintain physical fitness, an Army preoccupation that can also be said to have begun with the Light Division. As for the marksmanship, it laid the ground for a far more professional attitude to soldiering.

The 95th's founders also wanted to provide motivation in the shape of promotion and distinction for deserving soldiers. Here too they achieved remarkable results. Robert Fairfoot can be seen as a prototype. His father served almost twenty-nine years in the Army without escaping the rank of private. But young Fairfoot ended his days as a commissioned officer and a perfect model for young riflemen to emulate. William Brotherwood might well also have ended up as a sergeant major or even an officer had he not been killed in 1813. The Rifles did not invent this type of promotion, but in trying to extend it widely, by educating privates and non-commissioned officers, the 95th was quite directly subverting the class system. Conservatives did not like it one bit: Wellington himself commented that this 'new fangled school mastering' would be the cause of revolution in England if there ever was one.

The way that the 95th undermined the old social hierarchy during its Iberian campaigns may be seen, along with its innovative tactics, as its most lasting and significant achievement. A life on outposts or in the skirmish line meant officers and soldiers shared the same hardships. A captain of the Rifles or the 52nd usually slept out in the pouring rain, just like his men did. Their position in the advance guard meant they were not allowed the tents and other officers' camp comforts enjoyed in the eighteenth-century Army or even in many of the other Peninsular regiments. The spirit of mutual respect between battle-hardened soldiers became the cement that held the regiment together and that allowed it to enter battle again and again, to the admiration of so many others in Wellington's Army.

In the Rifles, a passionate bond emerged between fighting soldiers, and it usually extended to the leaders as well as the led. While such feelings became quite a common hallmark of the twentieth-century experience of war, this was a strange new feeling to men of the early nineteenth century. Costello summed up these feelings admirably when telling the tale of how the soldiers had given their last biscuits to a sobbing toff, eighteen-year-old Second Lieutenant the Honourable Charles Spencer, as they all starved during the retreat to Portugal in November 1812: 'These are times when Lords find that they are men and men that they are comrades.' John Kincaid even referred to the 95th as a 'band of brothers'.

The bonds were all the stronger between those who came through the 95th's final trials without succumbing to battle exhaustion or stress. Between August 1813 and the battle of Quatre Bras in June 1815, more than thirty men deserted the 1st Battalion of the 95th, many of them veterans. This marked a significant proportion of those who had survived the Peninsular campaign and set the scene for the flight of something like a hundred rieflemen at Waterloo. Clearly they had been pushed by years of fighting beyond some personal cracking point. But for those who had not – still the majority of the old hands – there was all the more reason to marvel at the depth of their own camaraderie and forbearance.

Officers of the Rifles were unusual, even within the Light Division, in that they often fought with firearms. This was another decided break with custom – for most commissioned men considered the sword to be the only gentlemanly weapon. There were no illusions of this kind in the 95th, particularly among the young subalterns, at least one of whom managed to bayonet a French soldier to death. While all officers died like common soldiers, and those of the Light Division often lived like them, those of the 95th actually *killed* like them too.

Some of the officers did not know how to respond to this subversion of the usual assumptions about the social divide. A man who had raised himself by his bootstraps, like Peter O'Hare, was therefore more likely to respond to carping in the ranks by cuffing the culprit, bellowing obscenities at him or even having him flogged. The officers most respected by the men were those who were comfortable with the exercise of their authority in this relatively informal atmosphere. For their part, these successful leaders – like Simmons, Leach or Harry Smith – lived for the esteem of a soldiery whom others derided as scum. The friendship between Simmons and Fairfoot, it is clear, was lifelong and intense.

In February 1856, an old soldier stiff from his many wounds, George Simmons received a letter. He had retired to Saint Helier in Jersey. There Simmons grew used to reading of the passing of the old riflemen whose campaigns had ended more than forty years back. Leach had died the year before. Fairfoot had crossed the Styx way back in 1838, but his widow Catherine had moved to Jersey, where Simmons was able to keep a protective eye on her. He could see from the back of the letter that it was from an old Peninsular comrade, Charlie Beckwith, who had commanded a company of the 95th. Beckwith had been perturbed to read of the deaths of two old regimental friends the previous year. He told Simmons:

Our friends it is true are fast descending into the tomb and we shall soon follow; but we shall lay down by the side of brothers who loved us during our lives. [They] and a long list down to the rank and file were all united in one common bond of common danger and suffering. God Bless them all!

Those words are an excellent epitaph for the 1st Battalion, 95th. They became legendary not just because of their training and tactics – which *were* truly innovative. Their real secret, however, was that they lived and died for one another and in doing so unlocked a true fighting spirit: that precious unity that inspires men to suffer the worst of hardships, to maintain the respect of their brothers in arms, in pursuit of victory.

Notes on Sources

ONE Departures

1 'Just before 6 a.m.': general descriptive detail of the embarkation has
   come from several eyewitnesses, including George Simmons, *A British
   Rifleman*, Greenhill edition, 1986; William Green, *A Brief Outline of
   Travels and Adventures of William Green*, Coventry, 1857; and notes
   from the manuscript journals of Jonathan Leach and some other officers
   held at the Royal Green Jacket Museum in Winchester.
– 'This, my dear parents, is the happiest moment of my life': Simmons's
   letter is one of those, along with his campaign journal, reproduced in *A
   British Rifleman*.
– 'the commanding officer's intent': so says Simmons.
2 'Private Robert Fairfoot marched in the ranks': details of Fairfoot's
   background come from various official documents in the Public Record
   Office, Kew. His age and other information are in WO 25/559, details
   of his Surrey Militia service in WO 13/2089 to 13/2095.
3 'One of the old hands commented contemptuously': Green.
– 'assert they were headed to help the Austrians': Simmons's letter says the
   destination is a 'profound secret', although it is supposed to be Portugal
   or Austria.
– 'There had been wives on the last expedition': their fates are suggested
   by Benjamin Harris, a 1st Battalion rifleman who served in the Corunna
   campaign of 1808/9 but did not embark with the others on 25 May
   1809. I have used the edition of Harris's memoirs edited and published
   by Eileen Hathaway's Shinglepicker Press in 1995 as *A Dorset Rifleman*.
– 'It was such a parting scene': Green.
4 'O'Hare's 3rd Company . . . went aboard the *Fortune*': Simmons.
– 'For some of the men, like Private Joseph Almond': details of Almond's
   service have been extracted from the pay and muster lists, WO 12/9522,
   WO 17/217, WO 25/2139.

4 'some of the young officers took the opportunity to go ashore': including Captain Jonathan Leach, *Rough Sketches of An Old Soldier*, London, 1831. Leach was to prove the most prolific of the 95th's later author-officers; in addition to his books I have had access to the copy of his unpublished manuscript journal produced by Willoughby Verner when working on his *History and Campaigns of the Rifle Brigade*.

5 'Private Fairfoot knew a fair bit about desertion': details of Fairfoot's vicissitudes emerge from the Royal Surrey paylists, WO 13/2089 to 2095

6 'A very amusing plaything': this description of the 95th came from Lord Cornwallis in a letter of 24 October 1800, and was reproduced in the *Rifle Brigade Chronicle*, 1893, and subsequently in Verner's *History*. Quite why Cornwallis, a veteran of much irregular fighting in America and India, should have been so short-sighted about the value of a rifle regiment is a mystery.

– 'The order of the day was to bombard the sea-fowl': this description comes from Leach, *Rough Sketches*.

– 'Tom Plunket, in 3rd Company, along with Fairfoot': Tom Plunket's saga is contained in Costello, *The True Story of a Peninsular Rifleman*, the Shinglepicker version of Costello's memoirs, published in 1997.

7 'he'd loaded his razor and fired that at the French': this anecdote of Brotherwood, along with comments on his character, is contained in Harris.

– 'Costello had been seduced by the yarns his uncle spun': Costello.

– 'it was a deeply unhappy battalion run on the lash and fear': Capt. B. H. Liddell Hart (ed.), *The Letters of Private Wheeler*, London, 1951. By a stroke of serendipity, Wheeler served in the same militia battalion as Fairfoot and describes its unhappiness under a regime of fear in his early letters. Wheeler volunteered in the 51st.

– 'the fickle dictates of fashion led to hundreds like him being cast out of work': F. A. Wells, *The British Hosiery and Knitwear Industry*, London, 1935, describes the depression in this trade and its causes. Pay lists and casualty returns reveal that dozens of the Leicester Militia men had been weavers. WO 25/2139 gives Brotherwood's trade as 'stocking weaver'.

8 'the great majority had never purchased a commission': this is my own research based on many sources, including War Office files and Royal Green Jackets archives. The one-time purchasers included Harry Smith and Hercules Pakenham.

– 'officers and men alike knew him as a foul-tempered old Turk': the term 'obstinate old Turk' is used by Harry Smith to describe O'Hare in *The Autobiography of Lieutenant General Sir Harry Smith*, London, 1901.

– 'An allowance of £70 or £80 was considered quite normal': see, for example, Cooke of the 43rd, one of the battalions brigaded with the Rifles.

8 'One young lieutenant . . . was the main provider for his widowed mother and his eight siblings': this was John Uniacke. His family circumstances emerge from WO 42/47U3, papers relating to the later financial distress of his mother.

9 'can never be taught to be a perfect judge of distance': Colonel George Hanger, a veteran of the American wars, in his 1808 *Letter to Lord Castlereagh*, cited by David Gates in his *The British Light Infantry Arm*, London, 1987.

TWO Talavera

11 'The quartermaster and a party of helpers soon appeared with dozens of mules they had bought in Lisbon': this detail and many others in this opening passage from Simmons's journal and letters.

– 'There was an official allowance of pack animals': these are set out in the volumes of General Orders published by Wellington's headquarters. These papers, printed on an Army press, were collected and bound by various staff officers and individuals in the Peninsular Army, and quite a few have survived. I consulted those in the National Army Museum and the stupendous private collection of John Sandler.

– 'The subaltern officers – thirty-three of them in the battalion': this is my count of these officers on the 1st/95th's pay rolls, not the standard establishment.

– 'A pack animal might cost £10 or £12': figures on the costs of various items emerge in many journals or sets of letters, including Cooke, Hennell and Gairdner.

12 'his "black muzzle" peered over': this description of Craufurd belongs to Harry Smith in his autobiography. Smith also comments on the squeaky voice.

– 'Craufurd's character was . . . described by one newspaper': *Cobbett's Political Register*, 25 October 1806.

– 'he would find himself again and again coming back to the memory of Buenos Aires': this letter from Craufurd to his wife is dated 3 December 1811 and is quoted in a biography of Black Bob written by Michael Spurrier, which drew extensively on family papers. The unpublished typescript was kindly loaned to me by Caroline Craufurd, one of the general's descendants. The key Craufurd letters remain in the family's possession.

13 'Captain Jonathan Leach, commander of 2nd Company, wrote in his diary': Leach's MS Journal, RGJ Archive, this passage is also quoted in Verner.

13 'The Standing Orders set out': I used 'The Standing Orders of the Light Division', Dublin, 1844.

15 'You have heard how universally General Craufurd was detested': Leach MS Journal, RGJ Archive. Verner's typescript of Leach's journal is not complete (it is missing early 1812) but the great majority of his narrative can be found scattered in many different packets of Box 1 of the RGJ Archive.

 – 'We each had to carry a great weight': this passage and the preceding comment about filling water bottles, Costello.

 – 'They began at 2 a.m. on the': details, Leach MS Journal.

18 'They had drawn up their forces in two waves': this passage on the centre at Talavera relies pretty heavily on Sir Charles Oman's synthesis of eyewitness accounts in Vol. II of *A History of the Peninsular War*, Oxford, 1903.

21 'the last ten miles the road was covered': John Cox MS Journal. Cox was a lieutenant in the 1st/95th at the time. His handwritten journals reside in Dublin, but Verner copies certain passages and these remain in the RGJ Archive.

 – 'The horrid sights were beyond anything I could have imagined': Simmons.

22 'the feelings which constant hunger produces': Leach, *Rough Sketches*.

23 'This will perhaps be a subject of joy to you': Craufurd's letter to his wife is in the British Library, MSS Add 69441.

THREE Guadiana

24 'The diary of one company commander read': Leach MS Journal.

 – 'Brigadier Craufurd allowed his Light Brigade soldiers to shoot some pigs': this incident appears in various accounts, including Leach, *Rough Sketches*.

25 'Here we remained a miserable fortnight': this was William Cox, brother of John, also of the 1st/95th, MS Journal, Verner's copies in the RGJ Archive.

27 'Captain Jonathan Leach wrote in his diary on 27 August': MS Journal.

 – 'Before Simmons knew it, he'd been collared by Craufurd': Simmons.

28 'Beckwith was a model of self-control': this picture of Beckwith is a collage drawn from Kincaid, Leach, Simmons, Smith and other Light Division diarists.

29 'Not a little disgusted, Beckwith asked him': this priceless anecdote was evidently related by Barclay to Colborne, a subsequent CO of the 52nd, and is contained in his biography, *The Life of John Colborne, Field Marshal Lord Seaton*, by G. C. Moore Smith, London, 1903.

 – 'One 95th officer described why it worked so admirably': this description of the 95th's system is contained in *Recollections and Reflections Relative to the Duties of Troops Composing the Advanced Corps of An Army*, by Lieutenant Colonel Leach, London, 1835 – one of Jonathan Leach's lesser-known works, but full of interesting detail nevertheless.

30 'Every corps did harness and march forth to the river in that form except our own': Leach, *Rough Sketches*.

– 'British generals had learned many valuable lessons': these lessons of America are culled from various sources, but principally General Sir William Howe's orders of 1 August 1776.

31 'Craufurd felt the Army was guilty of forgetting many valuable lessons of the American war': this point was made by Craufurd in speeches he made as a Member of Parliament in December 1803 and is quoted by Spurrier.

– 'His Lordship . . . approves of your expending, for practice': letter from the Adjutant General to Craufurd, 13 November 1809, in the published *Dispatches of the Duke of Wellington*, London, 1852.

– 'Many of the battalion's subalterns and even captains carried a rifle': Costello states wrongly in his memoir (written many years later, of course) that he cannot see why officers did not carry rifles too. It is obvious from various accounts that Leach and Crampton among captains in the first battalion did, likewise many subalterns.

– 'As soon as the rifleman has fixed upon his object': this quotation comes from *Regulations for the Exercise of Riflemen and Light Infantry and Instructions for Their Conduct in the Field*, London, 1803. This was a translated and slightly edited version of the first regulations produced five years earlier by the commanding officer of the new 5th/60th, Colonel Rottenburg.

32 'posted behind thickets, and scattered wide in the country': this account of the American war is related in an article about the formation of the Rifle Corps (which became the 95th) in *The English Military Library*, no. XXIX, Feb 1801.

– 'Rules and Regulations for the Army as a whole': these are General Dundas's *Rules and Regulations for the Formation, Field Exercise and Movement of His Majesty's Forces*, 1792.

– 'Dundas thought any large-scale skirmishing': these quotations come from Dundas's *Principles of Military Movements, Chiefly Applied to Infantry*, London, 1788, a work that formed the basis of the later *Rules and Regulations*. The fight between conservatives and reformers on tactics is also debated at length in David Gates's *The British Light Infantry Arm c. 1790–1815*, London, 1987. Moore's quotation is also cited in Gates.

– 'ape grenadiers': this phrase was used by Leach in *Rough Sketches* to deride the orthodoxy.

33 'One was to stress the limited roles of the light-infantry': this and the 'born not made' explanation emerge in *Essai Historique sur l'Infanterie Légère*, Comte Duhesme, Paris, 1814. Colonel F. de Brack, an experienced French officer, stated in his classic *Light Cavalry Outposts* that 'a man must be born a light cavalry soldier'.

– 'The rifle, in its present excellence, assumes the place of the bow': this quotation is from *Scloppetaria: or Considerations on the Nature and Use of Rifled Barrel Guns*, London, 1808, published by Egerton. The author is given as 'a Corporal of Riflemen' but was actually Captain Henry Beaufroy of the 95th. The references to Egypt and Calabria are to recent British military expeditions (of 1801 and 1806) in which the British had acquitted themselves well against the French.

– 'No printers, bookbinders, taylors, shoemakers or weavers should be enlisted': this is Colonel Von Ehwald (sometimes spelt Ewald) in *A Treatise Upon the Duties of Light Troops*, London, 1803. This work, another of Egerton's, was translated from German and contains many fascinating ideas. Colonel William Stewart's notions on recruiting in Ireland, cited later, seem to owe something to Ehwald. The decision to publish his works in English was a deliberate attempt to keep alive lessons of the American war, in which Ehwald had served as an officer in the Hessian Jaeger Corps.

– 'if it were smaller the unpractised recruit would be apt to miss': another quotation from the 1803 *Regulations for the Exercise of Riflemen*.

– 'The more experienced riflemen had trained in techniques for shooting at running enemy': the use of little trolleys with targets mounted on them is described both by Beaufroy and Sergeant Weddeburne of the 95th, *Observations on the Exercise of Riflemen*, Norwich, 1804.

– 'Eight out of ten soldiers in our regular regiments will aim in the same manner': William Surtees, *Twenty Five Years in the Rifle Brigade*. I used the 1973 reprint.

– 'One of the 95th's founders had written in 1806': this was Sir William Stewart, and his outline for the reform of the Army is quoted from in the Cumloden Papers, privately printed in 1871.

34 'Plunket, however, swore blind he would shoot the first officer': this is based on Costello's version of the incident.

35 'back in 1805 Beckwith had proven his aversion to flogging': this anecdote in Surtees.

– 'despite the wish of some officers to develop a more selective recruitment system': e.g. Beaufroy in his book suggests the Rifles should be recruited only from the light companies of line regiments.

– 'its composition had been roughly six Englishmen to two Scots and two Irish': these estimates for 1809 are my own and are necessarily approximate, based on the details in muster rolls and casualty returns. My work on the Casualty Returns for January 1811 to December 1812 showed ninety-five English (including Welsh), thirty-three Irish and thirty-two Scots. Later things changed somewhat. WO 17/282, a Monthly Return dated 25 July 1814, gives a rare national breakdown of soldiers in the 1st Battalion 95th. Its lists: 63 sergeants (of which 31 English, 20 Scotch and 12 Irish); 48 corporals (of which 24 English, 8 Scotch and 16 Irish); 15 buglers (11 English, 2 Scotch, 2 Irish); and 748 privates (523 English, 87 Scotch, 138 Irish). The points of notes here are (a) that the rank and file of the regiment had become even more 'English' by 1814 due to recruiting efforts (b) the Scottish element had declined relative to the Irish because – I believe – of higher losses due to sickness, desertion and capture in the Peninsula, and (c) the pattern of heavier Scottish recruit-ment during 1800–5 and Irish in 1805–8 is reflected in the respective national 'bulges' for sergeants and corporals.

35 'Many officers felt the Irish were particularly prone to thieving': the evi-dence of this stereotype can be found in several memoirs or diaries where an officer (e.g. Kincaid) notes that his Irish servant has stolen from him. We do not see similar records of English or Scottish thieving. It is worth noting that in General Orders the 88th or Connaught Rangers feature in scores of courts martial for theft and other misdemeanours during 1809–11. How far this represents a prejudice against this regiment with its strong Irish character, or how far it substantiates General Picton's view of them as 'robbers and footpads', we can only guess.

36 'except in cases of infamy': another quotation from Stewart's 'outline'.

– 'Officers of the 95th were sensitive to cases which might damage the reg-iment's good name': this point is made by Costello relative to the later flogging of a rifleman named Stratton – it explains however why the many punishments of this kind that he and others like Leach refer to do not appear in the Army's General Orders.

37 'The training at Campo Maior reached a peak on 23 September': Leach mentions the field day in his MS Journal.

– 'The tactics taught to the 43rd and 52nd by Moore back in England . . . were a hybrid of orthodox and rifle ones': the best evidence of this comes from A System of Drill and Manoeuvres As Practised in the 52nd Light Infantry Regiment, by Captain John Cross, London, 1823. Cross makes clear that the system described in the book was adopted during the Shorncliffe camp exercises of 1804. The quotation on the 52nd's method of aiming is from the Cross text.

38 'My case was really pitiable, my appetite and hearing gone': this was not a 95th man, but another sufferer, Sergeant Cooper of the 7th Fusiliers, in his Rough Notes on Seven Campaigns, Carlisle, 1869.

38 'We were ordered to sit up with the sick in our turns': William Green.
 – 'Dozens died in the 95th, with O'Hare's company, for example, losing
   twelve soldiers': this comes from the pay and muster roll research conducted by Eileen Hathaway and myself.

FOUR Barba del Puerco

40 'It was beyond anything I could have conceived': Simmons.
41 'This extraordinary undertaking': James Shaw Kennedy, whose essay on
   the outpost line appears in Lord Fitzclarence's *Manual of Outpost
   Duties*, London, 1849.
42 'by the over-eagerness of the riflemen': *Wellington's Dispatches*, letter of
   16 August 1808 to the Duke of Richmond.
43 'They in turn thought highly of him': Simmons and Leach praised
   Wellington highly in their journals well before his great Peninsular
   victories.
 – 'He rejected, for example, the old system of forming ad hoc battalions':
   this emerges from a letter to General William Stewart of 27 March
   1810, in the Cumloden Papers, Edinburgh, 1871.
 – 'Wellington soon realised that these regiments – the 43rd, 52nd and 95th
   – were among the very best troops': Charles Napier, in a letter home of
   21 March 1811, describes the Light Division as 'great favourites' of
   Wellington's.
 – 'He also rejected the doctrine of many conservative generals that riflemen, by virtue of their slower rate of fire and skirmishers' vulnerability
   to cavalry, could only ever be deployed in penny packets, supporting
   regular infantry': in a letter of 11 July 1803, General Clinton (Military
   Secretary at Horse Guards) wrote, 'I cannot help thinking that a corps
   armed with rifles, unless it is supported, would be exposed in a very
   short time to be cut to pieces.' He is cited by Gates.
 – 'with him the field officers must first be steady': these comments about
   William Stewart's time as commanding officer were made by Charles
   Napier (then an officer in the 95th) in his journal and reproduced in *The
   Life and Opinions of General Sir Charles James Napier*, by Lieutenant
   General Sir W. Napier, 4 vols., London, 1857.
44 'he had begun his military career as a surgeon's mate': see WO 12/7695,
   muster roll of 69th Foot.
 _ 'He had been promoted to captain in 1803': Sir William Stewart's letter
   to the Commander in Chief, see WO 31/143.
45 'His brother officers were ignorant of the wife, Mary, and daughter,
   Marianne': their ignorance is shown by the Register of Officers' Effects,
   WO 25/2964 where it says it is 'not known' whether he is married.
   Mary's existence emerges from PROB 6/189 Acts of Administrations

(these are probate records), and Marianne's from WO 25/3080 which are Abstracts of Compassionate Allowance Claims for 1814.

45 'O'Hare had spent some time pursuing a young lady in Hythe': Costello, who also provides the quotations about flogging the next man who makes an attempt, and about O'Hare's extremely ugly countenance.

– 'having enjoyed the wine very much': this quotation and the saga of the stolen boots come from Simmons.

46 'Whereas, for example, Lieutenant Harry Smith, a dashing young English subaltern': these forms of address come from Smith's memoirs. Costello says O'Hare's men usually called him Peter.

– 'We had but a slender sprinkling of the aristocracy among us': John Kincaid, *Random Shots From a Rifleman*, first published London, 1835.

– 'They soon took over the small *cantinas*, inviting local girls to join them in nightly drinking, dancing and song': tales of their carousing emerge from Leach, *Rough Sketches*, and *The Peninsula and Waterloo, Memories of an Old Rifleman*, a memoir of John Molloy, of the 95th, by Edmund F. Du Cane, published in *Cornhill Magazine*, Vol. 76, December 1897.

– 'Various amusements were exhibited this morning in our village': Leach, MS Journal, entry for 4 February.

– 'that to divert and to amuse his men and to allow them every possible indulgence': Leach, *Rough Sketches*, where the rifleman also cheerfully admits to stealing honey and poaching pigeons.

48 'There was great uncertainty in the French command about whether Craufurd's line of outposts was at all supported': that Ferey's raid was some sort of reconnaissance in force emerges from General Loison, his divisional commander's report of the event. This is found in the general's letterbook in French Army archives at Vincennes, dated 21 March 1810, letter 344.

– 'Early in the evening of 19 March': this account of Barba del Puerco relies on Simmons, Costello, Green, John Cox's MS Journal (RGJ Archives, Box 1, Item 34) and the official French report of the action above.

– 'O'Hare, who had "been taken unwell"': these are Simmons's words. My own suspicion, given some of the other material in this chapter, is that O'Hare was drunk. I have no direct proof, so I have refrained from making such an emotive allegation in the text itself. Clearly, whatever was wrong with him, it was not a serious enough illness to stop him bellowing about the battlefield just a few hours after he had retired.

51 'Our swords were soon fixed and giving the war cheer': John Cox MS Journal.

– 'Ferey's dispatch reported the losses: twelve dead and thirteen wounded':

actually Loison's dispatch alluded to earlier, but it was the custom simply to incorporate the details sent up by your subordinates in their own accounts.

52 'Had the drunken carousing of the 95th's officers alienated the locals': both Molloy and Leach speculated along these lines. The quotation about them being 'blind drunk' comes from Leach's *Rough Sketches*.

– 'we . . . looked upon it as no inconsiderable addition to our regimental feather': Kincaid, *Random Shots*.

– 'The action reflects honour on Lieutenant Colonel Beckwith': Craufurd's order has been reproduced in many places, including Simmons.

54 'Eventually, though, the brigadier set off regardless': Wellington told his brother-in-law in a letter of 31 July 1810 (in *Dispatches*) that 'I knew nothing before it happened'.

– 'Craufurd cruelly tried to cut up a handful of brave men, and they thrashed him': Charles Napier.

FIVE The Coa

55 'Craufurd had posted his division': this has been pieced together from various accounts, including Leach's MS Journal and Simmons.

56 'Some riflemen came around with dry cartridges': according to Green. This looks like interesting evidence that, even this early in their campaign, the riflemen had abandoned the pre-war style of loading. Instead of a loose ball, powder poured from the horn that symbolised their corps and a leather patch to give the bullet a snug fit, they were using paper cartridges with ball and powder wrapped up in them. This made for faster shooting.

– 'As the morning fog cleared away we observed the extensive plains': John Cox, MS Journal.

57 'If the enemy was enterprising we should be cut to pieces': these quotations from the journal come from Sir William Napier's life of his brother.

– 'Wellington himself had echoed these views': apologists for Craufurd, notably Alexander Craufurd in *General Craufurd and his Light Division*, London, 1891, suggest there was some ambiguity in Wellington's orders. I can't see that Wellington's missives of June and July 1810, culminating with one two days before the battle stating, 'I am not desirous of engaging in an affair beyond the Coa' (these can all be found in the volumes of *Wellington's Dispatches*), leave any room for doubt about his intentions.

– 'He sent his aide-de-camp, Major Napier, around the battalion commanders, telling them': Napier, life of Charles Napier.

58 'He ordered half his company, Lieutenant Coane's platoon (under Simmons now)': Simmons.

– 'The French cavalry are upon us!': Costello.

59 'Captain Vogt, one of their squadron commanders, fell dead': Capitaine R. Dupuy, *Historique du 3e Régiment de Hussards de 1764 à 1887*, Paris 1887.

– 'One of the Portuguese battalions started to disintegrate': Wellington's letter of 29 July 1810 to William Beresford (the British officer seconded to command the Portuguese army) reveals the flight of about half of the 1st *Cacadores*. An inquiry into their conduct was subsequently ordered by Beresford, which concluded, rather feebly, that those who fled across the bridge had been left without orders.

– 'They sent their light infantry in abundance like swarms of bees': Jonathan Leach MS, from the letter account of the Coa sent home to an (unknown) friend and later copied by Willoughby Verner while researching his history.

60 'Beckwith saw Major Napier nearby, and ordered him to get through to the 52nd': this is evident from Napier's journal and Harry Smith's comments.

– 'they had run out of ammunition': Leach MS Journal.

61 'Captain Alexander Cameron's men of the 7th or Highland Company': Cameron's positions vis-à-vis the 43rd were discussed in a letter to him from Christopher Patrickson, late 43rd, written in 1844, RGJ Archive, Box 1A, Item 40.

– 'This is an officer of ours, and we must see him in safety before we leave him': Simmons.

– 'The French in a second occupied the hill which we left': Leach MS Journal.

62 'Colonel Jean-Pierre Bechaud called out to the grenadiers of his *66ème Régiment*': Capitaine Dumay, *Historique du 66e Régiment d'Infanterie (1672–1900)*, Tours, 1900.

– 'Captain Ninon, commander of the *82éme*'s grenadier company': Capitaine P. Arvers *et al.*, *Historique du 82e Regiment d'Infanterie de Ligne*, Paris, 1876, contains a report by Ferey dated 10 September 1810 which relates the grenadiers' attack.

63 'The 95th had accounted for 129 of them: including 12 killed and 54 missing': Oman.

– 'all this blood was shed for no purpose whatsoever': John Cox MS Journal.

– 'But for Colonel Beckwith our whole force would have been sacrificed': Harry Smith.

64 'The Combat of the 24th proves to [the British] there is no position the French infantry cannot take': Loison's report of 26 July, contained in his letterbook in the SHAT Vincennes C 720.

- 'that a very unusual degree of severity is exercised towards the soldiers': this letter from the Adjutant General, Harry Calvert, to Wellington, dated 5 January 1810, is cited by Spurrier, apparently from the Wellington Papers at Southampton University.

64 'I never thought any good was to be expected from any thing of which General R. Craufurd had the direction': Charles Gordon, letter of 1 August 1810, in family papers relayed to me by Air Commodore John Tomes.

- 'If I am to be hanged for it, I cannot accuse a man who I think has meant well': Wellington to Wellesley-Pole, as above.

65 'The command of your advanced guard appears to be founded in more ignorance': Torrens to Colonel Bathurst (Military Secretary in Wellington's HQ), 14 August 1810, Spurrier citing WO 3/597.

- 'reports flew about that Craufurd would any moment be replaced by another general': Sir Brent Spencer was fancied for the job, according to a letter by Lieutenant Henry Booth, of the 43rd, to his brother in England, 30 July 1810, reproduced in Levinge's 'Historical Records of the 43rd'.

SIX Wounded

66 'In the churches or barns where Wellington's few surgeons struggled to cope with the Coa wounded': the main sources for the first part of this chapter are Simmons, Smith and Costello.

68 'The surgeons had neither the time nor opportunity to look after us': Costello.

69 'The people are not worthy of notice. I met with great barbarity all the way': Simmons sent this letter home on 10 August 1810.

- 'A lieutenant who had lost an eye or one of his arms could augment his income to the tune of £70 per annum': see *A Gentleman Volunteer, The Letters of George Hennell*, ed. Michael Glover, London, 1979. Hennell came out to the Peninsula as a volunteer and was commissioned into the 43rd in 1812. His observations were often deeply perceptive, but we must wait several more chapters before his letters regularly inform this narrative.

- 'a one-off gratuity of a year's pay': several 95th officers were to become eligible for this bounty, by virtue of serious wounds, but remain serving with their regiment. John FitzMaurice, a young subaltern who joined in 1811, on the other hand, went home for a year after being wounded at Badajoz.

70 'some got as much as ninepence a day': this was William Green's pension. There are various stories of soldiers getting less than this. The awards were usually decided by a board at somewhere like the Royal Hospital (Chelsea or Dublin).

- 'It was a place noted for every species of skulk': Costello.

70 'Late in the summer of 1810, Brigadier Craufurd wrote to Wellington estimating that': Craufurd's letter, 22 October 1810, cited by Spurrier.

– 'Some of the younger soldiers, benefiting by the instruction given to them by old malingerers': this was a surgeon called William Gibney, actually describing practices in Chelsea, where the interest in staying in hospital might well have been greater than in Portugal, where Belem barracks was a superior alternative. Gibney is quoted by Dr Martin Howard in *Wellington's Doctors*, Spellmount, 2002, a very useful study of army medicine at this time.

71 'On 23 October, Headquarters issued a General Order': in *Wellington's Dispatches*. The narrative does not proceed in strict chronological order here, for I consider this General Order from late October, then Simmons, writing early in September, before moving on in the next chapter to Busaco in late September.

– 'Private Billy McNabb of the 95th was one such': his basic story is told by Costello. However, various details gleaned from regimental muster rolls have been added.

SEVEN Busaco

74 'the *voltigeurs* of the *69ème Régiment*': *Campagnes du Capitaine Marcel*, ed. Le Commandant Var, Paris, 1913, is the source of information on Marcel and his battle.

– 'Their generals could observe all our movements and even count the number of files': François-Nicholas Fririon, *Journal Historique de la Campagne de Portugal*, Paris, 1841.

75 'There had been a heated discussion the night before': various French sources give different versions of this, including Fririon and J. Marbot, *Mémoires du General Baron Marbot*, Paris, 1892.

76 'preceded by its skirmishers. Arriving on the mountain's crest it will form in [battle] line': Masséna's orders are reproduced in Vol. III of Oman's *History*.

– 'No cartridges, go in with the bayonet!': Marcel.

78 'Simon's six battalions, marching behind in tight, long columns little more than thirty or forty men across the front': Leach in his MS letter home mentions the French battalions coming up in 'column of sections', which would mean half a company's width, the French companies being somewhat under strength.

– 'We must give the French their due and say that no men could come up in a more resolute manner': Leach MS letter.

– 'Simon had got his guns': the British sources say little about this, but since Fririon, Marbot and other French ones are adamant, I believe that they fell briefly into the power of the French.

78 'I turned about to the 43rd and 52nd Regiments and ordered them to charge': Craufurd's account of the battle, in a letter to his wife, undated, cited by Spurrier.

– 'An officer of the 52nd recounted': George Napier, another of the military brothers – his account is contained in *Passages in the Early Military Life*, ed. Gen. W. Napier, London, 1884.

79 'they loosed off a ragged volley at the chargers': George Napier.

– 'We kept firing and bayoneting till we reached the bottom': George Napier.

80 'it is clear that the six battalions taken forward by Simon suffered terrible casualties among their officers': details from A. Martinien, *Tableaux par Corps et par Batailles des officiers tués et blessés pendant les guerres de l'Empire*, Paris, 1899, a monumental standard work and the starting point for much analysis of Napoleonic battles.

– 'Colonel Bechaud of the 66ème, for example, having recovered from his chest wound in July at the Coa': Fririon.

– 'the English were the only troops who were perfectly practised in the use of small arms': Marbot, a man generally regarded as something of a romancer with regard to his own exploits, but quite right in this context, even if this reflection may have been made some years later.

81 'The French did not want to issue rifles to their men': *Neuf Mois de Campagnes à la Suite du Maréchal Soult*, by Lt Col J. B. Dumas, Paris, c. 1900. Although a history of the later (1813–14) campaign, the introductory chapter contains one of the most impressive and detailed analyses, from a French perspective, of the French Army's failure to match British firepower.

– 'The French also considered the rifle a very suspect thing if it just caused the soldier to sit, trying to pick off his enemy at long range': Duhesme.

– 'It was an unsuitable weapon for the French soldier, and would only have suited phlegmatic, patient, assassins': Comte Jean-Jacques Gassendi, *Aide-Mémoire des Officiers d'Artillerie de France*, Paris, 1809. Gassendi reminds us of the deep influence of such notions of national character in this epoch.

– 'The consumption of this munition is quite incredible': this comment was made by General Éblé, commander of French artillery and engineers during the siege, in a letter to the Minister of War in Paris dated 20 July 1810. It is reproduced in Capt. M. Griod de L'Ain's *Le Général Éblé*, Paris, 1893. Éblé later died of exhaustion having led his engineers into the freezing waters of the River Berezina, saving the remnants of Napoleon's army during the Retreat from Moscow in 1812.

82 'enormous loss of officers': Fririon.

– 'Our heavy losses at Busaco had chilled the ardour of Masséna's lieutenants': Marbot.

82 'In his official Busaco dispatch, Wellington praised Craufurd':
Wellington's letter to the Earl of Liverpool, 30 September 1810, in
Wellington's Dispatches.

83 'the 26th, 66th and 82nd are Bridge of Lodi boys, but of the heights of
Busaco I daresay they will be less proud': Leach MS Journal.

EIGHT The Corporal's Stripes

84 'This day's march was about as miserable as I wish to see': Leach MS
Journal.
– 'lines of fortifications stretching twenty-nine miles from the Atlantic
coast in the west': details of Torres Vedras, Oman.

85 'After such a miserable march, Captain O'Hare's pleasure': Simmons.
– 'Never was a town more completely deserted than Arruda': Leach,
Rough Sketches.
– 'This was the only instance during the war in which the light division
had reason to blush for their conduct': John Kincaid, *Adventures in the
Rifle Brigade*.
– 'the rifleman, who celebrated his twenty-seventh birthday in Arruda, had
become something of a friend and a personal project': Fairfoot is mentioned in Simmons's letters and journals, which is highly unusual for
officers in this period. In a later memorandum about the Waterloo campaign, dated 15 October 1850 (Sir William Cope's letter book, National
Army Museum MSS 6804-2 Vol. I), Simmons pays Fairfoot many compliments. My own suspicion is that Simmons may even have taught
Fairfoot to read and write, for Fairfoot's promotions in the militia were
only to the rank of drummer – i.e. to a station not requiring literacy.

86 'as great a tyrant as ever disgraced the Army': this is Wheeler's description in Liddell Hart, as is the following quotation about volunteering
and the general description of life in the Royal Surreys.
– 'frequent opportunities are afforded for the display of personal courage':
Sergeant William Weddeburne, *Observations on the Exercise of
Riflemen and the Movements of Light Troops in General*, Norwich,
1804. This text is very rare, and I am grateful to Ron Cassidy for copying the one in the RGJ Museum for me.

87 'His company had set sail in May 1809 with six sergeants and six corp
orals': this comes from my own work, and that of Eileen Hathaway, on
the regimental muster rolls.
– 'Esau Jackson . . . got himself appointed to a comfy sinecure in charge
of stores at Belem': this is borne out by both Costello and the muster
rolls.

87 'the "Green Book" written by Colonel Coote Manningham': a copy survives in the RGJ Museum.

88 'the non-commissioned officer will make the most minute inspection of the men': this quotation comes not from the Green Book but from Manningham's *Military Lectures Delivered to the 95th (Rifle) Regiment 1803*, first published in the *Rifle Brigade Chronicle*, 1896, and republished by Ken Trotman, 2002, under the same covers as *Light Cavalry Outposts* by F. de Brack.

– 'But while bright enough, and no skulker on the battlefield, Almond's company commander had taken against him': Costello.

89 'If I ever have any occasion to observe any man of the Brigade pick his road': these notes survived in Leach's papers and were reproduced in Verner.

90 'in time enough to save us from total annihilation': Leach MS Journal, ditto the preceding quotation.

– 'Are you aware, General, that the whole of Junot's corps is close': Simmons, who clearly loved seeing Craufurd humiliated by Wellington as much as Leach did.

– 'Craufurd had been making representations to Horse Guards for some time about the need for more troops': Spurrier.

– 'The company with which I had just arrived were much distressed to keep pace': Kincaid, *Random Shots*.

91 'The early part of their evenings was generally spent in witticisms and tales': Kincaid, *Random Shots*.

92 'Had sentence of death been pronounced, it could not have sounded more harsh': the tales of Plunket's grog and the still, Costello.

– 'If a man in England . . . fancies that he really knows the comfort of tobacco': Leach, *Rough Sketches*.

– 'Books were in short supply': the Gairdner diary (NAM MSS) makes clear that he was one of the French speakers who read *Nouvelle Héloïse*. As to *Don Quixote*, Costello uses the term 'Dulcinea' and Leach refers to his 'Rosinante'. There are numerous references to *Gil Blas* in Peninsular writings, including a couple by Wellington himself. In Page's 'Intelligence Officer in the Peninsula', there is a list of reading matter in the possession of Captain Edward Cocks. It includes Spenser's *Faerie Queen*, Warton's *History of English Poetry*, Milford's *Grecian History* and a number of titles of professional military interest. Cocks, however, was an officer of unusual education and wealth.

93 'He wrote to them of his "miserable position"': letter from Craufurd to his wife, 5 September 1810, cited by Spurrier.

– 'I would beg you to reflect whether, considering the situation in which you stand in the Army': Wellington to Craufurd, 9 December 1810, in *Wellington's Dispatches*.

– 'without reducing me to the painful alternative which I have at present to contemplate': Craufurd's reply to Wellington, 17 December 1810, cited by Spurrier.

94 'Brigadier General Craufurd has sailed for England': Leach MS Journal, entry for 3 February.

NINE Pombal

95 'constant reports brought in that they cannot remain much longer in their present positions as the soldiery are suffering sad privations': Simmons, as is the following quotation.

96 'looked like a city of the plague, represented by empty dogs and empty houses': a characteristically elegant turn of phrase from Kincaid, *Adventures*.

– 'sixty-five thousand when it entered Portugal, to just over forty thousand as it left': Oman's figures, based on careful analysis of French returns.

– 'The Peninsular Army had become chronically short of cash during the winter': there are various letters in *Wellington's Dispatches* averting to the shortage of specie or ready money at this time. The regimental muster rolls show the 95th's periods without pay.

97 'Go kill a Frenchman for yourself!': Costello.

– 'It was a sunshiny morning, and the red coats and pipeclayed belts and glittering of men's arms in the sun looked beautiful': Simmons.

– 'The files (a pair of men in each case) would then move apart – anything from two to six paces between them': this section is based on Rottemburg's regulations plus some other texts of the kind.

98 'most of the Light Division adopted skirmishing tactics too': the MS version of Simmons's diary was edited by Verner and his starting copy remains in the RGJ Archive. He says of the advance 'the remaining part of the Division [i.e. not the 95th] were nearly all advancing in skirmishing order'.

99 'but was refused because he had gone out of action with the wounded': Allen's story is told in Costello.

100 'He is very blind, which is against him at the head of the cavalry': one of my favourite Iron Duke quotations, because it is so utterly dry and mordant. It comes from his letter to Beresford, 24 April 1811, in *Dispatches*.

– 'checked with ninety-four casualties, including two officers and three soldiers of the 95th killed': the officers of the 95th were Major Stewart and Lieutenant Strode. Technically they both 'died of wounds' rather than being killed in action.

– 'they soon began referring to him as "Ass-skin"': Verner is the source of this gem. Smith, rather knowingly, calls Erskine an 'ass' at one point in his narrative.

101 'pressing us harder than usual': Marcel.

101 'From 5 to 15 March, that is to say in eleven days, [the corps] sped across thirty-three leagues': Fririon.

102 'If you ask me whether we might not have done more than we have, I have no hesitation in answering certainly yes': my old friend George Scovell, in a letter to Colonel Le Marchant, 11 April 1811, contained in the Le Marchant Papers, Packet 1a, Item 4.

103 'Our regiment gets terribly cut up': Simmons, letter of 26 March.
  – 'Pillaging is expressly forbidden, and pillagers will be punished': this order was dated 3 April and is reprinted in Fririon.

TEN Sabugal

104 'An eerie sound penetrated the early-morning fog': Harry Smith described it.
  – 'Wellington issued orders for a large-scale attack': the orders, written up by his Quarter Master General, are reproduced in Vol. IV of the 1852 *Wellington's Dispatches*.
  – 'soon enough, they were wading up to their waists': according to Simmons in a letter home. In his journal, oddly, Simmons says the water came up to their armpits.

105 'three companies of the 3rd *Cacadores*, generally reckoned the best Portuguese troops': Verner argues they were not present, but they are referred to in *Wellington's Dispatches* so I think we must assume they were.

106 'short-sighted old ass': Smith.
  – 'A brigade of dragoons under Sir William Erskine, who were to have covered our right': Kincaid, *Adventures*.
  – 'the whole of Right Wing formed one long skirmish line': Simmons.

107 'the galling fire of the 95th Rifles at point blank [soon] compelled them to retire': John Cox MS Journal, also the following quotation.
  – 'Beckwith, finding himself alone and unsupported, in close action, with only hundreds to oppose the enemy's thousands': Kincaid, *Random Shots*.

108 'Having come forward in columns, they could not now deploy into firing lines': Cox and Simmons are quite specific about the French coming forward in columns. The point about not deploying into line derives from study of the ground and of the frontage that would have been required for this.
  – 'Now my lads, we'll just go back a little if you please': the Beckwith quotations in this section come from Simmons and Kincaid.

109 'Their officers are certainly very prodigal of life, often exposing themselves ridiculously': Simmons.
  – 'Shoot that fellow, will you?': these Beckwith quotations are from Smith.

109 'The regiments facing the British brigade in this part of the fight had eighteen officers shot': Martinien and Oman.

110 'our loss is much less than one would have supposed possible, scarcely two hundred men': letter of 4 April 1811 to Beresford, in *Dispatches*.

– 'Of the five French colonels who led their regiments against the Light Division': Martinien. The colonels of the *2ème Léger* and *70ème* Line both died of wounds received at Sabugal, the *6ème* and *17ème Léger* had their colonels wounded.

– 'If anything brilliant has been done, it will be to a certain degree mortifying': Craufurd letter, cited by Spurrier as 'early April'.

111 'I consider the action that was fought by the Light Division': Wellington's dispatch to the Earl of Liverpool is dated 9 April 1811, in *Dispatches*.

– 'it would be stupid to pretend to persuade you that I did not feel any regret that the events': Craufurd to his wife, 13 April 1811, Spurrier.

– 'On 11 April, Peter O'Hare was given an in-field promotion, or brevet, to the rank of major': this data, and much else in the subsequent paragraphs, comes from the Challis Index, a biographical goldmine on Peninsular officers kept at the Royal United Services Institute in London.

113 'supposing I got into the most desirable Regt. in the service, I should be happy to leave it the moment I could get a step': this letter is contained in *The Pakenham Letters 1800 to 1815*, privately printed 1914.

– 'as to remaining an English full-pay lieutenant for ten or twelve years!': letter from Charles Napier, quoted by William Napier.

– 'Layton and Grant argued until, pistols being produced, they determined to fight a duel': details of this fascinating case emerge from Green and the *Rifle Brigade Chronicle*, 1947.

114 'A contest of this kind had caused one officer of the 95th to leave the regiment': Captain Travers – the case is described in the *Rifle Brigade Chronicle*, 1895.

– 'But Layton's fate was to serve on without the possibility of promotion': this is evident from the fact that he was never promoted, even though others less senior were, without purchase.

ELEVEN Fuentes d'Onoro

116 'I found my Division under arms, and was received with the most hearty appearance of satisfaction': Craufurd's letter to his wife dates from 8 May 1811, another one cited by Spurrier.

– 'they had the sense that Craufurd attended keenly to his duty': Costello and Harris are examples of this. Interestingly both books were (ghost)written long after the Napoleonic wars and Craufurd's mention of the three cheers is the only one I can find in any contemporary document. The same applies to more general remarks about his qualities: they do not appear in the contemporary journals or letters of characters like Simmons, Leach and John Cox.

117 'formed column at quarter distance, ready to form square at any moment if charged by cavalry': Simmons. This account of the Light Division's battle differs somewhat from that of Oman, the great authority, and indeed from my own Oman-influenced version in *The Man Who Broke Napoleon's Codes*, Faber, 2001. The changes reflect careful study of Light Division accounts.

118 'While we were retiring with the order and precision of a common field day': Kincaid, *Adventures*.

– 'One of these riflemen, named Flynn, was a good specimen of the hard-fighting Irish': both tales of Flynn come from an officer called John FitzMaurice, who joined the 95th in 1811 and whose son privately published a volume of reminiscences called *Biographical Sketch of Major General John FitzMaurice* in Italy in 1908.

119 'this was the first charge of cavalry most of us had seen': Costello.

– 'a company of the Guards, who did not get out of the wood': Simmons.

– 'Lieutenant Colonel Hill's men were unable to form square': Oman quotes Hall of the Guards at length on this incident.

120 'The town presented a shocking sight': William Grattan of the 88th, 'Adventures with the Connaught Rangers, 1809–1814', London, 1902.

– 'Such was the fury of the 79th': FitzRoy Somerset writing to his brother, the Duke of Beaufort on 8 May 1811, unpublished, residing in the family archive at Badminton House, Beaufort Papers FmM 4/1/6.

121 'Most of the Peninsular veteran regiments . . . had adopted the movement and firing tactics of the Light Brigade': Major General John Colville, commanding the British brigade most heavily engaged at El Bodon in September 1811, for example, wrote home that the drills his battalions used to form square during that battle were, 'the Light Infantry or Sir John Moore's', i.e. not the old regulations. Colville's letter, retained in family papers, is reproduced in *The Portrait of a General*, by John Colville, Salisbury, 1980 – a very useful volume. As for the regiments adopting Light Division firing practice, this is evident in Simmons's comments about the losses to the 79th.

– 'firing volleys in sections according to the old drill': this point is made by Simmons.

– 'a ball had passed through the back part of the head': Kincaid, *Adventures*.

– 'endless euphemisms were coined to provide a little conversational variety': Kincaid's *Random Shots* is the best single source of these, but they appear in many different places.

123 'to be in the Light Division is sufficient to stamp a man as a good soldier': Wyndham Madden, an officer of the 43rd, writing home to his mother on 5 August 1811, RGJ archive box 1A /455.

– 'Lord Wellington conceives there he might be treated to more shots than his friends would wish': letter from FitzRoy Somerset, 23 May 1811, Beaufort Papers FmM 4/1/6, as is the recommendation of the Fusiliers. In his next letter, Somerset changed this to the Guards ('as I am persuaded it is the only part of the Army where there is now good society'). The identity of the young aristocrat receiving this advice via the Duke of Beaufort is not entirely clear from the letters.

124 'the last named officer, I beg leave in a particular manner to recommend to Lord Wellington's notice': Beckwith's letter to Somerset, 3 July 1811, in WO31/327.

TWELVE The Gentleman Volunteer

125 'I hope to see a great number of volunteers come out soon': Simmons.

– 'your memorialist, a native of Scotland, aged 19, is a son of respectable parentage': Mitchell's notes survives in the Mitchell Papers, cited by William C. Foster in his *Sir Thomas Mitchell and His World 1792–1855*, published by the New South Wales Institution of Surveyors.

126 'A volunteer – be it known to all who know it not': Kincaid, *Random Shots*. Kincaid calls Sarsfield 'Dangerfield' in his book, presumably to safeguard against the threat of litigation or a challenge to a duel.

– 'John FitzMaurice . . . had come out a few months before his countryman Sarsfield': his recommendation was from Judge Day. The story of FitzMaurice's arrival in his regiment was told by his son, cited above.

127 'While they are treated as gentlemen out of the field': Kincaid, *Random Shots*.

– 'That young devil FitzMaurice is covered with blood from head to foot': FitzMaurice *fils*.

128 'Sarsfeld's brother had been killed at Albuera': this detail emerges from Beckwith's letter to Somerset of 4 July 1811 in WO31/327.

129 'the usual sinister cast of the eye worn by common Irish country countenances': Kincaid, *Random Shots*.

– 'His original good natured simplicity gave way to experience': Costello, who calls Sarsfield 'Searchfied' in his book.

130 'General Murray who commands the garrison . . . is very fond of shew and parade': Gairdner's letter to his father 26 May 1811. The other quotation comes from a letter of 10 September 1810. Both are contained, along with Gairdner's journal, in the archives of the National Army Museum MSS 7011-21. Gairdner's impressions form a vital and hardly ever used primary source on the 95th.

130 'the laughing stock of the whole army, and particularly of the Light
Division': Charles Napier, in William Napier's book of his life.
– 'Ensign William Hay joined the 52nd only to witness the following':
Captain William Hay, *Reminiscences, 1809–1815, Under Wellington,*
London, 1901.
131 'Order upon orders of the most damnable nature were issued': Leach
MS Journal.
– 'I am glad to see you safe, Craufurd': this is one of the better-known
Craufurd anecdotes, first described by F. Larpent, *Private Journal of F.
Seymour Larpent, Judge Advocate General,* London, 1853.

THIRTEEN Deserters

134 'A Spanish peasant girl has an address about her': Kincaid, *Adventures.*
135 'characters like Leach or Johnston strolling down the lanes with a pet
wolf': Leach, *Rough Sketches* and 'Anecdotes in the Life of the Late
Major Johnstone, of the Rifle Brigade', by a Brother Officer [in fact
Kincaid], *United Service Journal,* 1837, Part I.
– '21 August, when half of the 3rd Battalion – four companies comprising
its Right Wing': Leach MS Journal.
136 'One evening, returning from an inspection of the outposts, General
Craufurd rode straight into a scene of near riot': Costello is the source
of this entire anecdote.
– 'The corporal was broken to the ranks and awarded 150 lashes':
Costello says the man was called Corporal Miles, a name that does not
appear in the 1st Battalion lists. It is possible he was in another battalion
of the 95th. He is also unclear about when exactly the incident happened, but Leach in his MS Journal makes reference to the flogging of
two men on 11 October 1811.
137 'I am labouring under a fit of the blue devils': Craufurd to his wife, 3
December 1811, cited by Spurrier.
– 'Headquarters was putting the squeeze on skulkers in the hospitals
again': with a General Order of 15 November 1811, in *Dispatches.*
138 'Three men had absconded from the 1st/95th within a year of its landing': they were Neil MacLean and Ronald MacDonald, 7th Company,
and Allan Cumming, 3rd Company, according to returns. Cumming
returned later, as we shall see. Kincaid, in *Adventures,* reports the death
in battle of another 95th deserter, which circumstantial evidence suggests may have been MacDonald.
– 'A private of the 43rd had tried desertion back in the summer of 1810':
these examples come from the court-martial records in *General Orders,
Spain and Portugal,* London, 1811–14.
– 'Well, Rifles, you will remember the 24th of July': the source of this fas-

cinating anecdote and the quotation at the end of this passage is Green.

138 'The case of Allan Cummings may have also persuaded them': Cummings' desertion and pardon is described by Harris in his recollections. WO 25/2139, Casualty Returns, lists him as a deserter, as do the muster rolls, which show him having gone on 27 October 1810. WO 25/2139 is also the source of the information on MacFarlane and other deserters, including for example Almond's debts when he deserted.

139 'On 17 November, Almond decided to take his chance': the dates of the desertions come from subsequent proceedings in the volumes of General Orders and from WO 25/2139.

140 'one of his mad freaks': Harry Smith, who, like Wellington, was evidently unable to accept the genuine privations described by Costello and others.

 – 'The Commander of the Forces is much concerned to learn from your letter': this letter and the Adjutant General's of 21 December are in *Wellington's Dispatches*.

 – 'Craufurd, you are late': these quotations are from Smith.

141 'I cannot say that Lord Wellington and I are quite so cordial': this comes from the Rev. A. Craufurd's book.

142 'I expect in a few months, very few, to be with you': this was Craufurd's last letter to his wife, dated 8 January 1812, cited by Spurrier.

FOURTEEN The Storm of Ciudad Rodrigo

143 'Lieutenant Colonel Colborne led his column forward': G. C. Moore Smith's life of Colborne contains extensive details of this enterprise.

144 'Corporal Robert Fairfoot had joined the party': this emerges from Fairfoot's service record in the 2nd Battalion Description Book for 1830, WO25/559.

 – 'What's that drunken man doing?': Moore Smith again.

145 'Yer honour, I'll lend him my greatcoat if ye'll allow me': Costello.

 – 'Uniacke enjoyed his men's renown for his handsome looks and athletic prowess': e.g. Costello. Others make mention of him too, like Harry Smith and Simmons.

 – 'His mother had long been a widow, and her survival and that of John's eight siblings depended on his remittances from the Peninsula': details of Uniacke's family circumstances emerge in WO 42/47U3, an application by Mrs Uniacke for a pension.

146 'When that young subaltern eventually reached the battalion, on 13 January, he exhibited the whey face': Gairdner's journal, NAM MSS 6902-5-1.

148 'Gairdner, another officer, and thirty men were sent down to their position at about 8 p.m.': details of this operation and the subsequent quota-

tion are in a letter to his father of 19 January 1812, NAM MSS 7101-20.

149 'the Royal Wagon Train supported by the *mounted* 14th Light Dragoons': these words come from *Rambles along the Styx*, by Lieutenant Colonel Leach, London, 1847. This work, a curious combination of fact and fiction, takes the form of dialogues between old soldiers in the after-life. Leach suggests this wind-up was perpetrated on a volunteer just before Ciudad Rodrigo. I cannot be completely sure it was Gairdner, hence my weasel 'it would seem', but the circumstantial details fit neatly with Gairdner's arrival during the siege.

150 'Craufurd and Picton did not intend to throw their divisions forwards in the usual order': these details of the Light Division storming arrangements from Verner.

– 'while the subaltern commanding the forlorn hope may look for death or a company': Kincaid, *Random Shots*.

151 'The advantage of being on a storming party': Kincaid, *Adventures*.

– 'Move on, will you, 95th? or we will get some who will!': Moore Smith, Colborne recalled that Craufurd 'squeaked out' this insult, an example of the pitch in his voice produced by anger.

– 'Go back, sir, and get others; I am astonished at such stupidity': Simmons.

152 'Look there, Fitz, what would our mothers say, if they saw what was preparing for us?': FitzMaurice.

– 'Soldiers! the eyes of your country are upon you': these words of Craufurd's come from Costello, written long after the event. It seems a little surprising that none of the other Light Division diarists recorded them at the time, but on the other hand it is likely that he would have said something inspiring to his men.

– 'I mounted with a ferocious intent': Kincaid, *Adventures*.

153 'Gurwood was making his way up one of the ladders when he was either thrown or knocked off': Smith.

– 'Looking up in the murk, they could see the mouth of a cannon facing down and across the breach': Green.

– 'When the battle is over, and crowned with victory, he finds himself elevated for a while into the regions of absolute bliss': Kincaid at his descriptive best.

154 'broke into different squads, which went in different directions': Costello.

– 'If I had not seen it, I never could have supposed that British soldiers would become so wild and furious': John Cooke, of the 43rd, from *A True Soldier and Gentleman*, the version edited by Eileen Hathaway and published by her Shinglepicker Press, 2000. Cooke records the unfortunate private as Evans.

– 'What, sir, are you firing at?': Kincaid, *Adventures*.

FIFTEEN The Reckoning

156 'We marched over the bridge dressed in all variety of clothes imaginable': Costello.

– 'I walked around the ramparts that morning at daybreak': Gairdner MS letter, dated 19 January, but like many officers in these campaigns, he started the letter on that day and finished it, with various postscripts, somewhat later.

– 'The general's coffin was borne by sergeant majors from each of the Light Division's battalions': from the account by G. R. Gleig, published in *The Gem*, London, 1829.

157 'some Light Division men marching straight through a great slushy puddle': this is Gleig again, speculating about the soldiers' motivation on the basis of a few days with the Army since he had only joined during the siege. Personally I'm sceptical, but the muddy puddle has been a part of many subsequent accounts of Craufurd. Gleig's account is generally colourful, almost to the point of Victorian high camp.

– 'He is a man of a very extraordinary temper and disposition': Somerset's letter to his brother, 22nd January 1812, Beaufort Papers FmM 4/1/8.

– 'His honour guard was formed of several dozen men of the 3rd Company': Gairdner MS Journal.

– 'Fairfoot assured the priest that Uniacke was Irish': this fascinating anecdote was first published in F. M. FitzMaurice's *Recollections of a Rifleman's Wife at Home and Abroad*, London, 1851. Mrs FitzMaurice was the wife of John, who was serving at the time of Uniacke's funeral as a subaltern in his company.

– 'an evasion made necessary by the British laws against Papists holding commissions': the laws concerning Catholics holding officers' rank had been modified away from an absolute ban in the last decades of the eighteenth century. However, it was to be some time before they were formally allowed to be commissioned and so a system of 'don't ask, don't tell' had emerged. I am grateful to Dr Rory Muir for bringing to my attention an article in the *English Historical Review*, Vol. 70, 1955, on 'Roman Catholics holding Military Commissions in 1798', for a description of this state of affairs.

158 'There had been around two dozen turncoats serving the French garrison there': Green puts the figure as high as forty. I'm sceptical that it was that high, given the numbers of men returned in the previous months as having deserted. On the other hand, the 1st/95th returned five deserters in November and December 1811 and with Mills, McInnes, Hogdson and Almond accounted for, that still leaves one rifleman who either died in the siege or successfully escaped.

159 'Murphy of the 95th had been sentenced to six months': this emerges in

General Orders, the court martial having taken place on 5 January
1812. Neither Murphy nor the man he killed seems to have been a 1st
Battalion man.

159 'The court having considered the evidence': General Orders.

– 'Miles Hodgson of the 95th was among those saved': this emerges in
Costello, who gives an account of Hodgson's later wounding in battle. It
was Surtees who said McInnes was seduced into desertion.

– 'everyone was pretty much agreed that they would get what was due to
them': those who showed no compassion towards the deserters included
Green and Simmons.

– 'Some held that the deserters had fought twice as well as any Frenchers':
Surtees reports these feelings among the soldiers. To me, the tale of the
soldiers taunting their former comrades in English during the storm has
the whiff of an urban myth about it. None of the many diarists reported
hearing such calls, first person, and the fondness for morbid tales
around the camp fire (described by such Light Division types as Kincaid,
Cooke and Hennell) probably accounts for these claims.

160 'They soon after appeared, poor wretches, moving towards the square':
Surtees.

– 'Oh, Mr Smith, put me out of my misery': Smith. Given his unpleasant
role in these proceedings, Smith's omission of any mention of his duty as
prosecutor in the subsequent trial of Almond is curious.

161 'Joseph Almond had been captured by a patrol of Spanish guerrillas':
Costello, who provides the basis for much of this section.

162 'The Court having duly considered the evidence': General Orders, 7
March 1812.

– 'the execution could not be carried out until these several pounds had
been received': Kincaid.

SIXTEEN Badajoz

165 'This had the desired effect; and the field pieces were withdrawn into the
fort': Leach, *Rough Sketches*.

166 'He'd developed a thirst for action that, on that very day, got him promoted to sergeant': the date of the promotion and the fact of Fairfoot's
volunteering for the Picurina storm emerge from the description book
WO25/559; Brotherwood's volunteering emerges in Harry Smith's autobiography.

– 'Damn your eyes!': Smith, evidently one of those who heard the story
from Brotherwood himself.

– 'the Russian army is 400 thousand strong': Cameron's friend wrote his
letter on 15 May, a little later, but war with Russia was confidently
expected by many in the Peninsular army. The letter resides in the

Cameron Head Papers at the Highland Region Archive office in Inverness.

167 'Major O'Hare . . . greeted the returnees, including Sergeant Esau Jackson': Costello. This is my favourite O'Hare anecdote.

– 'Private Thomas Mayberry was one of those readying himself for the moment': Harris is the source of this story and of the quotation about Mayberry being held in contempt.

– 'one of those wild untamable animals that, the moment the place was carried, would run to every species of excess': Kincaid on Burke, *Random Shots*. His Kilkenny origins emerge from the muster rolls.

168 'The more the danger, the more the honour': this phrase was used by Simmons in a letter home late in 1810. He wrote it inside inverted commas, suggesting that it was a common saying in the Army at the time.

– 'so great was the rage for passports to eternity in our battalion': another nice turn of phrase from Kincaid, *Adventures*.

– 'Lieutenant Willie Johnston would not be put off': Kincaid, *Random Shots*.

– 'He insisted on his right as going as senior lieutenant': this comment on Harvest comes from Surtees, but Cooke of the 43rd also mentions his conduct.

169 'One subaltern of the 43rd chanced upon Horatio Harvest': Cooke.

– 'Bell . . . had joined the 1st/95th in February, just after Rodrigo, with two other subalterns': the arrival of these three officers (Bell, Austen and Foster) is mentioned in the monthly return, 25th February 1812, WO 17/217. The return lists officers in order of seniority within each rank, hence the comment about Bell's superiority to Kincaid.

– 'Lieutenant Bell chose this moment to complain of feeling sick': Bell's feigning illness is reported in a letter from James Gairdner, part of the NAM MS, and will be dealt with more fully in the next chapter.

– 'O'Hare was ill at ease. Captain Jones, of the 52nd, asked him': this exchange is quoted by Costello, who couldn't resist morbid portents of this kind.

171 'A lieutenant colonel or cold meat in a few hours': O'Hare's comment is quoted by Simmons and has been seized upon, quite rightly I think, by various historians as an extraordinary expression of the fatalism prevalent among these men.

– 'Instantly a volley of grape-shot, canister, and small arms poured in': Costello.

– 'What a sight! The enemy crowding the ramparts': Cooke of the 43rd.

172 'Lieutenant James Gairdner fell on this slope': Gairdner MS Journal.

– 'the musket ball hit the peak of his cap, going through it into his left temple': this is described by Green and the injury appears in WO 25/559.

172 'No going to the rear for me': Harris.
173 'Another man of ours (resolved to win or die)': Kincaid, *Random Shots*.
 – 'French troops were standing upon the walls taunting and inviting our men to come up and try again': Cooke.
 – 'Why don't you come into Badajoz?': William Napier's *History*.
174 'In the awful charnel pit we were then traversing': Kincaid, *Random Shots*.
 – 'The men were not so eager to go up the ladders as I expected them to be': Hennell in a letter home dated 5 April 1812, but with postscripts describing that awful night. Hennell had been sent to the 94th as a volunteer and, for his heroic conduct at Badajoz, was commissioned as an ensign in the 43rd.

SEVENTEEN The Disgrace

176 'Major Cameron walked slowly and deliberately up and down the ranks of riflemen': this scene is described by Kincaid, *Random Shots*.
177 'who by this time were tolerably drunk': Costello.
 – 'I hear our soldiers in some instances behaved very ill': Hennell's comments were made in letters – the best kind of record. I've used the volume edited by Michael Glover throughout.
178 'Every atom of furniture was broken and mattresses ripped open in search of treasure': Cooke.
179 'O'Hare's property at home was more substantial': PROB 6/189 Acts of Administrations. The £20 figure comes from the register of Officers' Effects.
180 'in place of the usual tattoo report of all present, it was all absent': Kincaid, *Random Shots*.
181 'The defences on the tops of the breaches ought to have been cleared': Kincaid, *Random Shots*.
 – 'They blamed Wellington and his engineers': Verner discovered some interesting, if unsourced, evidence of this, an angry comment about Wellington, clearly from a Light Division veteran, scribbled in the margins of a Rifles memoir.
 – 'I was before this last action sixth from the top of the Second Lieutenants': Gairdner MS letter, 25 April 1812.
 – 'This regimental havoc will give me promotion': this was Lieutenant Robert Fernyhough quoted in Thomas Fernyhough, *Military Memoirs of Four Brothers*, London, 1829. Although Fernyhough served in the 95th, this is the only quotation of his I have used in this book. His record of service was in fact a series of missed opportunities and illnesses that resulted in him missing every significant moment of the regiment's campaigns.

EIGHTEEN The Salamanca Campaign

183 'He and Captain McDearmid were the only two of the thirteen senior officers . . . left fit to march': my own research with the monthly returns, WO 17/217, and the Challis Index. The figures for men fit to march and invalided home also come from the monthly returns.

184 'a subtle and unmistakable change in the conduct of quite a few old sweats in the battalion': this is such a sensitive subject, being connected with powerful concepts of courage and honour, that it is hard to find direct evidence for it. Kincaid, in comments made about Vitoria (see Chapter 20) is one of the few to tackle it explicitly, stating that a man who survives a great battle wants to be able to tell the tale. Leach and Cooke (of the 43rd) both, for example, measured subsequent battles in comparison to Badajoz and one only has to look at the pattern of volunteering for the Salamanca forts and San Sebastian to see that most of those who came forward at Rodrigo or Badajoz did not go on these later storming parties.

– 'a couple of men committed suicide and quite a few fell into deep depression': according to Surtees.

– 'Cameron was born and grew up in Lochaber': an article on Cameron's background and career appeared in the *Rifle Brigade Chronicle*, 1931.

– 'His relatives had kept too tight a grip on the family funds': this detail about Cameron emerges from Charles Napier's journal in Napier's *History*.

185 'perhaps from being less spoiled and more hardy than British soldiers': Cumloden Papers.

– 'As a *friend*, his heart was in the right place': Kincaid, *Adventures*.

186 'Now Smith dined alone as acting commander of 3rd Company': good detail of the reorganisation emerges from Gairdner's MS Journal.

– 'was in his choice of his profession': Kincaid, *Random Shots*. Sarsfield's departure is noted in the monthly return.

– 'not suited to our *specie of troop*': Beckwith's letter to Cameron, 10 October 1813, referring to Sarsfield's later transfer out of the 95th. The letter resides in the Cameron Head Papers.

187 'The march was commenced with precisely the same regularity': Leach, *Recollections and Reflections*.

189 'A trooper of the 14th Light Dragoons captured a French cavalier': Costello.

190 'Our division, very much to our annoyance': Kincaid, *Adventures*.

– 'The public buildings are really splendid': Simmons.

– 'It is here the stranger may examine, with advantage, the costume, style and gait': Cooke.

– 'A fine meal could be had in Madrid, but it would cost you six shillings': Hennell.

191 'I have been very unwell, add to that I never had money': Gairdner MS Journal, entry for 20 October 1812.

– 'I sold some silver spoons and a watch': Leach, *Rough Sketches*.

– 'Lieutenant Samuel Hobkirk of the 43rd . . . was rumoured to spend £1,000 a year on his uniforms': Cooke and Hennell are among those who were transfixed by Hobkirk's wealth.

192 'In Madrid, they were able to find a proper theatre': Cooke.

– 'I was truly glad to get away from this unfortunate place': Simmons.

– 'The conversation among the men is interspersed with the most horrid oaths': Hennell.

194 'The road was covered with carcasses of all descriptions': Simmons.

– 'It is impossible to conceive of anything more regular': Leach MS Journal.

– 'which was fun for them but death to us': Simmons.

– 'Cameron sent the Highland and 1st Companies out to the water's edge as skirmishers': Gairdner and Leach provide good accounts of this fight in their MS journals. Gairdner notes the four supporting companies of the 95th were 'formed in line'.

196 'Charles Spencer, distraught at the prospect, burst into tears': Costello.

– 'sentries with fixed bayonets placed around the piles': Leach MS Journal.

NINETEEN The Regimental Mess

197 'Fire places of no small dimensions were made by our soldiers': Leach MS Journal.

– 'Having ransacked the canteens of each company for knives, forks, spoons, &c.': Leach, *Rough Sketches*.

198 'after a great deal of needless and ungentlemanly blustering': Gairdner MS Journal, as is the quotation of Cameron.

199 'Between field sports by day and harmony and conviviality at night': Leach MS Journal.

– 'Up to this period Lord Wellington had been adored by the army', Kincaid, *Adventures*.

200 'the most ultra of all ultra-Tories': Kincaid's (anonymous) sketch of Johnston in the *United Services Journal*, 1837, Part I.

– 'he was the type who might easily have called out some Scot': FitzMaurice, in the work about his father, also the source of the above quotation, describes him as a man who could never be shaken from his conviction that duelling was an honourable way to settle matters of honour, saying he was raised in the tradition of the '*duello*'.

201 'take advantage of his superior rank, not only to decline giving me that satisfaction': this passage is by William Surtees about an officer in another Rifles battalion who tormented him. I have included it because

it is an unusually candid consideration of some of the factors weighed up before calling someone out.

201 'the conduct of our Commandant and a few of his adherents is tending to establish *parties*': this passage was written in a common or simple cipher in Gairdner's MS Journal and is dated 25 March 1813. A *Newsnight* colleague, Meirion Jones, and I broke the code in about twenty-five minutes during a quiet afternoon in the office. In *The Man Who Broke Napoleon's Codes*, Faber, 2001, I wrote about the techniques used to break these types of cipher so quickly.

– 'Lieutenant Gore and Lord Charles Spencer who are both good looking': Leach MS Journal. This is also the source of the following quotation about Wellington crying out 'Bravo!'.

202 'He is equally delightful at the festive board as at the head of his Division': Leach MS Journal.

203 'Alten's attempts to assert his authority were rather weak': Gairdner MS Journal.

204 'If there is one school worse than another for a youngster': Leach, *Rough Sketches*.

– 'Cameron tried to obtain the recall of Second Lieutenant Thomas Mitchell': this saga comes from the Mitchell Papers cited in his biography above. Cameron's angry letter, dated 12 November 1812, was addressed to the Adjutant General. The reply from Colonel Gordon, the QMG, was fired back the following day. Gordon was replaced a few weeks later by George Murray, an officer who had previously held the same position and was much more to Wellington's liking.

205 'I ought to have had you tried by General Court Martial': this Cameron quotation comes from Costello's account. Costello states that he can only think of six men of his battalion flogged during the Peninsular War. This is nonsense: my own researches would suggest there were dozens of such punishments, particularly during Craufurd's command of the Light Division. Evidently Costello's memory of this had been dimmed by the passing years. The Costello quotation, along with various statements by Moore, Manningham and Stewart about their dislike of corporal punishment, have sustained something of a myth that the Rifles were rarely flogged.

206 'Only one is a native of Great Britain': monthly return WO 17/217.

– 'A few dozen men in the 95th took Spanish or Portuguese wives': the real measure of this was in the desertions at the end of the Peninsular War, when some of the soldiers disappeared rather than forsake their Iberian sweethearts.

207 'We have acted some plays . . . with various success': this letter was written by Captain Charles Beckwith, 95th, to his friend William Napier of

the 43rd who was on leave at the time. It is reproduced in Verner.

207 'Barnard took the setback philosophically, and began plotting':
Barnard's thoughts emerge in letters home in 'Letters of a Peninsular
War Commanding Officer', ed. M. C. Spurrier, *Journal for the Society
of Army Historical Research*, Vol. XLIV, pp63–76.

– 'We had a brigade field day this day on the plain between': Gairdner MS
Journal. Leach MS Journal suggests Kempt was rather impressed with
his new brigade. Perhaps on first seeing it, he was just underestimating
its potential (for evidence of how impressed he was later, see the following chapter).

208 'Officers would offer up the latest theory with an *"on dit"*' : Leach MS
Journal.

– 'Rumour says that we are about to retrace our steps': this comes from
the Beckwith letter of 1 May 1813. It is worth pointing out that
Beckwith was on the staff and therefore might reasonably have been
supposed to be a little more in the know than the average regimental
officer. Evidently this was some years before the Army had a department
called the Directorate of Corporate Communications.

– 'We now only require that the canteens of each Company's mess should
be well supplied': Leach MS Journal.

209 'Such a review in England would have been attended by crowds':
Hennell.

TWENTY Vitoria

210 'We encamped today in a most heavenly May morning': Leach MS
Journal.

– 'Well, here we go again. We shall go so far and then have our arses
kicked and come back again': he said it to Jock Molloy and it is contained in the memoir of that officer written by Du Cane.

212 'it had three battalions of 95th, three of foreign riflemen, six battalions
of light infantry': I am counting the 5th/60th and two battalions of KGL
Light Troops as 'foreign riflemen', although there could be some debate
over whether all of the latter had the Baker rifle, and the 43rd, 51st,
52nd, 68th, 71st and Chasseurs Britaniques as light infantry.

213 'Wellington, wrote one company commander, "suddenly appeared
amongst us . . ."': Leach MS Journal.

– 'The 1st Batt 95th extended over their flanks within pistol shot of them':
John Cox MS Journal.

– 'Lord Wellington ordered four of the companies of our first battalion to
attack': Leach MS Journal.

– 'A few hundred skirmishers were not meant to be able to drive off a similar number of men in a formed line': the formation of this French line is

noted by Leach, Cox and Simmons. The last says the Riflemen got 'several discharges from a well formed line'. San Millan was one of several incidents during 1813–14 when the Light Division achieved such skill that they inverted the usual 'rules' of warfare.

214 'Our men became outrageous': a nice comment in one of Hennell's letters.

– 'They were purchased by some of the officers either as *momentos*': Leach MS Journal.

215 'I do not like the idea of forcing the bridge': quoted by Hennell.

– 'Others thought the Rifles would soon be able to pick off the French gunners': Cooke.

– 'More jokes pass then than at a halt on a wet day': Hennell.

216 'Yes my Lord, I see smoke and dust in that direction': Du Cane quoting Molloy.

– 'This little path, clinging to the craggy rock face, led them around the right-angled bend': this detail comes from one of Hennell's letters which contains full details and a sketch map. If only we could find accounts of other Napoleonic battles made at the time and in such detail!

– 'The 3rd Division, at a run, crossed the bridge of Trespuentes': Cooke.

217 'two of our companies lost two officers and thirty men, chiefly from the fire of artillery': Kincaid, *Adventures*. He uses 'lost' to mean both killed and wounded. A careful analysis of casualties and accounts allowed me to pinpoint those as the 2nd and 6th Companies.

218 'FitzMaurice was running at a cracking pace': these details come from his son's narrative – presumably they had heard it enough times around the dinner table to know it by heart. John Cox, MS Journal, also has some details on this memorable feat.

219 'It was impossible to deny ourselves the satisfaction of cursing them': Kincaid, *Adventures*.

– 'One other rifleman was rumoured to have taken £3,000 in coin': Du Cane.

220 'Do any of you know where Jack Connor is?': this passage comes from Costello. Eileen Hathaway did some reasearch into the names mentioned for her edition of his memoirs. The quotations and casualty records did not match up in all cases. I have included it nevertheless as one of the longest passages of authentic riflemen's dialogue included in any of the memoirs. It always moves me, despite having read it dozens of times.

221 'After surviving a great day, I always felt I had a right to live': Kincaid, Adventures.

– 'This renewed report of disorder committed by soldiers': Adjudant General's letter to Alten, 29 June 1813, in *Wellington's Dispatches*.

221 'You sweep everything before you': Simmons.
   – 'By God I never saw fellows march so well': Leach MS Journal.

TWENTY-ONE The Nivelle

223 'By throwing up redoubts on the heights one regiment may hold up':
   Hennell, letter of 16 July 1813.
224 'Marshal Soult predicted that his enemy would suffer 25,000 casualties':
   this emerges in a letter of Soult's quoted in *Campagne du Maréchal Soult dans Les Pyrénées Occidentales 1813–1814*, Le Commandant Clerc, Paris, 1894.
   – 'Our cavalry therefore and I understand a considerable part of our artillery': Leach MS Journal.
225 'an enthusiastic apostle of light troops and the rifle': one example of Barnard's zeal in this respect is the story told by Harry Smith of how the colonel took Wellington to see the aftermath of the Combat of Tarbes, a tale which will be told in Chapter 23.
226 'actually flogged the infantry with their sabres to drive them before the rearguard': John Cox MS Journal.
227 'In truth, though, neither of the officers who went from the 95th were original members of the battalion either': these officers were Lieutenants Percival and Hamilton. The first was an experienced officer but neither had been serving as long in the Peninsula as the likes of Leach, Simmons, MacNamara *et al.* of the 1st Battalion. Kincaid says even Hamilton had seen enough fighting to satisfy any reasonable man, which is as maybe, but I still think the absence of the *real* veterans interesting in this case.
   – 'This affair caused lasting rancour between the Rifles and Skerrett': Harry Smith is the prime example of this feud.
228 'They are expressly told to fire first at officers and in particular commanders and generals': this fascinating quotation of Soult's comes from a letter dated 1 September 1813 to Clarke, the Minister of War, and is reproduced in Clerc. Soult attributed all the killing to the 5th/60th – an error since the bridge of Vera was an affair fought entirely by the 2nd/95th and some men of the 3rd/95th and was mentioned in Soult's letter as part of the phenomenon he was discussing. Evidently the French High Command knew that the assassination of their officers by riflemen had reached epic proportions, but they were fuzzy on the details of exactly *who* was doing it. The 5th/60th may have been held responsible because they had more desertions than the 95th and much French knowledge of this kind would have been based on deserters. It is also worth pointing out that Soult was exaggerating his officer losses for effect, just as he understated them on other occasions when he

wished to minimise the magnitude of his setbacks.

229 'Kempt's attack, however, was ordered almost entirely in skirmish order': Leach's MS Journal, Hennell and Cooke are good sources on this.

– 'The 95th moved regularly (I do not mean in a line) up the hill': Hennell's letter to his brothers of 13 October 1813; ditto the following quotation about the 95th's prowess.

– 'they fired off some ineffective volleys which all went too high': a good deal of detail in this passage comes from Moore Smith's life of Colborne.

230 'The only way was to put a brave face on the matter': Moore Smith.

– 'We remained a whole month idle spectators of their preparations': Kincaid, *Adventures*.

– 'One soldier of the 3rd Battalion, 95th, for example, . . . transported for life': Private John Howley of the 3rd/95th was tried on 3 November 1813, according to General Orders. The 1st Battalion's desertions are recorded in WO 25/2139.

231 'The successes in Germany are most exhilarating': this letter from Judge Day is quoted in FitzMaurice's book.

– 'Peace is now I think fairly beyond doubt': this letter was written by Hennell on 25 November 1813. I've taken a slight liberty with the timings here, but there was plenty of speculation about the downfall of Napoleon even before late November. Hennell is also the source of the lovely phrase about 'gaping for news'.

232 'I have been thinking of visiting you this winter after the campaign is over': Simmons, letter of 30 August 1813.

– 'These fellows think themselves invulnerable': this Wellington 'O Group' is recounted in Moore Smith.

233 'That this was an anxious, I might say awful moment': Leach MS Journal.

– 'Eh, but Fitz, just see how easy it slips in': FitzMaurice. It is curious how similar this anecdote of Church is to some of those later (e.g. Vietnam) accounts of soldiers who, when asked the question 'How can you shoot women and children?' replied 'You just lead a little less.'

– 'One of our officers gallantly jumped into the second fort': Cooke.

235 '"a swarm of skirmishers" had made the attack': this is General Marinsin's report of the battle, quoted by Clerc.

TWENTY-TWO The Nive

236 'opened his mouth and well and truly said the wrong thing': the accounts of Cooke and Hennell of this bloody incident are both gripping. Neither explicitly blames Hobkirk but he was the senior officer of

the two companies concerned and his guilt is implied in certain passages.

236 'to the front of the wood, each man to his tree, and kept up a fire':
Cooke.

– 'Hobkirk's bugler sounded the advance': Hennell.

237 'Some young sanguine officers who are more vain than good': Major
William Napier's letter is quoted in Glover's edition of Hennell's letters.

238 'Some Light Division officers having received *The Times* of 8
November': Hennell.

– 'the pickets would approach tapping the stocks of their weapons': this
signalling is discussed in various places, including Napier's *History*.

– 'Well, I won't kill these unfortunate rascals': Gairdner is quoted by
Kincaid in his *Adventures* and he is the source for this entire anecdote.

239 'The night before the French attack had been one of heavy, driving rain':
detailed French accounts of this appear in Clerc.

240 'The enemy are going to attack us': Harry Smith.

– 'where the Highland Company had made its outposts': WO 25/2139
records the prisoners' names and details. Ten of the fourteen are listed
with Scottish places of birth, evidence that 7th Company retained its
Highland character until the end of the Peninsular War.

– 'Lieutenant Gairdner was mustered along with the reserve for the outlying picket': the Gairdner MS Journal is the source of these details and
the subsequent quotations.

241 'Although Clausel . . . got to the base of the church walls': this report of
the fighting (undated) was written by one Colonel Lapene and found its
way into the French Army archives. It is quoted at length by Clerc.

– 'the French wheeled up twelve cannon': Clerc.

242 'Riflemen may be employed also with great success against field
artillery': Manningham's lectures.

– 'We kept up an incessant discharge of small arms': Cooke. Kincaid also
mentions the long-range firing in *Adventures*.

– 'The artillerymen fled back over to the safe side of the ridge': see the
French version of this in Lieutenant Colonel Dumas' book.

243 'Hopwood and Brotherwood had been stripped of all their belongings':
Costello.

– 'whether we had been surprised on 10 December': Cooke.

TWENTY-THREE Tarbes

245 'Colonel Barnard . . . had managed to scrounge them enough shakoes':
the issue of new uniforms happened on 23–4 February, according to the
diarists. The headgear situation is described by Barnard in a letter to
Alexander Cameron of 1 April 1813 and included in the *Rifle Brigade
Chronicle*, 1931. This long letter (sadly few from Barnard on military

matters survive) is the source of much information on Tarbes, including a long quotation near the end of this chapter.

245 'The general quickly ordered the 2nd Battalion': Barnard, above, noted that Wellington personally ordered the Rifles into the attack.

246 'On gaining the summit of the hill we found a much larger force': William Cox MS Journal. This Cox sailed with the 1st Battalion in May 1809 but had been promoted as captain into the 2nd.
 – 'The whole of their heavy infantry [was] drawn up on a steep acclivity': William Surtees.
 – 'having been accustomed for many years to oppose imperfectly organised Spaniards': Leach, *Rough Sketches*.
 – 'This column was driven back by a rapid advance of the 1st Batt 95th Rifles': John Cox MS Journal.

247 'a heavy tirallade was then kept up in the vineyards': William Cox.
 – 'Ah, there you are, as usual, just where you should be': Du Cane citing Molloy.
 – 'The loss of the enemy from the fire of our Rifles was so great': Harry Smith, as is the Wellington quotation immediately before it.
 – 'Official French returns indicate only around 180 killed and wounded': these figures are contained in the histories of the 45th and 116th regiments. I am grateful to Tony Broughton for his help on the issue of French casualties at Tarbes. It would be easy to conclude that the Rifles officers were exaggerating. However, I have found them sufficiently honest about such matters during the writing of this book that I suspect some statistical error or sleight of hand in the French figures (which was quite common). It may be that certain men were returned as casualties for the battles of Orthez in February or Toulouse in May rather than Tarbes or listed as having deserted rather than being battle casualties.
 – 'Their estimates ranged from asserting that the French suffered as many casualties': the high estimate is Surtees, the low one William Cox.

248 'I never saw such skirmishers as the 95th, now the Rifle Brigade': Major J. Blakiston, *Twelve Years' Military Adventure*, London, 1829.

249 'one of the intruders, flying into a fury, killed him on the spot': this saga is told by a number of the diarists, including Simmons, Surtees and Costello.
 – 'We tried every means to find out the villain, but to no purpose': Simmons.

TWENTY-FOUR Castel Sarrazin

251 'They walked along the banks of the Garonne, escorted the prettiest French girls to dances': life there is described by Simmons, Leach (*Rough Sketches*), Kincaid (*Adventures*), Harry Smith, Cooke and Gairdner.

252 'was most confoundedly annoyed when the officers of the Rifle corps were taken for Portuguese': Cooke.

253 'Great regret was expressed when the order arrived which obliged us to leave': Leach, *Rough Sketches*.

254 'In six cases though, the riflemen chose to desert': the names are in WO 25/2139, casualty returns for the 1st Battalion, 95th Regiment. Given the writing off of twenty-one names in the March 1814 return (see Chapter 27), it is quite possible that more than just the named six deserted at this time.

– 'Some of the followers, evidently feeling cheated, stole before they went': Surtees being one victim of such theft.

– 'the role of his British or Irish accomplices in the company was to remain a secret': Costello is the source of this information. It is quite possible that in choosing to blame Blanco for the crime, the 2nd Company men were shielding themselves and Costello was complicit in this deception.

– 'William MacFarlane, a soldier who had deserted the regiment': his return is shown by the 25 May pay list.

255 'The British rank of colour sergeant had been introduced': by General Order, 6 July 1813.

– 'One subaltern of the 43rd calculated his net loss at £70': Cooke.

256 'three cheers . . . from the yardarms': Costello.

– 'only six were still serving with the Peninsular Army at the end of the campaigns': names followed through to WO 17/282, the monthly returns for 1814.

– 'the vagaries of Army record keeping do not allow every man's fate to be precisely determined': the difficulties are compounded by the fact that the 1st/95th received drafts of new recruits in 1812 and in May 1814, just after the fighting had stopped but before they embarked for England. A small number of men – perhaps a dozen – were also transferred between different Rifle battalions in the field. In making my calculations, I have had to discount these numbers.

257 'those for whom no satisfactory account could be given': the period ending 25 March 1814 in WO25/2139.

– 'it is to be presumed that nearly the whole of these men have died in hospitals': Adjutant General's letter of 28 May 1814, in *Wellington's Dispatches*.

– 'about 180 were sent home during the course of the war': these figures are obtained by following through the monthly returns in WO 17.

– 'The largest portion of the original group, 421, were those who had died in Iberia': research conducted by Eileen Hathaway and myself from pay lists and casualty returns.

257 'Here we enjoyed the luxuries of London life for a short time, having three years' pay to receive': William Cox MS Journal.

258 'there was a strong desire to resume some sort of quiet domesticity': this becomes apparent from the case of the married Corporal Pitt, which will be described in the following chapter.

– 'Fairfoot married Catherine Campbell, a slip of a girl of sixteen, on 2 October 1814': this comes from the description book cited earlier. My speculation about it being a happy union arises from the five children it produced.

TWENTY-FIVE Quatre Bras

260 'about one soldier in four was new to the battalion': this is my own analysis of the muster rolls.

– 'Simmons's brother Joseph had been left behind': the process of senior men taking priority, etc. is described in one of Simmons's letters.

– 'the old sweats were calling them "recruits"': Costello.

261 'This cursed war has knocked all my plans in the head': Gairdner MS letter, dated 23 April 1815, with various postscripts.

– 'my wife was separated from me when I went to the Peninsular War': the story of Pitt and many other fascinating details and quotations in this chapter come from a long memorandum on the Waterloo campaign written by Simmons for Sir William Cope when he was writing his early history of the Rifle Brigade. Simmons's document, which runs to many pages, can be found in Cope's letter book, National Army Museum MSS 6804-2, Vol. I. Although written decades after the event (dated 15 August 1855) Simmons's statement is consistent in every detail with his letters and journal and amplifies many points. I shall refer to material from this statement as Cope MS. After writing this passage, I came across the following in Field Marshal Lord Carver's memoirs, *Out of Step*, a description of what happened when his regiment returned to Britain in 1944 after several years' fighting in North Africa: 'several senior non-commissioned officers who had splendid records of gallantry and devotion to duty as tank commanders, applied to transfer to units less likely to be in the front line again. They were undoubtedly influenced by their wives, from whom they had been separated for several years and who resented their husbands going into the heat of battle again.' The similarities with Pitt and Underwood are interesting, I think.

– 'disliked flogging as much as any man': Cope MS.

– 'my legs will never carry me through a long campaign': Simmons's letter home of 19 May 1815, as is the quotation about entering Brussels.

262 'some riflemen were even attacked by the locals': this incident is described both in the Gairdner MS Journal and Cope MS.

262 'for we were all aware that Napoleon was about to make a dash':
Kincaid, *Adventures*.
  – 'in consequence of the difficulty of assembling the division': Gairdner
MS Journal.
263 'Barnard, these fellows are coming on; you must stop them by throwing
yourselves into that wood': FitzMaurice.
  – 'Ah! My boys, you are opening the ball in good style!': Cope MS.
  – 'Why man! You are like a fine lady!' Cope MS, as is the following quotation of Simmons about pushing Underwood through the hedge.
  – 'We were saluted by a fusillade of extreme violence': Colonel Trefcon,
Carnet de Campagne du Colonel Trefcon, Paris, 1914.
264 'Look at that glorious fellow, our comrade and brother soldier': Cope
MS.
265 'Oh Mr Simmons, the game is up with me, for this campaign anyhow':
Cope MS.
  – 'the news of this disastrous defeat of our allies was calculated to throw a
damp on the prospects': Leach, *Rough Sketches*.

TWENTY-SIX Waterloo

267 'camp kettles were boiling away outside Barnard's billet': Kincaid,
Adventures.
  – 'It was here that Captain Leach was initially posted with two companies': dispositions pieced together from Leach, *Rough Sketches*,
Simmons and the Cope MS.
268 'we perceived our adversaries bringing into position, on the heights
opposite': Leach, *Rough Sketches*.
  – 'the very first shot from the grand battery taking off a rifleman's head':
this is described by Kincaid and Simmons in the Cope MS.
  – 'This rush and enthusiasm were becoming disastrous': Capitaine Duthilt,
Memoires du Capitaine Duthilt, Lille, 1909.
269 'French cuirassiers cantering up to a Hanoverian militia battalion':
Leach and Simmons.
  – 'many of the riflemen panicked': this story emerges from Barnard's letter
quoted later in this chapter.
271 'Oh lift me up, I am suffocating!': Cope MS which also says Fairfoot
was crying. Simmons's published letter says only that the sergeant
became highly agitated.
272 'I regret to say that a *great* number of our men went to the rear without
cause': this letter, of 23 June 1815 addressed to Cameron, is deeply
compromising in a way memoirs almost never were. It survives in copy
form in the RGJ Archive, Box 1A, item 35. The copy, evidently made by
Verner, was of an original in the Cameron family papers.

273 '*all* soldiers ran away sometimes': Wellington's remark was quoted by
Croker in recounting dinner on 27 April 1828. '[Wellington was] very
frank and amusing. He said all troops ran away – that he never minded;
all he cared about was whether they would come back again, and he
added that he always had a succession of lines for the purpose of rallying fugitives.' It is contained in his two-volume set of reminiscences of
the Duke.

275 'George Baller was another veteran of O'Hare's company': details from
Rifle Brigade Chronicle, 1930.

TWENTY-SEVEN The Legend is Born

279 'The bayonet may, in truth, be termed the grand mystifier of modern
tactics': this phrase was used by Mitchell in the *United Services Journal*
and his book *Thoughts on Tactics and Military Organisation*, London,
1838. The quotations here come from the book.

280 'It is discipline, which is nothing but each man, shoulder-to-shoulder':
this letter by W.D.B. is in the *United Service Journal*, 1838, Part 3.

– 'Our corps gained the reputation . . . not by aping the drill of
grenadiers': Leach, *Rough Sketches*.

281 'Kincaid for example arguing that skirmishing soldiers needed to be kept
moving': he did this in *Random Shots*, not the *United Services Journal*.
The book was published in 1835 and the *USJ* bayonet debate took place
in 1838–40.

284 'there, perhaps, never was, nor ever again will be, such a war brigade':
Kincaid, *Adventures*.

286 'the most celebrated old fighting corps in the Army or perhaps the
world': Major General G. Bell, *Rough Notes by an Old Soldier*,
London, 1867.

– 'A remarkable revival of curiosity in the events of the time of Napoleon
has lately arisen': Du Cane in his article on Molloy.

288 'new fangled school mastering': Wellington made this remark in a letter
to his friend Rev. Gleig.

Bibliography

In several cases the dates given are those of the edition used in the compilation of this book rather than of the first edition.

Arvers, Capitaine P., *et al*, *Historique du 82e Regiment D'Infanterie de Ligne*, Paris, 1876

Baker, Ezekiel, *33 Years Practice and Observation . . . with Rifle Guns*, London, 1813

Bell, Major General G., *Rough Notes by an Old Soldier*, London, 1867

Blakiston, Major J., *Twelve Years' Military Adventure*, London, 1829

de Brack, Colonel F., *Light Cavalry Outposts*, reprinted in English translation by Brown and Buckland (Ken Trotman), 2002

Beaufroy, Captain Henry, *Scloppetaria: or Considerations on the Nature and Use of Rifled Barrel Guns*, London, 1808 (Beaufroy has been identified as author; the work was published as being 'by a Corporal of Riflemen')

Boyle, Colonel Gerald Edmund, *The Rifle Brigade Century*, London 1905

Campbell, Colonel Neil, *A Course of Drill and Instruction in the Movements and Duties of Light Infantry*, London, 1808 (Campbell, an early member of the 95th who later served with Wellesley in Denmark, was asked by the general to produce this volume to create some sort of standard drill for light companies from line battalions)

Clerc, Commandant, *Campagne du Marechal Soult Dans Les Pyrennees Occidentales 1813–1814*, Paris 1894.

Cooke, John, *A True Soldier and Gentleman*, ed. Eileen Hathaway, Shinglepicker Press, 2000

Colville, John, *The Portrait of a General*, Salisbury, 1980

Cooper, Sergeant J., *Rough Notes on Seven Campaigns*, Carlisle 1869.

Cope, Sir William, *History of the Rifle Brigade (the 95th)*, London, 1877

Costello, Edward, *The True Story of a Peninsular Rifleman* (edited version of his earlier memoir), Shinglepicker Press, 1997

Craufurd, Rev. Alexander, *General Craufurd and his Light Division*, London 1891.

Croker, John Wilson, *The Croker Papers*, London 1885

Cross, Captain John, *A System of Drill and Manoeuvres as Practised in the 52nd Light Infantry Regiment*, London, 1823.

Derrecagaix, General, *Le Marechal de France Comte Harispe, 1768–1855*, Paris, 1916

Duhesme, Comte P. G., *Essai Historique sur l'Infanterie Legère*, Paris, 1814

Dumay, Capitaine, *Historique du 66e Regiment d'Infanterie (1672–1900)*, Tours, 1900

Dumas, Lt Colonel J. B., *Neuf Mois de Campagnes a la Suite du Marechal Soult*, Paris, *c.*1900

Dundas, Colonel D., *Principles of Military Movements, Chiefly Applied to Infantry*, London, 1788

Dupuy, Capitaine R., *Historique du 3e Regiment de Hussards de 1764 a 1887*, Paris, 1887.

Duthilt, Capitaine, *Memoires du Capitaine Duthilt*, Lille, 1909

Ehwald (sometimes sp. Ewald), Colonel Von, *A Treatise upon the Duties of Light Troops*, London, 1803

Fare, Charles, *Lettres d'Un Jeune Officier à Sa Mère 1803–1814*, Paris, 1889

Fernyhough, Thomas, *Military Memoirs of Four Brothers*, London, 1829

Fitzclarence, Lord, *Manual of Outpost Duties*, London, 1849

FitzMaurice, F. M., *Recollections of a Rifleman's Wife at Home and Abroad*, London 1851

FitzMaurice, J., *Biographical Sketch of Major General John FitzMaurice*, Italy, 1908

Foster, William C., *Sir Thomas Mitchell and His World, 1792-1855*, New South Wales Institution of Surveyors

Fririon, François-Nicholas, *Journal Historique de la Campagne de Portugal*, Paris, 1841

Fuller, J. F. C., *Sir John Moore's System of Training*, London, 1924

Gassendi, Comte Jean Jacques, *Aide-Memoire des Officiers d'Artillerie de France*, Paris, 1809

Gates, David, *The British Light Infantry Arm, c.1790–1815*, London, 1987

Girod de L'Ain, Capitaine M., *Le General Eble*, Paris, 1893

Gleig, 'Account of Robert Craufurd's Funeral', first published in *The Gem*, 1829, reprinted in *A Memoir of the Late Major General Robert Craufurd*, privately published, 1842

Glover, Michael, ed., *A Gentleman Volunteer: The Letters of George Hennell*, London, 1979

Godbert, Capitaine H., *Historique du 70ème Regiment d'Infanterie de Ligne, 1792–1815*, Leguyers, 1890

Grattan, William, *Adventures with the Connaught Rangers*, London, 1853

Green, William, *A Brief Outline of Travels and Adventures of William Green*, Coventry, 1857

Griffiths, Paddy, ed., *A History of the Peninsular War*, Vol. ix: *Modern Studies of the War in Spain and Portugal, 1808–1814*, London, 1999

Hall, John A., *A History of the Peninsular War*, Vol. viii: *The Biographical Dictionary of British Officers Killed and Wounded, 1808–1814*, London, 1998

Harris, Benjamin, *A Dorset Rifleman*, ed. Eileen Hathaway, Shinglepicker Press, 1995.

Hay, Captain William, *Reminiscences, 1809–1815, under Wellington*, London, 1901

Haythornthwaite, Philip J., *The Armies of Wellington*, London, 1994

Howard, Dr Martin, *Wellington's Doctors*, Spellmount, 2002

James, C., *A Collection of the Charges, Opinions and Sentences of General Courts Martial*, London, 1820

Kincaid, John, *Random Shots from a Rifleman*, London, 1835

MacDonald, John, *Instructions for the Conduct of Infantry*, London (a translation of French regulations, but contains an introduction)

Larpent, F., *Private Journal of F. Seymour Larpent, Judge Advocate General*, London, 1853

Leach, Jonathan, *Rough Sketches of an Old Soldier*, London, 1831

– *Recollections and Reflections Relative to the Duties of Troops Composing the Advanced Corps of an Army*, London, 1835

– *Sketch of the Field Services of the Rifle Brigade from its Formation to the Battle of Waterloo*, London, 1838

– *Rambles Along the Styx*, London, 1847

Liddell Hart, B. H., ed., *The Letters of Private Wheeler*, London, 1951

Macdonald, J., *Rules and Regulation of the Field Exercise*, 1803 (a translation of the French 1791 regulations but contains interesting remarks on French light troop tactics by the translator)

Mannigham, Colonel Coote, *Military Lectures Delivered to the 95th (Rifle) Regiment, 1803*, first published in the *Rifle Brigade Chronicle*, 1896, republished by Ken Trotman, 2002.

Marbot, Baron J., *Memoires du General Baron Marbot*, Paris, 1892

Martinien, A., *Tableaux par Corps et par Batailles des Officiers Tués et Blessés pendant les Guerres de l'Empire*, Paris, 1899

Mitchell, Lieutenant Colonel J., *Thoughts on Tactics and Military Organisation*, London, 1838

Moore Smith, G. C., *The Autobiography of Lieutenant General Sir Harry Smith*, London, 1901

– *The Life of John Colborne, Field Marshal Lord Seaton*, London, 1903

Muir, Rory, *Britain and the Defeat of Napoleon 1807–1815*, New Haven
   and London, 1996
– *Salamanca 1812*, New Haven and London, 2001
Nafziger, George, *Imperial Bayonets: Tactics of the Napoleonic Battery,
   Battalion and Brigade as Found in Contemporary Regulations*, London,
   1995
Napier, General W., *Passages in the Early Military Life*, ed. George Napier,
   London 1884.
Napier, Sir William, *History of the War in the Peninsula and in the South of
   France*, 1807–14, 6 Vols., London, 1851
– *The Life and Opinions of General Sir Charles James Napier*, 4 Vols.,
   London, 1857
Oman, Sir Charles, *A History of the Peninsular War*, 7 Vols., Oxford,
   1902–30
– *Wellington's Army 1809–1814*, London, 1913
Rottenburg, Colonel, *Regulations for the Exercise of Riflemen and Light
   Infantry and Instructions for Their Conduct in the Field*, London, 1803 (a
   translated and slightly edited version of the first regulations produced five
   years earlier by the Commanding Officer of the new 5th/60th;
   Rottenburg's name does not appear, although he was undoubtedly the
   author)
Pelet, Jean Jacques, *The French Campaign in Portugal 1810-11*, ed. Donald
   Horward, Minneapolis, 1973
Simmons, George, *A British Rifleman*, Greenhill edition, 1986.
Six, Georges, *Dictionnaire Biographique des Generaux et Amiraux Français
   de la Revolution et de l'Empire, 1792–1814*, Paris, 1934
Sontag, Colonel, Hints for Non-Commissioned Officer on Actual Service,
   London, 1803
Stevens, Crosbie, 'The Rifle Brigade 1800–1870: A Study of Social, Cultural
   and Religious Activity', PhD thesis, Sheffield University, 1996
Stewart, Sir William, *The Cumloden Papers*, privately printed, 1871
Surtees, William, *Twenty-Five Years in the Rifle Brigade*, 1973 reprint of
   1833 edition
Torrens, Major General Sir Henry, *Field Exercise and Evolutions of the
   Army*, London, 1824
Trefcon, Colonel, *Carnet de Campagne du Colonel Trefcon*, Paris, 1914
Var, Le Commandant, ed., *Campagnes du Capitaine Marcel*, Paris, 1913
Vassais, Capitaine J. G., *Historique du 69ème Regiment d'Infanterie
   (1672–1912)*, Paris, 1913
Verner, Willoughby, *History and Campaigns of the Rifle Brigade*, 1912–19.
Weddeburne, Sergeant William, *Observations on the Exercise of Riflemen*,
   Norwich, 1804

BIBLIOGRAPHY

Wellesley, Arthur, Duke of Wellington, Dispatches of the Duke of
  Wellington, London, 1852
Wyld, James, *Maps and Plans Showing the Principal Movements, Battles,
  and Sieges* . . . , London, 1840

*Rules and Regulations for the Formation, Field Exercise and Movement of
  His Majesty's Forces*, London, 1792
General Orders, Spain and Portugal, London, 1811–14
The Standing Orders of the Light Division, Dublin, 1844
The Pakenham Letters 1800 to 1815, privately printed, 1914

Index